T0391845

Water and Development

Water and Development

The Troubled Economic History of the Arid Tropics

TIRTHANKAR ROY

OXFORD
UNIVERSITY PRESS

Oxford University Press is a department of the University of Oxford.
It furthers the University's objective of excellence in research, scholarship,
and education by publishing worldwide. Oxford is a registered trade mark of
Oxford University Press in the UK and in certain other countries.

Published in the United States of America by Oxford University Press
198 Madison Avenue, New York, NY 10016, United States of America.

© Oxford University Press 2025

All rights reserved. No part of this publication may be reproduced, stored in a retrieval system, transmitted, used for text and data mining, or used for training artificial intelligence, in any form or by any means, without the prior permission in writing of Oxford University Press, or as expressly permitted by law, by license or under terms agreed with the appropriate reprographics rights organization. Inquiries concerning reproduction outside the scope of the above should be sent to the Rights Department, Oxford University Press, at the address above.

You must not circulate this work in any other form
and you must impose this same condition on any acquirer

Names: Roy, Tirthankar author
Title: Water : the troubled economic history of the arid tropics / Tirthankar Roy.
Description: New York, NY : Oxford University Press, [2025] | Includes bibliographical
references and index. |
Identifiers: LCCN 2024055731 (print) | LCCN 2024055732 (ebook) | ISBN 9780197802397 hardback |
ISBN 9780197802403 epub | ISBN 9780197802427
Subjects: LCSH: Tropics—Economic conditions | Tropics—Environmental conditions |
Arid regions—Economic aspects | Water—Storage | Water reuse
Classification: LCC HC695 .R69 2025 (print) | LCC HC695 (ebook) |
DDC 330.915/4—dc23/eng/20250326
LC record available at https://lccn.loc.gov/2024055731
LC ebook record available at https://lccn.loc.gov/2024055732

DOI: 10.1093/oso/9780197802397.001.0001

Printed by Marquis, Canada

The manufacturer's authorised representative in the EU for product safety is Oxford University Press España S.A. of El Parque Empresarial San Fernando de Henares, Avenida de Castilla, 2 – 28830 Madrid (www.oup.es/en or product.safety@oup.com). OUP España S.A. also acts as importer into Spain of products made by the manufacturer.

For

Kaoru Sugihara

Contents

Maps	viii
Figures	ix
Acknowledgments	x

One. Introduction	1
Two. The History of a Concept	29
Three. The Arid Regions	48
Four. Dry Seasons and Disastrous Ones	90
Five. Ancient Assets	104
Six. The Colonial Era: Property Rights	115
Seven. Dams and Drills	133
Eight. The Big Push	164
Nine. Paying For Green Revolutions	193
Ten. Inequality And Discord	205
Eleven. Tropical Pastoralism	222
Twelve. The Future of the Trade-Off	247
Thirteen. Conclusion	261

References	264
Index	287

Maps

1.1.	Arid Tropics	4
1.2.	Water Stress	24
3.1.	West Africa	57
3.2.	East Africa	70
3.3.	North Africa and West Asia	76
3.4.	Southern Africa	80
3.5.	South Asia	85
3.6.	Tropical North America	88
11.1.	Grasslands	225

Figures

1.1. Seasonality: Comparing Tropical and Temperate Areas	6
1.2. The Water Cross	25
3.1. "Picturesque View of the River Niger," 1840 engraving	55
5.1. Lothal	106
5.2. Bhikha Behram Well, 1725	110
7.1. The Gunnaram Sluice on the Godavari	137
7.2. Richard Baird Smith (1818–1861)	141
7.3. The Gezira Cotton Scheme, 1951	144
8.1. Jawaharlal Nehru and M. Visvesvaraya, c. 1947	169
8.2. Variations in Lake Chad	172
8.3. Annual Freshwater Withdrawal 1901–2000 (billion cubic meters)	174
8.4. Monument to Honor the Derg Army in Ethiopia	186
9.1. The Old Shoolpaneshwar Temple	196
10.1. An Arax Airlines cargo plane bringing relief supplies during the Sahel famine, 1972	215
11.1. *Nomads of Bechar,* by Antonio Beato, 1864	233
11.2. "Halt of a Boer's Family," 1804 engraving by Samuel Daniel	238

Acknowledgments

Since 2019, I have explored, through several connected projects, this book's core thesis that the economic emergence of societies in arid and semi-arid tropical regions depended on their ability to extract and recycle water and, in turn, on manipulating the environment in certain ways. The process has been politically tense and has tested federal democracies.

From the start, my idea, or parts of it, were presented in seminars and conferences. The PowerPoint slides steadily augmented as I received suggestions and comments from the audience, making writing it all up both a challenge and a pleasure. I want to thank the participants and organizers of the Social and Economic History seminar at Utrecht University (2020); the D. D. Kosambi Lecture, Mumbai (2021); the Bengal Club, Kolkata (2021); a Cambridge University history seminar (2021); a panel on environment-economy interactions at the World Economic History Congress, Paris (2022); the R. C. Dutt Memorial Lecture at the Centre for Studies in Social Sciences, Kolkata (2022); the Frontier Research in Economic and Social History meeting at the University of Gothenburg (2022); the Research Institute of History and Nature, Kyoto (2023); Kansai University (2022, 2024); the Orissa Economics Association (2023); a University of Sussex seminar (2023); and Waseda University (2024).

Partly through these interactions, a series of publications emerged, initially focused on India and gradually expanding to a global scale. These include two papers in the *Journal of Interdisciplinary History* (2021) and *Economic History of Developing Regions* (2022) and a book, *Monsoon Economies: India's History in a Changing Climate* (MIT Press, 2022). A book titled *Monsoon Economy*, a revised version of the previous one, was published by Penguin India in 2023. I am grateful to the referees, editors, series editors (Michael Egan for MIT Press and Gurcharan Das for Penguin), and publishers for their advice and support throughout the publication process.

The manuscript improved substantially and became significantly bigger while dealing with the detailed comments received from two anonymous readers for OUP, both supportive and critical, in the way I needed. Conversations, some that have occurred over several years, contributed positively to the project. I want to thank Bharat Punjabi, Gareth Austin, Hugh Roberts, Jean-Yves Puyo, Kaoru Sugihara, Kazuo Kobayashi, Kenneth Pomeranz, Maanik Nath, and Michiel de Haas particularly. V. Yogesh and Bhaskar Das prepared some of the maps. I want to thank them also.

Chapter One
Introduction

From the early twentieth century, a big part of our world—the arid tropics—began to extract, store, and recycle vast quantities of water to sustain population growth and economic development. These regions worked on water to deal with seasonality, or concentrated seasons of rain and flooding combined with extreme aridity for the rest of the year. The idea of water recycling was not a new one in this geography. Indeed, it was an intrinsic part of ancient culture, statecraft, and technology. Most ancient projects, however, were local and small in scale. The capability of water extraction on a scale large enough to transform whole regions, societies, and countries and create new cities improved in the early twentieth century. The process gave rise to a sharp break in the long-term population and economic growth pattern from the mid-twentieth century.

The world knows that rapid economic growth must take a toll on the environment, and the tropics were no exception. However, the economic emergence of the arid tropics reinforces the message differently from how climate activists imagine it. The geography of the arid tropics makes transforming landscapes to extract and recycle large quantities of water damaging to the environment and disputatious. The book is about that troubled history of economic emergence.

This book is not about water scarcity. That water scarcity obstructs economic growth is not its message. That message is so obvious that it would not need a book. The message instead is that the tropical arid regions face a *seasonal* water scarcity *that has a solution*, trapping or mining water on a large scale, one that has been used more extensively in the twentieth century. It is expensive in money, damages the environment, and generates conflicts, but there is no known better way to sustain economic growth in the presence of seasonality.

That message should fundamentally change our understanding of global economic history. According to this new understanding, the economic emergence of societies in arid and semi-arid regions did not stem from learning the tricks to build the institutions of capitalism from the West. Instead, it

Water and Development. Tirthankar Roy, Oxford University Press. © Oxford University Press (2025).
DOI: 10.1093/oso/9780197802397.003.0001

2   WATER AND DEVELOPMENT

depended on water by manipulating the environment in specific ways. That understanding makes the price of economic emergence clearer.

Why is seasonality a problem that needs a solution?

The Problem of Seasonality

Locating Arid

Arid refers to climate. Classifying climatic zones has been going on for over a century. The first approximation of the climatic zone for economic purposes must start from geography because geographers handle seasonality better than economists and historians. However, there are two issues with any geography-based classification system. First, the variables that define a zone (seasonality of precipitation, for example) do not occur equally strongly from one year to the next. Nor do these occur similarly in identical spaces every year. The borders of a zone are changeable. This is a minor issue and does not ask us to give up using the classification system. The second issue is messier. Climatic zones do not neatly overlap with political zones. Similar climatic conditions may appear in two neighboring states, but one may have a more prosperous government (because the country has oil or diamonds) than the other. How do we tell the story of the challenge and response? Should we use the climatic zone (to illustrate the challenge) or the nation-state (to illustrate the response) as the basic unit?

I do not have a solution to this problem. Instead of complicating the zoning, the book mainly follows a geographical approach when discussing regions in terms of the environment (Chapter 3). It switches to national boundaries when dealing with institutional reforms or geoengineering. Effectively, from Chapter 5 and the formation of European colonial states in Asia and Africa, the reference changes from mainly environmental or eco-logical zones to primarily political ones. *West Africa* may be used in both cases, with slightly different meanings. We must live with this awkwardness.

Let's start with the environmental zoning. The part of the world that this book is interested in is the arid tropics. The area is large in extent, about a third or more of the globe's land surface (Map 1.1). One section of it, the hyper-arid zone, has few rainy days in a year and is desert or so thinly pop-ulated that a story of economic emergence seems impossible. And yet, like Egypt-Sudan, served by the Nile floods, or the Mexican northwest, served by groundwater, areas within the hyper-arid do have thriving economies. I do not exclude these hyper-arid water-rich areas from the study, even though the concept of seasonality applies with more force in the semi-arid regions. Seasonality works directly in semi-arid spaces and indirectly via the recharge mechanism in hyper-arid ones with a river or an aquifer. Despite this difference, the responses to aridity and seasonality are often similar between these areas.

Of more direct interest is the climate class called the *semi-arid tropics*. The geographer Carl Troll used this term to mean places where rainfall exceeded potential evaporation for a limited time in the year. The moist equatorial areas like Amazonia are intertropical but outside this definition. So are the deserts. Semi-arid, however, combines features of both these zones—very wet and dry—at different times of the year. Roughly located between 15° and 25° north and south latitudes, the semi-arid tropics have one-sixth of the world's population, the world's highest population density, lower-than-average Gross Domestic Product per head, above-average infant mortality, and the world's lowest levels of water availability.[1] These features are interrelated.

In development studies, *semi-arid tropics* refers to areas with enough rainfall to enable rainfed farming but where the rain is uncertain from season to season.[2] I use a broader definition that is less rooted in the monsoonal cycle. Semi-arid tropics are areas where high temperatures dry up surface water faster than in temperate climates, in addition to erratic but significant moisture inflow. Arid and moist seasons alternate, making economic and demographic transition dependent on water recycling between seasons.

Tropical seasonality with "high temperatures and evaporation rates in addition to highly variable and unreliable rainfall" is a distinct climate type.[3] "The degree of seasonality in precipitation [is the] most pronounced in the tropical and subtropical ecoregions and generally low in the predominant ecoregions of the northern hemisphere."[4] By contrast, the temperate

---

[1] Matti Kummu and Olli Varis, "The World by Latitudes: A Global Analysis of Human Population, Development Level and Environment across the North-South Axis over the Past Half Century," *Applied Geography*, 31(2), 2011, 495–507.

[2] Thomas S. Walker and James G. Ryan, *Village and Household Economies in India's Semi-arid Tropics*, Baltimore: Johns Hopkins University Press, 1990.

[3] C.T. Agnew, "Water Availability and the Development of Rainfed Agriculture in South-West Niger, West Africa," *Transactions of the Institute of British Geographers*, 7(4), 1982, 419–457, cited text on p. 423.

[4] Simeon Lisovski, Marilyn Ramenofsky and John C. Wingfield, "Defining the Degree of Seasonality and its Significance for Future Research," *Integrative and Comparative Biology*, 57(5), 2017, 934–942.

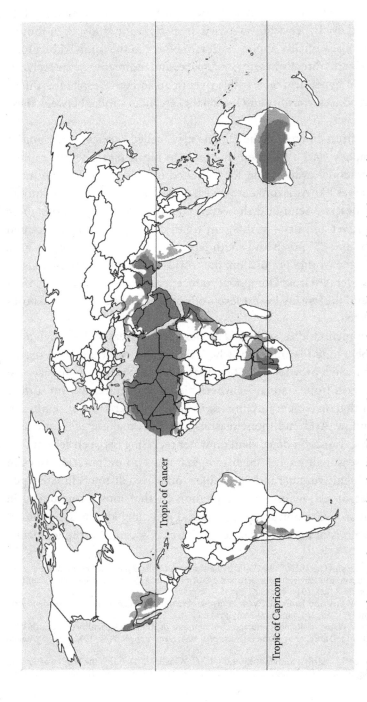

Map 1.1 Arid tropics, hyper-arid including deserts shown in darker shade, semi-arid in lighter shade
Source: Based on Köppen-Geiger data in the public domain

zones are temperate because of lower average heat (low evapotranspiration rates) and an even distribution of rains during the year. *Evapotranspiration* is the process by which water is transferred from the Earth's surface to the atmosphere. The rate depends on solar radiation, air temperature, vapor pressure deficit, wind speed, and the characteristics of plants and vegetation.[5]

Thirty-three countries in Asia and Africa have an average annual rainfall level of less than five hundred millimeters or twenty inches. The tropics pass through fourteen of these, and twelve more contain extremely arid lands within five hundred miles of the 23°27′ latitudes. In most countries (eighteen of twenty-six), the maximum summer temperature exceeds 50° Celsius (122° Fahrenheit). Excessive heat evaporates surface water rapidly, and occasional rains on baked soil cause high runoffs. A 1970s book on the desert fringes of western India described a semi-arid land in this way: "Extremely low (5–20 inches or 12–50 cm) and uncertain rainfall, widely fluctuating temperature, low atmospheric humidity, desiccating winds, sandy soils susceptible to erosion, generally brackish or saline and inadequate subsoil water, . . . low and sparse vegetation consisting of drought-hardy trees, shrubs, and perennial grasses."[6] The semi-arid tropics display these conditions for some months in a year (in the northern hemisphere, November until June) when the heat dries up surface water (evapotranspiration rates exceed the rate of moisture inflow), usually the most accessible type of water.

High aridity would turn these lands into a desert but for the intertropical convergence zone (ITCZ)—or the area where the trade winds of both hemispheres converge, causing rainfall. The ITCZ is a low-pressure and high-rainfall belt that shifts northward or southward with the thermal equator and at variable speeds over land and sea. These rainfall episodes are concentrated in a few months, sometimes a few weeks, of the year and are often called *monsoons*. The temperate zones do not experience the combination of aridity and a bell-shaped rainfall pattern (for an illustration, see Figure 1.1).

For the three or four months when moisture influx exceeds evapotranspiration, groundwater pools are recharged, and vegetation proliferates. The

---

[5] The vapor pressure deficit is the difference between the amount of moisture in the air and the moisture the air could potentially hold. A relatively high value indicates that the air is too dry, resulting in faster transpiration and drying of plants.

[6] N.S. Jodha and V.S. Vyas, *Conditions of Stability and Growth in Arid Agriculture*, Vallabh Vidyanagar: Agroeconomic Research Centre, 1969.

6 WATER AND DEVELOPMENT

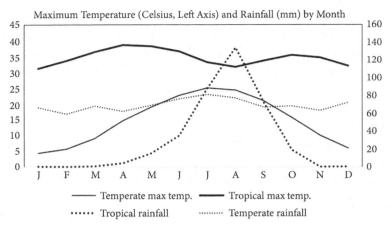

Figure 1.1 Seasonality: Comparing Tropical and Temperate Areas

Notes: The samples consist of the capitals of six countries in Sahel-Sudan (tropical), and New York, London, and Berlin (temperate). In each case, the figures are the average maximum monthly temperatures and monthly rainfall.
Source: https://en.climate-data.org/

western Indian area that the citation refers to received rain but of a quantity just enough to sustain livestock and insufficient to grow high-valued grains. In even drier regions, the pastures are so precarious that a small herd buildup would cause overgrazing or the pasture shrinking fast. In other monsoonal areas, the rain would permit growing one crop or two with relatively little artificial irrigation effort.

Over a big part of the intertropical area, the heat-rain balance is enough to create a *savanna*—also known as *range, prairie,* or *steppe*—sustaining herding but not agriculture. A rainfall level of 250 mm is considered the minimum necessary for any farming to exist at all.[7] Most of North Africa and the Middle East, the Horn of Africa, and Namibia have less; other tropical countries have extensive areas with less rainfall than that. Elsewhere, the monsoon and seasonal floods shape crop choices. Monsoons come in variable strengths. South and Southeast Asia experience powerful monsoons. On average, the African monsoons bring less rain. In sub-Saharan Africa and South Asia, 50 percent of the land is tropical savanna. Like all other livelihoods in these lands, pastoralism is "defined by the presence of water

---

[7] Thomas Vettera and Anna-Katharina Rieger, "Ancient Water Harvesting in the Old World Dry Belt—Synopsis and Outlook," *Journal of Arid Environments* 169, 2019, 42–53.

sources."[8] Herders must access fields, sometimes hundreds of miles apart, that stay moist at different times of the year.

In the remaining areas, seasonal rainfall or flooding is sufficient to enable rainfed and "flush" or recessionary agriculture. Of the total annual moisture inflow of about four thousand cubic kilometers in India, 100 percent comes from seasonal rains.[9] In the inland Niger Delta, of the total yearly moisture inflow of forty cubic kilometers, 13 percent comes from rains, and 87 percent comes from flooding of the larger rivers that receive rains near their sources.[10] Much of the Niger River plains is semi-arid. However, in the inland delta of Mali, a land of lakes formed by annual river flooding sustains cultivation and fishing over thousands of square miles. In both South Asia and the West African Sahel, evaporation and seepage losses are significant. It is 50 percent of India's inflow (as mentioned) and 43 percent in the inland Niger Delta.

The semi-arid (next section) is particularly interesting to this book and economic historians for its seasonality. I use this word analytically as a possible cause of poverty and stagnation, which needs some explanation.

What Is Seasonality?

An everyday meaning of seasonality is the existence of a busy and slack season in rain or flood-dependent agricultural economies. In tropical monsoon areas, the high temperatures that cause aridity also cause the slack season, whereas concentrated rainfall in the monsoons creates the prospect of an economically active time within the year. The main rainfed crops reach the markets during the busy season, when consumption and investment peak, and everybody spends more money and borrows more money to fund these expenditures. Seasonality is universal. Extreme seasonality is not. Monthly interest rate fluctuations are a crude measure of the seasonality of business activity. The economist Simon Kuznets estimated an index

---

[8] Pauline Peters, cited in Frances Cleaver, "Water as a Weapon: The History of Water Supply Development in Nkayi District, Zimbabwe," *Environment and History*, 1(3), 1995, 313–333.

[9] "India's Water," The Economic Times, accessed December 5. 2024. https://economictimes.indiatimes.com/news/politics-and-nation/the-precarious-situation-of-indias-water-problem/articleshow/57965416.cms?from=mdrInland.

[10] Moussa Ibrahim, Dominik Wisser, Abdou Ali, Bernd Diekkrüger, Ousmane Seidou, Adama Mariko, and Abel Afouda, "Water Balance Analysis over the Niger Inland Delta—Mali: Spatio-Temporal Dynamics of the Flooded Area and Water Losses," *Hydrology*, 4(1), 2017, 1–23.

8 WATER AND DEVELOPMENT

for the pre-Depression United States.[11] The busy-season interest rate was 2 to 5 percent more than the slack-season rate. It was 250 to 300 percent of the slack-season rate in India in the 1920s. Both countries had similar banks and similar laws related to banking in the 1920s. Their difference stemmed not from institutional conditions but from the climate.

Tropical seasonality was more than a modulation. The monsoons made agriculture possible with little investment in irrigation infrastructure, a cheap and easy way to grow food. Yet geographers, almost without exception, would describe the climate as "hostile" to human life and not ideal for economic growth.[12] Why? Because rainfed agriculture also shortened the economically productive season in the arid areas. The climate constrained economic and population growth in this way. Water matters to all societies: to sustain lives, for intensive agriculture, and for industries and cities—and mattered in a specific way in the semi-arid tropics. The combination of wetness and aridity shortened the cultivation season. The closer one gets to the two tropics, "production [of food] is limited by insufficient water, for everywhere in the [semi-arid tropics] the annual potential evapotranspiration exceeds rainfall."[13] Water mattered by running out for an extended time during the year, whereas enormous volumes of water came in free of charge for a concentrated time during the year.

The climate constrained economic and population growth in other ways too. The temperature and the high radiation are suitable for vegetation growth, so biodiversity is the greatest in the tropics. However, aridity tends to depress land yield in rainfed farming. "Water is a major factor limiting agricultural productivity."[14] Although average soil quality in the major arid or semi-arid tropics varies, most soils in the arid areas are of the entisols type, sandy soil, low in organic matter, and with low water retention capacity—or aridisols, again dry with low concentration of organic matter.[15] Most aridisols contain water for plant growth for no more than ninety days. These soils can be suitable for crop production with irrigation and additional nutrients. Managing land yield, however, is not just a matter of applying more water but also controlling the water addition so that nutrients do not leach away.

---

[11] Simon Kuznets 1993, "Seasonal Variations in Industry and Trade: Appendices," NBER Working Paper No. 2204, accessed on October 10, 2019, www.nber.org/chapters/c2204.pdf.
[12] Lisovski, Ramenofsky, and Wingfield, "Defining the Degree of Seasonality."
[13] S. Jeevananda Reddy, "Climatic Classification: The Semi-Arid Tropics and Its Environment—A Review," *Pesquisa Agropecuária Brasileira*, 18(8), 1983, 823–847, cited text on p. 843.
[14] Agnew, "Water Availability."
[15] Classifications developed by the US Department of Agriculture.

INTRODUCTION 9

Doing this is easier with groundwater and more complicated with canal water, floodwater, and rainwater.

Tropical biodiversity entails an elevated risk of death and debilitation from diseases. This is so not only because seasonal water scarcity would raise the risk that many people would use contaminated water sources. There was another factor: the distinctness of tropical disease conditions lies in the agency of the environmental reservoir in disease transmission. Compared with colder climates, disease transmission occurs relatively more due to the pathogens' occurrence in the environment and relatively less due to the number of infected people. Pathogen occurrence in soil, water, vectors, and food sources contributes to the spread of diseases like schistosomiasis, leprosy, trachoma, malaria, and a variety of lesser-known diseases.[16] Because many infectious diseases pass through environmental pathways in the tropics, even temporary environmental changes, like droughts and floods, can quickly unleash epidemics. In the past, these epidemics started in two ways: water quality or food sources changed, or reduced nutrition made people more vulnerable to pathogens already present in the environmental reservoir. Droughts, in these ways, could cause mass deaths with or without a persistent shortage of food.

Besides land yield, a second way seasonality might constrain economic growth was by limiting the size of cities to adjust to the size of the available local and perennial water sources. Perennial rivers were a rarity in the semi-arid tropics, but thanks to monsoonal rains, there were plenty of rivers. I cannot offer numbers to prove this correlation between scale of flow, seasonality of flow, and city size. Economic historians have not explored the link, and reconstructing the database is beyond this book's scope, but impressions confirm the connection. Contrast premodern city size between the north and the south of India. In the eighteenth century, Mughal imperial cities were much larger than those in the Deccan Plateau for one apparent reason: the former was situated next to Himalayan rivers, fed by snowmelt and with water throughout the year. Similarly, the robust urbanism in West Africa, where the deltas of major rivers receive water from the wet highlands, contrasts with the weaker urbanism of the Horn of Africa, where rivers of similar scale are absent.

[16] A. Garchitorena, S.H. Sokolow, B. Roche, C.N. Ngonghala, M. Jocque, A. Lund, M. Barry, E.A. Mordecai, G.C. Daily, J.H. Jones, J.R. Andrews, E. Bendavid, S.P. Luby, A.D. LaBeaud, K. Seetah, J.F. Guégan, M.H. Bonds, and G.A. De Leo, "Disease Ecology, Health and the Environment: A Framework to Account for Ecological and Socio-Economic Drivers in the Control of Neglected Tropical Diseases," *Philosophical Transactions: Biological Sciences*, 372(1722), 2017, 1–12.

10 WATER AND DEVELOPMENT

Another indirect way to test the association is to consider consumption. In the 1970s, Sudanese towns' daily per-capita water consumption was about 20 gallons. A study suggested that industrial and business growth prospects improved only when the average exceeded that figure.[17] Around 1950, the average water consumption in India's cities was about 20 gallons per day. Large metropolises had about two and a half times that level, small towns much less. In 1950, an average American consumed 145 gallons daily, and an average Briton consumed a slightly smaller quantity. Both countries were significantly more urban than India or Sudan. The difference in consumption level stemmed partly from evaporation rates and seasonal variation in the reservoirs from which the cities drew water.

A third way that seasonality constrained economic growth was by elevating drought risk. Although monsoons are a certainty, the quantity of moisture inflow is uncertain and unpredictable because the ITCZ does not follow a fixed pathway. Drought means dryness. While the world's drought map is changing due to climate change, on average and in the long run, the chronically drought-prone regions of the world are still concentrated in the arid tropics. Dryness sometimes causes famines or acute food shortages. In the past, when food trade was more limited and costlier, the relationship between drought and famine was closer. Drought and famine occurred in many geographies, not just the arid tropical ones. In the tropics, the risk of the combined event was relatively high because, for the same percentage shortfall in moisture inflow, the semi-arid tropics experience more significant surface water loss. On average, two severe droughts should occur yearly somewhere in the tropics. Droughts seriously affected nearly two billion people in Asia, Africa, and the Middle East in the twentieth century. The corresponding number in Europe, the Americas, and Oceania was 5 percent of that figure, even though the rainfall shortages were often quite similar between these two regions.[18]

A high drought risk would induce people to invest in insurance assets like animals or gold. Some evidence of the prediction that the semi-arid tropics raised risk aversion and led to underinvestment came from research done after the green revolution in the 1970s. Farmers in the semi-arid tropics seemed reluctant to adopt the new seeds. With their rain dependence,

[17] El-Sayed El-Bushra and Mohammed Osman El Sammani, "Urban and Rural Water Supplies in the Sudan," *Ekistics*, 43, 1977, 36–42.

[18] Regina Below, Emily Grover-Kopec, and Maxx Dilley, "Documenting Drought-Related Disasters: A Global Reassessment," *Journal of Environment and Development*, 16(3), 2007, 328–344.

INTRODUCTION 11

they stuck to indigenous cultivars that delivered low but assured yields.[19] More generally, pervasive risk aversion could mean keeping stocks of food (instead of selling them) and livestock, holding liquid assets like silver, and an aversion to investing in land improvement.

Fourth, seasonality limited the size and capability of states. In discussing premodern China, Prasannan Parthasarathi suggests that the natural priorities of premodern states ruling lands with famine-prone areas were to avoid famines rather than generate economic growth.[20] The only way most states could deal with famines was to commute taxes—that is, by becoming weaker for the time being. Premodern and colonial states in Asia and Africa earned too little money per head to sustain a robust public goods drive.[21] Premodern states, and many modern ones, found it more challenging to tax herders than farmers. Farmers were no great resource either, for land yield was low. "With few exceptions," writes Richard Roberts, "African precolonial states were not very powerful." Although they were "states," in the sense of possessing coercive capacity that many who lived under them saw to be legitimate, "their ability to transform societies . . . were limited. Analogies to European state forms are not very helpful." They were also "essentially fragile," being exposed to drought and famine risk. A prolonged drought in the mid-eighteenth century led to a political collapse in the middle Niger Basin.[22] Limited state capacity derived from the poverty of the rural livelihoods that were taxed.

Seasonality elevated mortality from famines and droughts and depressed population growth. The population growth rate in Asia and Africa was close to zero until the second quarter of the twentieth century. Disease deaths were the leading cause of high mortality. Many of the diseases were related to drought. Drought reduced water quality and led to outbreaks of waterborne diseases like cholera. Food shortages reduced resistance to common infectious diseases. The relatively low capacity to produce food would depress nutritional intake and population growth in normal conditions. Again, in recent times, evidence shows that calorie sources varied drastically between seasons in the arid tropics.

[19] Hans P. Binswanger, "Risk Attitudes of Rural Households in Semi-arid Tropical India," *Economic and Political Weekly*, 13(25), 1978, A49–A62.

[20] Prasannan Parthasarathi, *Why Europe Grew Rich and Asia Did Not: Global Economic Divergence, 1600–1850*, Cambridge: Cambridge University Press, 2011, 172–175.

[21] K.K. Karaman and Sevket Pamuk, "Ottoman State Finances in European Perspective, 1500–1914," *Journal of Economic History*, 70, 2010, 593–629. See also http://www.ata.boun.edu.tr/sevketpamuk/JEH2010articledatabase.

[22] Richard Roberts, *Warriors, Merchants and Slaves: The State and the Economy in the Middle Niger Valley 1700–1914*, Stanford, CA: Standford University Press, 1987, 9–11.

12   WATER AND DEVELOPMENT

The world's water databases register estimates of freshwater withdrawal and freshwater sources.[23] The Sahel-Sudan region of the tropics (Chad, Mali, Niger, Burkina Faso, Mauritania, and Sudan) has a low land yield, low GDP per head, and low per-capita renewable water. As a proportion of the world average, per-capita renewable water ranges from 5 percent in Sudan and Mauritania to 30 percent in Mali. This measure is based on seasonal rainfall, cross-border flows, floodwater, and upper aquifer withdrawals. South Asia falls in between with 20 percent. On the other end of the water curve, the United States, Canada, and Scandinavia are water-rich, income-rich, and have high land yields. So do Japan and Europe. There is, however, considerable variation in all three indices within Europe. Like Europe, there is a wide dispersion among middle-income countries. The data do not tell us that the more arid a country is, the poorer it must be. The data tell us that a dry country can be so far from the norm that strategies to overcome aridity must be prioritized.

All geographies experience seasonality. Its form differs, and therefore, ways for humans to adapt vary. In parts of monsoon Asia, such as Japan and Korea, rainfall has a bell shape, but the bell looks like a longer and flatter hill than a sharp spike, as in South Asia. Japan is also a temperate zone region by aridity or evaporation loss. In other words, not all monsoon areas are alike, and the tropical monsoon is a distinct package formed of alternating periods of moisture flow and moisture stress or alternating risk of flood and drought.

In places with extreme winters, such as northern Europe or the north of North America, surviving and working through the winter would require, in the past, burning a lot of wood and coal. In the warm, arid tropics— where rains appear for a few weeks a year, leaving the rest of the year dry and hot—surviving and working throughout the year requires water stored from the wet-season supplies. These strategies may sound symmetric, but they were not. There are two crucial distinctions between cold climate seasonality and warm climate seasonality. Without adequate water storage and recycling facilities, tropical seasonality entails long periods of unemployment and potential starvation in the countryside, low land yield, and a high risk of droughts and famines. The cold winter zones do not necessarily share these conditions. The land, on average, yielded a lot more food and fodder.

---

[23] The dataset has a limitation: it does not adjust for the costs of accessing different sources.

Food was stored through the winter, there was little moisture stress, and famines were rarer (but certainly not unknown) in the temperate zones.

Another issue relating to response marks tropical seasonality as distinct. Heating homes in the past did not involve significant economies of scale, and private resources were adequate for the purpose. Water storage and recycling, by contrast, are expensive and cannot usually be done with private resources. Still, everybody tried to do it. People living in the semi-arid tropics knew that seasonality limited economic opportunities. A whole pattern of response to seasonality developed over the past centuries.

A History of Response

Trade and Technology before Colonialism

Two patterns of response to aridity and seasonality were widespread in the past: trade in goods intensive in moisture in different degrees (economists call this type of trade *virtual trade in water*) and capture of excess moisture during the wet seasons for use in the dry season. When economists think of trade between regions, they think of resource endowments. Regions produce goods for market exchange on the principle that the goods use more of the relatively cheap and abundant resource (labor or land) in that area. History is a narrative of what happens when the relative price of resources or the cost of trade changes. Economists, however, do not know how the story should proceed when the most critical resource in the endowment set is moisture, when the moisture supply is seasonally modulated, and when a significant risk attaches to the supply.

The history of Africa and South Asia suggests alternative modes of analysis when moisture is a critical resource. The trans-Saharan caravan trade was partly an example of moisture-bound specialization and exchange (examples of similar specialization in the Horn of Africa and Australia figure in Chapter 7). An account of the middle Niger Basin before and during French colonization uses the term *ecological specialization*.[24] Arid and wet zones in this account traded specific goods intensive in more moisture or less—for example, millet or animals for rice. Arid zones also appear in the account as areas of monoproduction rather than producers of a diversified basket

[24] Roberts, *Warriors, Merchants and Slaves.*

14   WATER AND DEVELOPMENT

of goods. States in the arid zones were fiscally weak and fragile because the scope to earn much money from land or transit taxes was limited. Therefore, trade did not respond much to political controls or changes in control.

The ecological zones, moreover, not only traded but were tied via non-trade links like sanctioned or forced migration during droughts. "Geographical sectors," according to another study of the West African Sahel, or the pastoral and desert sectors, developed trading relationships and interdependence.[25] In Niger in the nineteenth century, trade and dependence between the desert-edge herders (Tuareg) and the farmlands (Hausa) was systematic. The commodity composition of the trade depended on geology (mining, for example) and climate (moisture supply and fluctuations). This interdependence, which factored in both costs of goods and security during droughts, changed in the twentieth century with closer connections developing between the savanna and the coast.

Similar distinctions and focus upon trade and nontrade links appear in studies of pastoralism and agriculture—implicitly marking the vegetal, plant-oriented spheres from the pastoral, animal-oriented ones. From semi-arid South India comes the distinction between dry and wet agriculture—that is, rainfed and irrigated agriculture—and the finding that in irrigated areas, turnover in the land market and changes in patterns of inequality were faster and more profound in impact.[26]

These works caution against drawing too sharp boundaries between these zones. Haruka Yanagisawa thought the "intermediate" zone between the wet and the dry in South India, with mixed farming methods, a fascinating ecological zone because it saw considerable changes in agricultural methods and landownership. Between the vegetal and the pastoral, some lands were usable for growing plants in one season and grazing animals in another. Since the nineteenth century, the intermediate zone saw some of the most dramatic changes, like converting combined use to single-purpose use, nomadic pastoralists to sedentary livestock breeders, and so on.

Locally, the solution to seasonality was an obvious one. By trapping the runoff and excess rains of the wet season and recycling in the dry, the dry months and the desert-edge areas could grow crops and create economic

[25] Stephen Baier, "Economic History and Development: Drought and the Sahelian Economies of Niger," *African Economic History*, 1, 1976, 1–16.

[26] Haruka Yanagisawa, "Mixed Trends in Landholding in Lalgudi Taluk: 1895–1925," *Indian Economic and Social History Review*, 26(4), 1989, 405–435. Beyond these specific findings, the wet-dry contrast has not played as prominent a role in South Asian historiography as in its African counterparts.

opportunities. The storage would sustain towns and cities if enough were stored to withstand evaporation. None knew that better than the people who lived in these regions. That "successful agriculture . . . depends on irrigation from reservoirs filled during the monsoon . . . was recognized by the Indian people long before the coming of the Europeans."[27]

However, mass storage was expensive to build and maintain. Most systems that archaeologists have discovered tend to be minor, the biggest serving a small region, even a cluster of villages or a part of the capital city, or built for flood control. Ancient storage and retention systems—like the ahar-pyne in eastern India, acequia in Mexico, or qanat in the Jordan Valley—were local and context-bound and often crumbled away with population growth, dispersal of communities, and withdrawal of patronage. Most premodern states did not have the financial or technological capability to build large systems, though some tried. Some of the most significant examples from the tropical drylands, like the canals in the pre-fourteenth-century Sri Lankan north and east, Sultanate canals in Punjab and the prehistoric canals of Mesoamerica were of a scale that was more exceptional than the norm and fell into disuse with shifts in politics.

More often, the response to seasonality was circulatory migration, transhumance, and a combination of herding and farming. When droughts struck, movements covered longer distances, became semipermanent, and changed the relationship between settlers and Indigenous peoples. Movement is a constant theme in the economic history of tropical Asia and Africa before the colonial era. A substantial share of the Indian population was mobile during certain seasons until recently. In Africa, more water-secure lands next to the drought-hit ones provided insurance, sometimes resettlement, and farmland development opportunities.

Some movements depended on prior arrangements; for example, farmers offered refuge to nomadic herders south of the Sahara Desert fringe during droughts of exceptional intensity. Animals enriched farmlands in an average year. Without a compatible arrangement, movements would entail significant costs. Forced migrations, by contrast, did not follow rules. Hierarchies emerged during forced migrations. People with insufficient means to cope with shortages became dependent upon strangers during crises, sometimes accepting a degree of unfreedom. Cutting across the scholarship on

---

[27] Charles Comstock, "The Mir Alum Dam," *Military Engineer*, 26(148), 1934, 254–257, cited text on p. 254.

16 WATER AND DEVELOPMENT

Atlantic and Indigenous slave trades and across Asia and Africa, premodern migrations, historians claim, reinforced caste, inequality, and trading in enslaved people.

Trade and technology reached a new level in the nineteenth century.

The Colonial Period: Trade, Technology, Disease, Property Rights, and River Water

In the nineteenth century, European colonial regimes ruled much of arid Asia and Africa. These states did not share many similarities except that all had to struggle to raise financial resources to fund their expensive military and administrative setup. They were, however, militarily strong states, stronger than most Indigenous states, and could consider the development of resources occurring within the territories they firmly controlled. And while the regimes sometimes misread the geography, they unfailingly understood the value of water. Significant changes happened when they did.

European colonialism prioritized the vegetal, and made laws and invested in infrastructure to strengthen it. The vegetal and the pastoral spheres also became sharply marked due to the remapping of territories during colonial rule and because private property rights worked for the peasants and did not work for the herders whose "property" was not fixed geographically. Colonialism imposed political boundaries upon these ecological ones and sometimes tried to use its superior military capacity to create economic regions corresponding to the new boundaries. These attempts were a partial success at best.[28] The failure stemmed from the limits that ecology imposed on the scope of intensive agriculture and crop diversification. In the longer run, of course, borders did matter. They did most decisively when states stepped in to invest seriously in water infrastructure that could change land use or create big cities. That transition took shape from the late interwar period.

Transport was a critical area of intervention, partly for military reasons and partly an implicit policy to encourage trade between interior drier areas

---

[28] Richard L. Roberts, *Two Worlds of Cotton: Colonialism and the Regional Economy in the French Soudan, 1800–1946*, Stanford, CA: Stanford University Press, 1996.

and seaboard ones, a kind of virtual trade in goods intensive in water in different degrees. Market forces changed the relationship between ecological zones. It is not easy to offer a straightforward narrative of a decline of the older patterns of trade. We do know that the trans-Saharan caravan trade changed in the West African Sahel in the nineteenth century. The climate probably became more arid, inducing some pastoralist groups to go south. European trade forged closer connections between overland and overseas trades. European merchants on the seaboard supplied cloth, tea, sugar, and firearms. Guns aided religious and imperialist wars as well as piratic raids on the caravans. But guns also aided the protection of the caravans.[29] The Atlantic slave trade declined, yet regional demand inside Africa for enslaved people continued. If these contradictory developments leave the average trend in overland trade open to interpretation, technology did change its status forcefully around 1900.

From the turn of the twentieth century, the railway considerably reduced trade costs between the semi-arid savanna and the seaboard. In eastern and southern Africa, the railway and the expansion of French and British colonial administrations led to the speedy growth of livestock trade for export and domestic markets, to which merchants and pastoralists redirected their resources. Several arid-land products entered export trades—animals, cotton, and groundnut being some of the more famous examples. Cotton and groundnut from rainfed or dry lands emerged as major export commodities in India. The trans-Saharan trade, whatever its scale, was no longer a powerful integrating force between regions.

Engineers and agronomists advising or working for the colonial administration insisted that large waterworks were essential to sustain cities and deliver on the ambition to extend cultivation. In the nineteenth century, engineers could plan extensive works over a river basin because the territorial extent over which these states ruled was larger than that of the Indigenous states that preceded or survived colonial expansion. When geography permitted such actions, some states (notably Egypt, India, and Sudan) diverted river water to promote commercial agriculture. The impact on land yield and urban growth was limited because large-scale storage or reservoirs

---

[29] Ghislaine Lydon, *On Trans-Saharan Trails: Islamic Law, Trade Networks, and Cross-Cultural Exchange in Nineteenth-Century Western Africa*, Cambridge: Cambridge University Press, 2009.

18   WATER AND DEVELOPMENT

were not yet a part of the plan. The concepts—like canals taken from a perennial source—were not a European import either. In many cases, ancient works were revived.

Transportation, settlements, and urban development initiated a demographic transition. Across Asia and Africa, the initial effect of colonialism was a rise in epidemics, especially cholera, malaria, trypanosomiasis, and rinderpest, as people and herds began to move around more and congregate in smaller spaces. But by 1920, a turnaround had set in owing to concentrated attention to water quality. In the towns and cities, authorities invested in water storage and piped water supply. Although a limited step, the new infrastructure made sanitation easier and, together with the fruits of bacteriological studies, reduced epidemic deaths. Throughout the tropical world, death rates from climate shocks fell after 1900, not because droughts became less frequent, nor because of better famine relief, but because of epidemic control measures and, in some cases, railways transporting food faster and cheaper. Before 1900, the population growth rate was near zero. In a drought-prone country, initially, "people would have clustered . . . in the best-watered parts of this semi-arid region, and would have grown more numerous there."[30] As that happened, the drive to settle in the drier lands escalated, exposing more and more people to droughts and intense competition for limited land and water. This "climate-sensitive demographic model" of population growth was finally broken in the early decades of the twentieth century.

A better understanding of famines contributed to the shift in mortality. British colonial rulers in nineteenth-century India developed an intuition about why droughts sometimes blew up into famines by studying three late-nineteenth-century famines in the Deccan Plateau. Their findings were that interyear variation in moisture supply and the cost of transporting food mattered to the equation and that famines were a local event with a broad impact. The impact stemmed from movements of people who often died on their way to a less stressed area or spread diseases. The intuition that famines had a spatial-climatic element led to more emphasis on artificial irrigation, cholera control, railways, and data collection on weather and harvests. Aspects of the package were transplanted in different countries throughout the tropical world in the twentieth century.

[30] Joseph C. Miller, "The Significance of Drought, Disease and Famine in the Agriculturally Marginal Zones of West-Central Africa," *Journal of African History*, 23(1), 1982, 17–61, cited text on p. 22.

INTRODUCTION   19

Famine and drought studies also suggested that "hunger does not kill, it is sickness that kills."[31] With advances in bacteriology and the growing understanding of vectors of common diseases, a significant shift occurred in the tropical medical research outlook, from observing people, their habits, and their landscapes to researching the habits and the habitats of the vectors and the bacterial reservoirs. For historians of empires, the shift was of particular interest as a lens into the process that made an unfamiliar environment familiar and potentially controllable.[32] This enterprise may appear to be a political one, and most historians read it as such. On the contrary, it was consistent with the fundamental nature of disease generation in the tropical world: the environmental reservoir was a richer, bigger, and more potent agent in causing disease outbreaks in the tropics than in the temperate world. The medical research paradigm needed to engage with the reservoir concept in some form. That started in colonial times, and scientists employed by the colonial bureaucracies led that new science. A new understanding of disease led to attention to sanitation and water quality. Public health and medicine to tackle just a few waterborne diseases could substantially bring down deaths from droughts.

Besides transport and disease, sharing river water by agreed-upon rules was another area of intervention. Colonial powers could collaborate and create more treaties, which sometimes formed a template for postcolonial states, for a geographical reason. All states, colonial or Indigenous, understood the importance of perennial rivers in the tropical landscape in combating seasonality. Because their power extended beyond one country's borders, and thanks to antecedents available in Roman law, the colonial authorities were readier to strike transboundary fluvial treaties.

Fourth, where they could, these states consolidated titles to property directly by redefining private property rights and indirectly by recognizing the authority of clans and chiefs to allocate rights in a manner consistent with the broad economic aims of the state. Coding property rights in land by default defined some of the rights of the pastoralists, which encouraged growth in herding. The desperate drive to raise money imparted a pattern upon their economic plans. The colonial regimes started promoting settled agriculture, plantations, and long-distance trade, hoping to create more business for expatriate firms and settlers or collect more money from land

[31] Ibid., 23.
[32] Helen Tilley, "Ecologies of Complexity: Tropical Environments, African Trypanosomiasis, and the Science of Disease Control in British Colonial Africa, 1900–1940," *Osiris*, 19, 2004, 21–38.

20 WATER AND DEVELOPMENT

and trade. The drives to encourage settled farming and boost trade converged in those areas where forests could be cleared or pastures resettled to create commodity-exporting farms.

While generating a population transition, the infrastructure projects were too few and far between to deliver economic growth. Regional inequality became sharper because moist coastal areas gained more from global trade in export crops and agricultural commercialization than arid ones. Herders remained poor, and some lost access to prime pastures. The joint outcome was increased population growth, limited income gains, and low *per-capita* income growth. We see these societies as failures if we assess performance by observing per-capita income. The real story is that they solved one problem (short lives) better than another (low income).

For the postcolonial states, raising income was the prime challenge.

The Challenge of Development

Since the 1920s, rainfed agriculture has not been economically unsustainable anymore because of population growth and the growing nationalist desire to catch up with the developed Western world. Some late colonial states set the ambition to build big and gain complete control over moisture influx; the independent states took that dream much further. The prewar and the postwar periods, therefore, were very different times. One difference was the formation of new international borders. Independence from imperial rule marked a significant break so far as new borders redefined the role of the state. Unlike the river basin–wide models the British had worked with in Egypt, Sudan, or India, the postindependence constructions tended to be located within a border. Canals fell out of favor. Dams and reservoirs became the preferred mode of investment.

When, in the 1950s and 1960s, states in Asia and Africa became independent, the demographic transition made the production of more food and the provision of jobs outside agriculture and pastoralism in urban industries in the cities of critical importance. Ambitious geoengineering took over. Deep drilling, dams, and reservoirs to trap water where runoff was high, interbasin transfers, basin management, and hydroelectric power generation for cities and industries—all had a twentieth-century origin. The states took the project much further with greater access to foreign aid and control over domestic financial markets. They partnered with engineers, a politically

INTRODUCTION 21

neutral lobby that would perform a critical role in economic modernization. The desire to catch up with the West pushed these states to use available technologies fully.

Enormous river valley projects were designed to generate water and power for the cities and the countryside. The idea of impounding water during excess inflow was an old one. From the twentieth century, the states were inspired by American interwar projects to develop the capability in Asia and Africa to put the impounding idea into practice on an infinitely larger scale than in earlier times. The ability to raise dam heights substantially enabled that shift in scale. To illustrate, possibly the world's largest ancient artificial reservoir, Kala Wewa in fifth-century Anuradhapura in Sri Lanka, had a peak capacity of 125 million cubic meters. The Hoover Dam reservoir has a peak capacity of 35 billion cubic meters. The average large dam built in India in the 1950s and 1960s had a capacity exceeding 1 billion cubic meters. The ability to generate electric power made the postwar different again and linked their development more to the United States rather than Europe or Indigenous precedents.

The scale of dam building around the tropical world between 1965 and 1990 was staggering. Western European governments and the World Bank offered cheap loans to finance these dams. Massive works appeared on the Nile, Niger, Volta, Senegal, Zambezi, Jordan, Euphrates, and Indus Basins. By 1990, there were over two thousand dams across Indian rivers. Most of these had appeared in the Deccan region.

If the dams, reservoirs, and canals prevailed in South Asia and West Africa, a different model would emerge wherever groundwater was plentiful. In northwestern Mexico, for example, wealthy private families owned ranches. Shallow aquifers had long been used in this otherwise hyper-arid place; the scale of the enterprise expanded from the 1940s. Securing the assistance of American engineering firms, landowners drilled deeper and bigger to tap groundwater from deep aquifers. Private capital went into drilling for water where it was present below ground.

Dams and drilling gave rise to a "golden age of agriculture" in different parts of the tropics.[33] The volume of annual freshwater withdrawal rose slowly in many of the world's poorer countries between 1900 and 1950. After that, the growth was explosive and steady, increasing by 200 to 270 percent

---

[33] José Luis Moreno, "'A Never-Ending Source of Water': Agriculture, Society, and Aquifer Depletion on the Coast of Hermosillo, Sonora," *Journal of the Southwest*, 54(4), 2012, 545–568.

in the next fifty-five years. In the poorer countries, much of the extra water went into agriculture. As it did, cereal production in sub-Saharan Africa and South Asia increased from a little less than two hundred million tons to six hundred million tons (1970–2020), a faster rise than in the world. Land yield rose three times in South Asia and 60 percent in sub-Saharan Africa. The gap in the tropical and temperate countries' per-capita incomes closed somewhat in the late twentieth century.

Economic development came at a high environmental and political cost, however. So high was the price that the golden age of agriculture practically ended in the new millennium.

Costs

The colonial accent on intensive agriculture set off a series of adverse outcomes. Canals for irrigation in Egypt, the Indo-Gangetic Basin, and Punjab sometimes degraded land, changed the disease environment, pushed pastoralists farther away, and caused obsolescence of useful local knowledge about the riparian environment.[34] Contests and competition between farmers and nonfarm users of land intensified, breaking out into violent clashes from the mid-twentieth century. It was not always the scarcity of land that generated these conflicts. The land-use patterns in pastoralism and agriculture can be mutually contradictory. Herding needs access to pastures that are viable in different seasons. Herding is at risk if one of these tracts starts growing crops year-round. In Africa, extensive areas that turned from pastures to potential farmland had undefined property rights and no inherited rights. These lands were up for grabs. Conflict had been in the making since commercial agriculture began to spread. Droughts and population dispersal worsened these. In recent times, civil wars in Chad, Mali, Ivory Coast, and Darfur in Sudan testify to the disruptive legacies of the 1970s and 1980s droughts.

By the end of the twentieth century, the dam drive was starting to flag, as the massive environmental and economic costs of river-valley projects made these an unsustainable pathway. These expensive projects caused displacements of people and ecological destruction on a large scale. Dams

---

[34] For a study, see Jennifer L. Derr, *The Lived Nile: Environment, Disease, and Material Colonial Economy in Egypt*, Stanford, CA: Stanford University Press, 2019.

INTRODUCTION   23

encouraged shifts in cropping patterns, with damaging long-term consequences. In a water-scarce economy, cheap or free water leads to wasteful resource use. The change to water-intensive but profitable paddy in arid areas is a good example of the syndrome. Canals also contributed to inequality and were potentially a source of discords. A feature of any water project that uses gravity (like canals drawn from a reservoir in a basin) is that it creates inequality between upstream and downstream users. The colonial legacy of strong property rights on land and weak rights over water further escalated this inequality.

As the dam drive slowed, countries moved to drilling. Since India's economic reforms began (1980s), most urban-industrial water has come from underground rather than surface water recycling projects. In the new millennium, one study after another revealed clear evidence that overextraction was depleting underground water sources in many areas of India and Pakistan. This prospect had already materialized in Mexico, where the primary aquifer came under severe strain at the end of the twentieth century.

Basin-sharing treaties—some inherited from colonial times (between Egypt and Sudan, in West Africa, between Madras province and Mysore state in India), and some designed anew (Indus Waters Treaty)—came under strain by the end of the twentieth century. A new source of tension was China's draft on Himalayan rivers. The upstream state par excellence, China's water policy set store on bilateral rather than multilateral treaties and was often seen by excluded parties as an obstacle to cooperation.

Some of these discords are hard to solve. This is so because any rise in basic living standards in the semi-arid tropics risks increased water stress (Map 1.2). In contrast with a popular narrative of climate change—that overconsumption damages the environment—in this case, the damage to the environment via a collective rise in water stress was a price paid to redress dangerous levels of underconsumption. To ask water-deprived populations to consume less water makes little sense. Therefore, the trade-off between water stress and development entails a moral dilemma.

The narrative that I offer in this book resembles a cross. Access to water increased in the long run, whereas stress increased simultaneously, or the usable water reserve fell sharply. This is not a specifically tropical experience. Most societies in the twentieth century would have experienced such a cross. Population growth alone would have caused one. It is likely, though, that the access curve was steeper in the tropics, and the stress curve fell to a level that has huge adverse consequences and raises serious questions about

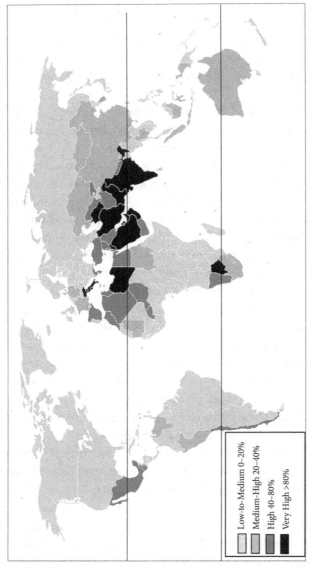

Map 1.2 Water stress (usually measured as a ratio of water extraction to renewable water available). The horizontal lines represent the Tropics.

Source: Based on World Bank data in the public domain.

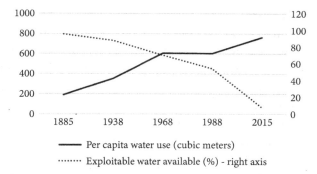

Figure 1.2 The Water Cross, India

Notes: For details on sources and construction, see Tirthankar Roy, "Water, Climate and the Economy in India from 1850 to the Present," *Journal of Interdisciplinary History*, 11(4), 2021, 565–594. Exploitable resource = Total renewable resource (surface water + groundwater − overlap) − environmental flow requirement for the sustainability of the aquatic system. The figure for India is 1089 bcm during the year 2015. I hold this constant for all times. Usable resource is (1 − use/resource)

sustainability. For now, we can illustrate the narrative with data calculated for the Indian subcontinent (Figure 1.2). These propositions find some confirmation from other statistical work on long-term water access (though not stress; see Figure 8.3). However, international comparisons await further search for long-term statistics of the kind the British colonial authority in India started collecting.

Who Is This Book For?

The book has two lessons for two types of readers: economic historians and development specialists. Economic historians think the deep roots of modern economic growth can be found by studying the Western economies. Doing so will show us the factor that generated "modern" or productivity-driven economic growth from the nineteenth century. By this logic, the tropics fell behind in average income growth because they did not have the factor accounting for the Rise of the West. For those who think about economic history in this way, the book has a message. The arid tropics fell behind not because they were insufficiently like the West but because they were arid. Whatever worked for Europe would not have worked for them. Cheap coal and steam engines would not make economic growth happen

26 WATER AND DEVELOPMENT

there. The arid tropics needed to arrive at economic growth by solving a *different* problem from those the Europeans and most North Americans faced. That problem was gaining control over moisture enough to overcome seasonality. They did solve it to some extent in recent decades, overturning a persistent inequality between the temperate and the tropical from the 1950s, but at a significant cost.

The evidence of a persistent tropical-temperate inequality that weakened in the late twentieth century seems robust enough. "In 1992," we read in an NBER blog post, "GNP per capita in the tropical regions was 25 per cent of that in the temperate zone."[35] Angus Maddison's data suggest that inequality had been present in the early nineteenth century. In 1820, GDP per capita in major intertropical regions (South Asia, the Middle East, sub-Saharan Africa, and Latin America [excluding Argentina and Chile] was 30 to 32 percent of that in Europe and European settler regions.[36] Indeed, it was present, less starkly, from much before that. In 1600, the average income in Africa was 47 percent of that in Western Europe, and in India, 60 percent of the latter.[37] In other words, the three great nineteenth-century forces that economic historians sometimes cite to explain the origin of modern world inequality—industrialization, globalization, and European colonial rule—would not explain this inequality. The persistence had owed to geographical factors, the force of which began to weaken from the 1950s. The second half of the twentieth century has seen more convergence than divergence in average incomes across countries.[38]

How do we explain the divergence followed by convergence? The results will be meaningless if we try to explain the recent convergence using the Rise of the West stories. We would be forced to assume that whichever factor accounted for the rise was missing in the poorer world until the 1970s—be these good institutions or good politics—but magically appeared after that. That approach is absurd and untestable. The theory that does work must start with the premise that seasonality constrained incomes in the past, and

---

[35] Andrew Balls, 'Why Tropical Countries are Underdeveloped,' 2001, https://www.nber.org/digest/jun01/why-tropical-countries-are-underdeveloped (accessed on December 5, 2024).

[36] Maddison Project Database (University of Groningen) https://www.rug.nl/ggdc/historicaldevelopment/maddison/releases/maddison-project-database-2020?lang=en. (accessed on December 5, 2024) [published data will not work because it is a database under constant updating]

[37] http://www.ggdc.net › horizontal-file_02-2010. (accessed on December 5, 2024).

[38] François Bourguignon and Christian Morrisson, "Inequality among World Citizens: 1820–1992," *American Economic Review*, 92(4), 2002, 727–744.

the solution to seasonality began to work on a large scale in the late twentieth century.

The book has a message for development specialists who define their field as a bundle of theories and instruments capable of generating modern economic growth in developing countries. It is common in this field to think that in the 1950s and the 1960s, economic policy, instruments, and priorities took shape in the developing world in sharp contrast with the dark ages of colonial domination and as a radical departure from it. This is true so far as European imperial states were generally indifferent about industrialization in the colonies, whereas the newly independent nations wanted industrialization. It is not true anywhere else.

There was another side to state intervention, one we see more clearly in agriculture, urban growth, and pastoralism. Production conditions in agriculture were so dependent on uncertain moisture supplies that the productivity was too low. Changing these conditions required intervention in water. Water was also critical to generating electric power for industrialization and cities. Inspired by that prospect, the postcolonial nation-states invested significant money in dam building. When they did, they pursued a path designed and implemented by engineers in the colonial service and before them by the Indigenous states and communities. All understood development—or its equivalent: "progress"—to mean regulating and conserving natural resources like land and water, especially water. History shows that modern development is rooted in ancient ideas of development. Fiscal, technological, and institutional contexts changed. However, the idea did not change much during ancient, colonial, and postcolonial times. As in the old times, in recent ones, water intervention solved a problem that was the tropics' own: seasonality.

Conclusion

Economic historians are familiar with the claim that cheap energy from fossil fuels and their efficient use enabled the economic emergence of Britain. The growth impulse spread to the Atlantic world through trade, investment, and migration. The book's message is that the economic emergence of the arid tropics similarly depended on solving a critical resource problem, but the resource was different. It was water, not energy. The ambition to permanently alter the landscape to solve seasonality was part of the history of the semi-arid tropics. The partially successful drive to meet that ambition had adverse consequences. The book is about that costly transition to modernity. The complete narrative tells us there is no cheap, reliable, and peaceful response to moisture stress and that economically successful responses have adverse environmental effects.

To tell this story, I draw on contributions from geographers; environmental studies experts; specialists in pastoralism, hydroengineering, and rural development; and climate history experts. There is little available within economic history on aridity and tropical conditions, let alone seasonality. Still, there are connected scholarships that economic historians sometimes rely on. I need to discuss these to restate clearly what this book is aiming to do differently. Chapter 2 does that survey. Chapter 3 discusses the most relevant regions and their political histories, and Chapter 4 deals with responses to seasonality in the precolonial and early colonial eras. Chapters 5 to 7 deal with modern tools and ideas for sharing, recycling, storing, and extracting water. Chapters 8 to 10 illustrate the claim that the generation of modern economic growth in the tropics depended on an expensive, conflict-ridden, and potentially unsustainable pathway to recycle and redistribute water. Chapter 11 considers tropical pastoralism and the conversion of savannas.

Climate change makes the interdependence between water and development shift to some extent. Would the capability to sustain consumption, subsistence, and growth in the arid tropics change? The answer depends on credible predictions of evapotranspiration and peak streamflow (net water flow into waterbodies). The book ends (Chapter 12) with a survey of studies on these two benchmarks.

How new is this inquiry?

Chapter Two
The History of a Concept

The concept of the tropical sometimes interested historians. A credible theory of the economic history of this geographical space does not emerge from their speculations because most writers chose to concentrate on one dimension, either aridity or seasonality of rainfall, not both together. Ellsworth Huntington's attempt to marry geography with history, Karl Wittfogel's hydraulic societies, and famine historiography tilt toward an aridity-based definition. Monsoon Asia, an idea popularized in the 1980s, considers precipitation seasonality and overlooks aridity. Some of this scholarship is still useful in suggesting that water matters, an accent I retain. And it is necessary to see where this scholarship falls short to define the book's scope more precisely. Chapter 2 addresses that task.

Geographical History

In *Pulse of Asia*, Huntington discussed how climate history acted as a driver in the political history of Africa and Asia. He saw the arid regions surrounding wet ones as a persistent threat to "civilizations." The threat materialized during periods of extreme drought and increased aridity. Similarly, Arnold Toynbee, another contemporary writer who considered the rise and fall of civilizations, believed that a challenging (but not too challenging) geographical setting made some societies more creative than others. Until the 1970s, geographers and archaeologists in the Soviet Union, many sharing an interest in Central Asia, delved into the geographical agency behind the rise and fall of ancient settlements.[1] By then, a substantial body of geographers in the Western world had dismissed Huntington's ideas of a climate agency behind the "destiny of nations" as speculative and possibly wrong. Toynbee was regarded more as an entertaining writer with epic ambitions than a reliable

---

[1] John E. Chappell Jr., "Climatic Change Reconsidered: Another Look at 'The Pulse of Asia,'" *Geographical Review*, 60(3), 1970, 347–373.

Water and Development. Tirthankar Roy, Oxford University Press. © Oxford University Press (2025).
DOI: 10.1093/oso/9780197802397.003.0002

30   WATER AND DEVELOPMENT

user of data.[2] Their shared fascination with "civilizations" and Huntington's late obsession with race did not serve either writer well.

Early works like these represented a mode of thinking in which the non-Western experience helped to understand better the West's successes in transforming nature and generating mass prosperity. Pierre Gourou took that project much further, observing that landscape organization happened differently between climatic zones, and that the ability to live longer under tropical disease conditions was a more appropriate measure of adaptation to the environment than income or consumption. The idea that tropical biodiversity was a mixed blessing for human well-being (see Chapter 1) can be traced to his thoughts.[3] Still, his work lacked a precise definition of climatic conditions. The tropics appeared somewhat flat, a weakness to which the civilizational mode of thinking was susceptible. The near-contemporary Karl Wittfogel, while not free from the syndrome, became more famous through his accent on water, calling societies and states in the arid tropics "hydraulic" or "hydraulic civilizations" (his major work used "civilization" sixty times). Wittfogel was a historian of China, just as Gourou started as a scholar of northern Vietnam. Both writers saw the deep interdependence between rivers and peoples in these geographies.

Wittfogel's interest was not geography but polity. A Marxist schooled in Weimar Germany, Wittfogel moved to the United States in 1934 and turned his back on communism. A thread ran through the various phases of his intellectual trajectory: we must include the geographical context of societies to understand the enduring appeal of totalitarianism.

In his most famous work, Wittfogel made three points. First, in "a landscape characterized by full aridity," the possibility of agricultural societies depended on artificial irrigation. Second, the typical form of irrigation was a canal drawn from a river. Third, arid regions saw the emergence of despotic states because canal systems required considerable political, bureaucratic, and military resources. "The administrative officialdom [in China, Egypt,

---

[2] O.H.K. Spate, "Toynbee and Huntington: A Study in Determinism," *Geographical Journal*, 118(4), 1952, 406–424.
[3] Pierre Gourou, "Qu'est-ce que: Le monde tropical?," *Annales. Histoire, Sciences Sociales*, 4(2), 1949, 140–148. The discourse inspired works that defined the arid and semi-arid climate more precisely and in a similar fashion to my book. Little of that output was historical, however. For example, Jean Demangeot, *Les espaces naturels tropicaux: Essai de geographie physique*, Paris: Masson, 1976. Other geographers in that tradition, especially Jean Gallais, studied the aridity. The scholarship represents the French tropical geography school of thought.

and India formed a] mighty hydraulic bureaucracy."[4] At the same time, the power of nonstate institutions, like courts of law, was relatively weak in such societies, hence low levels of development in these places.

Wittfogel is not directly useful for this book for three reasons. Two of these are well known. There was indeed a deep connection between aridity and waterworks. Archaeologists studying the Indus Valley, Jordan Valley, and Mesopotamia drew this connection long before him. One of them, Grahame Clark, famously said that "from the stone age to the 20th century, water has reflected the image of society."[5] Most historians and archaeologists do not see a systematic connection between climate and large scale, or between the environment and concentration of political power.

One of the early critics of the scale point showed that in ancient (pre-thirteenth-century) Sri Lanka, a village reservoir was the typical response to aridity.[6] India offers plentiful examples of "[a] rich historical tradition of local water harvesting."[7] So does tropical Africa. Irfan Habib says that cultivation in the Indo-Gangetic Basin relied mainly on rainwater, with minimal effort spent on artificial irrigation until recent centuries.[8]

Of course, more prominent political actors built more ambitious monuments, dams, canals, or stepwells. However, the claim that these constructions stood for concentrated political power lacks credibility. Nor is it credible that these projects served mass welfare; more likely, access was limited to particular groups. Evidence suggests that most state-made works were maintained by local agents like monasteries in medieval Sri Lanka or peasant communities and warlords in India, meaning that sovereign power was dispersed rather than concentrated. The Sri Lankan water scholarship suggests that the states that built the most famous works became weak from infighting and relied on mercenary soldiers to fight their battles, showing that large works could empower local landholders and warlords to the detriment of the king. Early modern China had a "hydraulic bureaucracy." However, it was

---

[4] Karl Wittfogel, *Oriental Despotism: A Comparative Study of Total Power*, New Haven, CT: Yale University Press, 1957, 8.

[5] Cited in Steven Mithen, "The Domestication of Water: Water Management in the Ancient World and Its Prehistoric Origins in the Jordan Valley," *Philosophical Transactions: Mathematical, Physical and Engineering Sciences*, 368(1931), 2010, 5249–5274.

[6] R.A.L.H. Gunawardene, "Irrigation and Hydraulic Society in Early Medieval Ceylon," *Past and Present*, 53, 1971, 3–27.

[7] Mihir Shah, "Water: Towards a Paradigm Shift in the Twelfth Plan," *Economic and Political Weekly*, 48, 2013, 40–52, cited text on p. 44.

[8] Irfan Habib, "An Examination of Wittfogel's Theory of 'Oriental Despotism,'" in K.S. Lal, ed., *Studies in Asian History, Proceedings of the Asian History Congress, New Delhi*, London: Asia Publishing, 1969, 378–392.

32   WATER AND DEVELOPMENT

not a hierarchical command system; it was fragmented into a federal and a local sphere, as one would expect in the presence of a great diversity of works.[9]

The construction of large-scale waterworks happened over centuries. The present-day viewer looking at the ruins may not realize that "many of the modern ruins simply represent replacements of still older ruins dependent upon the same water supply."[10] The idea that large systems were created by coercing many people may be wrong. The Sri Lankan canals and reservoirs were built with hired labor. But raw labor was hardly the critical resource. Some of these systems required sophisticated knowledge of geology, engineering, and materials. Patterns of intellectual exchange among early empires might better explain what systems would be built.

So, the climate-scale link and the scale-power link were both overstated in Wittfogel. My criticism is that the model misreads climate. The semi-arid tropics are not just hot and dry. They are hot and dry *with a rainy season*. The challenge is not distributing water over space but trapping more to spread it over seasons. Wittfogel, who mentioned monsoons only once in a huge book, did not see this. He was obsessed with the evidence of ancient canals, but canals did not solve the tropical problem. Most canals did not trap water. He was right to note that the variable mediating between people and power was water. However, the water problem was not scarcity as he thought; it was seasonality.

Wittfogel's canal fetish carried over into economic history. The term *hydraulic state* was thrown at random whenever ancient canals were discovered in the developing world, be it India, the Nile Basin, the Yellow River and Yangtze Basins, Siem Reap, the Jordan Valley, the Maya-ruled area of Mesoamerica, or the Peruvian coast, thus bringing into a false equivalence regions as different from one another as Egypt with 14 rainy days in a year and Siem Reap with 155 rainy days in a year.

Modern-day environmental history is not more convincing when dealing with climate. But it does offer one helpful idea.

---

[9] Combined with "an inflexible fiscal system that did not place adequate funds [with regional administrators]," the division of duties did not consistently deliver results. Wenkai He, "Public Interest and the Financing of Local Water Control in Qing China, 1750–1850," *Social Science History*, 39(3), 2015, 409–430.

[10] E.R. Leach, "Hydraulic Society in Ceylon," *Past and Present*, 15, 1959, 2–26.

THE HISTORY OF A CONCEPT   33

Environmental History

European rule in unfamiliar geographies led to numerous attempts to theorize the tropical climate, based on which new plans for agricultural intensification or famine relief could be designed. Aridity was central to how the tropics were imagined or researched, while seasonality remained more obscure. Some historians insist that tropicality was a "discourse that constructs the tropical world as the West's environmental Other."[11] Colonial imagination does enter in this book via land and pastures. In recent environmental history scholarship, climate finds a central place.[12] Again, while aridity is acknowledged more readily, seasonality remains obscure in the sources and the interpretations of what the imperialists thought they were doing.

In one set of studies on pastures and pastoralism, attention falls on the savanna. A stylized chronological narrative says there was once a golden age when communities lived on natural resources. The pastoralists had rights over grazing lands and waterholes; the states recognized these rights, and the pastoralists sustainably used these resources.[13] In the past, a study of Sudan says, "Historically evolved resource-regulating institutions based on traditions, customs, kinship relations, moral pressure and restraints" made sustainable use of land and common property resources possible.[14] Expressing a similar sentiment, a study of Puntland in the nineteenth century says that "interdependence, and a conservation ethic" protected herder clans from death during famines until wider markets made them lose the ethic.[15]

---

[11] For a discussion of this perspective, Daniel Clayton, "Militant Tropicality: War, Revolution and the Reconfiguration of 'The Tropics' c. 1940–c. 1975," *Transactions of the Institute of British Geographers*, 38(1), 2012, 180–192, cited text on p. 180. See also Martin Mahony and Georgina Endfield, "Climate and Colonialism," *Climate Change*, 9, 2018, 1–16; and David Arnold, "'Illusory Riches': Representations of the Tropical World, 1840–1950," *Singapore Journal of Tropical Geography*, 21(1), 2000, 6–18.

[12] Two representative collections are Edmund Burke III and Kenneth Pomeranz, eds., *The Environment and World History*, Berkeley: University of California Press, 2009; Alan Mikhail, ed., *Water on Sand: Environmental Histories of the Middle East and North Africa*, Oxford: Oxford University Press, 2013.

[13] In nonriparian Sudan, until the 1960s, "all land and the associated renewable resources were controlled by communities." These clan networks followed informal rules and "traditional value systems." They excluded outsiders from access and practiced sustainable use among themselves. Gaim Kibreab, "Property Rights, Development Policy and Depletion of Resources: The Case of the Central Rainlands of Sudan, 1940s–1980s," *Environment and History*, 7(1), 2001, 57–108, cited text on p. 63.

[14] Kibreab, "Property Rights." Cited text on p. 59.

[15] Wayne K. Durrill, "Atrocious Misery: The African Origins of Famine in Northern Somalia, 1839–1884," *American Historical Review*, 91(2), 1986, 287–306, cited text on p. 293.

34 WATER AND DEVELOPMENT

In the same way, a history of famines in India writes, "In most of India water had *always* been a communally managed common resource."[16] It follows that European colonialists destroyed the golden age by promoting capitalism and private property, the "ultimate cause of . . . environmental degradation."[17] "Economic changes," writes a historian of Sudan, "set into motion during the colonial period and exacerbated by post-independence policies led to major famine and caused a major crisis of legitimacy for the contemporary state."[18] The story repeats for Ethiopia, the Sahel, and British India.

The premise that once there was a benign and inclusive property rights regime is unverifiable and almost certainly wrong. All forms of property rights presuppose a powerful state. Some pastoralist environments were "societies where states do not fit well" or "economies without states."[19] There was no force above to make groups cooperate. Only low population growth would stem a breakdown into anarchy. When rural communities controlled local resources, the allocation rules were not egalitarian. In precolonial India, the "untouchable" peoples had no recognized right to humanmade water bodies.

The part of the story that is true is that the European imperialists laid claim to all territory and all resources within their borders. To do that, they drew the borders carefully. Present-day national borders in Asia and Africa are usually an imperial legacy. Declaring ownership over open-access lands would mean little without an adequate legal and administrative infrastructure. However, unlike the local communities, these states could think of working on the landscape on a bigger scale than before. Nation-states inherited that thinking with better hardware (dams and drills) and software (property rights, tax reforms, and foreign aid). To sum up, the colonial agency needs to be qualified. It needs to be contextualized with reference to the tropical geography and knowledge that the imperialists were at least partly doing the same thing (dealing with seasonality) that the ancient states and societies had done.

[16] Mike Davis, *Late Victorian Holocausts: El Niño Famines and the Making of the Third World*, London: Verso, 2001, 331, emphasis added.

[17] Durrill, "Atrocious Misery," 63.

[18] Lidwien Kapteijns, "The Historiography of the Northern Sudan from 1500 to the Establishment of British Colonial Rule: A Critical Overview," *International Journal of African Historical Studies*, 22(2), 1989, 251–266, cited text on p. 254.

[19] William Reno, review of Peter D. Little, *Somalia: Economy without State*, Bloomington: Indian University Press, 2003, *Journal of Modern African Studies*, 42(3), 2004, 474–475.

THE HISTORY OF A CONCEPT 35

While environmental history does not show much interest in comparative economic growth questions, in 1997, Jared Diamond's *Guns, Germs, and Steel* advanced a bold argument linking the environment and economic history, describing a pattern of knowledge transfer in the preindustrial world.[20] A package of crops and techniques travelled along a route where new crop adaptations were possible. These were usually movements along latitudes. On the other hand, exchanges between northern and southern latitudes remained rare. Few northern European tools and cultivars successfully adapted to the tropics. In short, premodern agricultural adaptation borrowed cultigen and rarely, if ever, used a different set of tools to raise yield in old cultigens. This idea helps show why the tropical agricultural problem (low yield, extensive pastoralism) remained tropical in the long run. Beyond that, *Guns, Germs, and Steel* is not applicable. It does not define tropical seasonality nor engage with that concept. David Landes's *Wealth and Poverty of Nations* has the same problem. The book starts with the observation "On a map of the world in terms of product or income per head, the rich countries lie in the temperate zones, particularly in the northern hemisphere; the poor countries, in the tropics and semitropics."[21] The discussion of the tropics then loses its way into triviality.

Certain strands in development studies engage with the tropical condition, which deserve a look.

Tropical Development

I discuss here five clusters dealing with resources, trade, risk, monsoons, and conflicts. The birth of formal economics happened by purging water from the production function. "Water and air," wrote David Ricardo, "are ... indispensable to existence, yet, under ordinary circumstances, nothing can be obtained in exchange for them."[22] A free resource, water did not matter, permitting us to concentrate on the "original and indestructible powers of land." Ricardo's book—and the almost contemporary works of Johann Heinrich von Thünen, an agriculturist and economist—gave rise to the concept of the

---

[20] Jared M. Diamond, *Guns, Germs, and Steel: The Fates of Human Societies*, New York: W.W. Norton & Company, 2017.

[21] *Wealth and Poverty of Nations*, Cambridge, MA: Belknap Press of Harvard University Press, 1998, 15–16.

[22] David Ricardo, *On the Principles of Political Economy and Taxation*, London: J. Murray, 1821, 1–2.

36 WATER AND DEVELOPMENT

aggregate production function, a critical but controversial tool in economic theory, one in which output is expressed as the function of land and labor. In later neoclassical abstractions, a general notion of "capital" replaced land.[23] In the 1950s, development economists, many trained in the Ricardian tradition, assumed that land and labor were the critical inputs in agriculture. There was little role for water, climate, or drought in the following analytical debates.

In the early years of development economics, the problem with land was that it yielded little output per unit of land at that time. Although some saw this syndrome as a symptom of geography or technological backwardness, most saw it as an institutional issue. Incentives were the matter. Redistribution of land from the wealthy landowner to the poor tenant farmer would raise production in the aggregate because the latter applied himself or herself harder on land. Ownership patterns needed to change to use that asymmetry. "Ownership of land," wrote K.N. Raj, "determines to a considerable degree . . . the range of choices effectively open to different members of agrarian societies."[24] Gunnar Myrdal said of India, "To own the land is the highest mark of esteem."[25] The mystique about the land was largely missing in Africa, where land was often of poor quality, pastoralism extensive, and clan titles were more secure than public or private rights. In any case, the advocates of land redistribution did not consider that land and labor were not substitutable resources in a tropical land when there was little water.

Some writers approached the problem with a theory of history. Ester Boserup, an economist who worked for the United Nations, reinforced the hope that land and labor were substitutes. The "Malthusian scissors," a phrase the historian Emmanuel Le Roy Ladurie coined, meant a pattern of long-term change that started with relatively abundant land in a new agricultural zone. Agricultural productivity would fall as the population grew quickly and options ran out for raising more food with the available land. Boserup questioned the premise that population growth always puts pressure on resources, suggesting instead that population growth could encourage the search for new techniques to raise agricultural productivity.[26]

---

[23] John Hicks, "The Production Function," in *Capital and Time: A Neo-Austrian Theory*, Oxford: Oxford University Press, 1987, 177–184.

[24] K.N. Raj, "Agricultural Development and Distribution of Landholdings," *Indian Journal of Agricultural Economics*, 31(1), 1975, 1–13, cited text on p. 7.

[25] Gunnar Myrdal, *Asian Drama*, London: Allen Lane, 1968, 1057.

[26] Ester Boserup, "The Impact of Scarcity and Plenty on Development," *Journal of Interdisciplinary History*, 14(2), 1983, 383–407.

THE HISTORY OF A CONCEPT   37

Such "induced" innovation did not just happen. Sometimes an assured water supply is needed as a precondition. That step was a formidable challenge in arid tropics because waterworks cost money and were beyond the individual farmer to build. Evidence from the world's drylands shows that population growth led to emigration more often than innovation.[27] Boserup seemed to acknowledge that more labor would not solve water problems but did not take that idea forward.

In the 1960s, studies on green revolution technology that came into wider use in the tropical world stressed the role of water as a complementary input. In one such book, Vernon W. Ruttan showed that technological ideas must be ecologically adaptive.[28] Imported seeds failed in Southeast Asian agriculture without irrigation and drainage. "Technology borrowed from research conducted in temperate climates or tropical research conducted in a limited variety of ecological zones" thus had a high likelihood of failure.[29] Indeed, tropical green revolutions showed time and again that investment in water supply was a precondition, and agencies outside the village had to fund and implement the kind of waterworks needed.

The tropical condition was more central in some writings on trade-based growth. In the 1950s, the economist Hla Myint said that since the nineteenth century, the availability of surplus land in the developing world had fed a global trade boom.[30] By saying this, Myint advocated the virtues of openness rather than protectionism. Myint concentrated on Southeast Asia, which was not an arid tropic. In 1970, W. Arthur Lewis published an edited collection of essays called *Tropical Development*.[31] Contributors to the book explored a proposal that Lewis had set out in a lecture the year before, that the nineteenth-century history of the tropical regions was quite distinct from the European pathway. Whereas "the engine of growth in the temperate world has been industrial production, the engine of growth in the tropical

---

[27] For example, northern and central Ethiopia in the twentieth century: James C. McCann, "A Great Agrarian Cycle? Productivity in Highland Ethiopia, 1900 to 1987," *Journal of Interdisciplinary History*, 20(3), 1990, 389–416.

[28] John C.H. Fei and Alpha C. Chiang, "The Fundamental Cause of Economic Stagnation," in W.W. McPherson, ed., *Economic Development of Tropical Agriculture: Theory, Policy, Strategy, and Organization*, Gainesville: University of Florida Press, 1968, 23–45. A reviewer drily remarked, "nothing novel," Hiromitsu Kaneda, Review of McPherson, *Economic Development*, *Pakistan Development Review*, 9(3), 1969, 346–349.

[29] Charles R. Frank Jr., review of John de Wilde, ed., *Agricultural Development in Tropical Africa*, Baltimore: Johns Hopkins University Press, 1967, *Economic Development and Cultural Change*, 17(3), 1969, 438–441, cited text on p. 439.

[30] Hla Myint, *The Economics of the Developing Countries*, New York: Praeger, 1965.

[31] W.A. Lewis, ed., *Tropical Development 1880–1913: Studies in Economic Progress*, London: George Allen and Unwin, 1970.

38   WATER AND DEVELOPMENT

world until quite recently has been exports to the temperate world."[32] Nearly all the chapters in Lewis's book attributed the export growth to the transport revolution, which reduced the cost of trading bulky agricultural goods. Some also considered institutional and political shifts enabling or forcing market integration. Ecology was not a strength of the book, however. The "tropical" merely meant certain latitudes.

Lewis and Myint were optimistic about trade. That optimism begged the question: if tropical export agriculture was almost as good a development pathway as industrialization, why did many tropical countries stay poor? Lewis's answer was inefficient agriculture, an idea that did not see much elaboration beyond a few suggestive remarks. Myint's historical analysis did not tackle the question either.

Economic historians continue to examine Lewis's intuition about trade and its transformative potentials.[33] However, the trade-based concept of tropicality is relevant for a limited time in history and is not rooted in geography. Lewis's account of inefficient agriculture is undeveloped at best. Still, one interesting idea in Lewis carries over into the subject of this book. Unnoticed by most reviewers of *Tropical Development*, Lewis had added a twist to his history of tropical agricultural trade. "The richness or poverty of a tropical agriculture," he said, "depends *more than anything else* on water."[34] When countries contained wet and dry zones, the former—formed of deltas, forest edges, and estuaries—commercialized, and the latter fell behind or exported labor. As trade grew, the axis of capitalism shifted from overland trade in the dry zones to maritime trade in the wet zones. That idea of a growth-generating transfer of resources between sectors had already found fuller expression in a growth model Lewis was famous for.

Tropicality as drought risk was central in 1980s scholarship on famines. The benchmark was a 1981 book by Amartya Sen, which suggests that

---

[32] Harry G. Johnson, "Review of W.A. Lewis, *Aspects of Tropical Trade, 1883–1965*," in *Journal of International Economics*, 1, 131–136, cited text on p. 132.

[33] "A tropical location did prove advantageous for . . . the agricultural and forestry products which could be most easily produced in the tropics (such as palm oil, cocoa, rubber, citrus fruits and spices amongst many others) did not have temperate zone substitutes," Michael Havinden and David Meredith, *Colonialism and Development: Britain and Its Tropical Colonies, 1850–1960*, London: Routledge, 1996, 18. See also Jeffrey G. Williamson, *Trade and Poverty: When the Third World Fell Behind*, Cambridge, MA: MIT Press, 2013, and Giovanni Federico and Antonio Tena-Junguito, "Lewis Revisited: Tropical Polities Competing on the World Market, 1830–1938," *Economic History Review*, 70(4), 2017, 1244–1267.

[34] Lewis, *Tropical Development 1880–1913*, 17, emphasis added.

THE HISTORY OF A CONCEPT   39

droughts are more frequent in arid geographies and can cause famines.[35] The proposition for which the book became famous is that droughts, while a sufficient cause, are unnecessary for famines to occur. Legal access to available food can also cause famines. This latter argument became so influential that it shifted the attention of famine historians away from the environmental agency behind these shocks. Droughts are crucial to the present study because these events are intrinsically climatic, and frequent droughts can depress economic growth (Chapter 1). But droughts are moisture stress, and famines are shortages of food. The two things are different. Famine deaths were less than half a percent of the more than two billion people affected by droughts in the twentieth century. We should understand droughts without being trapped by the urge to explain mass death. In this book, droughts are an integral part of seasonality.

Monsoon seasonality played a role in the economist Harry Oshima's concept of the economic emergence of East Asia. Because the Asian monsoon ensured that rural labor found employment for a short cultivation season, the development problem was not how to accumulate capital, as in Western Europe, but how to employ more people gainfully. The answer was labor-intensive nonfarm activities, where Japanese industrialization originated.[36] Japan was the first miracle economy of Asia and a monsoon economy as with much of Southeast and South Asia, so the theory had an appeal in the rest of Asia. But did it have broader relevance? Oshima faced a challenge explaining the wide divergence between India and Japan in the twentieth century when both countries were poor, densely populated, agricultural, and monsoon-dependent in the late 1800s.[37] Oshima overlooked aridity. Villagers in India and Japan needed to deal with seasonality for a similar reason (rainfall concentrated), but they did not have similar means to deal with the dry season. The dry season was too dry in India to sustain work and consumption locally. The only option was to leave home and go away, not find work near home. There was no work near home.

[35] Amartya Sen, *Poverty and Famines: An Essay on Entitlement and Deprivation*, Oxford: Clarendon Press, 1981.

[36] Harry T. Oshima, *Economic Growth in Monsoon Asia: A Comparative Study*, Tokyo: University of Tokyo Press, 1987. The phrase had already entered school geography texts with E.H.G. Dobby, *Monsoon Asia*, Chicago: Quadrangle Books, 1961.

[37] The "low growth" of India - another monsoon Asiatic region - had owed to inappropriate policy choices, and its "socialist/caste institutions," an undefined concept, "The Transition from an Agricultural to an Industrial Economy in East Asia," *Economic Development and Cultural Change*, 34(4), 783–809,' cited text on p. 809.

40   WATER AND DEVELOPMENT

Despite the limitations of the concept as a tool for comparative economic history, it is impossible to study East and Southeast Asian economic history without a modified version of the concept of the monsoon, which is an exceptionally powerful phenomenon that deeply impacts the production possibilities in this part of the world. Kaoru Sugihara has contributed greatly to reinventing "monsoon Asia" as a conceptual category and integrating monsoons into the notion of factor endowments. His work shows the distinctive pattern of change in East Asia compared with Western Europe and also, usefully, shows how long-run trajectories varied within Asia consistent with resource endowment variations.[38]

Not all developmental discourses were unmindful of aridity. In the 1950s, a small circle of American economists coined the term "hydroeconomics," which they thought should become a field. Their fundamental intuition was, "The higher the standard of living, the greater the degree of industrialization, the greater is the per capita rate of water utilization."[39] The field did not take off. The geographical context was not well developed. Arid regions are not alike. Monsoons, seasonality, prehistory of settlement, government and law, drought risk—all differ. In the 1970s, the accent in agricultural innovation shifted from water to high-yielding seeds. Still, consistent with the same intuition, a potential link between water and growth became an attractive idea for individual writers on the third world. In the 1960s, the French agronomist and environmentalist René Dumont's writings on Africa saw geography as an obstacle to development.[40] He was, however, mainly interested in politics rather than climate.

In the 1980s, the British anthropologist Polly Hill invented a concept she called "dry grain farming mode" and thought areas in Hausaland, northern Nigeria, and Karnataka state in India were similar enough to be characterized as dry grain farming regions.[41] Hill recognized semi-aridity as a common feature of the two areas but did not use climate as an analytical tool, even though, as any climatic map will show, much of Karnataka and all of northern Nigeria are semi-arid. Among the features of the "dry"

[38] Kaoru Sugihara, "Varieties of Industrialization: An Asian Regional Perspective," in Giorgio Riello and Tirthankar Roy, eds., *Global Economic History*, London: Bloomsbury, 2nd ed., 2024, 249–269.

[39] Abraham M. Hirsch, "Some Aspects of River Utilization in Arid Areas: The Hydro-Economics of Inadequate Supply," *American Journal of Economics and Sociology*, 20(3), 1961, 271–286.

[40] René Dumont, "Le développement agricole spécialement tropical exige un enseignement totalement repensé," *Revue Tiers Monde*, 5(1), 1964, 13–38.

[41] Polly Hill, *Dry Grain Farming Families: Hausaland (Nigeria) and Karnataka (India) Compared*, New York: Cambridge University Press, 1982.

mode that the work identified, the predominance of rainfed millet growing, low land yield, systemic underemployment, and migration were obviously linked to the climatic condition (Chapter 1). Only one main crop was possible. Farm households tried to send some male family members away from the farm. Those families who did so more often were the rich; those who could not send men away were the poor and the most underemployed. Usually, the success of sending family members out depended on some asset-holding. However, land, the main asset, was not valuable (there was not much of a market in land, Hill found); instead, how landholders invested in people and the connections that created the prospects of leaving the village for employment outside had more effect on employment and earning opportunities.

An interesting concept—and one linked to aridity and seasonality—the dry farming mode had little impact as far as one can ascertain on academic work on development and history. The reason, I believe, is that Hill did not strengthen the bond between geography and economy. Her explanation for poverty descended into a Marxist-type cliché about surplus extraction by the urban economy rather than building on the environment that made dry farming the only mode possible.

In the 2000s, some statistical studies on comparative development revived this line of thinking, showing that "location and climate have significant effects on income levels and income growth through their impact on transport costs, disease burdens, and agricultural productivity."[42] The scholarship did not engage in serious economic history. Cross-country correlations would not tell us how the people subjected to tropicality tried to overcome their condition. This scholarship barely recognized seasonality.[43]

Seasonality forms a small but significant literature in applied development economics. For example, scholars who study nonfarm activities as insurance against the risks and low returns from rainfed agriculture recognize seasonality and lack of work for months in a year (see the earlier discussion on monsoon Asia). Martha Chen's fieldwork of a village in the semi-arid Gujarat state in India in the 1980s revealed how profoundly monsoon seasonality affected employment and earnings and how the meaning

[42] John Luke Gallup, Jeffrey D. Sachs, and Andrew D. Mellinger, "Geography and Economic Development," *International Regional Science Review*, 22(2), 1999, 179–223; Sachs, "Tropical Underdevelopment," Center for International Development (Harvard University) Working Paper, 2000.

[43] David E. Bloom and Jeffrey D. Sachs, "Geography, Demography, and Economic Growth in Africa," *Brookings Papers on Economic Activity*, 2, 1998, 207–295.

42   WATER AND DEVELOPMENT

of seasonality shifted between farming groups, pastoralists, and laborers.[44] Most households needed to combine occupations. Migration to the towns was an integral part of this strategy. One strand in this literature also acknowledges that seasonality could lead to inequality if the nonfarm opportunities were restricted to, say, those few who were more creditworthy than others.[45] None of this contains much history. However, works like this point toward the many sources of conflict in a seasonal world, besides the contest for access to land or water.

Political Ecology

Political ecology offers a fruitful way to understand some of these conflicts. It emerged as a field in the 2000s, driven by a single idea: disputes over access to natural resources are fundamentally disputes over access to political power, and these tensions leave profound legacies on politics and governance. These are distributional conflicts rather than a reflection of scarcities. The tenet that resource conflicts are essentially political is common among intellectuals who believed in land reforms, those who explained why famines happened, and the political ecologists who discuss water or pollution. Political ecologists have produced rich narratives on water disputes, especially after a big drive in the early 2000s to privatize urban water systems worldwide. Perhaps no other field is so responsive to the contestations over water. They show how disagreements shaped discourses and institutions, and "social movements born from such conflicts are creatively generating new modalities of water management and governance."[46]

The book benefits from political ecology and cites many papers in that tradition, but it also approaches contestations over water from a different standpoint. I do not believe that "water scarcity [in the world] is the result of failed policies and not of the environmental characteristics of different regions." It follows that "there is enough water, enough technology and easily enough money around to ensure that everyone in the world has access to

---

[44] Martha Alter Chen, *Coping with Seasonality and Drought*, New Delhi: Sage, 1991.

[45] Agnes Andersson Djurfeldt, "Seasonality and Farm/Non-farm Interactions in Western Kenya," *Journal of Modern African Studies*, 50(1), 2012, 1–23.

[46] Beatriz Rodríguez-Labajos and Joan Martínez-Alier, "Political Ecology of Water Conflicts," *WIREs Water*, 2, 2015, 537–558, cited text on p. 537.

THE HISTORY OF A CONCEPT 43

water: the key issue is how to choreograph the necessary politics."[47] Accepting this would amount to discarding, even denying, the climatic map shown in Map 1.1, from which this book starts.

The recently published *Divided Environments* is a different type of work within the political ecology tradition, with which *Water and Development* shares some common ground.[48] *Divided Environments* is an investigation into the claim, "orthodoxy-dominated and scientifically contested," that climate change causes and aggravates conflicts via resource access and availability. The book by Hoffmann and colleagues examines the link between climate change and water in five geographical regions where water policy has been a priority for the states. Four things I share with this book—the accent on water, the international angle, the focus on arid and semi-arid tropics, and the rejection of an unsubtle alarmist position that things are only getting worse. What I do not share are the three central arguments of the book: that "modern hydraulics" is a form of state building, that "hydraulic projects repeatedly involve conflict and everywhere create new forms of insecurity," and that "the renewal of hydraulic missions in response to real or imagined fears of climate change . . . presage a resurgence of hydraulic . . . conflicts and insecurities."[49] No matter how well these claims are established in the book, these three arguments show how political ecology informs *Divided Environments'* mission and, indeed, how field experts define the field's scope.

These arguments help me to show how this book—*Water and Development*—departs from political ecology despite the apparent overlap of interest in water as a developmental priority. Political ecology thinks water projects are primarily about state-building. Development paradigms have power because of the political weight that attaches to them. And because state power is contested, water projects breed conflict. Perceiving history in this way, in my opinion, is wrong. Water projects of the kind the modern tropical world has been familiar with stem from a climatic condition: the combination of extreme heat and extreme seasonality of moisture influx. Dealing with the challenge required big states. This was not the only thing that pushed postcolonial states to grow big, but it was one of the critical

---

[47] Alex Loftus, "Rethinking Political Ecologies of Water," *Third World Quarterly*, 30(5), 2009, 953–968, cited text on p. 953.

[48] Clemens Hoffmann, Gabrielle Daoust, and Jan Selby, *Divided Environments: An International Political Ecology of Climate Change, Water and Security*, Cambridge: Cambridge University Press, 2022, cited text on p. 9.

[49] Ibid., 140–141.

44 WATER AND DEVELOPMENT

factors. State-building did not come first and water second. Water came first, and state-building had to adapt.

Water projects are primarily about tropical monsoon seasonality. It does not require economists and report-writers to advance a statist "paradigm" for water projects to kick in. It is common sense that trapping excess monsoonal inflow would help people live and stay economically productive in seasons when excessive heat dries up all surface water. This idea is not an idea that somebody invented. Nobody invented this developmental paradigm. It's been a deeply embedded practice for millennia. The colonial states picked it up, as did Indigenous communities for a long time. Postcolonial states aided its implementation on a large scale, with better access to international money and availability of engineering capability.

That premise makes for a different reading of most conflicts. Not the distribution of political power, but geoengineering itself generates conflicts because the environment cannot be manipulated without creating losses. Dams displace people; dams deprive soils of silts; projects can be high capacity (borewells in city apartments) or low (one municipal tap shared between hundreds of slum dwellers); aquifers run out of water; canals live on sources that can dry up, and so on. Above all, practically no large water projects known in the developing world pay for themselves. All are subsidized, which means that some claimants to subsidies get less than others. Politics kicks in in every case, but the root of these inequalities is not political.

Return of Water

In recent decades, water has made a return to world history. Two chapters on the "hydrosphere" in John McNeill's environmental history of the world are a good point to start.[50] One fact that stands out in these chapters is that the world used much more water per head for personal and economic use in the twentieth century than in the past, as far as we can measure. Water was an essential resource, almost a precondition for economic emergence, an effect most tellingly shown in the histories of cities that grew based on water security. The book's scope is global rather than regional; neither the tropics nor climatic constraints are central in the hydrosphere chapters.

---

[50] John McNeill, *Something New under the Sun: An Environmental History of the Twentieth-Century World*, New York: W.W. Norton, 2000.

THE HISTORY OF A CONCEPT   45

Another route through which water returned in environmental history was the history of the arid areas, especially those in colonial Africa. Aridity and water figure centrally in Alan Mikhail's edited volume, *Water on Sand*. Several essays in the book show how worries over water and droughts shaped national policy in the Middle East in the twentieth century, with far-reaching consequences.[51] Mikhail's book on Egypt presents a rich account of irrigation and knowledge about water regulation in early modern Egypt.[52] Diana Davis's *Arid Lands* is the most significant book-length treatment of a theme explored in the literature on colonial water policy, paying particular attention to French North Africa.[53] The scholarship shows how nineteenth-century interpretations of tropicality produced far-reaching consequences for contemporary politics and future developmentalism.

Two books on South Asia place rivers at their center. Between the two, Sunil Amrith's *Unruly Waters* is more concerned with climate. The book shows how the alternating risks of floods and famines in a monsoon land led India to begin developing its weather reporting infrastructure, maturing into an advanced system of meteorological monitoring by the later decades of the twentieth century and a greater understanding of the link between the monsoon and the Indian Ocean.[54] On the other hand, Asian politicians utilized the nation-building potential of big dams, which became symbols of political authority and ways to mitigate the extreme events the monsoons would cause. Sudipta Sen's *Ganges*, by contrast, is a long-period study of one river that has shaped the destiny of one of the world's most densely populated regions, the Indo-Gangetic Basin.[55] Sen's *Ganges* is, in spirit, similar to Robert O. Collins's *The Nile*, and like that book, shows how one river stood at the intersection of many forms of material and cultural traditions.[56] Both books describe changes happening in colonial times that resonate with *Water and Development*.

So does Heather J. Hoag's 2014 book, *Developing the Rivers of East and West Africa*, a sweeping study of the British colonial and postcolonial efforts

---

[51] Alan Mikhail, ed., *Water on Sand: Environmental Histories of the Middle East and North Africa*, New York: Oxford University Press, 2013.

[52] Alan Mikhail, *Nature and Empire in Ottoman Egypt: Studies in Environment and History*, New York: Cambridge University Press, 2011.

[53] Diana K. Davis, *The Arid Lands: History, Power, Knowledge*, Cambridge, MA: MIT Press, 2016.

[54] Sunil Amrith, *Unruly Waters: How Rains, Rivers, Coasts, and Seas Have Shaped Asia's History*, New York: Basic Books, 2018.

[55] Sudipta Sen, *Ganges: The Many Pasts of an Indian River*, New Haven, CT: Yale University Press, 2019.

[56] Robert O. Collins, *The Nile*, New Haven, CT: Yale University Press, 2002.

46   WATER AND DEVELOPMENT

to extend the productive use of a set of African rivers.[57] Although commercial navigation and irrigation were colonial priorities, Hoag shows how rivers emerged as a focus of developmental action—increasingly, in some cases, for electricity generation to sustain growing cities. Communities dependent on rivers for a range of livelihoods engaged with that process rather than resisting it. This theme of rivers and economic emergence is a core interest of my book and appears in later chapters with data from other river basins and empires to illustrate the trajectory.

Still, my project is a different one. *Water and Development* is rooted in a global economic history discourse about the origins of economic and demographic growth and divergence. None of these books shares that entry point. *Water and Development* starts from a definition of arid tropical climate rooted in geography. None of these books engages with tropicality enough, nor in a conceptually satisfactory way. Finally, *Water and Development* is doing global history. Its coverage is more comprehensive, whereas the other books mentioned here (except for Davis's to some extent) engage with the environment because of a primary interest in one world region. In my book, the environment comes before the regional experiences.

Conclusion

The chapter discussed writings connecting geography with development and history. In most of these, the concept of seasonality is missing; therefore, a precise definition of the arid tropics usable by economic historians is missing too. And yet, it is not all irrelevant.

One might ask how far removed this book is from Wittfogel's hydraulic society. A short answer is that it *is* about hydraulic societies, minus Wittfogel's political baggage and weakness for megaprojects, and with a more precise definition of tropicality added. The lack of a good definition of tropicality that works for the economic historian characterizes most economic studies of tropical development and welfare, environmental history, and political ecology. Drought risk in famine historiography is useful. Lewis's intuition that tropical development entailed regional differentiation finds confirmation. The accent on discords in political ecology has produced

---

[57] Heather J. Hoag, *Developing the Rivers of East and West Africa: An Environmental History*, New York: Bloomsbury Academic, 2013.

literature that I cite a lot. Still, the review confirms that defining the tropical condition with climatic classification tools makes sense for a historical inquiry. Chapters 4 to 11 do that. The regions that supply raw materials for it deserve a brief background.

Chapter Three
The Arid Regions

The book concentrates on regions well served by scholarship in geography and history. Many places are excluded from this account because the scholarship is too thin or does not reference geography enough. The chronological frame (concentrating on the time after 1850) and the choice of places depend partly on the presence of European colonial rule in these lands. These regimes collected a lot of data on the prehistory and ecology of the regions of interest, among other reasons, because the ecology differed from that of the temperate zones.

A descriptive account of the places is needed for several reasons: to show that geographical regions and country borders do not coincide and, therefore, to show which regions within countries are of particular interest. It is necessary to show how some countries emerged in the first place as we know them. The accent on countries is another way of acknowledging that the actions of the states matter critically. The European colonial states left more documentation on water and the environment than Indigenous states. They also designed some large-scale projects and property rights regimes that the nation-states inherited. Therefore, a chronological history from the nineteenth century can be handy.

But how do we write it? By following a climatic map, a hydrogeological map, or a political one? Countries came into being through colonization, and using countries to describe precolonial processes would be an anomaly. Regions have no fixed boundaries, especially in the semi-arid tropics, where the monsoonal rainfall does not follow a fixed season or path. In the hyper-arid areas, we can adopt a simple rule to tell most stories: follow the river. Most political and economic actions concentrated in river basins. The idea of thus using the basin as an organizing framework makes sense for the Nile, Senegal, and Niger. But it does not work so well for most other semi-arid tropics. The Horn of Africa or southwestern Africa were places without seasonal rivers that carried enough water. The Volta and Zambezi were used more for electricity than water in the postcolonial times. Lakes, shallow pools, and flooded plains were important in areas fed by rivers,

Water and Development. Tirthankar Roy, Oxford University Press. © Oxford University Press (2025).
DOI: 10.1093/oso/9780197802397.003.0003

even if the rivers started far away or were not perennial. In parts of the world, groundwater made rivers irrelevant, even though riverbeds did make digging underground for water somewhat promising.

To avoid missing out on the information that different ways of mapping offer us, I first discuss the climate map and identify the regions of interest. I then bring in geology and hydrology to qualify the character of these climate-based zones and suggest why some areas do not figure in this narrative much or at all. Finally, I describe the political and economic history of eight world regions by frequently referring to modern political boundaries. Switching to politics is necessary when discussing state-led large-scale responses to the seasonality problem.

The regions that figure prominently in this book's narrative are West Africa, the Nile Basin (Egypt and Sudan), East Africa, North Africa and West Asia, Southern Africa, Southern Asia, the Americas, and Australia. In three of these regions, the follow-the-river technique pays off: Senegal and Niger for West Africa, the Nile Basin, and the Indo-Gangetic Basin for South Asia. In two other regions, the Americas and Australia, groundwater takes the place that rivers occupy elsewhere. In East Africa, North Africa, and Southern Africa, geology figures more than rivers or groundwater.

Let us start with climate zone mapping.

Mapping Arid Climates

The Russian-German geographer and meteorologist Wladimir Köppen used temperature values and precipitation volumes as boundaries to classify world climatic zones. This system divided the arid tropics into two main parts: regions with high summer temperatures and seasonal precipitation or monsoon (semi-arid) and regions without significant rainfall. The Köppen classification was first developed in 1884, and it has undergone several modifications since then. The Köppen system has been revised based on data collected later. To the extent that variability (in rainfall and temperature) is a part of the definition, much more data collected in recent decades have led to modifications in the classification of some border zones.[1] However, the system is still robust and remains an essential tool for teaching and research,

---

[1] M.C. Peel, B.L. Finlayson and T.A. McMahon, "Updated World Map of the Koppen-Geiger Climate Classification," *Hydrology and Earth System Sciences*, 11, 2007, 1633–1644.

50 WATER AND DEVELOPMENT

because it is easy to understand. It also has a significant limitation. To measure moisture intensity as rainfall intensity overlooks the fact that the effect of moisture on life depends not only on volume but also on distribution.

In 1931, Charles Warren Thornthwaite, an American climatologist, created a conceptually new system. The key difference was that Thornthwaite used evapotranspiration (representing the temperature impact that matters to humans, animals, and biodiversity) along with temperature values. The measures, however, are too complex for everyday use and do not vitally affect the macroregional classification. A final major index was that of the German geographer Carl Troll. In the Troll system, the length of the humidity period became a variable. Seasonality was a crucial concept in Troll, whose system is widely seen to supply the most direct definition of the semi-arid tropics.

Following the Köppen or the Köppen-Geiger system, the climate type that dominates the earth's surface is B, arid (30.2 percent), which is almost equally distributed into hyper-arid (BWh) and semi-arid (BSh, or arid with some seasonal moisture influx) types. Type B is not always tropical, but predominantly so. Besides this, the Köppen system defines type A (tropical) to include equatorial rainforests (Af), regions experiencing heavy monsoons and moderate temperature rise (Am), and grasslands. Of particular interest for this book is the subtype BSh within B. In Africa, this zone has hyper-arid areas on one side and the savanna on the other. In southern India, this zone is surrounded by savanna and monsoon tropics (Af and Am). The BSh or the extent of the semi-arid varies in strength depending on the strength of the monsoon. The BSh in the Deccan Plateau is milder than that in the Northern Sahel and does not border a desert.

How can we think of the connections between tropical climatic zones and livelihood patterns? Think of two main livelihood zones: vegetal or plant-based, and pastoral or animal-based. The Am is mainly associated with the vegetal, and the BSh with the pastoral. Along their border, the vegetal and the pastoral may complement one another; that is, the same resource is usable for growing plants and sustaining animals at different times of the year or in different years. The geographer John Innes Clarke explained that people who lived here were designated "semi-nomadic," a category that did not mean "a . . . transitional phase between nomadism and agriculture; it is a distinct mode of life."[2] Or they may compete, with people with a primary

[2] John I. Clarke, "Studies of Semi-nomadism in North Africa," *Economic Geography*, 35(2), 1959, 95–108.

THE ARID REGIONS   51

interest in one of the two things fighting over the same resource. As we can see later, many developmental actions in the late twentieth century targeted the border between the Am and the BSh, and therefore land conversion and conflicts have also been intense on this border.

In the northern hemisphere, the major semi-arid tropics (BSh + BWh) include India and Pakistan in South Asia; parts of Mali, Chad, Senegal, Niger, Mauritania, Burkina Faso, Nigeria, and Cameroon in West-Central Africa; the Horn of Africa, including parts of Ethiopia and Eritrea; North Africa and the Middle East; the Mexican Northwest; and the southwestern United States. In the southern hemisphere, the semi-arid tropics contain the Australian desert fringe; Kalahari and Namib desert fringe falling in Namibia, Botswana, South Africa, Angola, and southwest Mozambique; Sertão in Brazil; and the southern coast of Madagascar.

But then the semi-arid or BSh is not one homogeneous type. Regional inequality today can be quite extreme in the tropical world, and one dimension of that inequality is geographical, as we see next.

Exceptions within the Norm

Moisture influx is not the only variable shaping access to water. Also significant are hydraulic conductivity and transmissivity, or how well water transmits over the area, a variable that depends on soil structure and geological formations. Wind patterns and oceans can create microclimates. It is worthwhile to consider five such variations: coast, mountain, river, groundwater, and monsoon quality. Many tropical deserts and near deserts border the sea.[3] But even in the harshest climates, the seaboard has a better chance to overcome seasonality, sometimes thanks to the more stable flows of a deltaic river and sometimes by trading with the rest of the world, which reduces its dependence on agriculture and pastoralism.

Microclimates in the highlands can sustain a different economy from the plains. For example, the Ethiopian plateau did not suffer famines and droughts with the same intensity observed in the desert fringes. Similarly, in precolonial and colonial Eritrea, Namibia, and Madagascar, the political elite lived in mountains that moderated aridity, whereas much of the surrounding country experienced it. Taiwan, through which the Tropic of

[3] Western Sahara, Northwestern Australia, Peruvian and Atacama deserts, Sonora, the Namib, the Middle East, and North Africa.

52   WATER AND DEVELOPMENT

Cancer passes, has an extensive highland zone. The High Atlas in Morocco moderates the effects of a climate that exposed the plains in the south to droughts.

Perennial rivers can moderate seasonality. The Blue Nile originates in the equatorial highlands, which receive significant quantities of rain throughout the year. Its annual floods enabled intensive agriculture in a narrow strip of land that extended hundreds of miles. The rivers of the Fertile Crescent, fed by snowmelt, carry large volumes of water. In the dry savanna of the Sahel, the Niger Basin created a scope of intensive agriculture, mixed farming zones, extensive livestock breeding, and commercial fishing. The Indo-Gangetic Basin experiences intense heat but developed agricultural societies because the heat melts Himalayan snow and recharges the Indus and Ganges River systems. Similarly, the eastern Red River Delta sustained agricultural communities in an otherwise dry climate in northwestern Vietnam. Against the relentless aridity of the Horn of Africa, strong political centers emerged on the Benadir coast, in the well-watered coastal agrarian belt of Lower Shabelle (and in the cooler uplands in Eritrea and Somaliland).

Lastly, the chances of mining water moderated the effect of climate. In the southwestern drylands of North America and Australia, groundwater resources partly compensated for the high evapotranspiration rates that reduced surface water supplies. Resources underground can act wonders in other ways. Much of Botswana is very dry; so are the Middle East and North Africa. However, oil and diamonds create enough export income to combat drought and subsidize vulnerable livelihoods. Finally, the monsoon of the Indian Ocean is powerful and occurs twice. Regions in its pathway—South and Southeast Asia, Taiwan—receive a larger volume of seasonal rainfall than most arid tropics.

West Africa

The Sahel refers to the west-to-east stretch of land that borders the Sahara in the south and in the north, though in common parlance, the Sahel usually refers to the southern belt. The Sahel is dry, but its aridity is broken by seasonal rains, large perennial rivers, lakes, and annual floods. Much of the Niger River plains is semi-arid, yet yearly floods in the river and its branches sustained cultivation and fishing over thousands of square miles. In the inland Niger Delta in Mali—a land of lakes formed by annual flooding of the river—the level of water in the lakes varied from year to year, depending on rainfall patterns. Severe drought years would mean a drying up of the lakes, which happened at about twenty-year intervals in the twentieth century. In "normal" years, the inundation pattern would shape land use. Neither agriculture sustained by annual flooding nor the rivers could support intensive year-round cultivation. The fluctuations in the water level were too extreme for that.

The pattern of land use in the inland delta followed the four major occupations that the lacustrine ecology could sustain: fishing—or more accurately, nomadic fishing, that is, following fish shoals as they migrated; irrigated rice cultivation; herding that involved migration from the flood-prone active delta during the rains toward the drier inactive delta and return during dry seasons; and cultivation of millets on higher and sandier soils. Marshland rice grew on clayey soil after the floodwaters receded. In some low areas that retained floodwaters from the previous year, rice could grow if mud dykes would protect the land from the current flood. The fast-maturing rice *Oryza glaberimma* was cultivated in flooded lands. Both crops were sensitive to the balance between flood level and elevation of the ground. Since flood levels varied at different heights, the chance of a lost crop was significantly high.

Outside the areas of flush agriculture, rainfed cultivation and pastoralism existed. Both livelihoods needed to adapt to shifts in rainfall patterns. It rarely involved a fixed point-to-point movement. Herds moved to dry-season pastures, where grass and water were available in pools. The return journey involved settling temporarily in a series of *zones d'attente*, or waiting areas, to allow floodwaters to recede before moving on. Beyond the grasslands, the desert began.

The historiography of the Sahara acknowledges that the desert was an obstacle to overcome in forging links between distant regions, but not an insurmountable one. For two thousand years, camels connected the northern and southern desert fringes and the many oases and settlements in between. For a thousand years, Islam, often carried farther by merchants, again built bridges between the north and the south. While nineteenth-century European scholarship, informed by travelers-explorers, saw the connections, European reading of African political history often overstated the difference between the northern and the southern Sahel, between an "Arab" and a "black" Islam. These categories were partly a European construct and partly a carryover from Indigenous discourses in the Sahel "as ideological buttresses to struggles for power amongst nomadic groups. . . .

54   WATER AND DEVELOPMENT

'Race' was a corollary of the heightened ideological importance of lineage."[4] Therefore, the idea of a space unified by culture or trade may be as exaggerated as that of geographically determined separateness.

The two images—exchange and an unstable diversity—suggest that the connections created by religion and commerce did not translate into states that centralized military and fiscal power, thus enforcing an integration. Geography did pose a barrier to the formation of fiscal states. The desert was an insurmountable obstacle to the formation of cities and farmlands. There was never enough water to sustain large garrisons or taxpaying farmers. All explorers, especially Heinrich Barth, registered how traveling even a few miles was a project conditional on receiving news about the state of the next well ahead on the road.

Around 1850, when Barth traversed the Sahara until reaching the Chad Basin and the Niger-Benue River system where the Sokoto Caliphate ruled, political power was fragmented into small units that lived in areas where there was enough water to sustain settlements. The word "water" appears frequently in both Barth's narrative and Mungo Park's fifty years earlier (Figure 3.1).

Geography constrained state formation in another way. Animal herding was a common livelihood form in the desert fringe. Pastoralism is incompatible with territorial states. One of the uses of a state is to protect property, but pastoralist property—neither fixed in space nor permanent nor in year-round usage—is hard to define and protect. The herders had to be armed to defend their rights. "None of [the common forms of social grouping such as clan or tribe]," wrote a 1957 study of the nomadic Fulani herders of northern Nigeria, "had, or has, any *de jure* rights to ownership of pasture, water, or cattle tracks enforceable either by the sanctions of Pastoral Fulani society, or those of the alien political entities within which the Pastoral Fulani move. The nomadic movements of Pastoral Fulani are a constant adjustment to the changing demands of the natural habitat."[5] Merchants, likewise, relied on breeders and mobility and had no fixed territorial space to live on.

States—as the Europeans understood that concept in the nineteenth century—did not exist, and "a political praxis based in tribal alliances"

---

[4] Bruce S. Hall, "The Question of 'Race' in the Pre-colonial Southern Sahara," *Journal of North African Studies*, 10(3–4), 2005, 339–367, cited text on p. 339.

[5] Derrick J. Stenning, "Transhumance, Migratory Drift, Migration: Patterns of Pastoral Fulani Nomadism," *Journal of the Royal Anthropological Institute of Great Britain and Ireland*, 87(1), 1957, 57–73, cited text on p. 57.

Figure 3.1 "Picturesque View of the River Niger," 1840 engraving
While making sense of inland Africa, early-nineteenth-century cartographers and geographers often started with the river basin, which was easier to know than mountains and deserts because of information that flowed via trade. The rivers inland, however, presented a harsh environment for a traveler and were dangerous to navigate. The Scottish surgeon and explorer Mungo Park (1771–1806) tried to get to the source of the Niger, drowning during an attack on the second attempt.
Source: British Library

ruled.[6] The words *clan* and *tribe*, used to describe the political structures, cannot be defined precisely. Broadly, a clan is a lineage, usually agnatic, whereas a tribe is an identity marker. Both elements were present in securing alliances, though identity was also changeable. Nomadic tribal alliances that traded across the desert contained relatively few people living in one place. The towns nearer the greener and wetter regions were larger and more permanent settlements. Despite the small numbers, nomadic groups were formidable military forces, for within these, "nearly every (adult) man could serve in war, a very high proportion of armed men indeed."[7] Islam and commerce notwithstanding, the tribal alliances did not necessarily regard

---

[6] Baz Lecocq, "Distant Shores: A Historiographic View on Trans-Saharan Space," *Journal of African History*, 56(1), 2015, 23–36, cited text on p. 35.

[7] Georg Klute, "The Coming State: Reactions of Nomadic Groups in the Western Sudan to the Expansion of the Colonial Powers," *Nomadic Peoples*, 38, 1996, 49–71, cited text on p. 59.

56   WATER AND DEVELOPMENT

each other as either equals or alike. Clashes and rivalries were present, and because they were present, European conquest was not a simple matter but was reliant on forming alliances with one group against another. Under French colonial rule, this vast area maintained peace because a superior military force backed up the partnerships.

The Senegal originates from several sources, including the heavy rainfall in mountainous and semiequatorial central Guinea. The Senegal proper is of relatively short length. Most of its length (about four hundred miles) marks the border between Mauritania and Senegal. The shared basin region, located between 15° and 17° north latitude, is semi-arid and exposed to significant heat throughout the year and extreme heat in summer (Map 3.1). The seasonal floods in the rivers enabled cultivation in some parts of the basin and the delta.

French colonial authorities did not take a serious interest in the agricultural potential of the river basin, though its value for inland navigation was recognized. The main export crop was groundnut, which grew in central and western Senegal, well south of the river basin. Private property rights were strong in basin lands. So secure were peasant property that some thought in the interwar period that private property would obstruct state investment in the basin.[8] A persistent rice shortage during and after World War II induced the colonial government to encourage rice cultivation in the basin lands. Elsewhere, cultivation existed with herding. As recently as the 1990s, it was common for farmers to keep herds. Specialized Fulbe herders also visited farming villages to seek dry-season pastures, where they had developed "preferential relations with a [farmer] family."[9]

The accent on rice continued after independence in 1960. A state-sponsored land development company formed in 1965 took charge of the mission, invested in infrastructure, and subsidized inputs to rice growers. The scheme was a partial success at best. Saltwater intrusion into delta lands and the unsustainable cost of the subsidies derailed it. With the population growing faster and no solution to the pervasive water insecurity in sight, emigration levels increased. In the 1960s, migrants from the Senegal valley formed the largest ethnic group of immigrants in France. Then came the

[8] Adrian Adams, "The Senegal River Valley: What Kind of Change?" *Review of African Political Economy*, 10, 1977, 33–59.

[9] Monique Chastanet, "Survival Strategies of a Sahelian Society: The Case of the Soninke in Senegal from the Middle of the Nineteenth Century to the Present," *Food and Foodways*, 5(2), 1992, 127–149, cited text on p. 133.

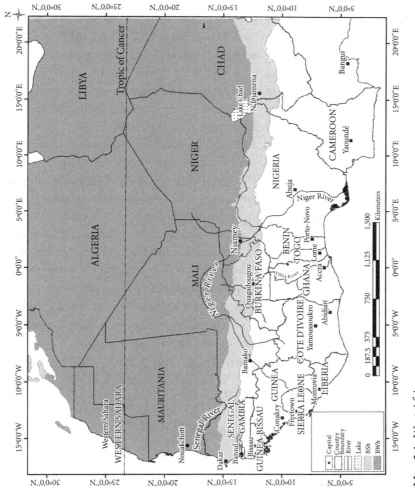

Map 3.1 West Africa

58 WATER AND DEVELOPMENT

1972 drought, which kicked in the drive to construct big water projects in the river's upper reaches (Chapter 8).

The two basins form part of the West African Sahel, which has seen a rise in aridity (average temperature and decline in rainfall) for over fifty years (since the 1950s). In the Senegal basin, the number of rainy days in the peak rainy stretch (August 11–20) fell from 3.17 in 1919–1959 to 2.85 in 1960–1985.[10] In the wake of the two prolonged Sahelian droughts of the 1970s and 1980s, studies emerged to explain the climatic conditions that caused exceptional dryness. One explanation was that human interventions changing the land surface fed back into the regional climate. This position now stands modified. It seems clear that the droughts were part of a periodic movement of the intertropical convergence zone, though land surface changes may have modulated the impact of the variations.

In discussing the West African Sahel, the follow-the-river technique that I have so far used with Niger and Senegal must adapt when we come to the area around Lake Chad, a shallow and seasonally variable lake formed of water drained from the Logon Basin. This lake sustained flush agriculture and fishing before French colonialism brought it into closer contact with the seaboard. The early twentieth century saw a thriving traditional trade centered on cattle export to British West African colonies. After World War II, Chad's economy moved more firmly toward export crop production. Similarly, Mali established itself as a leading cotton producer in Africa. The introduction of Egyptian and American varieties and mechanized ginning stimulated cotton production. Considerable assistance with transporting and processing raw cotton initially came from the colonial state.[11]

If French colonialism in Senegal and Niger was not particularly interventionist, British colonialism in the Nile Basin was different.

The Nile Basin

The Blue Nile descends from Lake Tana in the Ethiopian highlands and joins the White Nile in Khartoum. The White Nile originates in the Equatorial Plateau and is fed by the snowmelt of the Ruwenzori mountains. The two

[10] Richard Black and Mohamed F. Sessay, "Refugees, Land Cover, and Environmental Change in the Senegal River Valley," *GeoJournal*, 41(1), 1997, 55–67.

[11] Abdoulaye Abakar Kassambara, "La Situation Économique et Sociale du Tchad de 1900 à 1960," PhD dissertation, Université de Strasbourg, 2010.

branches and their tributaries traverse eleven countries. Some are equatorial or semiequatorial (Rwanda, Burundi, Congo, Tanzania, Kenya, South Sudan, and Uganda), others with mixed geographies (Ethiopia and Eritrea, which contain a mix of dry tropical and wet highlands), and still others mainly dry tropical (Sudan, Egypt). The countries with extensive hyper-arid lands rely crucially on the river. The survival of Egypt and Sudan depends on it.

Of the four countries that face significant aridity, Eritrea had a marginal role in regional foreign policy negotiations, in which the Nile loomed large, until the 1990s. Since its contribution to the Nile is small (mainly through the Atbara, a tributary), its claims were weaker, too.[12] Its highlands form a small part of the country but are home to most towns and farmlands. Herding is more common in semi-arid regions. Rivers are few, and groundwater is exploited extensively. Ethiopia has a similar geography. Agriculture is mainly rainfed in both countries, and land yield is small.

During the northern hemisphere summer (May–August), monsoon rains in the Ethiopian highlands cause floods in Egypt. The silt-laden water sustains fertile farmlands. In the rest of the year, the water level drops. The flow varied a lot more in the past before a series of dams and canals were built in the twentieth century. The White Nile, being partly snow-fed, retains its flow in the summer months.

The northern border of Sudan is a straight line along the 22° north and within a hundred miles of the Tropic of Cancer. More than two-thirds of the population is concentrated in the Nile Corridor, where the major cities and most industrial units are based. The Nile Corridor gains water security from the river and soil conditions near the river. Here, shallow wells can be dug more easily as they receive river water via seepage. The two highlands, the Nuba Mountains in the south and Jebel Marra in the west, have more surface water. An ancient system called hafirs or rock cisterns captured rainwater. Shallow wells excavated to a depth of fifteen to thirty feet near seasonal streams yielded enough water, but digging deeper to access the deep aquifers was costly because of the sedimentary rock layer underneath. In the 1930s, the government constructed deeper wells and sometimes installed pumps to extract water. The scale of the enterprise was small, and many of

---

[12] Adams Oloo, "The Quest for Cooperation in the Nile Water Conflicts: The Case of Eritrea," *African Sociological Review*, 11(1), 2007, 95–105.

60 WATER AND DEVELOPMENT

these reservoirs appeared in the tract between the two Niles, where there was more water overall. The rest of the country consists of desert or savanna.

The genesis of modern Sudan goes back to the start of Turco-Egyptian rule (1821–1881). In theory, the rule integrated a political system divided into separate kingdoms. These kingdoms were the Funj Sultanate in the Blue Nile and Atbara floodplains, which succumbed to the Turco-Egyptian invasion without much resistance; the Darfur Sultanate, which continued until incorporation in the 1880s; the Taqali Sultanate absorbed in the Mahdist regime after 1881; and a few smaller ones. The tax base of these states, an agricultural tax or a levy on livestock, was never adequate. "Foreign trade in these kingdoms," therefore, "was largely controlled by the rulers."[13] Slave raids were also a source of income.

Islam was a weak unifying force over this collection of states. According to one interpretation, "the coming of capitalism" from the eighteenth century had more unifying power as overland and overseas trades expanded. The main axis was east-west, between Egypt and western Sudan, and involved an exchange of textiles and other goods for slaves, ivory, ostrich feathers, and livestock. The empowerment of the merchants and middle classes "undermine[d] royal control of trade, land, taxes, and justice," setting the stage for new states to form, where these classes would command more power.[14] Essentially an account of the urban economy and society, the coming-of-capitalism narrative tells us little about whether the rise and fall of states through the Turco-Egyptian, Mahdist, and finally British rule changed anything in the countryside. Except for livestock to a limited extent, none of the other newly traded goods could profoundly affect livelihoods in the village.

British colonial rule was established around 1882 and remained in place until 1952. During this time, modern business and intensive agriculture developed in the riverine areas and the main urban-industrial center, Khartoum. The colonial accent on commercialization aided the process, though it did not create it. The "alliance of riverine, northern Arab elites" sustained an ethnic-religious nationalism formed in reaction to British rule.[15] Colonialism ruled the villages with a light touch, which left land titles weak. Successive failure in land titling initiatives left landed property vulnerable

---

[13] Lidwien Kapteijns, "The Historiography of the Northern Sudan from 1500 to the Establishment of British Colonial Rule: A Critical Overview," *International Journal of African Historical Studies*, 22(2), 1989, 251–266, cited text on p. 253.

[14] Ibid.

[15] Scott Straus, *Making and Unmaking of Nations. War, Leadership, and Genocide in Modern Africa* (Ithaca, NY: Cornell University Press, 2015).

to capture. Outside the corridor, geological conditions (basement complex or a substratum of igneous and metamorphic rocks) made sinking wells an unprofitable enterprise. Deep boreholes and open wells were rare, whereas most natural or humanmade surface water bodies were impermanent and polluted during droughts.

Egypt's dependence on the Nile was as great as Sudan's, with the difference that the annual flooding in the river's lower reaches created highly fertile agricultural land there. Egypt became an Ottoman province in the sixteenth century and, following a brief French occupation during the Napoleonic wars, went back to that status, albeit ruled by a practically autonomous viceroy. The new regime embarked on a modernization program in the first half of the nineteenth century, the cornerstone of which was irrigated cotton farming. In 1869, a French joint stock company built the Suez Canal, a project with the backing of the court and European merchants. In 1882, an indirect form of British colonial rule was established in Egypt. The concept of dams and canals was ancient. The British pursued the idea with considerable energy and a more developed theory of basin management, which initiated a new era of water control in the Nile Basin. Later chapters discuss the initiative.

The economic history of the Nile Basin is inextricably linked with the history of Ethiopia.

East Africa

The Tropic of Cancer runs a few hundred miles north of the northern border of Ethiopia. The Abyssinian Massif that dominates the northwest and center sustained rainfed agriculture using the ox plow. Much of the lowlands, except narrow river basins like Awash, were too arid to make agriculture possible. The lowlands in the country's east sustained animal herding or a combination of farming and herding. The lowlands were also exposed to diseases of human and animal populations. The region receives seasonal rains but of erratic frequency. Rains die away in the east, giving rise to the Danakil desert in the northeast and the Ogaden desert in the southeast. Throughout recorded history, imperial states and religious establishments thrived in the northern highlands. The lowlands were not closely integrated into the imperial state and were ruled by practically independent rulers. Islam was more common here, though hardly a unifying force in an ethnically diverse population.

62   WATER AND DEVELOPMENT

Much of Ethiopian agriculture was rainfed as late as the end of the twentieth century. Irrigation was poor; less than a quarter of the arable land was cultivated, and about 3 percent had irrigation. Rainfall, even when "abundant," was seasonal. The Ethiopian monsoon occurred during the June-to-September period, as in southern Asia. The strength of the subsidiary spring rains was highly uncertain, and its failure caused devastation.

European travelers held a rosy view of Ethiopia based on their impression of the highlands. These accounts observed the "richness of soil," "good climate," "never-failing water supply," and the prospect of raising agricultural production and productivity if only more hands were available.[16] Economic geography long agreed with the Europeans in insisting that Ethiopia enjoyed "abundant arable land and water resources" and was a "land of plenty."[17] They believed Ethiopia's rich natural resources were not fully exploited because of a labor shortage or "a low density of population."[18] If that were the case, then the massive famines that broke out in 1974 and again in 1985 would seem like a puzzle, created by humans and state rather than nature. "There is nothing in the resource base of the country that suggests that famine ought to have been a problem for its inhabitants."[19]

The reality is that most impressions of "plenty" were based on the highlands. These views typically excluded the area of low rainfall—the Tigrayan plateau and Danakil Depression in the north and east—where droughts happened. Over these regions, the migration of nomadic groups who ordinarily lived on the savanna lands was a regular occurrence, and during long droughts, it was an irregular and disputatious one. In the sixteenth century, the invasion of Ahmed Gran and subsequent wars and migrations had an element of "attempts of nomadic and pastoralist lowlanders to gain access to more or better land."[20]

Ethiopia was landlocked, so living conditions relied more on local resources than the prospect of trade. Commerce and access to the sea were not absent, however. On a smaller scale than most parts of Africa, overland trade flourished in the Afar Imamate of Aussa (Awsa) in the northeast and

[16] Cited in Sven Rubenson, "Conflict and Environmental Stress in Ethiopian History: Looking for Correlations," *Journal of Ethiopian Studies*, 24, 1991, 71–96.

[17] Girma Kebbede, "Cycles of Famine in a Country of Plenty: The Case of Ethiopia," *GeoJournal*, 17(1), 1988, 125–132, cited text on p. 125.

[18] Ibid., 87.

[19] Ibid.

[20] Rubenson, "Conflict and Environmental Stress in Ethiopian History: Looking for Correlations," 77.

was a source of revenue. The region provided relatively easy access to the seaboard via the Massawa port. The sultan's economic interest was remotely linked to the herders but firmly to that of the urban elites and farmers.

The northeast was dry, dependent on seasonal rains, and mainly sustained herding except on the banks of the Awash River. The livelihood of the leading ethnic group (Afar) in the drylands of Ethiopia was a mixture of farming near the rivers and herding and animal breeding in the drier areas away from the rivers. The herders would migrate seasonally between wet pastures in the higher lands and dry-season wetlands nearer the rivers. Where farming was possible, the farmers also kept herds. In a good year, the animal herding business demanded good cooperation between households, clans, and villages. But in years of abnormal rainfall, the forced dispersal weakened these institutions. Even as late as the late twentieth century, the common grazing lands they lived on carried substantial user rights; the lands could not be enclosed, purchased, or sold because the clans that used these had their rights commonly recognized. Marriage practices cemented interclan cooperation in the use of grazing lands.

Northern and Eastern Kenya share the tropical semi-desert climate zone of the Horn of Africa, stretching into three countries: Ethiopia, Somalia, and Kenya. British colonization of East Africa proceeded via antislavery movements initially and later from a drive to build trade links with India and between the seaboard and the interior, especially the lake region of Africa. Following the Berlin Conference (1885) and several treaties with the local rulers, Britain began to colonize the Kenyan coast in 1885. Progress into the interior was erratic and happened through conflicts and alliances. In 1886, after an agreement between the shipping magnate William Mackinnon with the British Foreign Office, the Imperial British East Africa Company (IBEA) was established. The company's interest was trade in ivory, among other goods. Suppression of the slave trade from Zanzibar by controlling the hinterland of the trade was also a stated objective. Many individuals engaged in extending British and German power in East Africa believed in that aim. Still, antislavery actions mixed up with other aims. The company failed in 1894, but its work was done. In 1895, the British formally took over power in Kenya (East Africa Protectorate) and Uganda.[21]

---

[21] Jonas Fossli Gjersø, "The Scramble for East Africa: British Motives Reconsidered, 1884–95," *Journal of Imperial and Commonwealth History*, 43(5), 2015, 831–860.

64   WATER AND DEVELOPMENT

Over much of this land, pastoralism ruled. The emergence of colonial borders in the region cut up the pastoral orbits in this vast area and brought within the colonial borders places where pastoral groups or clans substituted for states. The British who ruled Kenya did not like territories that were difficult to control even when there was no overt conflict or resistance, and worried about integrating these places. One of the early areas of action was to create reserves and discourage population movements, which was unenforceable and did not change things much. That ambition received money after the Colonial Development and Welfare Act of 1940 started.

According to maritime trade patterns, the Horn of Africa can be divided into two segments, north and south. On the northern side, the major ports before European rule were Berbera and Zeila (Saylac) in present-day Somaliland, Suakin in Sudan, Massawa in present-day Eritrea, and Mocha in Yemen. These ports traded in gold, ivory, slaves, Indian textiles, and coffee. On the southern side, the Benadir coast, Mogadishu was a major seaport. This is the coast, which has a milder climate. The inland is mostly hyper-arid (Map 3.2). The entire region is on the pathway of the Southwest monsoon of the northern hemisphere. Monsoon rains, however, were of significant quantity only in the far south of the Benadir coast. The only area of Somalia that offered prospects of commercial agriculture was a strip of land between the Shabelle (Shebelle or Shebeli) and Jubba Rivers, roughly the territory of the Lower Shabelle province where the capital, Mogadishu (Mogadiscio) is located. Here, on the floodplains of the two rivers, agriculture could develop. Salt marshes on the coasts made agriculture and town-building demanding enterprises. Still, in the interfluve of the rivers and near the seaboard between Mogadishu and Kismayo towns, floods, underground water in the alluvium, and the prospect of storing excess river water enabled agriculture. Arable land was more or less confined to a narrow area near these rivers.

In the remaining area, animal husbandry was the dominant livelihood, even the only form of livelihood. Pastoralism took over only a short distance from the area. Herders were mobile and dispersed if the rains were good and concentrated near secure water sources when the season was bad. Here, the basis of clan authority was control of wells and acacia clusters where gum could be harvested. Droughts visited this population regularly. During these episodes, the herders reduced consumption and lived on hunting.

The Horn represents something like a puzzle to the historian. "When we think of the formation of the nation/state in Sub-Saharan African history," writes Irma Taddia, historian of Eritrea, "we tend to isolate the Horn of Africa from other African ex-colonial societies and to analyze it as a peculiar phenomenon."[22] Statements like these refer to the specific nature of the imperial impact and postcolonial history marked by episodes of state collapse. In fact, what made the region special was also aridity so fierce that agricultural and urban growth became and remained a struggle. Consequently, state formation was a struggle.

A significant part of the historiography of precolonial and colonial Somaliland concerns the absence of statelike institutions almost anywhere before European colonization.[23] Instead, the "political structure . . . reflected the decentralised nature of the production base," and one may add demography.[24] The absence of statelike authority is also significant to understanding the concept of a protectorate as opposed to a colony—a colony is acquired from a ruler; a protectorate is a declaration to be a caretaker until a worthy ruler is found. The Horn of Africa saw mainly the latter type of colonial rule.

By contrast with Somalia, Eritrea's geography was a little different, with a cordillera running northwest by southeast dividing the country into two halves. Although narrow in the north, the uplands spread wider in the south. The east and west of the uplands are arid and semi-arid, but the mountainous south received good rainfall. Before the region became a European protectorate, around 1890, the Eritrean inland was under a loose form of control by the Ethiopian state. Somalia had a collection of statelike entities around clans and tribal councils. Toward the south, the sultanates had features of states in the Jubba and Shebelle Basins. In the Puntland in the north, where the Ismaan Sultanate formed of the Majeerteen peoples prevailed, the state was little more than a collection of clan networks. All states or clans tried to collect money from trade. With the Majeerteen, that activity included raiding European ships wrecked on the dangerous bit of the Indian Ocean near the Ras Haafuun (or Xaafuun) promontory. Indeed, this was so profitable—or the clans otherwise so starved of money—that piracy and raids supplied a significant income for the Majeerteen. Clashes with rival clans over the control of this activity intensified in the nineteenth century as shipping density rose.[25]

[22] Irma Taddia, "At the Origin of the State/Nation Dilemma: Ethiopia, Eritrea, Ogaden in 1941," *Northeast African Studies*, 12(2–3), 1990, 157–170.
[23] See discussion on the subject in David D. Laitin and Said S. Samatar, *Somalia: Nation in Search of a State*, Boulder, CO: Westview Press, 1987.
[24] A. Samatar, "The State, Agrarian Change and Crisis of Hegemony in Somalia," *Review of African Political Economy*, 43, 1988, 26–41, cited text on p. 29.
[25] Wayne K. Durrill, "Atrocious Misery: The African Origins of Famine in Northern Somalia, 1839–1884," *American Historical Review*, 91(2), 1986, 287–306.

66 WATER AND DEVELOPMENT

Before European colonization, the Horn coastland had a string of ports from which the Ottoman Empire collected customs. The climate was so dry and seasonally variable—and the rivers of such uncertain value for navigation or irrigation—that the ports did not possess a significant rural hinterland. The coastland was governed, if loosely and from a distance, by the Ottoman Empire in the northern segment and the Zanzibar Sultanate in the southern segment. Power was held by local chiefs ruling over smaller areas. Neither of these two overlords had much interest in the inland.

The Italians in the 1880s acquired from the Zanzibar sultanate the right to manage the Red Sea ports. These ports received goods carried to them by caravan trade—gum, skins, livestock, myrrh, ostrich feathers, and ivory— and exported these in exchange for mainly manufactured goods from Asia. In the 1890s, Italy formally took over management of the Benadir coastland from Zanzibar. Vincenzo Filonardi, a naval commander with experience of the East African coast and a shipping entrepreneur, was invited by the Italian government to run the government of the coastland. He stayed in this post for only a few years. Italy and Filonardi were interested in the transit ports of Benadir, though these were losing some trade to Aden and Mombasa. However, the Italians had little inclination to develop and prepare the countryside for settlers. Although settlement was a cornerstone of Italian colonization in Africa, Somalia was considered too unattractive and harsh for investment.

A contender for the Ethiopian throne, Menelik, handed over the territory of Eritrea to the Italians in 1889 against Italian military help. At about the same time, Filonardi established an Italian protectorate in Somalia. Although the Italians were more interested in the coastland for economic reasons, the Eritrean uplands drew in settlers. A construction boom followed in Asmara, attracting wage workers from the plains. Commercial agriculture grew in the southern uplands, the Seraye region, again bringing in migrants and settlers.

Italian colonization of the coastland was the first step to securing the ultimate prize, Ethiopia. Within a year of the start of an Italian protectorate, conflicts with Ethiopia became inevitable. The Italo-Ethiopian wars ended in 1896 with a decisive Italian defeat. An interesting fact is that though the Italian forces were vastly outnumbered, the deeper reason for their defeat was not a military one but their poor access to food in the arid northeastern region of Ethiopia, where they had gained territory. The recruitment strategy changed after this war, when Italian recruits had dominated the military force. The colonial government spent a great deal of energy on building the army, now mainly consisting of Eritrean recruits. The army became a resource to fight imperial wars in other parts of Africa.

Although Eritrea was held up in Italy as a promised farmland for poorer Italians, the settler policy was unsuccessful. One reason for the failure was that agriculture would require extensive private capital (in water) that did not come forth. Settlers were offered private property but little more in government aid.[26] The ambition of settler agriculture was practically abandoned in the first half of the twentieth century, making a brief return in the fascist period. On the other hand, there was an inflow of Yemeni capital in a part of the Red Sea littoral. These enterprises succeeded in the interwar period by practicing dry farming techniques in large farms. Small farmers on the coast diversified into cash crops, including coffee, feeding the business of the Red Sea ports.[27]

Despite these developments, Eritrea remained primarily a military-administrative outpost of the Italian empire. The significant economic legacy of Italian colonization was the growth of wage work in place of various types of tributary labor services. The army was a significant employer. Labor requirements were met with interregional migration. On a small scale, Indian (Parsi) labor agents based in Aden helped in the process. The urban society was divided along racial lines. In the hierarchy of rights and privileges, Europeans, locals, and migrant workers from other regions were placed unequally and in that order. There was little impact on the bedrock of the arid plains: pastoralism.

The British, who had a presence in the Red Sea and were nervous about rivals in the Suez, saw the Italians as a friend rather than a rival, and a state of some sort took shape. In 1936, when Italy occupied Ethiopia and stayed there for five years, scattered Italian possessions in Eritrea, Ethiopia, and Somalia came under the East African empire. The British acquisition of Aden (1839) and the Suez Canal (1869) stimulated trade between the Benadir and British India and Europe. The cost of livestock trade fell significantly, generating a boom in animal trade. In the later nineteenth century, a series of treaties with clans led to the emergence of a British protectorate in the northern

---

[26] Stefano Bellucci and Massimo Zacearia, "Wage Labor and Mobility in Colonial Eritrea, 1880s to 1920s," *International Labor and Working-Class History*, 86, 2014, 89–106.

[27] Steven Serels, "Small-Scale Farmers, Foreign Experts, and the Dynamics of Agricultural Change in Sudan, Eritrea, and Djibouti before the Second World War," *International Journal of African Historical Studies*, 52(2), 2019, 217–230.

68 WATER AND DEVELOPMENT

part, the area corresponding to the present territory of Somaliland. Between 1899 and 1920, an armed resistance (Dervish) kept the colonial authority busy. The British were fighting on behalf of the coastal merchants and some pastoralist groups against others. Something resembling colonialism emerged at the end of the resistance in 1920, until its end in 1960—but with little agricultural development possible, the regime took interest in development mainly in protecting the trade ties between the pastoralists and the coastal merchants.

Livestock trade, however, was hit by a series of disasters around 1900: rinderpest and drought, worsened by Dervish control of some critical pastures. Thus, although the Dervish resistance did not trouble or disrupt foreign trade much, it pushed many pastoralists to turn to farming. In the twentieth century, this became a general trend. Intermittently, herders would get into farming if possible. The supply of milk and meat from these agropastoral settings increased against the more distant and arid sources.[28]

Besides externally induced crises like drought, disease, and wars, the coastal-caravan trade was too dependent on one commodity, animals, to generate a sustainable and widely shared change in living standards. It strengthened the coastal bourgeoisie that led the nationalist movement in the mid-twentieth century. But the Benadir's growth impulse was weak in the long run.

The Horn became the site of a series of violent conflicts in the late twentieth century, through which process the modern political map of the region took shape. These conflicts had deep roots in the history of state formation and the way geography shaped state formation. States in the Horn of Africa were a precarious construction. The harsh climate and poor water and soil resources had made the Horn an unlikely site for the emergence of a robust fiscal state. In the 1960s, only 10 percent of the land in unified Somalia could sustain any agriculture, and a fraction of that land was cultivated in any year. The only sustainable livelihood was pastoralism. There was never a time in the past when an empire had ruled the Horn of Africa. Strong central power and pastoralist claims to territory would not easily go together. Colonialism left a light touch and mainly militaristic legacy upon the region's governance. Settler agriculture was a failure, and the army was one of the leading employers in the urban economy.

---

[28] Samatar, "The State, Agrarian Change and Crisis of Hegemony in Somalia."

THE ARID REGIONS   69

After colonial rule withdrew, therefore, state-making generated competition and conflicts. The inheritance of the colonial military enterprise made that contest more violent. After World War II and a brief British protectorate status, Eritrea joined a federation with Ethiopia. The federation was troubled almost from the start, partly because of a religious and cultural divide and partly related to disputes over finances. These problems only returned with greater force after 1962, when the Eritrean parliament voted to become a province of Ethiopia.[29] With armed rebel groups rising, that experiment collapsed in 1974. The Marxist regime in Ethiopia tried to regain Eritrea by violent and peaceful means, failing in the effort. In the bargain, the festering conflict drained the state's resources and left it ill-equipped to deal with the mid-1980s famine. In the 1980s, the Ethiopian forces tried to beat their enemy by destroying food reserves. Deliberate starving had been a military strategy in this region on many occasions. With the collapse of the regime in Ethiopia, Eritrea became an independent country.

During Italian colonialism, the economy received stimulus from infrastructure investments and the Red Sea trade. World War II made Eritrea a frontline and brought money into the region. During British rule after the war, investments went to industries. However, from 1960, for almost forty years, conflicts and a weak state left the economy struggling, except for intermittent years of peace. Eritrean nationalism was a reaction not to colonial rule but to Ethiopian ambitions, and therefore it was more a military-political than an economic movement. The army, sustained by compulsory conscription, was the core institution of the state, which had little money left over for investment in economic assets. Development effort, therefore, concentrated on land reform and pastoralism support rather than industrialization or big infrastructure projects.

In the 1990s, Eritrea became independent, and the rest of Somalia broke up to create Somaliland and Puntland, practically two countries. Puntland, the larger territory of the two, started around 1998 as a semi-independent part of the Somali federation but is effectively a country. Although dominated by one clan, Majeerteen, interclan conflicts have occurred in Puntland too. Puntland, Somalia, Somaliland, and Eritrea had a severely restricted

---

[29] John Markakis, "The Nationalist Revolution in Eritrea," *Journal of Modern African Studies*, 26(1), 1988, 51–70.

economic base.[30] Arid and pastoral in the interior, all states relied on livestock trade and a small tax take from trade. Puntland also had a reputation for organized piracy on the Red Sea, which is a historical legacy in a sense. Whereas Eritrea has a powerful army, the countries earn too little

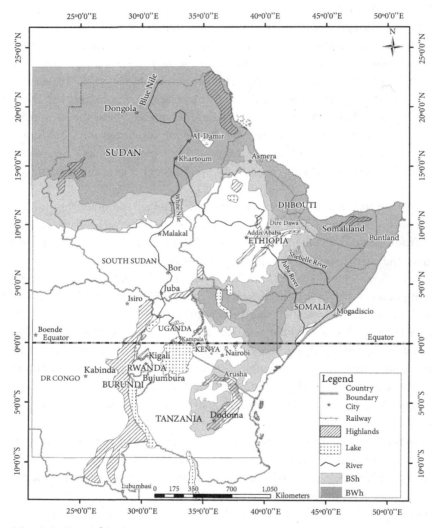

Map 3.2 East Africa

[30] Martha C. Johnson and Meg Smaker, "State Building in De Facto States: Somaliland and Puntland Compared," *Africa Today*, 60(4), 2014, 3–23.

revenue per head to run a militarily robust state. The ability to spend on public goods is minimal. Nevertheless, decades of emigration paid off richly in a steady and significant flow of remittances, usually bypassing government channels and going straight into businesses.

Postcolonial Somalia was a spectacular example of the collapse of a state. There were several elements in that collapse. Mohamed Siyad Barre, the dictator who ruled between 1969 and 1991, controlled the biggest of colonial legacies, the military. Using that power, he played clans against each other and converted the state offices into extensions of clan power. The military was not strong enough to hold a large and diverse country together without the backing of external agents, which colonialism had notionally offered. The politics of clan culture had divided the regions further.[31] Civil war and regional movements in the 1980s and 1990s led to the separation of Somaliland, formerly a British protectorate, and to effectively autonomous rule in Puntland, an Italian protectorate. In the remaining territory, state-making became a hard struggle, proximately due to the resurgence of radical Islam and, at a deeper level, due to the central state's weak fiscal and military power.

North Africa and West Asia

"If we draw on a map the rather flat arc from modern Tunis . . . to Agadir . . . in southern Morocco," Melvin Knight said, "nowhere is it more than two hundred miles from the coast to the southern frontier of a foot of annual rainfall." Well before that frontier of the arid belt, a dry farming regime started because even there, rains were too little and too seasonal "in this country of excessive evaporation."[32]

The Tropic of Cancer passes near the southern border of Morocco, yet Morocco, while facing acute water seasonality and shortage, had the mildest climatic conditions among the North African states (Map 3.3). On the southern Morocco coast, heavy dew reduced evaporation rates. Away from the coast, not only was any agriculture irrigation dependent, but the soils also required periodic fallowing and dispersed planting to recover fertility and

---

[31] Hussein M. Adam, *From Tyranny to Anarchy: The Somali Experience*, Trenton, NJ: Red Sea Press, 2008.

[32] Melvin M. Knight, "Water and the Course of Empire in North Africa," *Quarterly Journal of Economics*, 43(1), 1928, 44–93, cited text on p. 45.

72   WATER AND DEVELOPMENT

supply enough nutrients to the plants. Relatively milder climatic conditions with enough moisture and low evaporation occur only in parts of Morocco where the High Atlas generates snowmelt. The mountainous areas, however, had too little cultivable surface—not more than 10 percent of which received irrigation in the 1920s (Knight's estimate)—and these lands were not easily accessible by mass transportation to be integrated with long-distance trading systems. "Africa Minor has never afforded a cheap trade route to any valuable region beyond," Knight said about the precolonial past. He was disputing a myth created by the French imperialists that the Romans and their water projects had once turned all of North Africa into a breadbasket for the empire. The vestiges of Roman aqueducts and other works added up to "a multitude of little projects . . . on the whole less permanent," and did not stand for any extra irrigation capacity than the works in the 1920s could deliver, serving a tiny fraction of the cultivable lands.[33] Artesian wells, moreover, were poor insurance against seasonality, for their water levels rose and fell according to seasons.

Farther north, in Algeria, Tunisia, and Libya, a strip of land along the coast has a Mediterranean climate with mild summers and winter rains. Precipitation exceeds the evapotranspiration rate. This region has soil suitable for intensive cultivation and is home to most towns and cities. The southern frontier of this land merges into an arid band where the precipitation rate falls and temperatures rise to a degree that surface water dries up for a long stretch of the year. Farther south and southeast, the hyper-arid takes over. Water is still available, where geology permits runoffs from sudden bursts of rains to accumulate in fractures on the rocky surface.

Loosely under Ottoman rule in the nineteenth century, the region fell into French and Italian hands. Algeria became French after a messy diplomatic incident led to a war in 1830. In theory Ottoman-ruled, and in practice independent, Algeria north of the mountains benefited greatly from trade with Europe and Ottoman Empire in the eighteenth century. Trade provided the main revenue for the regional rulers and was controlled by them. Agriculture, by contrast, offered little value for the state, though the Ottoman administration did use land tenure and land grants to secure the loyalties of clans and chiefs. With the decline of seaborne and trans-Saharan trade in the nineteenth century and inadequate land taxes, the regime in Algeria was too weak to resist colonization.

---

[33] Knight, "Water and the Course of Empire," 58.

THE ARID REGIONS   73

Tunisia, which was not under Ottoman rule and had a regime struggling to get its finances in order, fell victim in 1881 to Franco-Italian rivalry to control the northern coast of Africa. Italy lost that battle but compensated for it by using its military capacity formed in the Horn of Africa to conquer Libya in 1911. The coastal areas of western and eastern Libya (the central coastal belt is a narrower strip) had existed as nominal Ottoman provinces until Italian occupation ended their independence. The attempt to unify the territory of the coastal greens and the arid interior led to a destructive conflict that took a heavy toll on the nomadic herder population. In 1943 Libya came under British control, and a constitutional monarchy followed in the 1950s.

The French stake in Morocco had risen from the 1840s, when the leader of the Algerian resistance went to Morocco and tried to raise an army. An Anglo-Moroccan treaty in 1856 and a war with Spain in 1859 further weakened the state to resist European expansion into Morocco. At the turn of the twentieth century, many Europeans lived and worked in Moroccan cities, and European advisers were influential in the court. The move to a French protectorate in 1912 was consistent with this development.

The European empires expected Morocco, Tunisia, Algeria, and Libya to become settlements of immigrant farmers practicing intensive agriculture and raising cash crops for export. Settlements did emerge. Spanish immigrants introduced dry farming methods. American dry farming also had an impact on European practices in Algeria. In the nineteenth century, intensive agriculture stayed confined to a small fraction of the cultivable land, and European settlers tended to "fall back largely upon native crops, methods and help."[34] However, in the early twentieth century, with greater investment in irrigation, settler agriculture diversified crops and improved capacity.

In the interwar period, between 5 and 12 percent of the population of these countries consisted of European settlers.[35] Farming was the most important occupation both for the settlers and the Indigenous people, but a divergence in the condition of the farmers emerged, thanks in part to a concentration of settler farming with better water access along the coast. Europeans rarely figured in dryland farming. On the other hand, Europeans held a disproportionate share of ownership of irrigated lands and

[34] Knight, "Water and the Course of Empire," 74.
[35] Philip D. Curtin, "The Black Experience of Colonialism and Imperialism," *Daedalus*, 103(2), 1974, 17–29, cited data on p. 24.

74 WATER AND DEVELOPMENT

embarked on plans for intensive agriculture even in less suitable lands. This "environmentally anomalous" pathway did not deliver significant results.[36]

The colonist settlers in North Africa were a mix of French and Spanish in Morocco and Algeria and French and Italian in Tunisia. The French held the largest farms in all three countries to grow vines, olives, and soft wheat. The state aided settlement by offering freehold titles and land grants, a practice later discontinued, and in Morocco by providing a loan to cover the purchase. The Moroccan system did not deliver much value to the state or the settlers because the wheat market experienced oversupply in the interwar years.

Economic change in the three belts—Mediterranean, semi-arid, and hyper-arid—were interdependent since the late nineteenth century. French colonization in Algeria saw the settlers capture lands in the fertile zone. Subsequent attempts to expand cultivation dealt with aridity and water shortage in the second zone. Rainfed agriculture continued in the second zone, supported by Indigenous techniques of storing or accessing water, and pastoralism ruled in the third. Hydraulic projects like dams and barrages started in colonial times and had a limited impact on agriculture. However, urban water supply systems changed radically, driven by the anxiety that water had a role in spreading epidemics.

If we follow latitudes, this region of North Africa belonged in the same arid tropical geography that extended into Syria, Iraq, Jordan, Israel, and the Arabian Peninsula. J.R. McNeill called land use in the Middle East and North Africa a "patchwork" of cultivable land, pastures, and forests in proximity, unlike the extensive savanna of sub-Saharan Africa or farmlands in India. Such a settlement pattern shaped social and political interactions in special ways. "The MENA was eccentric in the degree to which pastoral and agrarian communities interacted."[37] In McNeill's narrative, "pastoralist confederacies" emerged in lands where pastoralism was extensive, eventually to be subdued and coopted by agrarian empires. This process, encouraging nomads to turn to farming and supply soldiers, occurred in the Ottoman Empire between the seventeenth and nineteenth centuries. It was more

---

[36] Edmund Burke III, "The Transformation of the Middle Eastern Environment, 1500 B.C.E.–2000 C.E.," in Edmund Burke III and Kenneth Pomeranz, eds., *The Environment and World History*, Berkeley: University of California Press, 81–117, cited text on p. 105.

[37] J.R. McNeill, "The Eccentricity of the Middle East and North Africa's Environmental History," in Alan Mikhail, ed., *Water on Sand: Environmental Histories of the Middle East and North Africa*, Oxford: Oxford University Press, 2013, 27–50, cited text on p. 34.

successful in the east. It was incomplete in North Africa, and pastoralist confederations retained a great deal of autonomy.

On the eastern side, the areas to receive considerable attention in long-range environmental history are the Fertile Crescent, including the Jordan Valley and the Tigris-Euphrates Basin, and, to a more limited extent, southern Iran. The Tigris-Euphrates Basin consists of rivers that descend from the central Anatolian Plateau and the Zagros Mountains. Almost the entire basin (mainly in Iraq and Syria) is desert or arid with little rainfall. The 30° latitude crosses the southern end of the basin, its northern end having much cooler temperatures than the tropics proper. Like the Himalayan rivers in South Asia, these waterways are fed by snowmelt, carrying relatively larger volumes of water throughout the year. Irregular flooding created nutrient-rich alluvium in parts of the basin. One of the first regions of the world to see irrigated agriculture develop, it is also the water archaeologists' favorite site. Much of the Fertile Crescent from the sixteenth century was integrated into the Ottoman Empire. European powers did not colonize it except for a few years of Anglo-French rule after World War I.

Farther west, the Jordan River Valley, especially its western side, is arid tropical. Climatic conditions vary in the Levant, from more winter rains and moderate temperatures along the coast and the northern Esdraelon plains to the dry and hot Rift Valley along the river's west bank. Until the end of the nineteenth century, agriculture was mainly rainfed. A few areas had local storages and commercial farming. Technically, the Ottoman sultans claimed these as crown lands. However, state authority was light upon the large estates in the north and subsistence small-holder farming in the south.

Located on or near the 30° north latitude, southern Israel is arid or desert. The seaboard and the country's north are more water-secure, with more rainfall and groundwater. European settlements from the nineteenth century marked a change in this region's politics and agricultural conditions. Whereas Jerusalem had an Indigenous Jewish population, the countryside was mainly Arab until Jewish settlers from Eastern Europe arrived in the 1880s. The settlers purchased land from the Arabs, created small agricultural settlements, and practiced dry farming (Chapter 7). Some early settlements could not make ends meet because the settlers ran out of money to develop the land. The survival of the others depended on Baron James de Rothschild's personal interest in the colonization project. That interest took the form of sponsoring viticulture, fruit trees, and olive groves—in short, commercial agriculture and monoculture. A significant investment went into constructing wells and water control systems.[38] During the British occupation of Palestine in the interwar period, more investment and workforce extended commercial agriculture and contributed to urbanization.

From the 1930s, Jewish organizations and philanthropists who sponsored settlements started thinking about pan-regional water schemes, including dams, reservoirs, and pipelines to distribute water from the Jordan Valley to drier fields. The State of Israel had an advantage, with no obligation to defend an inherited Indigenous institutional tradition and the ability to create a law that declared all forms of water sources public property (1952–1959). Armed with the law, the government cross-subsidized the water-poor areas. The state also had access to significant foreign funding.

Much of Iran is too far from the Tropic of Cancer to fit into this narrative. Also, the land is mainly mountainous, impacting precipitation and evaporation rates. The most tropical region is in the southwest, Khuzestan, over which the 30° north latitude passes. An arid near-desert plain, the deltas and river basins descending from the Zagros Mountains' eastern slope created potential for irrigated agriculture in this region. The ancient Elamite civilization was a product of that ecology. Since World War II, the government of Iran built a series of dams and reservoirs in this area to develop farming and industry.[39] In Iran (and Iraq), oil royalties contributed to the construction of dams in the 1960s.

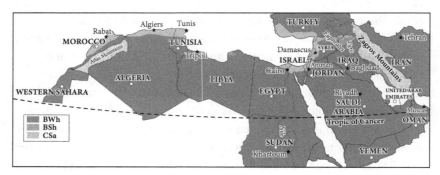

Map 3.3 North Africa and West Asia

---

[38] Ran Aaronsohn, "The Beginnings of Modern Jewish Agriculture in Palestine: 'Indigenous' versus 'Imported,'" *Agricultural History*, 69(3), 1995, 438–453.

[39] Peter Beaumont, "Water Resource Development in Iran," *Geographical Journal*, 140(3), 1974, 418–431.

Southern Africa

From a few hundred miles south of the equator, arid tracts become more frequent (Map 3.4). The nature and degree of aridity remain variable and take on a more standard character (high aridity and seasonality) as one reaches the Tropic of Capricorn. Almost all the major countries of southern Africa contain well-watered highlands or plains and arid zones; the balance varies. It is more favorable in Zimbabwe, which consists of water-rich uplands to the north and east and a semi-arid area to the southwest. The Tropic of Capricorn passes just south of its southern border. In the colonial period, the fertile, watered highland agricultural zones developed large-scale private farms producing export crops. Most, though not all, reserves allocated to the Indigenous population were in the arid areas during colonial rule in the early twentieth century, followed by white settler rule.

Tanzania belongs in an intermediate zone and is a land of contrasts. It is not exactly tropical by latitude, but like Mozambique in the south, it contains large areas inland that receive little rainfall. Its seaboard had land suitable for agriculture, did a lot of fishing, and participated in the Arabian Sea trade. The highlands are a source of several rivers that flow to the Arabian Sea. The rivers, their tributaries, and the marshes and swamps where some short rivers end up are subject to significant seasonal variation. Their narrow floodplains and the inadequate dry season flow cannot sustain intensive cultivation. But the deltas are water-rich. The northern areas bordering Lake Victoria are equatorial.

Hyper-aridity prevails in the central part of the country and toward the south. In the colonial era, low rainfall and other climatic and geological conditions in arid areas discouraged intensive cultivation. A lot of the stormwater was lost in runoff and evapotranspiration. The Basement Complex soil was not very fertile. After colonial rule ended in the 1960s and the 1970s (1961 in Tanzania; in Zanzibar, 1963), pastoralism expanded because of population growth and migration of people formerly living in the mountainous lands in the southwest and the northeast. Expansion of cultivation based on the water of the major rivers led to deforestation. Overgrazing and soil erosion reduced the returns from pastoralism.[40]

---

[40] J.P. Msangi, "Water Resources Conservation in the Semi-arid Parts of Tanzania," *Journal of East African Research and Development*, 17, 1987, 63–73.

The map of Tanzania is a product of European colonial rule, which began in the late nineteenth century in this region through alliances with the Zanzibar Sultans who loosely controlled a string of port cities. The ports conducted maritime trade in the Indian Ocean and caravan trade with the areas ruled by smaller kingdoms in the Great Lakes region. The slave trade was a significant business. The German East Africa Company, with protection of the state, established territorial control over both the coast and the interior. After World War I, the British took over the government.

Namibia is too dry to sustain arable lands and intensive agriculture, except in a narrow area to the country's north and the highlands. Much of the rainfall, which occurs between January and April, quickly evaporates under extreme heat. The agriculture that takes place at all occurs in an extremely short growing season. Most of the territory of modern Namibia sustained pastoralism. The migration of mixed-race populations from the east in the eighteenth and nineteenth centuries led to tensions over control of water sources, eventually ending in German colonization in 1884. The expectation that the colony would sustain settler agriculture was never quite fulfilled.

Early German settlers in waterless southern Namibia, where they had established a foothold, manipulated photo albums to feed the fantasy that even in the desert, water was available to transform the landscape. For these settlers, the principal article of trade was water, brought from as far away as Cape Town. German colonizers lived in the "dream of riches beyond the dunes."[41] With confidence in the ability of German engineering to turn barren landscapes into green gardens, a handful of people backed by private investment and political sponsors spoke of drilling riverbeds, installing condensers to trap moisture in the air, building cisterns, planting trees, and going inland to search for moist lands and minerals. Nothing worked. The German colonization drive became dependent on its British counterpart and had to scale down its ambitions.

Much of South Africa—and Gaza in southern Mozambique—is arid. The South African geography is a complex combination of rainfall zones and elevation. The summer rainfall zone on the western coast sustains intensively cultivated croplands and viticulture. The eastern coastal winter rainfall zone grows sugarcane, among other commercial crops. The highlands parallel to the east coast have moderate temperatures and much-reduced evaporation.

---

[41] Martin Kalb, *Environing Empire: Nature, Infrastructure and the Making of German Southwest Africa*, New York: Berghahn Books, 2022, cited text on p. 61.

THE ARID REGIONS 79

Together with two river basins, that condition sustains cultivation, the center of which is the present-day Free State province. Outside these lands, scrubs, bushes, and grass dominate the landscape of interior South Africa. Toward the northeast (Northern Cape), the savanna merges with the Kalahari Desert.

European settlers and mixed-race peoples in these areas adopted herding as their main occupation. Droughts and the constant search for pastures drove them to migrate long distances. These often movements triggered competition over pasture and wars with either Indigenous pastoralists or Indigenous states of the highlands. The discovery of diamonds, foreign investment, immigration, and the expansion of British power from the west to the east introduced new dynamics, especially from the late nineteenth century. However, herding remained the main livelihood for many in the interior.

Madagascar, the fourth largest island in the world, is about one thousand miles long from north to south, meaning that it is not ecologically uniform. The Central Massif is a mix of mountains and plateaus. It has a temperate climate and receives good rainfall. In the past, it was agricultural, constrained by poor soil and limited irrigation potential. The highlands were the seat of power before and after colonization. The French succeeded in colonizing the island (1895) by taking over the Merina Empire in the highlands, which had claimed to control the island except for the south.

French interest in the island was initially in provisioning ships bound for colonies in the Indian Ocean. From the 1860s, exaggerated accounts relayed back to France about the mineral resources and agricultural possibilities created a political interest in the island. The formal takeover was a response to the Merina imperial state's alleged reluctance to offer concessions to European planters. The Merina Empire did move to engage more with European investors, but wars with the French distracted it.[42]

The northern and eastern seaboard traded a lot in the Indian Ocean. In precolonial times, Europeans and other foreign merchants visited the ports of the north, which were integrated with the Arabian Sea trade and exchanged goods and slaves. The plains on the island's west face had an arid seasonal climate, and those on the east had a heavy monsoon. A few

---

[42] Phares M. Mutibwa, "Trade and Economic Development in Nineteenth-Century Madagascar," *Transafrican Journal of History*, 2(1), 1972, 32–63.

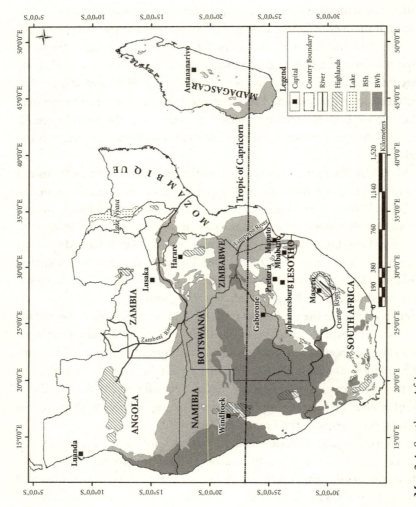

Map 3.4 Southern Africa

THE ARID REGIONS   81

European pirates took refuge on the island and married into elite families, and their progeny became rulers on the eastern seaboard.

Of direct interest to this book is the roughly twenty-thousand-square-mile section in the south and the west, over which the Tropic of Capricorn passes. It was a hyper-arid area with few rivers, and therefore no river ports, so it did not trade much. A shared interest before colonial times in trading guns made for a form of contact between the locals and the Europeans. However, such communication was limited and sporadic. Indeed, the region is an enigma for the historian for the almost total lack of documentary sources and the tragic fate of European visitors to this coast. Some in the sixteenth and seventeenth centuries reached these shores following shipwrecks. Large numbers died of disease or in the hands of the local people.[43] These drylands lived on herding, especially cattle, and relied on wells and the prickly pear cactus as human and animal food.

Southern Asia

The Tropic of Cancer cuts through northern India and Bangladesh and passes about one hundred miles south of the Pakistan coast (Map 3.5). The intense heat and the Indian Ocean produce a powerful hydrologic cycle and one of the strongest monsoons in the world. The Western Ghats Mountains and the Himalayas influence the path of the monsoon winds so that the western coast, eastern India and Bangladesh, and the foothills of the Himalayas receive the most annual rainfall (forty inches or more, or one thousand millimeters). The rain-bearing clouds of the southwest monsoon lose a lot of their moisture when crossing the Western Ghats Mountains. The hotter air of the plateau creates a convectional process that brings on storms and causes the air to cool. Still, seasonal rainfall reduces to less than a third of that on the windward side of the mountains. A north-south band through the center of the South Asian landmass receives fifteen to twenty inches (four hundred to seven hundred millimeters). That drier band extends into Sri Lanka. Much of Pakistan receives even less rain and, except for the highlands, is either semi-arid or hyper-arid.

For a region with low rainfall and intense heat, South Asia became significantly agricultural in the last two thousand–odd years, shedding its ancient

[43] Mike Parker Pearson, "Close Encounters of the Worst Kind: Malagasy Resistance and Colonial Disasters in Southern Madagascar," *World Archaeology*, 28(3), 1997, 393–417.

82   WATER AND DEVELOPMENT

attachment to animal herding. The Himalayan rivers that gave rise to the Indo-Gangetic Basin provided secure water throughout the year to those who lived near the banks of these rivers. Pastoralism persisted until recently in the Punjab, Rajasthan, and parts of the Deccan uplands.

The mountain range on the western side of the Deccan Plateau has few gaps along its north-south expanse for a thousand miles; a lot of the rainwater flows down the eastern slope into the plateau and forms the so-called Ghat-fed rivers. Godavari and Krishna—and the two tributaries of Krishna, Bhima and Tungabhadra—carry most of the monsoon flow. The Godavari and Krishna drainage areas cover more than two-thirds of the plateau between them. However, the water flow in the southern rivers varies significantly between seasons. The rivers do not carry much water for eight months in a year to sustain intensive agriculture or a large population.

Populations in the Deccan were exposed to a relatively high risk of droughts and famines. They could potentially access groundwater, but the sources were unreliable everywhere. The larger part of the plateau in its northwestern side, the so-called Traps, was formed by late-Mesozoic volcanic eruptions (sixty to sixty-five million years ago). The southern and eastern sides of the Deccan uplands formed parts of the Gondwana continent that drifted away from Africa and collided with the Eurasian plate about forty to fifty-five million years ago, creating the Himalayan mountains. Because of their different geological origins, the soil and rock types vary between these zones. Both regions, however, have hard rock formations. The aquifers that occur between these rock layers are expensive to access.

The southern parts of the plateau relied a great deal on humanmade lakes or "tanks." Local chiefs and warlords devoted money and power to constructing tanks, using forced labor. These tanks dotted the Tamil Nadu countryside and a large area in southern Karnataka, or the former Mysore state. The tanks were not wholly a credit to the regimes that ruled the region. Mysore, a plateau, was the only region in southern India with a milder summer and a relatively low evaporation rate. Humanmade lakes had a better chance in that area to withstand the summer aridity. Most survive today. The tanks came in a wide range of sizes and capacities. With a few exceptions, the best of them provided to the population a slightly higher level of water security than did rivers. When the rains failed, most smaller tanks dried up. The tank became a disease carrier when the subsoil water level fell during severe droughts. The conduct of "personal ablutions, washing of clothes and utensils, and watering of cattle" in the same place turned it into a "source of pestilence."[44]

The Indo-Gangetic Basin and the deltas of the southern rivers offered scope for digging wells at a low cost. In the alluvial Gangetic Basin, subsoil water could be found almost everywhere. In the Indus Basin, annual flooding and wells also provided security against droughts. Elsewhere in arid western India, agriculture was universally rainfed. Although the local chiefs did build storage tanks, the level of access that the poor or famine-stricken had to these tanks is an open question.

Hundreds of kingdoms ruled the South Asian mainland in the early eighteenth century. Some larger ones owed allegiance to the Mughal Empire in the Gangetic Basin lands. Others, especially in eastern and southern India, did not. That empire was slowly collapsing in the 1730s. Although technically entitled to the taxes paid by the farmers in some of the most fertile regions of India, the empire had grown militarily weak because provincial rulers did not send money to the central treasury or send soldiers. At the same time, in the Deccan plateau, formidable rivals emerged, the most important force being the Marathas. The British East India Company, operating from the seaboard, joined in on the broader conflict and eventually established a powerful rule in northern and eastern India. The company, however, left most princely rulers alone. With a few exceptions, almost all of them ruled in semi-arid central and southern India. With command over limited tax resources, these regimes did not threaten British India. Even more than their predecessors, the colonial government was keen to develop an agricultural tax base and convert pastures to cropland using the law, intimidation, and later canal technology. The conversion was a dramatic success in Punjab, begun in the 1870s and almost completed by the 1930s.

Sri Lanka is located about a thousand miles from the Tropic of Cancer but shares some features of a tropical region. Rainfall is seasonal and relatively weak on the leeward side of the central highlands. Therefore, the island's north and east are "dry." With annual rainfall well above forty inches, the dry zone is nowhere near as dry as the arid lands near the tropics (with fifteen inches rainfall or less). The dry zone was instead an area of rainfed agriculture with potential for irrigation development. Although not exactly

---

[44] India, *Report of the Indian Famine Commission. Part I: Famine Relief*, London: HMSO, 1880, 108.

84   WATER AND DEVELOPMENT

tropical, the arid zone in Sri Lanka became famous in the global history of water, thanks to an extensive network of ancient canals.

Although the maritime provinces of the island of Ceylon had been ruled by the Portuguese and the Dutch before 1800, British rule (1796–1948) was the first time a coastal state had established control over the entire island. The control was obtained after annexing the Kandyan Kingdom (1818) after nearly twenty years of intrigue, diplomacy, and warfare.[45] The colonial state took steps to develop land but concentrated its energy on highland plantations. The plains, especially agriculture in the dry zone, were left alone until independence in 1948.

On the other end of South Asia, Afghanistan shares some features of the tropics. The southern plateau of Afghanistan, about four hundred to five hundred miles north of the Tropic of Cancer, is one of the driest areas of South Asia—hot in summer and cold in winter. The southwest monsoon does not visit this area. However, the "western disturbance," a weather pattern that originates in the Mediterranean and travels southeast in the winter, causes a small quantity of rainfall in December and January. Pastoralism was the main livelihood here, except along the Helmand River, which flows in a broad arc through the plateau and sustains agriculture near its banks. The drive to convert the common lands into agricultural land was significantly weaker in Afghanistan, which was never colonized. The lack of radical change in land use also meant an inequality between areas of intensive cultivation near the northern rivers originating in the Pamir or Hindu Kush, and the dry southern savanna remained entrenched. The inequality would shape domestic politics in the future.

In southwestern Pakistan, aridity rules. The rainfall rarely exceeds ten inches, and in the Baluchistan plateau, it is usually half that. In the central, western, and northern parts of Baluchistan, mountains have moderate evaporation. In Quetta and Loralai, underground water channels, artesian wells, and streams irrigate fruit orchards. As elevation falls and near the Arabian Sea coast, aridity is extreme. The region known as Makran, once the largest district of Pakistan, sustained mainly dryland agriculture or nomadic sheepherding. A sedentary population would only exist in the oases and river valleys, raising date palms, among other crops. The rivers descend from the highlands. "Even the major streams of Makran . . . are meagre during the

---

[45] The process of state-making in the early nineteenth century is described in Sujit Sivasundaram, "Ethnicity, Indigeneity, and Migration in the Advent of British Rule to Sri Lanka," *American Historical Review*, 115(2), 2010, 428–452.

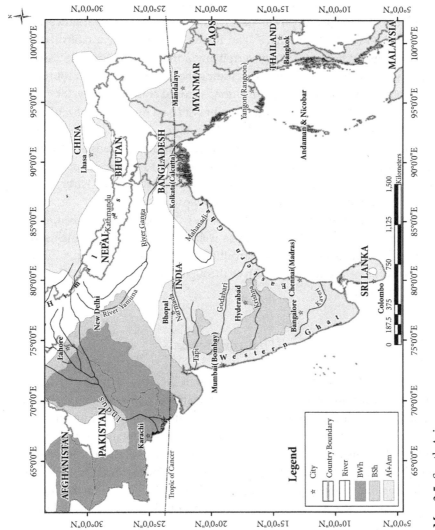

Map 3.5 South Asia

86   WATER AND DEVELOPMENT

best years," claimed an anthropological study from the early 1970s.[46] Qanats or a chain of wells dug into a single water table (see Chapter 4, locally *kahn* or *kahn-karez*), though expensive to build and which irrigated no more than a few hundred hectares, were a water source for date cultivation.

So inhospitable—and from the revenue point of view, unattractive—was the region that imperial power never grew roots here. Governance was largely left to the local populace. The British colonial state established an overlordship but did not try to govern it anymore than did its predecessors. Therefore, control over resources, including the kahns, remained a source of local political power. Tribal organizations secured control over water. "The shareholders," offered a 1995 study, "are pressurized not to sell the land and water share outside the tribe. To block the entry of other tribes, the women are not ordinarily given a share in the karez contrary to the Islamic law."[47] Droughts could severely test these norms created to enforce cooperation, as some members would want to increase the capacity of the karez, while exposing the entire system to the risk of collapse.

East of India, the Tropic of Cancer passes through Burma (Myanmar). Burma received a strong monsoon, as well as Himalayan snowmelt river water. Still, a roughly circular area around Mandalay is a semi-arid savanna. The presence of the Irrawaddy River through it significantly modifies the impact of aridity.

The Americas

The Tropic of Cancer passes through northern Mexico (Map 3.6). For hundreds of miles along the Sierra Madre Occidentale, moderate temperatures and adequate rainfall enable a temperate climate and intensive agriculture. However, the central plateau between the two mountain ranges, especially the northwestern plains and Baja California, were hyper-arid with some herding until the late nineteenth century. Underground water exists in this region. Sparsely populated, the Sonora River Valley in the northwest mainland saw an early green revolution on the back of groundwater exploitation.

---

[46] Stephen Pastner and Carroll McC. Pastner, "Agriculture, Kinship and Politics in Southern Baluchistan," *Man*, 7(1), 1972, 128–136.

[47] Muhammad Fazle Karim Khan and Muhammad Nawaz, "Karez Irrigation in Pakistan," *GeoJournal*, 37(1), 1995, 91–100, cited text on p. 94.

The Sonoran Desert is the southern extension of a vast arid tract extending into Arizona, Nevada, New Mexico, California, Utah, and Texas. The largest mass of the dry land occurs inside California. The state saw significant expansion of agriculture in the twentieth century, thanks to large river valley projects that diverted and impounded rivers. As population pressure on surface water increased, groundwater exploitation began. Some aquifers straddled Mexico and the United States and started depleting in the 1920s with rising agricultural use. Every drought was dealt with in a drought-prone state by drawing significant water underground. Ranching was a more extensive occupation in New Mexico and Arizona. Groundwater extraction was usually a private investment pursuit and required capital.

European settlements, the emergence of large landholders, and the expansion of the church induced a privatization of land and water resources in semi-arid northwest Mexico since the seventeenth century. Indigenous communities had formerly used these resources. In this backdrop, a prolonged period of climatic drying and frequent droughts from the late seventeenth century led to disputation over ownership and use of water.[48] The long-drawn elite encroachment on peasant farming property led the anthropologist Eric Wolf to invent the "closed corporate community" concept—a response to such encroachment. The concept offered a way to explain cultural practices with reference to resources. To resist encroachments, peasants formed communities restricting benefits to members. The community worked like a corporate body in the sense that members had well-defined rights. In a 1988 book, Thomas Sheridan argued that hydraulic control and politics were vital ingredients in building peasant communities in the dry northwestern environment.[49] This discussion has indirect relevance to the historiography of groundwater in Chapter 7.

In South America, northeastern Brazil—the territory of Ceara, Pernambuco, Alagoas, Paraiba, and Rio Grande do Norte—is classified mainly as tropical savanna and semi-arid. This vast area is predominantly grasslands or, toward the northeast, semi-arid scrubland. The Tropic of Capricorn lies about four hundred miles south of the southern border of the zone. The cool temperature of the Atlantic Ocean keeps the intertropical convergence zone farther away from here, causing desertlike conditions. Rainfall is scanty and

---

[48] Georgina H. Endfield and Sarah L. O'Hara, "Conflicts over Water in 'The Little Drought Age' in Central México," *Environment and History*, 3(3), 1997, 255–272.

[49] Thomas E. Sheridan, *Where the Dove Calls: The Political Ecology of a Peasant Corporate Community in Northwestern Mexico*, Tucson: University of Arizona Press, 1988.

88 WATER AND DEVELOPMENT

seasonal. The region's geology creates limited groundwater potential, and drought is endemic. Sandwiched between the Amazon rainforest and the relatively wet coastal areas, the region was known as Sertão or "backcountry." Highlands, river valleys, and marshes made the savanna geographically diverse, and nowhere wholly arid.

From the early sixteenth century, Portuguese settlers in Brazil discovered the prospect of growing sugarcane. The coastal parts of the northeast have some rains and produce the crop. To provide food and other produce for consumption in the coastal areas, settlers from the seventeenth century spread into the interior. In doing so, the settlers became more exposed to drought risk. "Because of the abundance of open spaces," such as more water-secure uplands to the west of the region, "the inhabitants of the northeast in the sixteenth and seventeenth centuries experienced no difficulty whatever in a dry season."[50] Just how bad these episodes were it is difficult to say. In the twentieth century, population growth posed a challenge to livelihoods. As in the Senegal Valley, emigration eased the pressure more than waterworks.

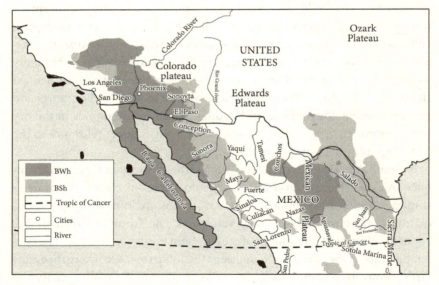

Map 3.6 Tropical North America

[50] Friedrich W. Freise, "The Drought Region of Northeastern Brazil," *Geographical Review*, 28(3), 1938, 363–378, cited text on p. 372.

Australia

In more than 80 percent of the land in Australia, the evaporation rate exceeds precipitation. This immense arid space is encircled on the west and southwest by "a ribbon of fertile country" between the mountains and the Pacific Ocean—the "real Australia," in one description.[51] Trade, towns, cattle breeding, and intensive agriculture developed in these parts from the time of early European settlement. Expansion of settler population into the interior began later. While plenty of land was available for the purpose, water and drought risks were severe obstacles to the growth of herding. The enterprise was intrinsically challenging and suffered from high animal mortality.

The story of relentless hardship changed with the discovery of highly productive aquifers in eastern-central Australia in the 1880s, spanning hundreds of thousands of square miles. Sixty percent of the land mass of Australia has a water-bearing sedimentary basin underneath. In common with northern Mexico and California, this dry tropical land could embark on intensive and sedentary ranching because of groundwater.

Conclusion

Is a thread running through these region studies? I believe so: the natural livelihood in the arid tropics with seasonal rainfall was animal herding. This occupation could adapt best to aridity, seasonality, and even drought risk since animals (if they survived the drought) were a better asset than parched land. Where agriculture existed, it depended on particular conditions—a heavy monsoon in India or Southeast Asia, or annual floods in rivers, deltas and river valleys, and highland or coastal temperate places. Chapter 6 describes from the late nineteenth century a range of attempts to free agriculture from dependence on these conditions, a movement we can call "modern." How did people live with tropicality before the modern?

---

[51] Geoffrey Blainey, "Australia: A Bird's-Eye View," *Daedalus*, 114, 1985, 1–27, cited text on p. 6.

Chapter Four
Dry Seasons and Disastrous Ones

Those living in the semi-arid tropics deal with seasonality every day. Only in the last 150 years have these actions taken the form of controlling moisture flow seriously using capital-intensive technologies. History reveals a range of adaptive responses before that. Virtual trade was mentioned in Chapter 1. Other primary responses involved chasing moisture over space during dry seasons, droughts, and famines. The relationship between droughts and famines has been discussed before; droughts are moisture stress, and famines are food shortages. In the semi-arid tropics, food shortages usually result from moisture stress. Famines can happen without that trigger, but most famines of the past we know of were set off by moisture stress. The connection between the two types of stress was closer in times past before the international food trade exploded.

Given the uneven nature of the sources and often the absence of precise dates, it is impossible to tell a chronological history of responses to droughts and dry seasons. I instead highlight three patterns or recurrent themes: movements over space, consolidation and emergence of hierarchies, and public relief. I identify patterns of response to seasonality and drought, an ever-present and universal condition of life. Future research could offer us ways to develop before-and-after scenarios.

Movements

"Mobility and migration," states a study of the present-day drylands, "are core adaptive strategies within dryland pastoral systems in response to unpredictable and irregularly distributed resources." Unpredictability refers to droughts. Irregularity refers to the seasonality of moisture flow, which makes lands in different places usable at different times of the year.[1]

[1] Andrea L. Balbo, Erik Gómez-Baggethun, Matthieu Salpeteur, Arnald Puy, Stefano Biagetti, and Jürgen Scheffran, "Resilience of Small-Scale Societies: A View from Drylands," *Ecology and Society*, 21(2), 2016, https://www.ecologyandsociety.org/vol21/iss2/art53/.

Water and Development. Tirthankar Roy, Oxford University Press. © Oxford University Press (2025).
DOI: 10.1093/oso/9780197802397.003.0004

DRY SEASONS AND DISASTROUS ONES 91

Movement is a constant theme in the economic history of tropical Asia and Africa before colonialism. "Half of India's population" in the eighteenth century, speculates the historian David Ludden, was mobile. We must add that the majority of such people were seasonal migrants.[2] Any number on the scale of migration in the eighteenth century is as good as any other. But Ludden sounds right. Throughout India, two occupations—soldiery and construction work—relied on seasonal migrants from the farming village who left home in winter to return there before the monsoon broke. Most battles in recorded history happened in winter when part-time peasants were ready to leave home. One of these fields, construction, continued to draw seasonal workers after the advent of British rule. Soldiery ceased to do so.

If seasonal migration in South Asia was a sign of lack of work at home, transhumance, or seasonal movements of animals and the people tending them, were moisture-seeking movements. Combining places and works to reduce unemployment is an intrinsic part of living in the semi-arid tropics. The form of the combination changed. The combination of herding and farming was one standard form. Another more recent pattern was to send members of the family abroad. A third form combines smallholding agriculture and laboring off-season in construction or artisanal activities.

Where herding was concerned, one would encounter specialist herders and farmers who owned herds. For both sets, the dry season posed a problem. In the savanna, pastures appear in contiguous areas at different times of the year, depending on the amount of rainfall, floods, and retained surface water. Stockkeepers must chase moisture. Like stockkeepers, whole agricultural systems would display considerable mobility, again chasing moisture.[3] In East Africa, the Sahel, or Nilotic Sudan, herders returned to the banks of the river in the dry months but traveled far inland in the rainier months when wells were full and pastures were green (Chapter 11).

Because dry-season or drought-hit pastoral orbit shrunk to a few places with secure water sources, migration during droughts had a distinctive character. It was not like movement from the distressed village to the city, but more and more people concentrated around boreholes and wells. In 1974, that happened on an extensive scale, and some people who moved in this way never returned, consolidating agropastoralism in the destination

[2] Cited by Ian J. Kerr, "On the Move: Circulating Labor in Pre-colonial, Colonial, and Post-colonial India," *International Review of Social History*, 51(1), 2006, 85–109, cited text on p. 89.

[3] John Iliffe, *Africans: The History of a Continent* (Cambridge: Cambridge University Press, 2007), describes examples of this.

92   WATER AND DEVELOPMENT

regions. So important were wells in the arid landscape that microenviron-
ments, "in the micro-est sense of the term," shaped significant demographic
shifts during disasters.[4]

Drought migration, in short, was a different kind of migration, with
much less regularity than seasonal movements. Drought-induced movements might ensure survival but did not always entail economic betterment
and might lead to a loss of political rights. Archaeological records for
agropastoral communities in arid western India suggest that storage of food
and livestock would last at least three years of scarce harvests and supplied nearly half of the calorie intake during droughts. Cattle domestication
became common from the time (Late Holocene, about four thousand years
before the present), and drought intensity and seasonality increased over
time due to climate change. More recent records suggest that these savings
disappeared quickly during droughts of great power. Indeed, a definition of
a modern famine, where death rates tend to be contained by timely medical
assistance, is a sudden loss of assets.[5]

Medieval (sixteenth- to eighteenth-century) Bengali poetic narratives
often mention famines as reasons to leave home. An unhappy and forced
decision, leaving home was the start of a new life and made a good story.
When famine struck, some of these narratives tell us that men sold their children and wives, died of indigestion from eating leaves and grass, or starved.
One of the oldest Bengali ballads, "Molua," begins with a famine. The pro-
tagonist, a young man called Chandbinod, finds cultivation impossible. He
then leaves home to hunt and wanders into unknown forests where the story
takes off.[6]

Like the forest in this story from India, in precolonial Africa, vast stretches
of less stressed and more water-secure lands could be found next to the
drought-hit ones. The seaboard, deltas, riparian floodplains, and lacustrine highlands like the Great Rift Valley provided insurance, sometimes as

[4] I copy the phrase from Clifford Geertz, "The Wet and the Dry: Traditional Irrigation in Bali
and Morocco," *Human Ecology*, 1(1), 1972, 23–39.

[5] Thanks to food aid and emergency relief, outright starvation and loss of life due to hunger have
almost disappeared, except in war zones where relief supplies cannot enter easily. This has changed
the meaning of such stressful events. "For Africans," writes a study of recent famines in Sahel, "the
essence of famine is a threat to their future economic viability. If adversity entailed widespread asset
liquidation and destitution, but conditions improved so that deaths were averted, a famine nonethe-
less took place." John Grolle, "Historical Case Studies of Famines and Migrations in the West African
Sahel and Their Possible Relevance Now and in the Future," *Population and Environment*, 37(2),
2015, 181–206, cited text on p. 183.

[6] Dinesh Chandra Sen, *Purba Banga Geetika*, 4 vols., Calcutta: University of Calcutta Press, 1923,
1:80–83.

opportunities for resettlement and farmland development. Tree rings, the Nile water level estimates, and oral traditions enable re-creation of the long history of some of these drought-generated migrations.[7]

Studies of twentieth-century practices suggest ways that tropical herders used to cope with droughts. Mobility, or micromobility, rather than migration, was the key instrument. It was used in diverse ways. A vital element in drought-induced mobility was the shift of herds closer to forest fringes, relatively wet areas that were open to access. During droughts again, pastoralists split up their herds to go in different directions. They lived as guests of settled agropastoralist peoples with whom the nomadic herders did business in good times. They would send scouts to look for forages that were still usable.[8]

In seventeenth and eighteenth century, large-scale movements occurred over more expansive spaces in response to climate change—like permanent shifts in the isohyet and shifts in the disease-prone zones. In turn, such drastic changes enabled military conquests that would have been impossible before. Shifts in desert edge and uprooting people in the seventeenth-century savanna zone in sub-Saharan Africa "had harsh consequences for many [as] ecological change . . . expanded zones of conflict and the loss of human freedom."[9]

The interdependence between the "desert-side" and the savanna has long been recognized as an essential characteristic of the Sahel. Before European rule emerged in this area, the interdependence was based on the trans-Saharan trade. The power of the Saharan trade to integrate regions and even forge ethnicities was greater than that of the states in this area and missing or weak in arid regions in other desert edges of the world. At the top of the commercial network were the Tuareg nomads and herders. The leaders among these groups headed large and diversified firms that organized stock breeding; conducted long-distance trade in salt and other goods exchanged for grain and textiles, among other commodities; owned slaves; financed commerce; and sometimes supplied soldiers in interstate wars and slave raids.

---

[7] J.B. Webster, "Drought, Migration and Chronology in the Lake Malawi Littoral," *Transafrican Journal of History*, 9(1), 1980, 70–90.

[8] Bilal Butt, Ashton Shortridge, and Antoinette M.G.A. WinklerPrins, "Pastoral Herd Management, Drought Coping Strategies, and Cattle Mobility in Southern Kenya," *Annals of the Association of American Geographers*, 99(2), 2009, 309–334.

[9] James C. McCann, "Climate and Causation in African History," *International Journal of African Historical Studies*, 32(2/3), 1999, 261–279, cited text on p. 269. Also, James L.A. Webb Jr., *Desert Frontier: Ecological and Economic Change along the Western Sahel, 1600–1850*, Madison: University of Wisconsin Press, 1995.

94 WATER AND DEVELOPMENT

Their businesses depended on the cooperation of the sedentary neighbors, who occupied the more fertile areas of the Sahel. The towns in these areas were the leading marketplaces for exchanging goods from different ecological regions and embodying different levels of water intensity. The sale of animals and using oxen and camels for transport provided a significant source of income for nomadic groups. The commercial infrastructure involved many groups who offered services as brokers and agents and part-time farmers on lands that could supply pasture for part of the year. Farmers in the desert edge, "midway between nomadic Tuareg society and sedentary . . . society," paid tribute to the former.[10] State authority was weak or notional, the land was of little value, and all households held animals.

These links between people of the marginal lands, and the savanna, urban groups, and the nomadic clans "provided a safety valve for the desert during droughts, particularly those lasting more than several years."[11] Except for a 1740s famine, most premodern droughts in this region can only be approximately dated and not studied in detail. From observing their effects during the more recent episodes, famines in the past would seem to induce a generally southward migration away from the desert fringe. These migrations were sometimes permanent ones, leading to the emergence of merchant groups in the urban centers of the Sahel, but more generally, they were temporary ones as wealthier northern people became guests of those managing their networks. The exact measure of the stress and the losses during these forced movements can only be guessed.

Unfreedom

A second theme that often shows up in accounts of movements is unfreedom. Economic historians often explain slavery with "factor endowments." Abundant low-quality land that needs a great deal of human effort to become productive and a relative scarcity of labor could induce employers and states to design rules that restrict the freedom of the worker. This stylized story has been used to explain Indigenous slave employment in Africa. An argument known as the land-abundance view of precolonial Africa suggests that

---

[10] Paul E. Lovejoy and Stephen Baier, "The Desert-Side Economy of the Central Sudan," *International Journal of African Historical Studies*, 8(4), 1975, 551–581, cited text on p. 563.
[11] Ibid., 572.

plentiful, low-quality land and labor scarcity encouraged labor coercion.[12] The key factors are land-labor balance and the coercive capacity of states and elites.

We can nuance the model by adding seasonality. Land quality varied with seasons. Rainfed or recession agriculture imposed prolonged idleness upon the workers and acute labor shortages during the few days or weeks when the moisture supply was just right for sowing. Coercive arrangements helped employers solve shortages on those days. Such arrangements usually entailed an obligation to provide subsistence to the workers when subsistence ran short. That risk was high.

The history of the arid tropics suggests another story about why slavery might emerge in specific environments, one connected with the frequency of drought and with spaces exposed to high levels of subsistence risk. The critical factor is the risk of death during droughts, not land-labor balance or coercion as a means of production. This alternative or supplemental narrative does not need to assume coercive state power to exist and yet can explain slavery and unfreedom. This is a more flexible theory of unfreedom in two ways. First, slavery did exist on an extensive scale where states were weak. Second, it can join the caste system in India with chattel slavery elsewhere into one broad movement from freedom to unfreedom in the face of extreme risk. Doing so helps to explain why some of the twentieth century's most significant popular political movements for freedom in South Asia joined water access with demand for equality.[13]

Famines broke up households and cooperation and made people accept dependence upon others at a cost. The Manusmrti, a code-of-conduct document for the Hindus composed in India in the early years of the Common Era, distinguishes categories of slaves, one category being slave-for-food.[14] Again, medieval Bengali ballads supply instances of children being sold during famines. In one case, an uncle sold a boy in exchange for rice to a gentleman who turned out to be the headman of a band of robbers.[15] European travelers in the sixteenth and the seventeenth centuries mentioned famines as an occasion that increased the supply of slaves. Chattel slavery was not

[12] Gareth Austin, "Cash Crops and Freedom: Export Agriculture and the Decline of Slavery in Colonial West Africa," *International Review of Social History*, 54(1), 2009, 1–37; James Fenske, "Does Land Abundance Explain African Institutions?" *Economic Journal*, 123(4), 2013, 1363–1390.

[13] Tirthankar Roy, *Monsoon Economies: India's History in a Changing Climate*, Cambridge, MA: MIT Press, 2022.

[14] P.V. Kane, cited in ibid.

[15] Sen, *Purba Banga Geetika*, 202–203.

96   WATER AND DEVELOPMENT

common in any part of India, but the sale of children was common enough during wars and famines. A Persian envoy of the sixteenth century took to Persia "a large number of Indian children, because famine had made them cheap during his visit. [Duarte] Barbosa tells us that when the people on the Coromandel coast were starving, the ships of Malabar used to carry food there and return laden with slaves, the people selling their own children for provisions."[16]

War, the traveler Mungo Park observed in 1796, was the first cause of slavery in the part of Sahel he visited. The second cause (sometimes, but not always, produced by wars) was famine, "in which case a free man becomes a slave to avoid a greater calamity."[17] A yet "third cause" was debt, and droughts added to indebtedness. In all cases, the shift of status was a form of transaction, according to Park: purchasing life by giving away liberty.[18] In this way, migration sometimes sharpened hierarchies and distinctiveness between ethnic groups, but not always. Relations of reciprocity and dependence governed some migration, as we have seen. In the middle Niger Basin, writes Richard Roberts, "ethnic boundaries were fluid."[19] Groups that moved also changed occupations. Being able to do that was necessary for survival in the semi-arid tropics because most smaller regions could sustain only a limited range of livelihoods.

There is a long-term dimension to this link between subsistence crises and unfreedom: persistent risk seemingly led to the consolidation of hierarchy. "Periodic waves of refugees from the surrounding dry land," wrote Miller on premodern Angolan droughts, "fled into these areas when the rain failed. There, the refugees often accepted subordinate civil status as 'guests' or 'slaves,' a price for asylum on the land of local communities of landowners. Many of these newcomers ended up later at the courts and markets of slave-selling kings and merchants."[20] An analytical narrative of Indian economic history in the longue durée contends that frequent famines in the ancient past drove "aboriginals [to contract] away their freedom for bare but regular subsistence."[21] A broad claim like this one is almost impossible

---

[16] William Moreland, *India at the Death of Akbar*, London: Macmillan, 1920, 92.

[17] Mungo Park, *The Travels of Mungo Park*, London: H. Milford, 1909, 226.

[18] Park, *Travels in the Interior of Africa*, 176–182.

[19] Richard Roberts, *Warriors, Merchants and Slaves: The State and the Economy in the Middle Niger Valley, 1700–1914*, Stanford, CA: Standford University Press, 1987, cited text on p. 7.

[20] Joseph C. Miller, "The Significance of Drought, Disease and Famine in the Agriculturally Marginal Zones of West-Central Africa," *Journal of African History*, 23(1), 1982, 17–61.

[21] Damodar Kosambi, *The Culture and Civilisation of Ancient India in Historical Outline*, London: Routledge and Kegan Paul, 1965, 88.

to verify with evidence, but there is an indirect confirmation of the link. With a significant rise in food production and water distribution in the Indian countryside from around 1900, many long-term and caste-based labor contracts crumbled quickly.[22]

Historians studying more recent famines explored with novel data the connection between climate shocks and unfreedom. The short-term nature of the effect is open to different interpretations depending on the evidence. "Famine," offered a study of early-nineteenth-century droughts in Mozambique, was "[a] major factor in filling the slave baracoons." "The Atlantic slave trade," Joseph C. Miller wrote, "flowed in part from the tides of drought and disease" in that the "historic peaks in exports" (from Angola) came when the most lasting and severe droughts were running their course. The link suggests that the slave trade was "in some ways less a cause of depopulation than a consequence of it when viewed in terms of droughts and demographic changes in West-Central Africa."[23] The message that famines could lead to slavery and labor scarcity does not discount that land quality also mattered. It is still a different approach, and explains better why some forms of unfreedom were difficult to end by legislative order.

Geography often forced Europeans in this time to rely heavily on the slave trade. Portuguese colonizers in Angola experienced such high death rates when they tried to settle or do business in the interior as to stop territorial conquests altogether, "lock[ing] Angola into its tragic dependence on slave exports."[24] Another study suggests that the relationship between famine and the slave trade was mediated by the cost of conducting raids, which was high during droughts.[25] The general point may still hold that people with insufficient means to cope with shortages during crises may become dependent upon strangers.

Distress sale of children and voluntary exchange of status for subsistence gave Sahelian slavery a peculiar character. Slavery consolidated in the nineteenth century and persisted in several Northwest African countries into the late twentieth century, in Morocco formally until 1961 and in Mauritania until 1981. In these cases, the last form of employment was domestic or household service. Although the societies practiced Islam, calling this

---

[22] Roy, *Monsoon Economies*.
[23] Miller, "The Significance of Drought, Disease and Famine."
[24] Ibid.
[25] James Fenske and Namrata Kala, "Climate and the Slave Trade," *Journal of Development Economics*, 112, 2015, 19–32.

98   WATER AND DEVELOPMENT

Islamic slavery would not make sense because slavery was not governed either by laws distinguishing free and unfree workers clearly or by religion, which is precisely the reason it could not be abolished in the same way that Atlantic slavery was. Instead of being a legal-religious concept, slavery was a part of the lived reality, and environmental risks were a core part of that reality. In Morocco, the end of slavery was gradual, as domestic slavery merged into the employment of servants; again, children were handed over to more affluent households when droughts struck, and there was not enough food and water for all.[26] In India, castes had comparable organic characters and were hard to eliminate for some of the same reasons, such as dependence during distress.

In the Mauritanian part of the Senegal River Basin, servile labor was pervasive in the early twentieth century, and possessing slaves "was a sign of wealth and represented one of the values of the aristocracy."[27] Droughts activated the slave trade before 1900. "The slaves were the first to be affected in times of crisis, especially . . . those who had just been bought or conquered. Pawned children were assimilated to slaves if their parents were unable to return the food that had been advanced to them."[28] Free people who moved and became dependent on others experienced a "loss of social status." Prolonged droughts that lasted for several years affected and broke up existing patterns of cooperation—for example, the extended family, an institution that protected the status and assets of free people and altered gender roles.

French colonization and a series of dry seasons reshaped these relationships. "The second half of the nineteenth century was a period of numerous crises of varying intensity. The years 1897–1915 saw an almost uninterrupted famine."[29] Farmers who lost their livelihoods would try to exchange their grains with milk from the herders and fish from the fishermen. The impact of droughts on the slave trade was asymmetric after 1900. French colonization changed the dynamics in the first half of the twentieth century. "Most of my informants," writes a scholar who surveyed the region in the 1980s, "considered the fiscal policy and the fight against slavery as

[26] R. David Goodman, "Demystifying 'Islamic Slavery': Using Legal Practices to Reconstruct the End of Slavery in Fes, Morocco," *History in Africa*, 39, 2012, 143–174.

[27] Monique Chastanet, "Survival Strategies of a Sahelian Society: The Case of the Soninke in Senegal from the Middle of the Nineteenth Century to the Present," *Food and Foodways*, 5(2), 1992, 127–149, cited text on p. 131.

[28] Ibid., 139.

[29] Ibid., 137.

outstanding features of the colonial system."[30] In the first half of the century, the government actively discouraged the sale of people, especially the pawning of children. Many formerly slave-owning aristocrats lost power and privilege. Trade and migrant remittances provided a cushion against harvest failure. Slavery was not formally abolished, but as people left the system, the owners had little practical way to bring them back.

The power of droughts and famines to remake societies is a frequent theme in the historiography of the tropics before European colonialism.

Disasters and Communities

Droughts are not food shortages or famine, but more complex conditions with diverse outcomes. The first-order effects may include reduced planting, livestock losses, drinking water shortages, and outbreaks of waterborne diseases as the surface water quality falls. Most droughts are mild, local, and end this way. One Africanist called these the "ubiquitous lesser drought."[31] When the rain failure is significant or affects larger areas, a series of second-order effects follow—famine, migration, loss of assets, and reduced consumption.

Occasionally, there were mega episodes. African and Asian history both register seven-year and ten-year droughts. The fourteenth-century Maghrebi traveler in India, Ibn Battuta, described one of these in graphic detail. Such events led to political disorder, institutional change, and cultural remaking. Sometimes famines followed political action. A few years before the 1335 famine broke out, an unhinged king in Delhi ordered the citizens to march to a new capital, an action that killed thousands of people from hunger, thirst, and disease. Episodes of severe and lasting drought weakened polities by reducing taxes and making it likely that the mercenary soldiers would switch sides depending on who could ensure food or wages.[32] In recent history, a series of violent civil wars in Chad, Mali, Ivory Coast, and Darfur in Sudan testifies to the disruptive legacies of the 1970s and 1980s droughts.

A study of Angolan history suggests that the nature of these processes changed according to how long a drought lasted.[33] A short, sharp rain

---

[30] Ibid., 140.

[31] Miller, "Significance," cited text on p. 32.

[32] For a nineteenth-century example of this dynamic from Southwest Africa, see Miller, "Significance."

[33] Ibid., cited text on p. 31.

100 WATER AND DEVELOPMENT

failure would force the affected population to fall back on reserves, kin networks, or business partners in more secure places, as discussed earlier. A two- to three-year shortfall would cause extensive population dispersal, a return to hunting and gathering, and perhaps banditry. These strategies were extraordinary, but, up to this point, "latently institutionalized and thus not perceived as entirely disruptive of the ongoing tempo of life." However, episodes of dryness that would last for eight or ten years (one of these occurred in the 1790s) "drove people to abandon and even to invert and pervert ordinary institutions."[34]

Disasters and States

In the semi-arid tropics, statecraft and famine relief were closely tied. This was not just a welfare duty. But famines seriously challenged state power, sometimes leading to collapse and dislocations. Severe and lasting droughts were more likely to aid the collapse of states, though they do not explain the nature of the disputes that followed or the formation of new states on the ashes of the old ones.

When made up of mercenaries and irregulars, armies shrank during famines. During the Bahmani king Ahmed Shah Wali's reign in the Deccan (India), "a grievous famine raged through all Dekkan [1421], and multitudes of cattle died on the parched plains, for want of water." The sultan's first step, perhaps wisely, was to "enlarge the pay of his troops."[35] In 1472, a failure of rains for two successive years in the Deccan again caused famine and migration on such a scale as to reduce the army greatly, making a foreign invasion likely.[36] Famines were also destabilizing because they induced riots and rebellions. During the 1421 episode, with rains failing again the following year, "people became seditious, complaining that the sultan's reign was unlucky, and displeasing to God." Most rebellions had warlord backers. Famines, therefore, caused a redistribution of power. The king could, in theory, offer more public relief by accepting a weaker position.

A famine of the 1530s is described in the *Mirat-i-Ahmadi*, which chronicles the last years of the Muzaffarid dynasty of Gujarat before the Mughal

[34] Ibid.
[35] Jonathan Scott, *Ferishta's History of Dekkan*, London: Shrewsbury, 1794, 102.
[36] Ibid, 162–163. During the Bahmani king Muhammad Shah's reign.

Empire annexed the region. Again, we hear that the famine made rebellions likely, causing a cycle to emerge that the ruler Bahadur Khan, with his resources depleting fast, was powerless to resist.[37] On two other occasions reported in the same work, once shortly after the death of Emperor Jahangir (1627) and the next one around 1700, severe scarcity developed in the town of Ahmedabad. On both occasions, the townspeople rose in revolt. The rumor in the second episode was that the grain merchants had bribed the town administration. A mystic saint and a *qazi* (judge in Islamic courts) led the people on these two occasions. The mystic was poisoned in a royal banquet, and the qazi escaped with his life on the Mughal prince Muhammad Azam Shah's intervention.[38] Famines could become occasions for palace rivalries to break out. A sixteenth-century Shekhawati Rajput king at the time of Akbar, Bhojraja, killed his nephew and started an internecine conflict over the manner of response to a violent famine.[39]

When their power was secure and their capacity not too impaired, kings intervened. Still, the intervention was usually limited to the towns and by the modes of transport available. Ibn Battuta's travel accounts mentioned the long famine around 1335 and the actions of Muhammad bin Tughlaq in dealing with it. The king ordered the state granary to be used to feed the poor, but state intervention did not seem to extend beyond Delhi city and its neighborhood (the sultan did offer cultivators near the city seed from the royal granary). At least the traveler's knowledge of it did not.[40],[41] Ferishta writes that Sultan Mahmud or Mahmud Gawan, the Bahamani king, arranged for a bullock caravan to transport grain. "A famine falling out during his reign, he kept ten thousand bullocks on his own account constantly going to and from Malwa and Guzarat for grain; which was sold out to the people at a cheap rate."[42] Ten thousand bullocks may sound a lot, but they could carry a minuscule proportion of the potential need for grain by the Deccan population.

---

[37] M.F. Lokhandwala, *Mirat-i-Ahmadi*, Baroda: Oriental Institute, 1965, 58

[38] Ibid., 268, 277.

[39] Haraprasad Sastri, *Preliminary Report on the Operation in Search of MSS of Bardic Chronicles*, Calcutta: Baptist Mission Press, 1913, 32.

[40] H.A.R. Gibb, *The Travels of Ibn Battuta, A.D. 1325–1354*, 3 vols., Cambridge, UK: Hakluyt Society, 1971, 3:695–696.

[41] The sixteenth century Persian historian Muhammad Qasim Hindu Shah was also known as Ferishta.

[42] Scott, *Ferishta*.

102   WATER AND DEVELOPMENT

The Indian sources also suggest that if famines weakened some kings, they encouraged other kings to attack, worsening a food crisis. "The calamities of war and its attendant famine," Ferishta writes, "had vexed Dekkan for a long series of years."[43] The Arab-Portuguese fights in the Arabian Sea in 1588–1589 caused a famine in Malabar, an otherwise well-resourced region.[44] A typical military action in the Deccan was a siege. The countryside being semi-arid, armies often gathered in a hill fort with a grain store. Sometimes these forts were centers of governance. Enemies then laid siege, hoping to starve those inside. The army that laid siege was vulnerable to the ability and willingness of the surrounding country to supply grain. It was not easy to concentrate on two fronts, and the camp followers, who were crucial agents in bringing food to these camps, often switched sides. The Ferishta mentions "famine" on many occasions to describe the unpredictable course of a siege. Several military campaigns in the region in the fifteenth and sixteenth centuries showed the risk of "famine and pestilential disorders . . . carrying off great numbers of men and animals."[45] A balance was thus restored. The weak king might face invasion, but if the strategy of starving the besieged king did not yield a quick result, the invaders would become weak in turn.

Famine documentation in Africa improved with the availability of European records. The first three decades of the nineteenth century were a period of repeated droughts in the southern hemisphere and left a deep legacy in southern Africa. In one disputed account, "climatic stress may have been one of the primary catalysts for the social revolution that produced the Zulu Kingdom under Shaka."[46] Kingdoms hit by a prolonged drought would have a reason to extend their boundaries, seeking moisture, often running into battles with settlers there. In the early nineteenth century, some movements involved going from the interior to the coast, where European colonists resisted the move.

A final lesson from these accounts is that, in the average years, people exposed to high risk of droughts chose to save assets that gave them little long-term return but were often valuable as food or for quick liquidity. It is a truism that animals are a better investment than the poor-quality land in the savanna. Economic historians have long wondered why rural Indians

---

[43] Ibid., 152.

[44] M.J. Rowlandson, *Tohfut-ul-Mujahideen*, London: Oriental Translation Fund, 1833, 178.

[45] Reference to the Ahmednagar ruler Burhan Shah's campaign in 1591. Scott, *Ferishta*, 327.

[46] Charles Ballard, "Drought and Economic Distress: South Africa in the 1800s," *Journal of Interdisciplinary History*, 17(2), 1986, 359–378, cited text on p. 359.

chose to save their windfall profits in the form of silver jewelry. Episodes of mass liquidation of these assets during acute economic stress showed why. Two such episodes occurred (in India) in the 1820s and the 1930s, though neither followed a drought event.

Conclusion

Why do I discuss famines so much in this chapter? For three reasons. First, almost without exception in recorded history, famines in the premodern world resulted from droughts or water stress. Large-scale conflicts were so bound up with seasonality that "war famine" cannot be defined as a distinct category. Droughts happened first, inviting wars either because the king had grown weak for fiscal reasons, the unpaid and starving part-time soldiers were unhappy, or the competition for food and water was too intense.

Second, famines created forms of inequality for which the arid tropics paid a price. Land quality was poor, and therefore the tax take was low. Weak states depended on trade in enslaved peoples. Forced dispersal consolidated unfreedom. Some groups voluntarily traded freedom for food.

Third, famine left a profound legacy in the minds of the rulers of this region. They saw the need to avoid these episodes to secure their survival. The precolonial states recognized that as clearly as the colonial and postcolonial states did. Much public goods and infrastructure in the ancient times or the recent past was designed to avoid famines, as we see next.

Chapter Five
Ancient Assets

Capturing water runoffs was a constant endeavor of societies. As mentioned earlier, the modern era did a more effective job, but the idea was old. We may think that the modern was a technology story mainly. It was not. Controlling moisture inflow on a large scale would involve public funds and capital markets. Most states, at most times, were too poor to embark on such plans. Capital markets for infrastructure were a recent innovation. Finance, not science per se, defined the modernity of public intervention in tropical water.

What could governments of such limited capacities do?

Dams, Tanks, Canals

Since the 1970s, geographers have studied water-harvesting technologies in the world's arid zones. That enterprise generated substantial data and descriptions of various methods to capture seasonal moisture inflow, using "diversion bunds, conduits, ditches, channels, micro-catchments, dams, embankments, spillways, reservoirs and cisterns."[1] India offers plentiful examples of a "rich historical tradition of local water harvesting ... from the *ahar-pyne* system in Bihar, the *tankas* of Rajasthan, the Himalayan *dharas*, the *talabs* in Bundelkhand to the *eries* of Tamil Nadu."[2] So does Africa.

The researchers faced a significant obstacle because these were small and local systems, and few were preserved intact for a long time. "In arid landscapes the remains of water harvesting cultures are neither impressive and spectacular, nor are they associated with great architectural or engineering installations."[3] There was a second reason for the obscurity of these systems. There is too little documentary information on small local works in state

---

[1] Thomas Vettera and Anna-Katharina Rieger, "Ancient Water Harvesting in the Old World Dry Belt—Synopsis and Outlook," *Journal of Arid Environments*, 169, 2019, 42–53, cited text on p. 43.

[2] Mihir Shah, "Water: Towards a Paradigm Shift in the Twelfth Plan," *Economic and Political Weekly*, 48, 2013, 40–52, cited text on p. 44. *Ahar-pyne*: network of channels and retention ponds; *tanka*: rainwater-harvesting tank; *dhara*: harvests natural spring water; *Talabs*: human-made ponds; *Eri*: another name for the tanks.

[3] Vettera and Rieger, "Ancient Water Harvesting," 52.

Water and Development. Tirthankar Roy, Oxford University Press. © Oxford University Press (2025).
DOI: 10.1093/oso/9780197802397.003.0005

archives. Arid lands were usually marginal to ancient states that relied on the resources of fertile lands. Most works were created without the king's help. Such small-scale systems were especially vulnerable to relatively small changes in regional geographical and political conditions that substantially impacted the benefits and costs of these projects. Desert agriculture, according to one study of the Negev in Israel, declined in the remote past due to "increased maintenance needs of terraces due to siltation, decreased value of export-oriented goods as olives and wine, neglectance [sic] of social-political agreements between farmers and herders, and a higher taxation."[4]

Larger works, sometimes serving hundreds of square miles, are better known. Orientalist scholars of Europe built their case about Asiatic despotism on such evidence (Chapter 2). One of the more well-known examples is the first major dam in Egypt, the Sadd-el-kafara, which was built in the third millennium BCE. Designed probably for flood control, the central part of the dam collapsed when a flood overtopped the structure not long after it was built. The damage this disaster would have caused might account for the rarity of large masonry projects. The structure remains significant in showing the scale at which dam buildings could be conceived even when no prior design existed.

In Mesopotamia, canals drawn from the perennial rivers irrigated lands. In Crete, wells, cisterns, aqueducts, and pipes served Minoan settlements. The Indus Valley sites were probably the first settlement in the Indian subcontinent to have constructed an elaborate network of drains and wells to supply drinking water, serve as bathing places, and provide effluent disposal (Figure 5.1).[5] These were brick-lined structures; the area was well-served with clay but was short on stone. The brick-built well was not essentially different from wells that appeared in the Indo-Gangetic Basin in recent times. Brick-built wells, cisterns, and tanks needed to be coated with minerals to prevent seepage. The Indus Valley systems displayed advanced knowledge of how to do that. The functional peak period for these sites was 5000–4400 BP (before the present), though older sites yet to be excavated exist. The climate was possibly wetter than it became after this time, but it was still tropical monsoonal, the pattern to emerge with the Holocene in South Asia. Indus Valley sites continued to exist for at least six hundred years after 4400 BP. It has never been firmly ascertained why they were abandoned after that,

[4] Ibid., 50.
[5] M. Jansen, "Water Supply and Sewage Disposal at Mohenjo-Daro," *World Archaeology*, 21(2), 1989, 177–192.

Figure 5.1 Lothal
One of the Indus Valley towns, Lothal in Gujarat state of India, was inhabited and active in trade and agriculture 4000 to 3500 BP (before the present). In common with similar sites, the town had a complex water supply and drainage system, a section shown in the photo. The depopulation of these sites is still unexplained, but the drying up of the environment is one theory.
Source: Alamy Stock Photos

whether due to climate change or an earthquake shifting the course of the rivers.

Unlike the Sadd-el-kafara, the first-millennium BCE Marib dam in Yemen, had gates to regulate water flow. The Sadd-el-kafara was probably built to control floods. The likely purpose of Marib was again flood control. In addition, the dam may have been used to divert the water of a stream into a fertile oasis. The state of Saba that built the dam controlled a crucial overland trade route of the time, connecting the Arab Peninsula with the Mediterranean. Marib, therefore, was a wealthy place. Late in the sixth century, an earthquake destroyed the dam's foundation, causing a devastating flash flood. Nothing can be said with certainty on how these dams connected to state formation in the area. Marib's commercial prosperity had long been over when the dam collapsed.

The Levant is a rich field for water archaeologists. Researchers in Israel contributed greatly to the global discourse on arid agriculture and economic development. They studied ancient systems to collect runoff water from slopes in catchment areas and channels directing the water to terraces.[6] Nabateans who lived in Petra in the south of Jordan stored water in cisterns that minimized evaporation and pollution (c. 300 BCE–100 CE). In the late twentieth century, excavations identified as a large water tank a place initially thought to be a market square. Ancient human-excavated depressions (*mahafirs*) in eastern Jordan collected water—with a near 100 percent evaporation rate—were unlikely to have retained water beyond six months.[7] More ambitious and carefully designed projects would include the *qanats*, some of which survive and are in use.

Qanats are human-made underground channels connecting into a natural water body or well in the uplands. The slope of the channel ensures water flows from upstream downward. Any well built above ground that is connected to the underground channel can tap into the water. Qanats appeared in Iran, the Levant, North Africa, Baluchistan, and Turkey, typically between the rain-abundant agricultural area with settled cultivators and the desert fringe and oases where nomadic herders lived. Many such small-scale works can be found in this frontier zone, scarce in rain but still promising in groundwater. They were built at various times, the oldest dating back to Roman settlements in the Levant. In this area, qanats were still used in the Byzantine period and some in the Umayyad period. Most were subsequently abandoned as the area lost economic significance after that. However, qanats in Iran continue to function today and remain significant as a tool to spread water over more expansive areas. Archaeologists and historians distinguish between "true" qanats that were often twenty to forty miles long and works that were called qanats but were actually short channels designed to increase the discharge in a natural spring.[8]

It is plausible that qanats required external sponsorship. They needed the labor of many people, and their construction was often dangerous. But more than power, qanats required specialist knowledge. A deep and long channel was expensive to build and could collapse unless the rock was firm enough. Knowing when the rock would support an underground canal and how close

---

[6] Anon, "Report of the Symposium on Arid Zone Development," *Bulletin of the American Academy of Arts and Sciences*, 29(7), 1976, 12–17.

[7] Clive T. Agnew, Ewan Anderson, W. Lancaster, and F. Lancaster, "Mahafir: A Water Harvesting System in the Eastern Jordan (Badia) Desert," *GeoJournal*, 37(1), 1995, 69–80. Also, Asit K. Biswas, "Ancient Urban Water Supply Systems," *GeoJournal*, 11(3), 1985, 207–213.

[8] Dale R. Lightfoot, "Qanats in the Levant: Hydraulic Technology at the Periphery of Early Empires," *Technology and Culture*, 38(2), 1997, 432–451.

108   WATER AND DEVELOPMENT

to the surface the channel could be was necessary. The disappearance of qanats had likely owed as much to lost skills as reduced sponsorship.

Eurocentric histories of the classical world of Greece and Rome saw these societies as creations of Europe, overlooking the deep ties of knowledge exchange that existed between these relatively drier parts of Europe and North Africa.[9] Given the shared geographies of dry lands, relations between Africa and the classical world might have been closer than the latter's ties with northern Europe. An important field of knowledge exchange was water storage. The *foggara* of North Africa almost certainly traveled from Algeria to Italy. In several oases of the Algerian Sahara, the qanat principle (foggara) was used to irrigate palm trees and farmlands. The great Intercalary Continental Aquifer is a vast underground waterbody beneath this part of the northern Sahara. It is too deep in most areas for commercially viable exploitation, but where near the surface, overground vertical shafts can access the water underground. Deep drilling more recently destroyed several of these ancient constructions.

Like qanats, ancient canals in Sri Lanka have generated considerable scholarship. While no part of Sri Lanka is arid in the same way as sub-Saharan Africa, monsoon rains are significantly smaller in volume in the east, north, and south of the island than in the southwest, around the highlands and southwestern coast. The wet zone receives annual rainfall above about one hundred inches, and the dry zone rainfall ranges from forty-seven to seventy-five inches.

Extraordinarily, the center of the Sinhala kingdoms ruling between the first millennium BCE and the thirteenth century CE was in the northeast before the axis of power shifted to the rain-rich southeast where the Kandyan kingdom emerged. Two ancient towns and political centers, Anuradhapura and Polonnaruwa, were in the dry zone. A colossal system of human-made canals and reservoirs served Anuradhapura. Classical Ceylon was a hydraulic, arid-area agricultural society reliant on large irrigation works. Not surprisingly, Sri Lanka became one of the earliest fields for the test of Karl Wittfogel's oriental despotism thesis, though Wittfogel had missed Sri Lanka.[10]

The Sri Lanka scholarship shows one fundamental problem with Wittfogel's conjecture: canals needed strong states. We can never know for sure how

[9] Baz Lecocq, "Distant Shores: A Historiographic View on Trans-Saharan Space," *Journal of African History*, 56(1), 2015, 23–36.
[10] E.R. Leach, "Hydraulic Society in Ceylon," *Past and Present*, 15, 1959, 2–26.

ANCIENT ASSETS 109

irrigation contributed to state formation or the other way around. We do not see how individual kings contributed to it. The construction was "haphazard and discontinuous and spread over many centuries."[11] Canals possibly empowered local chiefs and lords, who had more say in construction and maintenance than the king. No one knows how labor was harnessed and by whom. The gradual disuse and collapse of the system, even as irrigated agriculture continued, shows that villages relied more on local resources like small reservoirs than big dams.

Dams, canals, and ditches have been present in Mesoamerica from prehistoric times. Dams constructed in 1300–700 BCE in Mexico redirected seasonal streams. Various techniques were used to stop and control flows, but data to construct a connected history of the dams and canals are missing.[12] This technology predated European arrival in the region by hundreds of years. The Spanish colonizers, who had learned dryland irrigation technology from the Maghrebi people, sponsored digging watercourses known as acequia. The acequia's reputation came from its hydraulic properties and communal management, elements of which state law in the United States and Mexico incorporated later.

The reservoir idea was found to have the most systematic expression in southern India, especially in generally dry lands that received a stronger-than-average monsoon. The main regions were southern Karnataka (formerly Mysore) and northern Tamil Nadu. But reservoirs or "tanks" in Indian parlance appeared in other areas too, sometimes accompanied by a barrage to trap river water. Few of these tanks have a well-remembered history. Some of the more modern ones are an exception, such as the constructions of the eighteenth-century Hyderabad state officers. The Mir Alum tank, for example, was conceived by a general in the Nizam ul Mulk's army who fought alongside the British to defeat the Mysore warlord Tipu Sultan in 1798–1799. The tank supplied water to the town of Hyderabad before other larger constructions appeared in the nineteenth century. As political power decentralized in India in the eighteenth century, waterworks sprang up in many places. Usually, local landlords or merchants sponsored these. step wells in Rajasthan, or tanks in Mysore, and a few urban constructions testify to this display of wealth and charity by the local magnets (Figure 5.2).

---

[11] Ibid., 23.
[12] William E. Doolittle, "Indigenous Development of Mesoamerican Irrigation," *Geographical Review*, 85(3), 1995, 301–323.

Figure 5.2 Bhikha Behram Well, 1725

The well (with a place of worship) stands in one of the busiest parts of Mumbai (Bombay) city. It was built by a wealthy Parsi from Bharuch (Broach) when Bombay was little more than an overgrown village with a terrible reputation for the quality of its freshwater. Legend has it that the well supplied drinking water to the workers employed in constructing some of the magnificent buildings for which this area is now known.
Source: Alamy Stock Photos

Just how good were these systems in preventing droughts and famines? The archaeological studies suggest that most storages were of a scale small enough to provide slightly greater security than relying on insecure surface water. The best qanats would not irrigate more than a few hundred hectares of land. In qanats and channels, water discharge cannot be controlled. Western Indian step wells became easily polluted and a source of epidemic diseases. Many dried up or became contaminated during years of exceptional dryness, and almost none of these systems could sustain intensive or year-round cultivation. Geodetic satellite data show that the human-made lakes or tanks in southern India would shrink so much during exceptionally dry times that they would be unusable for human or livestock use.[13]

Most premodern systems would require vast amounts of communal or collective labor and were usually beyond the reach of most households.

---

[13] Tirthankar Roy, *Monsoon Economies. India's History in a Changing Climate*, Cambridge, MA: MIT Press, 2022.

ANCIENT ASSETS 111

Assessing rural society's economic potential by looking at the ruins of ancient dams and cisterns would be an error. Historiographies of dry regions, like interior Tamil Nadu, note the crucial importance of large constructions like tanks in organizing production, yet they were poor insurance against severe droughts.

Besides building reservoirs and ditches, farming societies in tropical lands adopted various farming methods to combat aridity. In East Africa, for example, these methods included terraces to slow runoffs along slopes, choice of water-saving crops and plants like millets, planting citrus trees, planting grass, mulching, and dew harvesting. In the extension of the Inland Niger Delta into northwestern Nigeria, recession agriculture in natural depressions (locally known as *fadama*) sustained an agricultural system under arid conditions. Temporarily waterlogged lands, even in a dry area, can produce rice well-adapted to flooding and, therefore, can create a profitable crop regime. In the 1990s, with help from World Bank loans, projects to revive the system and combine it with green revolution technology started.[14] Although the construction of dams in the area had changed flood patterns, recession agriculture held promise.

If one side of adaptation to moisture flow was coping with drought, the other side dealt with floods, where the seasonal rain was ordinarily quite intense (like the Bengal Delta). Again, we do not know enough about local works. However, some big works have survived to show how premodern states met that challenge.

Flood Control

Before British colonial rule emerged in Bengal in the late eighteenth century, several independent regimes and kingdoms ruled mainland South Asia. Few of these left many state papers on construction or paid systematic attention to public goods. Moreover, few faced the threat of seasonal flooding on a large scale. The Bengal delta, a lowland with heavy monsoonal rains, did present that risk.

The East India Company in Bengal formally took power in 1765. One of its first infrastructural plans was embankment construction and maintenance. None of their projects was new. It made economic and technical sense to build on older foundations. They collected some systematic data

---

[14] Throughout the book I use the phrase green revolution to mean a sharp rise in agricultural productivity brought about by the application of high-yielding seeds, fertilizers, and water together.

112 WATER AND DEVELOPMENT

on older constructions, which found that after the Mughal Empire annexed eastern Bengal (1580–1600), large construction works had been taken up, perhaps rebuilding on even earlier foundations. The government of the new province, for example, sponsored the construction of a causeway along the left bank of the River Surma in Sylhet to prevent inundations. Bir Bandh was a contemporary construction on the River Kosi in northern Bihar. Outside the empire, the Kaveri River delta had seen extensive embankment construction, again state-built and of uncertain antiquity. These projects aimed to protect agricultural land.

A second type of project to benefit from state investment protected capital cities exposed to storm surge. In Patna on the banks of the Ganges, the company's observer Francis Buchanan found evidence in the early nineteenth century of embankments of impressive size and strength of the foundation. The provincial capital of Orissa, Cuttack, which was exposed to tidal waves from the sea and frequent flooding of the Mahanadi, possessed evidence of ancient embankments. They were made of firmer material near towns and were frequently repaired in such locations. The value of this eight-hundred-year-old construction was evident in 1826. A European missionary who visited the town during a cyclonic storm that devastated the countryside saw an "immense volume of water" barely restrained by the embankment.[15]

The records tell us little about the broad division of duty in building and maintaining such works. The lack of documented sources suggests that unlike in the Yellow River in China, the Indian efforts were usually local, more minor in scale, and sporadic. It is also plausible that the fragmentation of state power in the eighteenth century led to neglect of the existing infrastructure, which had serious consequences in western Bengal. The last quarter of the eighteenth century was, ecologically speaking, a stressful time in the Indo-Gangetic Basin. Historians note the role that droughts played. Did floods also play a role?

The history of the Yellow River is a reminder of the crucial role of embankments in the survival of communities against the threat of seasonal floods.[16] These embankments, which were built and maintained by a diverse set of actors, came in a variety of types and scales. Recent disasters, like the

---

[15] For citation and more descriptive data, see Tirthankar Roy, *Natural Disasters in Indian History*, New Delhi: Oxford University Press, 2012.

[16] Kathryn Edgerton-Tarpley, "Between War and Water: Farmer, City, and State in China's Yellow River Flood of 1938–1947," *Agricultural History*, 90(1), 2016, 94–116.

1938–1947 floods in Henan and Jiangsu, also underscored that for a bank to work at all, it must be strong over hundreds of miles. One minor breach can collapse a large part of the edifice. In other words, the strongest banks might involve a supraregional authority, and crises in state formation could lead to demographic disasters. Few South Asian embankments, however, matched the scale of the one that protected the banks of the Yellow River.

Conclusion

In short, systematic response to seasonality was a global pattern. But most constructions served a local area. The minor exceptions were the canal networks and ancient dams. Most ancient reservoirs were not of a scale or type to reverse evaporation and percolation losses, where these were close to 100 percent. These projects did matter to the microregions they served, but collectively they were no match for the high average death rates that kept the population growth in the tropics close to zero, as far as we can measure).

A breakthrough took shape in the nineteenth century as technology permitted bigger dams to be built and made deep drilling for water feasible. Most local systems fell into disuse and disrepair, the state in which archaeologists found them in the twentieth century. Community-controlled systems similarly were victim to technologies that could harvest water from deeper underground. However, interest in premodern water storage and access systems revived in the 2000s as fields to study the usefulness of Elinor Ostrom's "design principles." Ostrom studied the conditions in which the tragedy of the commons could be averted. These conditions included a definite boundary to the commons, the possibility of participatory management, and dispute resolution systems. The examples included water harvesting systems in dry areas. One study of the foggaras of central Algeria in 2015–2016 found that the system tried to adapt to changing times through more exchange of information among the community.[17] On the other hand, they were under severe threats from commercial agriculture and deep drilling, and the risk of abandonment, degradation, and collapse.

---

[17] Salem Idda, Bruno Bonté, Marcel Kuper, and Hamidi Mansour, "Revealing the Foggara as a Living Irrigation System through an Institutional Analysis: Evidence from Oases in the Algerian Sahara," *International Journal of the Commons*, 15(1), 2021, 431–448.

114 WATER AND DEVELOPMENT

European colonial rule was an indirect agent in introducing and implementing the large-scale waterworks. But when it began, colonialism had a more limited ambition. All it wanted was to put its military and fiscal systems in order. Institutional interventions that left a legacy on water access were a side effect of that project.

Chapter Six
The Colonial Era

Property Rights

In neither Asia nor Africa did European rule (1800–1960) start a series of top-down interventions and revolutionary changes. These states did not share a single plan, origin, and ideology, and while militarily a success, they had too little tax revenues to do anything other than defend themselves. In some significant respects, they did differ from premodern states.

First, while all regimes believed that trade was good and a potential source for taxation, the colonial regimes acted on that belief by building railways and some roads, connecting the seaboard firmly with arid areas in the interior. The changes were profound. Not only did trade grow manifold, but trade in dry region exports grew too. In parallel, major overland trading systems weakened, further damaging polities in the interior and reinforcing colonialism. Market forces, droughts, transport projects, wars, and demographic pressure changed the relationship between ecological zones. Caravan trade was retreating in South Asia and West Africa. It is uncertain if the scale of trans-Saharan trade declined or how much it did. Still, the trade passing through the coast overshadowed overland trade from the nineteenth century. If towns in the Sahel had earlier looked north for trade, they looked south from 1900 or even before.[1] Chapters 1 and 4 talk about the market shifts. This chapter deals mainly with the second of the two differences that colonialism represented.

I refer to the belief that the environment could be managed and manipulated for economic gains. The expressions of that sentiment took varied forms, from transborder treaties on river basin sharing to allocating property rights on land and intervention in water quality to control epidemic outbreaks. Waterworks like canals and reservoirs, built with public funds, appeared too, though the scale was too small to make a dramatic difference in living standards. Still, these projects revealed another strength of the

---

[1] Stephen Baier, *An Economic History of Central Niger*, Oxford: Clarendon Press, 1980.

Water and Development. Tirthankar Roy, Oxford University Press. © Oxford University Press (2025).
DOI: 10.1093/oso/9780197802397.003.0006

116 WATER AND DEVELOPMENT

colonial regimes: some could command cheaper credit to fund fixed capital investment.

This shift was not "colonial." Independent countries like Ethiopia shared the same ambition. The confidence that geography could be radically reshaped had owed to science more than specific forms of power. Finance was a huge obstacle. The colonial territories were too poor to take the ambition much further. They often confined actions to the softer steps— property rights, sanitation, and fluvial treaties. Independent states followed the same model as they had even smaller chances of borrowing abroad. These moves had side effects. Property rights reforms created gainers and losers. In settler-dominated areas, the modern (settler) and the traditional (indigenous) became economically and culturally more distant, a divergence that added energy to the nationalist movement. Whereas "the modern economic sector was strong enough to fragment traditional ... society, it was too weak subsequently to deal with an uprooted population steadily increasing in numbers."[2]

The discussion should start with agricultural land, where some of the most far-reaching changes occurred.

The Super-Landlord

One universal feature of modern states is the drive to raise more taxes and make the administration self-sufficient. The need was desperate in the European-ruled states of Asia and Africa. Whether due to poor land yield, high costs of collection, or inadequate infrastructure, the tax earned per head was a fraction of what was raised in Europe. Where they could, these states encouraged private rights to farming or plantations. They encouraged trade, hoping to collect more money from assets or businesses sustained by using these assets.

Economic historians believe that landed property in the colonial territories was modeled after European law. Quite the opposite was the case. Colonial offices thought that customary tenure in Africa managed by clans was secure and that a clear ownership title in the British fashion would make them less so. Similarly, legislators associated with the East India Company wanted to base succession and inheritance laws upon Hindu and

[2] Tony Smith, "The French Economic Stake in Colonial Algeria," *French Historical Studies*, 9(1), 1975, 184–189, cited text on p. 189.

Indo-Islamic Scriptures in India. The law itself was a patchwork. However, the colonial states invested much more money and energy than previous regimes in creating a hierarchical system of courts. Litigants could sometimes choose the law they wanted to apply. Litigation possibilities increased significantly. There was also better codification of law. It became more of a public good than before.

There was another singular aspect of colonial law. These states explicitly asserted their authority on land administration and legislation. Politically, this would mean appropriating a super-landlord status, which invested the colonial state with symbolic power. Economically, the aim was to ensure that more land was used as a business asset and a potential tax source. In practice, acting on that ambition would entail the creation of recorded land titles. In some areas, the states took that road. Elsewhere, they backed off and permitted inclusive land management by clans and chiefs.

The readiness to assert a super-landlord status sometimes strengthened peasant proprietary title. British India saw the fullest development of ownership title. The Company inherited or could re-create land rights registers based on existing records. But the old rights were not of one type. At least in northern and eastern India, the right to own (and allocate, transfer, and inherit), to use, and to collect taxes from the same plot of land were held by different people. The company's reform aimed to privilege ownership over these other rights. Registering the owner sometimes favored the tax collector (the zamindar in Bengal) and sometimes the cultivator (the *ryot* in the Deccan). From the late nineteenth century, various user rights were recognized as tenancy in provincial legislation, and restrictions were imposed upon the mortgaged sale of agricultural land.

Like in British India, smallholder farming in West Africa developed based on customary land tenure. Land titles supposedly descended from lineages, meaning that, in theory, no outsider could buy land controlled by the lineages. As a cash crop export boom unfolded, the boundaries of custom broke often. Many chiefs allocated land to outsiders and businesses for a fee or transacted land among themselves as in a market. Transfer of rights did happen, but they were still rare. The colonial authorities maintained a commitment to keeping these tenures legally operative.

Like Gangetic North India, farming had been practiced in the Nile Basin for millennia. Here, the direction of reform was toward creating a clear ownership title. Two officers with India connections would transplant the idea. Herbert Kitchener, a military man who later served India and led the British

118   WATER AND DEVELOPMENT

army in World War I, worked for a short time as the first administrator of Anglo-Egyptian Sudan (1899) and set in motion a land tenure legislation at that time. The basic idea was that the relationship between the government and the taxpaying citizens needed to be based on the offer of a secure title in the land. In turn, such contracts could also distinguish the indigenous from the foreigner-migrant farmers, some of whom the British thought were too close to their enemy, the Mahdist regime.

Francis Wingate, another general-cum-administrator who had experience with Indian land titles before becoming Kitchener's successor, pursued the titling scheme and had more time in the job to expand its scope. He would use it to promote commercial agriculture. The legislation drafted under his rule recognized indigenous landholdings as legal ownership titles, though one of these laws applied to the towns. Another, Title of Lands Ordinance (1899), set out procedures for offering legal titles that were potentially applicable to rural and agricultural land. Registration was voluntary, based on people coming forward with a claim, and since few had the right type of certificates to support claims, the scheme covered little in the end.

The super-landlord status helped in land extension. The British in India generally did not encourage settler landholdings. But long-populated farmlands were one thing and forests another. When European capitalists were interested in developing tea estates in remote Assam, the government took over forest land and allocated it to the planters. By the mid-1800s, the colonial state started encouraging plantations in Ceylon to increase revenue and attract British investment. Wasteland development laws were introduced (Crown Lands [Encroachment] Ordinance No. 12 of 1840), and the highlands were settled with Europeans interested in making tea or coffee. Agricultural development followed a similar trajectory in the plains, especially the well-watered southwest where political power was concentrated. In 1863, the partition of rural landholdings was legally sanctioned, effectively establishing private property in land via the act of potential or actual sale. By what authority did the state do this in Assam or Ceylon? It was the idea that the state owned open access lands by default.

Forests were one thing; pastures and rainfed farming, when land needed long fallowing to recuperate, were another. Generally, land retitling followed the rule that the state would take over when private ownership did not exist in the juridical sense. Private ownership did not exist in that sense

THE COLONIAL ERA: PROPERTY RIGHTS 119

in pastures and fallows. If the Europeans wanted to grab such land, that stance could have enormous consequences for pastoralist and rainfed agriculture areas. Property allocation could have a magnified impact—and it did in North Africa.

Settlers in Africa

From the late nineteenth century, land titling was active in North Africa. The French colonizers in Algeria grappled with clan rights for over forty years, mainly to find out what land would be available to the settlers. They discovered that the clans claimed territories they did not use and that "there seldom existed any written document or property act sustaining their claims."[3] Land reform in 1873 established private ownership rights, overriding all preexisting rights. One effect of the reform was converting and selling grazing lands, weakening the economic position of the poorer peasants who combined farming and herding. At the same time, the land under settler cultivators increased.

The Italians in North and East Africa struggled with undefined and impossible-to-define rights to "vacant lands." In Tripolitania (Libya), a 1923 land reform decreed that "all land that had not been farmed in the previous 3 years was considered public and available for allotment, rent, and purchase by Italian farmers."[4] Italian immigrants formed a significant share of the population in the early twentieth century, possibly over 10 percent or about the same as the French in Algeria. Italians occupied some of the more fertile and well-watered lands near the coast, where considerable investment in transport and irrigation infrastructure was concentrated. The state stepped in with a property rights decree that turned all land not continuously occupied for several years into public land available for allocation. Indigenous farmers had used at least some of these lands as pastures or fallow. Long fallowing was critical to dryland farming to revive exhausted land. At any point in time, many of these lands would seem unoccupied and ownerless. The state engineered a redistribution of some of these assets. The extent of the shift remains unclear. In this case, neither state-led land grabbing nor labor

[3] Kjell H. Halvorsen, "Colonial Transformation of Agrarian Society in Algeria," *Journal of Peace Research*, 15(4), 1978, 323–343, cited text on p. 335.
[4] Mattia Bertazzini, "The Effect of Settler Farming on Indigenous Agriculture: Evidence from Italian Libya," *Economic History Review*, 76(1), 2023, 33–59, cited text on p. 37.

120   WATER AND DEVELOPMENT

reserves was practiced, only allocation of supposedly open access lands. In consequence, dry zone farming in indigenous hands lost laborers. With limited or no water for irrigation, these farmers could only expand cultivation to marginal lands, suffering a fall in yield.[5] The inequality between settlers and Africans deepened.

Decades later, the land titling project was repeated in East Africa, now relying on "an interpretation of African tenure that precluded any notion of 'ownership,' whether communal or individual."[6] This conception rested on another convenient myth: that kings alone delivered property rights, and if there was no king, there were no property rights. The planters received ownership of their estates but not the indigenous population. On the other hand, in the designated "native reserves" in East and South Africa, the definition of farmland rights was left to custom. Custom would mean joint, single, or family holdings but did not include allocation and transfer rights.

In Somalia, Vincenzo Filonardi's only major innovation in the countryside was the draft of a land property law, which recognized existing owners' private rights, ensured that settlers got a secure title if attracted to come, and claimed public ownership of "vacant lands." Although there was some disputation later over the principle on which such claims could be made, the law set a precedent.[7] In common with Libya, French Algeria, and Eritrea, vacant or apparently unoccupied lands were to be converted to the use of private investors, preferably settlers, though very few of them came to Somalia. Since much of the land was not suitable for farming anyway, the so-called tribal rights to the so-called unoccupied lands persisted. However, with new legislation in the twentieth century recognizing private and public rights, population growth, and market expansion, customary tenures tended to weaken and crumble.

European settlement was never a great success in Somalia, partly because the settler farmers wanted water that did not exist. However, the growing grain trade encouraged dry farming elsewhere. One significant example was the western part of British Somaliland, where pastoralist groups cleared bushes to start millet farming.

---

[5] Ibid.

[6] Fiona Mackenzie, "Conflicting Claims to Custom: Land and Law in Central Province, Kenya, 1912–52," *Journal of African Law*, 40(1), 1996, 62–77, cited text on p. 63.

[7] Marco M.G. Guadagni, "Colonial Origins of the Public Domain in Southern Somalia (1892–1912)," *Journal of African Law*, 22(1), 1978, 1–29.

In the interwar period, public discourse (mainly in Italian) on the economy of Somalia was torn between two visions; one of these looked toward the dry East Horn and advocated interventions to serve pastoralism, and the other looked toward the wetter west, river valleys, and the seaboard and advocated interventions to encourage farming by European settlers. In the end, the farming lobby prevailed. Around 1910, the government decided to extend its control and use it to develop agriculture beyond the few coastal towns in southwestern Somalia, or the Benadir coast, where its presence had so far been confined. The plan took off with the start of fascist rule in 1922, with the allocation of concessions to settlers willing to farm. The act to legalize the move established the principle that the government was the ultimate landowner and must use that status to improve land yield. "Farming in Somalia," wrote a study in 1931, "must be lifted out of the simple and primitive condition in which the natives practice it and, after a period of experimentation, be conducted along purely commercial lines. We have begun to see the situation in this light only very recently, but here alone lies the hope for the future."[8]

The catch was that for the vision to succeed and for commercial agriculture run by Europeans to become profitable, the government would have to invest in irrigation and force communities to supply labor to these farms.[9] In the end, few concessions were taken, for neither intervention was a dramatic success, and when tried at all, it did not extend beyond the narrow river basins. Pastoralism, believed by the colonial authorities to be the occupation of the ethnic Somalis, was left alone.

After World War II, the settler model was no longer feasible, and the pastoralist model returned. Help pastoralists "along sound, if simple, lines" became a refrain in the 1950s. Somalia was still an Italian enclave, though the colonial state called itself trustees for Somalia.[10] But how would the state help the pastoralists? The state did not collect much tax from them, and the herders regarded with suspicion any claim to territorial power. Government offices sometimes intervened in water by building or repairing borewells, a limited and indirect intervention at best.

[8] Giotto Dainelli, "The Agricultural Possibilities of Italian Somalia," *Geographical Review*, 21(1), 1931, 56–69, cited text on pp. 63–64.

[9] Annalisa Urbano, "A 'Grandiose Future for Italian Somalia': Colonial Developmentalist Discourse, Agricultural Planning, and Forced Labor (1900–1940)," *International Labor and Working-Class History*, 92(1), 2017, 69–88.

[10] A World Bank report, cited in Z.A. Konczacki, "Nomadism and Economic Development of Somalia: The Position of the Nomads in the Economy of Somalia," *Canadian Journal of African Studies*, 1(2), 1967, 163–175, cited text on p. 168.

122 WATER AND DEVELOPMENT

In this arm's-length relationship, one policy did have an effect. This was the campaign for animal health, a mixed package including epidemic control, breeding programs, and pasture management. Herd sizes began growing quickly, beyond the capacity of the available pastures. A theory became popular that herders accumulated animals as a precaution against famines, which made overgrazing inevitable. Even as survival rates improved due to the benefits of veterinary services, the precautionary impulse, rooted in herder culture, did not weaken.

The French did not radically change the landholding system in Morocco, in which communal, village, and state rights were dominant. Later assessments of the agricultural commercialization schemes in Morocco reflected a view that would have originated in the interwar years—the pervasive presence of "communal ownership, either public or tribal," which "encourages frozen patterns of exploitation that are both backward and uneconomic."[11] What the colonizers did was create a private property right for settlers and locals. To work at all, this right needed reclaimed land, either from communities or uncultivated frontiers, made cultivable by new infrastructure development. A fraction of the cultivable surface was converted in this way before independence. The French settlers commanded about 2.5 percent of the land at independence.

Morocco had a lot more water than the rest of North Africa or the Horn of Africa. At the time of colonization, there existed a complex set of water usage customs that derived from communal rights based on the occupation of the water source. The French colonial administration, keen to develop capitalist settler agriculture in the plains, asserted its right to the water. This meant creating a water law that would increase water allocation for colonial landowners and enclose old water rights that belonged to local irrigators. The legislation, in a way, relied on Islamic law to justify public authority.[12] Access to water became increasingly difficult for indigenous farmers. Some farming communities were forced to move to more marginal lands in the mountainous regions, where farming practices were less productive.

In 1884, Southwest Africa became a German colony. Although the colonial administrators disagreed on the best economic use of the new territorial possession, home pressure led to policies promoting settler agriculture. Only

[11] William Zartman, "Farming and Land Ownership in Morocco," *Land Economics*, 39(2), 1963, 187–198, cited text on pp. 197–198.
[12] Moulay Driss El Jihad, "L'eau de la montagne et le pouvoir étatique au Maroc: entre le passé et le present," *Annales de Géographie*, 110(622), 2001, 665–672.

THE COLONIAL ERA: PROPERTY RIGHTS   123

a few Europeans and South Africans moved into farmlands. In 1897, rinderpest devastated the herds of the indigenous pastoral groups, and war broke
out between the colonists and the herders. By 1904, the rebellion had been
brutally suppressed. Vast grazing lands were sequestereted to be handed over
to settler farmers on easy terms.

From the start, and even after the handover of the territory to South Africa
at the end of World War I, the land policy of the region persisted with settler
agriculture against the evidence that these lands were uneconomical for the
purpose without state support. The government propped up the "sheer fantasy" of settler farming with subsidization of credit, capital, and waterworks,
fanciful campaign photos, and forced labor. From the 1920s, Native Reserves
were created to supply cheap wage workers to the new estates. White farming
this way became "a drain on other resources of the country."[13] The experiment failed to become economically self-sufficient because soil and water
conditions were too poor to make intensive cultivation possible. Tropical
geography defeated colonialism.

A Dream That Died?

Why were the colonizing powers so keen on giving rights to the European
farmers? Settler colonialism in Africa, especially North Africa, stood for a
developmental ambition that did not deliver. What was the ideology? Did it
fail? Why did it fail?

The French imperial officers and intellectuals writing about Morocco,
Algeria, or Tunisia re-created the myth of a prosperous Roman realm of
well-cultivated, well-watered, vigorously trading North African economy of
two thousand years ago, which declined due to pastoralist incursions. It was
now the duty of the French to revive the Roman vision. The mythology of
the past reinforced belief in the superiority of European technology and science and a devaluation of indigenous knowledge about recycling water and
soil conservation.

That resurgence vision saw land reforms but did not produce a green
revolution. In the Horn of Africa, it was a spectacular failure. The white
settlers could not adapt to the heat, lack of water, and scarcity of labor.

---

[13] Wolfe W. Schmokel, "The Myth of the White Farmer: Commercial Agriculture in Namibia,
1900–1983," *International Journal of African Historical Studies*, 18(1), 1985, 93–108, cited text on
p. 106.

124   WATER AND DEVELOPMENT

Italian colonizers realized that it would be impossible to make this territory pay in any fashion. Government experimental farms had minimal impact. The only positive legacy was the introduction of a few new crops. By drawing irrigated land and workforce away from rainfed agriculture, settler farming caused inequality and regression in the latter. As Melvin Knight showed, the impact of "Europeanization" or settler cultivation on the economies of Tunisia, Algeria, and Morocco was limited because the environmental conditions the Europeans tried to overcome were too complex to solve.[14] A study of settler farming in Africa concludes that the commercial success of European farms depended on "the control over land, and above all the control over labour," both actions signifying that the colonial state stepped in with force to subsidize some costs otherwise borne by the settler farmer.[15] Even with subsidization, settler farming made small inroads in most places because of a crucial missing "control": water.

That negative assessment of settler enterprise should be qualified. Settler farming under the right conditions—good access to water, finance, and markets—created whole new businesses and produced significant gains for the economy. In all these regions in the twentieth century, there was population and livestock growth, increased irrigation intensity, crop diversification, a rise in food production, and a greater ability of economies to rebound after droughts. The French in Algeria extended viticulture and produced wines sold in the French market. "A century of French penetration has more than doubled the population and cultivated area in Algeria."[16] It would be a mistake to think that settlers alone gained from infrastructure investment and new laws. If water was available, cultivation practices changed across ethnic sets to raise land yield, for example, in irrigated compared with unirrigated wheat. While droughts were frequent and had serious effects on the crops, the rural economy gained greater capacity to withstand the worst effects. "Europeanization," said Knight, "has brought about a scattering of effort over more crops, with less danger of a total failure."[17] That said, the

[14] Melvin M. Knight, "Water and the Course of Empire in North Africa," *Quarterly Journal of Economics*, 43(1), 1928, 44–93.

[15] Ewout Frankema, Erik Green, and Ellen Hillbom, "Endogenous Processes of Colonial Settlement: The Success and Failure of European Settler Farming in Sub-Saharan Africa," *Revista de Historia Economica—Journal of Iberian and Latin American Economic History*, 34(2), 2016, 237–265, cited text on p. 261.

[16] Knight, "Water and the Course of Empire," 87.

[17] Ibid., 91.

overall effect, though often in the right direction, was not as impressive as expected.

The point was not that colonialism and settler farming were necessarily damaging but that any form of intensive agriculture needed a much more stable and controlled water supply than was available. The ambition to create a green revolution in the arid tropics died because the security of private property rights, the only weapon, did not make a big difference except for generating inequality. The challenge needed science and money.

Environmental historians suggest that the problem was cultural: the new rulers either misread the environment or read it through a European lens. Partly to make the territories attractive to settlers, the challenge of overcoming seasonality, water shortage, and thin soil was underplayed, and the prospect of intensive cultivation was overplayed. In French Algeria, colonial officers believed that "military control in the burgeoning colony necessitated a viable agriculture, and a viable agriculture was a 'European' agriculture, run by colonists who would farm and 'civilize' the land, taming it and healing it after centuries of destruction by the Arabs."[18] Similar sentiments prevailed in other colonies. Terms frequently used to criticize this discourse and the illusion of power that lay behind it—"representations," "meanings" assigned to landscapes, "images," and "imaginaries"—reinforce the notion that colonial knowledge was a distinct thing from nature, and that there was a disconnect between rhetoric and nature.[19]

That early colonial self-confidence came from a misreading of nature and an exaggerated sense of power is probably right. But we should not take it too far. Rhetoric and nature were not as distant as we may think from this discourse. Where colonial rule lasted a century or more, as in Algeria, knowledge adapted. The nature and rhetoric came significantly closer after famines and droughts. In the interwar years, colonial scientists and administrators in North Africa and South Asia delivered significant data and analysis on climate, weather, and hydrology. They correctly diagnosed that the seasonal influx of moisture and extreme aridity during certain seasons were obstacles to agricultural change. The Indian Famine Commission was right when it said that "atmospheric disturbances which prevent the occurrence of

[18] Diana K. Davis, *Resurrecting the Granary of Rome: Environmental History and French Colonial Expansion in North Africa*, Athens: Ohio University Press, 2007; and Brock Cutler, "Imperial Thirst: Water and Colonial Administration in Algeria, 1840–1880," *Review of Middle East Studies*, 44(2), 2010, 167–175, cited text on p. 170.

[19] See several essays in Diana K. Davis and Edmund Burke III, eds., *Environmental Imaginaries of the Middle East and North Africa*, Athens: Ohio University Press, 2011.

126 WATER AND DEVELOPMENT

the summer rains, and [the resultant] abnormal conditions of temperature and humidity [are] hostile to human life," an intuition that led to significant investment in railways, sanitation, and canals.[20] The colonial analysts did not doggedly misread tropical nature from an illusion about Europe. Tropical nature was too complex a thing for them to read.

Facing that problem, secure land title bestowed by the new states was not necessarily a great asset. However, the colonial states still pursued the titling project tenaciously almost everywhere. One area where the project was missing or appeared late was pastures and waterbodies.

Pastures and Waterbodies

The further one traveled away from the farmlands and the estates growing export crops, the meaning of property changed. Land lost value and taxpaying capacity. The vast savannas were cultivable in patches. Outside these patches, seasonal grasslands sustained mobile herders. The assets they depended on most crucially—wells, pastures—were not sufficiently, if at all, registered, let alone legislated; yet the definition of farmland rights also demarcated pastoralist domains, which was a positive thing for the herders. That status quo would be disturbed in the late twentieth century when pastoral domains started getting more water and could potentially convert into farmlands, and these new lands had no property rights.

Like pastures, the colonial states did little to address water access, yet the creation of ownership title in land, as in South Asia, had a curious dual effect: it created strong ownership rights to private waterbodies located inside the owned land, like a well or a pond, and led to the decline of commonly managed resources on which whole villages formerly subsisted.

Ceylon is a case in point. The island is not tropical but has a stretch of arid land at the center, an extension of the tropical climatic zone. Mid-nineteenth-century investigations into agricultural conditions revealed the deep dependence of the village upon reservoirs and common watercourses. These investigations also showed some form of joint or shared responsibility in maintaining the watercourses and tanks in the villages. At the time of the surveys, these were in disrepair and neglect. Anthropologists discovered only remnants of the jointly managed waterbodies a century later.

---

[20] India, *Report of the Famine Commission. Part I: Famine Relief*, London: HMSO, 1880, 28.

THE COLONIAL ERA: PROPERTY RIGHTS   127

In between, private property in land had appeared, ending cooperation and encouraging enclosures, though a chronological history of how this transition happened is not yet available.

Farther north, in the Tamil Nadu and Karnataka regions of India, East India Company officers in the early nineteenth century observed decaying tanks (artificial lakes). An estimated thirty thousand such tanks had once been in operation.[21] They presumed that the decline resulted from a decline in state power. More likely, local notables maintained the tanks and they lost their power to command labor.

Labor and employment contracts posed another set of problems. These projects had earlier been maintained not by cooperation but by forced labor, which by then had been outlawed. An 1857 report from Batticaloa in eastern Ceylon complained that British prohibition upon corvée led to the disrepair of common waterworks, fierce competition for dwindling water supplies, and frequent litigation.[22] To the detriment of the community, the village elite had lost access to the free labor of small farmers and workers. Examples like these suggest that forced labor to build dams and canals was sanctioned by tradition. The colonial states were ambivalent about the practice.

While locally, many indigenous waterbodies may have fallen into disrepair because, in the new property regime, no one knew how to maintain them, the colonial states were starting to experiment with the means to define and allocate water access over wider regions.

Rivers

The Treaty of Berlin (1885–1886), which set the territorial borders in Africa, also had an article about unimpeded access to rivers for navigation. The plan had as its inspiration a similar set of negotiations about the Rhine during the 1815 Congress of Vienna. In the 1880s, an International Commission of the Congo was modeled after the International Commission of the Rhine but did not take off. Other treaties, however, formed successfully. Whereas most colonial treaties were repealed and replaced in the mid-twentieth century,

---

[21] David Mosse, "Colonial and Contemporary Ideologies of 'Community Management': The Case of Tank Irrigation Development in South India," *Modern Asian Studies*, 33(2), 1999, 303–338.
[22] Bryan Pfaffenberger, "The Harsh Facts of Hydraulics: Technology and Society in Sri Lanka's Colonization Schemes," *Technology and Culture*, 31(3), 1990, 361–397, cited text on p. 381.

128   WATER AND DEVELOPMENT

old agreements became the basis for redrawing new ones. The major difference was that state priority shifted from navigation to the productive uses of
rivers.

The concept of basin sharing is perhaps as old as navigation itself. Still,
the *law* of basin sharing was a recent thing, taking shape since the nineteenth
century and seeing its fullest development in the twentieth. The modern law
derived from the concept of riparian rights in Roman law.[23] Riparian right
means that those with access to a waterbody due to possessing land next to it
have a right to use that body. When several parties have access to one waterbody, they share a right. The concept implies that all with riparian rights
must share the basin and that the basin has a unity that no right-holder can
singlehandedly endanger. Initially, the more common case of riparian rights
would be community control over a lake or a channel, like those in the Ceylon case discussed earlier. Transplanting the concept from communities to
the international stage and from the village channel to big rivers was never
straightforward. It had some success in colonial times because the French
and the British saw the need to agree on river sharing in Africa. Inland navigation was crucial for trade and army movements—and they did draw up
treaties.

Although colonial borders reflected inter-imperial relations more than
local history or geography—and the territories encompassed within these
borders were sometimes extremely diverse—the colonial era "did create a
kind of unity . . . [and this] unity was fundamentally economic."[24] Railways, steamships, and commercial laws advanced this integration during
European rule, but these tools appeared late and were not used similarly in different parts of the colonial world. More universally, military
treaties and naval protection of port sites promoted interregional market
exchange.

Consistent with that tendency, colonialism also facilitated cross-border
negotiations on water. All states, colonial or indigenous, understood the
economic importance of perennial rivers in the tropical landscape. However, the colonial ones went much further than the indigenous states on
transboundary treaties. As mentioned, following the start of "formal imperialism" after the 1885 conference, there was a systematic effort to develop

---

[23] Ludwik A. Teclaff, "Evolution of the River Basin Concept in National and International Water
Law," *Natural Resources Journal,* 36(2), 1996, 359–391.

[24] Gregory H. Maddox, "Networks and Frontiers in Colonial Tanzania," *Environmental History,*
3(4), 1998, 436–459, cited text on p. 438.

river treaties.[25] Implicitly, these moves recognized four rules of sharing river water: riparian rights, or the unity of basins; easement, or existing usage rights; public trust, or the state acting as a trustee of common property; and eminent domain, or the state asserting ownership of a natural resource.

Other fields of state intervention implied one or the other of these rules. The state did not apply any rule necessarily because it was the right thing to do or because the law came from Europe. A commercial motivation or a specific crisis was the common inducement. For example, the late-nineteenth-century famines in southern India led the relief authorities to take over many private wells. This was an expression of a public trust principle but an administrative emergency rather than an ideological move. The absence of any radical shift in law was evident in the almost total neglect of a vital commons, groundwater. "No substantive colonial water treaty mentions ground water."[26]

In Africa, the Nile Basin saw the most systematic and coordinated basin-sharing attempt. Egypt and Ethiopia fought a war in 1875–1876 over control of the source of the Nile, which Egypt lost. A few years later, the British colonized Egypt, governing it with a light touch. At the end of the nineteenth century, Britain and Italy had great influence among the main riparian countries that relied crucially on the Nile. In a series of moves, Britain and Italy, and Britain and Ethiopia, agreed to share some rules about the Nile. The main point of these early treaties was that upstream countries would not build dams. Later, influential among the semiequatorial riparian regions, France joined these treaties.

Egypt was a downstream country. The treaties did not stop Egypt from building two dams in Aswan in the south of the country to create reservoirs. The first was erected in 1889, and the second in 1928. The British wanted to expand cotton cultivation in the area served by the dam, but the interest in waterworks was not purely commercial. Egypt was crucial to Britain for strategic reasons. Colonial administrators saw that Egypt's existence and political independence from Ottoman influence would depend on economic freedom, which meant an expansion of intensive agriculture using river waters. Egypt's indigenous rulers, technically Ottoman viceroys, had reached the same conclusion from at least the mid-nineteenth century.

[25] Jonathan Lautze and Mark Giordano, "Transboundary Water Law in Africa: Development, Nature, and Geography," *Natural Resources Journal*, 45(4), 2005, 1053–1087.
[26] Ibid, 1061.

130   WATER AND DEVELOPMENT

The treaties created a discourse of cooperation to protect the entire basin. Instead of more wars, a framework for cooperation emerged. The 1929 Nile Waters Agreement between Egypt and Sudan went much further than earlier treaties and fixed the volumes of water that the two countries could claim.[27] Ironically, the only independent country in the region, Ethiopia, was excluded from most treaties because it was not part of any European empire.

What did these steps add up to? Directly, legislative reforms contributed little to production and productivity. However, these measures advanced regional inequality between the zones of intensive cultivation and the dry interior, just as Arthur Lewis had asserted (Chapter 2).

Inequality

The colonial ambition to transform the countryside mostly failed to deliver. But it did generate a variety of inequality. I have discussed the inequality between the settler and indigenous farmers in contexts where land was abundant, but land with secure water was extremely scarce. Even where European settler farming never emerged, a similar pattern of inequality did. It was more regional than ethnic. The two planks of colonial developmentalism—encourage agriculture and facilitate trade—reinforced one another in those areas where forests could be cleared or pastures resettled to create commodity-exporting farms. These farming clusters exported rubber, wheat, rice, tea, cocoa, coffee, palm oil, groundnut, and sisal. With small success as an African export, cotton was a semi-arid crop (though irrigation helped), and gum arabic came from the arid commons. Otherwise, the twin bias favored the water-rich deltas, basins, river valleys, and newly cleared forests.

General interpretations of the impact of colonial rule on economic development based on the commercialization of agriculture remain sharply divided. The works by scholars on the left (Immanuel Wallerstein, Paul Baran, André Gunder Frank, Walter Rodney, Samir Amin, and Amiya Kumar Bagchi) argue that trade and colonial rule ruined the colonies' economies. Market optimists like W. Arthur Lewis, Hla Myint, Celso Furtado, and D.K. Fieldhouse stand on the other side. They believe that the

[27] Ashok Swain, "Ethiopia, the Sudan, and Egypt: The Nile River Dispute," *Journal of Modern African Studies*, 35(4), 1997, 675–694.

THE COLONIAL ERA: PROPERTY RIGHTS   131

colonies made significant gains from the commodity exports. Both accounts overlook geography. The positive impact of agricultural intensification and commodity trade was present where water was secure, accompanied by business growth in port cities. There was more disruption in seasonal livelihoods in the savanna and drier lands, as deurbanization sometimes occurred where railways and ports took away trade and people. On average, nothing much changed except population growth rates. The colonial legacy was not growth or decline but the furtherance of regional inequality.

Thus, in the south of the Sahara Desert, from the time European colonial states consolidated in the region, the trans-Saharan trade declined, and the axis of international trade reoriented toward the Atlantic. Other examples of the retreat of caravans or pack-animal trains in semi-arid landscapes can be found in the Deccan Plateau in southern India and Sudan. "Population," W. Arthur Lewis wrote in an overview of tropical development, "started moving from the drier to the wetter areas, and this movement still continues today."[28]

Indian historical national income data help us quantify the inequality effect. India's port cities were a part of the Indian Ocean trade long before British colonization. The emergence of an empire consolidated their position as business cities, founded on different trades and supported by an extensive railway network. There were areas of dynamism in the countryside where irrigation water became available, but by and large, the rural economy was dominated by stagnant arid lands. Between 1900 and 1945, real income in industry and services increased by 133 percent, and real income in agriculture by 26 percent. In the same period, income per worker in manufacturing and services increased by 180 percent, and income per worker in agriculture grew by 6 percent.[29] The mainstay of business growth was long-distance commodity trade. Cargo carried by the railways and the ports increased from 5 to 140 million tons between 1871 and 1939. Finance and banking expanded to support the growth. Merchants and trading firms invested trading profits in cotton and jute textile factories. There was economic growth but it was regionally unequal.

European-ruled states in Asia and Africa tried to replicate the Indian story, foster agricultural commodity trade wherever they could, and build infrastructure to encourage trade. Few countries could do this on a significant

[28] W.A. Lewis, ed., *Tropical Development 1880–1913: Studies in Economic Progress*. London: George Allen and Unwin, 1970, 18.
[29] Tirthankar Roy, *The Economic History of India 1857–2010*, 4th ed. Delhi: Oxford University Press, 2020.

132 WATER AND DEVELOPMENT

scale, if a booming trade in animals is excluded. Given India's size, the commercializing policy could not but leave vast regions and many livelihoods untouched. A similar pattern of inequality arose between the commercializing ports and the agricultural hinterland and between the export economy and the interior economy of herders, nomads, and subsistence farmers in many other parts of the world.

Conclusion

In the end, colonialism had limited means to change land use. Pastoralism was a blind spot of law. For most of their duration, colonial states did not see it as their duty to develop the regions they controlled, nor did they have the money or the workforce to do such a thing. These states acted on a belief: encourage market integration, and growth would follow. Growth did follow, but like all market-based growth, it also generated stress for those with little to sell.

The colonial states' lasting legacy was to make water a field of intervention. From the twentieth century, civil engineers reinforced that effort.

Chapter Seven
Dams and Drills

Until recently, governmental authorities, economists, agronomists, botanists, naturalists, and engineers believed that the best use of arid lands was to bring them under cultivation. Colonial authorities in Asia and Africa designated open spaces as "wastes," meaning they were awaiting transformation into arable land with the proper injection of knowledge. A "global imaginary" of arid lands was emerging.[1] It sustained the hope that intensive cultivation in the Western European model was possible in the tropical regions.[2] As it turned out, the power of the colonial states was limited by an inadequate and often highly tentative understanding of what worked. European science was often at a loss when confronting dryland famines, Bay of Bengal cyclones, monsoon floods, and Himalayan rivers.

But science adapted. Around the turn of the twentieth century, a global scientific discourse emerged to offer credible pathways for transforming arid landscapes. A significant center of research and activism was the western states of the United States. From here, water-saving tools like dry farming traveled to North Africa and West Asia. Another hub was India, where the knowledge of how to build sturdy canals traveled to Egypt and Sudan. Civil and military engineers joined in economic development. The coming together of hydrodynamics, geology, and engineering made it feasible to conceive larger systems and handle complex problems. The professionalization of engineering and the creation of bodies like the Institution of Civil Engineers (1818) brought that capability more readily before governments worldwide. The two activities that would revolutionize the field were the multipurpose river valley project and drilling deep underground.

In the late nineteenth century, hydraulics and electric power generation came closer with the wider use of the water turbine. Hydropower was a familiar idea by the 1920s. But most projects were local, serving one city at

[1] Katherine G. Morrissey and Marcus A. Burtner, "Global Imaginary of Arid Lands," *Global Environment*, 12(1), 2019, 102–133.
[2] Corey Ross, *Ecology and Power in the Age of Empire: Europe and the Transformation of the Tropical World*, Oxford: Oxford University Press, 2019, 307–308.

Water and Development. Tirthankar Roy, Oxford University Press. © Oxford University Press (2025).
DOI: 10.1093/oso/9780197802397.003.0007

134 WATER AND DEVELOPMENT

the most. In the 1930s, a series of projects in the tropical United States took the developmental drive to another level. Late in the interwar period, the concept of the multipurpose dam traveled from the US southwest to India and then to Africa.

There were all sorts of political motivations tied to water. In North Africa, the settlers demanded the state help them. Initially advocates of minimal state intervention besides defense and law, the British Indian regime changed their attitude because famines in the Deccan Plateau between 1876 and 1899 gave rise to the fear that "water scarcity, internal conflicts linked to water usage, floods or epidemics are factors that could undermine the power and legitimacy of states."[3] Punjab canals rewarded a region where the British Indian army recruited many soldiers. Famines energized nationalist movements as powerfully as the desire for self-government: "The effective politicization of hunger by Irish and Indian nationalists . . . contributed to the late nineteenth-century shift in British understandings of famine."[4] Even at the end of the colonial timespan, Americans in northwestern Brazil and Italians in Libya saw World War II as a battle between European states and a hostile tropical nature.[5]

Still, geoengineering's appeal was not merely political. It came from a credible promise to end the tyranny of seasonality—and large-scale civil engineering was just one of an array of interventions that zeroed in on water. Sanitation measures to improve water quality (a function of fluctuations in water quantity) and dry farming ideas were parts of the same trajectory. This chapter deals with the early steps taken to apply science to seasonality.

Canals, Pumps, Boreholes, 1850–1930

The settlers in the semi-arid lands believed that European water management held great promise in the drylands. Colonial authorities listened to them. Historian Richard Roberts shows that policymakers in the French colonial empire disagreed over the intervention needed to promote commercial and intensive agriculture: market incentives for peasants with secure property rights or irrigation investment by the state. A policy

---

[3] Frans J. Padt and Juan Carlos Sanchez, "Creating New Spaces for Sustainable Water Management in the Senegal River Basin," *Natural Resources Journal*, 53, 265–284. Cited text on p. 284.

[4] Kathryn Edgerton-Tarpley, "Tough Choices: Grappling with Famine in Qing China, the British Empire, and Beyond," *Journal of World History*, 24(2), 2013, 135–176. Cited text on p. 159.

[5] Roberta Biasillo and Claiton Marcio da Silva, "Cultivating Arid Soils in Libya and Brazil during World War Two," *Global Environment*, 12(1), 2019, 154–181.

to encourage cotton farming in West Africa for export to France had to contend with robust domestic demand for cotton.[6] Even if not an immediate success story, the project underscored the need to work on water.

In Algeria, one of the first European colonies in Africa (established 1830–1848), the French administrators thought that colonization, which meant to them "attempting to re-create 'French' agriculture" in the Maghreb, crucially depended on water security. From the beginning, the French stressed the need to build water-powered mills and discussed dams and reservoirs, though real work along these lines had to wait until much later. The underlying idea was that secure and prosperous livelihoods would depend on trapping the excess flow in seasonal streams in this arid area with winter rainfall. The ambition to transform the landscape met with budgetary and ecological constraints and, in the end, did not deliver much. But the discourse survived.[7]

While fluvial treaties advanced in Africa, the productive use of rivers and monsoonal runoff expanded in British India. The large volumes of water that passed through the South Indian deltas and Himalayan rivers enabled the building of canals and reservoirs on a large scale. Military engineers stationed in arid zones gave shape to a model of development that involved the government building works to divert the water of the perennial Himalayan rivers and build barrages on the deltaic rivers to create canals. This, for many, was a win-win model. The farmers would pay more taxes while making money from new crops.

We may think that imperial public goods served as a political project, a demonstration of technological prowess, and power over the backward nations of Asia and Africa. The idea does not work with water projects. Droughts and famines exposed the weakness of imperialism and the worthlessness of its claims to serve Indian welfare. Indian nationalists saw that. The major water initiatives in India emerged as a damage control measure following a severe hit to the regime's credibility due to a famine. Because it came out of desperation rather than firm scientific understanding, there were fierce disputations within the imperial bureaucracy on what water projects were needed, and whether other ways of spending money might serve the purpose better.

[6] Richard L. Roberts, *Two Worlds of Cotton: Colonialism and the Regional Economy in the French Soudan, 1800–1946*, Stanford, CA: Stanford University Press, 1996.
[7] Sara B. Pritchard, "From Hydroimperialism to Hydrocapitalism: 'French' Hydraulics in France, North Africa, and Beyond," *Social Studies of Science*, 42(4), 2012, 591–615.

136 WATER AND DEVELOPMENT

The Indianist discourse on water started with Charles Dixon. Until the second or the third decade of the nineteenth century, the British Indian state understood water engineering to mean flood control rather than large-scale irrigation. This was so because the eastern Gangetic Delta, where the regime began, was not generally arid. A flat land that received a heavy monsoon, its usual problem was drainage and floods rather than dryness. From the 1830s, and after an enormous area in semi-arid southern and western India had joined the company's Indian empire, the accent of the water discourse changed from controlling floods to managing irrigation in dry lands.

Dixon, a Bengal Artillery lieutenant colonel, was appointed Ajmer-Merwara's superintendent in 1836. Following the Maratha wars, this western Indian province came under British rule. In the next twenty years, until he died in 1857, Dixon made it his mission to transform the economy of this region—one of the driest inhabited places of India with little groundwater— by creating artificial lakes to catch monsoon runoff. The memory of an 1832 famine and subsequent evacuation was still vivid when he began. When he died, the farmers gained sufficient control over moisture to grow more than one crop, and this small area saw a significant rise in population density. Dixon was not much of a writer or campaigner. Still, his intuition—that "it was manifest that water was the great desideratum. . . . It was the one thing necessary to bind the inhabitants to the soil, to attach them to our form of government, and to admit of our moulding them into the habits of life we desired"—inspired a section of the officialdom who had served in arid areas or seen a famine up close.[8] The most famous name in that set was Arthur Cotton.

Unlike most engineers and officers dealing with one small area they were familiar with, Cotton could design action plans spanning enormous river basins and deltas, and, based on that experience, lobby policymakers to spend more money on canals than railways. As he explained in a letter late in his life, on average, 97 percent of the water that the monsoon added into stream flow was lost to evaporation or runoff every year. It was a simple and telling argument that this flow must be conserved somehow, even if the statistics were overstated.

In the 1850s, Cotton successfully campaigned for projects to dam, trap, store, and divert monsoon rainwater flowing in the South Indian rivers. Indigenous regimes had demonstrated the feasibility of such projects in

[8] Charles George Dixon, *Sketch of Mairwara*, London: Smith, Elder, 1850, 85.

the Kaveri-Coleroon (Kollidam) basin. The earliest construction here is attributed to a king who ruled in the second century CE. A Google search for "Chola irrigation" brings up hundreds of websites and pictures that attribute a nineteenth-century British-Indian dam to this ancient king. Careful studies suggest the ancient construction was a flood control and river-water-diversion system, more an embankment than a dam. Tracing the original stone foundation requires expertise. In the early nineteenth century, the engineers of the East India Company saw the value of that construction because disrepair had caused silting of the riverbed.[9] Cotton proposed building a low-height "check dam" across the riverbed, which may have built on a seventeenth-century construction.

In the next stage, he proposed completely new projects built on a much larger scale in the deltas of the Krishna and Godavari Rivers (Figure 7.1).

Figure 7.1 The Gunnaram Sluice on the Godavari

Built around 1850 under Arthur Cotton's supervision, the sluice-cum-aqueduct became a showpiece of Cotton's philosophy, which was to build big works as cheaply as possible.
Source: British Library

---

[9] Chitra Krishnan and Srinivas V. Veeravalli, "Tanks and Anicuts of South India: Examples of an Alternative Science of Engineering," in A.V. Balasubramanian and T.D. Nirmala Devi, eds., *Traditional Knowledge Systems of India and Sri Lanka*, 220-226, Chennai: Centre for Indian Knowledge Systems, 2006.

138   WATER AND DEVELOPMENT

These rivers carried a lot more water during the monsoon. Still, the nature of the works was similar—a low wall constructed over the river to contain water when it was in full flow and construction of canals to divert the impounded water. Construction was a relatively easy proposition since the rivers ran almost dry in the summer months. All these projects came into being with government funding.

In the 1860s and 1870s, Cotton was a celebrity and the leading figure in a lobby advocating government investment in irrigation to develop Indian agriculture and disputing the claims of the railway lobby for money. In this mission, Cotton was not always successful. When he moved from the deltas to the drought-prone interior of the Deccan Plateau, the provincial government withdrew support. This was a far more challenging territory, for the monsoon was weaker, and the rivers were subject to extreme streamflow variation during the year.

After some hesitation, a private company, the Madras Irrigation Canal and Navigation Company, took up Cotton's plan to build dams over the Tungabhadra River, a tributary of the Krishna. The construction work for a dam started in 1860 in Sunkesula near Kurnool town. It soon turned out that the company had underestimated construction costs in a terrain formed of basaltic rock. The dam and the canal did start working, but the farmers did not know how to use the water. Most grew cotton in black soil that retained enough rainwater for cotton to grow. More water in the dry seasons might induce some farmers to grow rice. However, this was not a rice-consuming area, and there was hardly any way to sell cash crops in distant markets. The water projects did prove their utility in 1878 when large numbers of famine-stricken people migrated from neighboring districts into the dam area.[10] But drought relief did not bring the company any money. Unable to meet its welfare objective when farmers did not pay for water, the company had already gone bankrupt in 1865. Subsequently, the government took over the Sunkesula work. Almost a hundred years later, a canal link between Srisailam, one of the largest dams in South India over the Krishna, and Sunkesula strengthened the sustainability of the work.

Another private enterprise farther north had a similar experience. In Orissa (Odisha) the coastal canal projects built with private capital in the 1860s were aimed at diversion of monsoon floodwaters away from the deltaic

---

[10] M. Atchi Reddy, "Travails of an Irrigation Canal Company in South India, 1857–1882," *Economic and Political Weekly*, 25(12), 1990, 619–628.

rivers. Serving this welfare aim would not generate much revenue unless canal water was also available for irrigation for a fee. However, farmers in the deltas did not need this water—and were certainly not willing to pay for it. The company went bankrupt soon after its inception, and the government took over its assets. The government then tried to impose a water rate assuming that many farmers were drawing canal water without its knowledge. Whether that assumption was right or wrong, collecting a fee was never easy and often generated violence. For the farmers, merely the availability of canal water would not be enough incentive for growing cash crops because the transport system was still limited. The main aim of the canal system, to control floods, may have led the soil to lose fertility in some areas because the annual monsoonal inundation added rich silts to the soil.[11] After these failures, further canal construction followed two principles: canals would be built with public money, and navigation or flood control would be secondary objectives. Irrigation and food production would be the main goals.

Irrigation policy after Cotton became a battlefield. Cotton was a sharp critic of Proby Cautley (1802–1871), an army officer, engineer, and paleontologist who led canal construction in the Indo-Gangetic Basin. Cautley's basin projects were controversial because they took place in a region that was not exactly water-short and often led to waterlogging and salination.[12] But these also left large externalities—knowledge, for one. In the 1980s, Hirokazu Tada, in a series of research articles later compiled in a book, showed how seasonality induced public investment, and how it challenged the military engineers working in the Ganges Basin and made them adapt their tools to the local hydroclimatic conditions.[13] Other side effects were that brickmaking became big business, and the first school of engineering came up as an offshoot of training irrigation engineers. Officers who later supervised canal projects elsewhere learned their craft working with Cautley. Some would go to Sind to construct canals there. And having more water encouraged regional specialization, with sugarcane cultivation and the emergence of one of the world's largest sugar industry hubs.[14]

---

[11] Rohan D'Souza, "Canal Irrigation and the Conundrum of Flood Protection: The Failure of the Orissa Scheme of 1863 in Eastern India," *Studies in History*, 19(1), 2003, 41–68.

[12] Elizabeth Whitcombe, "Irrigation," in Dharma Kumar, ed., *Cambridge Economic History of India*, vol. 2, Cambridge: Cambridge University Press, 1983, 677–736.

[13] I am grateful to Kazuo Kobayashi for directing me to this research. Hirokazu Tada, *Indo no daichi to mizu* [Land and water in India], Tokyo: Nihon Keizai Hyouronsha, 1992.

[14] Ian Stone, *Canal Irrigation in British India*, Cambridge: Cambridge University Press, 1984.

140 WATER AND DEVELOPMENT

A third name of some significance in India's irrigation history was Richard Baird Smith (1818–1861), a Scottish army officer who became interested in the subject while assisting Cautley (Figure 7.2). Stationed in Punjab at the end of the Anglo-Sikh wars (1849), and with nothing to do, he measured water flows in the rivers and wrote a report. Thus began the story of the Punjab canals. Baird Smith was to head irrigation development and traveled to Italy and the South Indian deltas to gain more experience. But the 1857 rebellion, battle injury, and extreme stress cut his career plans and life short. He left behind an unfinished account of the siege of Delhi during the rebellion.

The 1876–1878 famine in South India and the subsequent reports on famines and irrigation pushed toward a public model aiming at more railways and canals. The biggest public projects had begun in the Punjab, on rivers fed by Himalayan snowmelt. The projects involved building canals rather than dams or barrages. The Punjab project took decades to be fully built. When construction was nearly done, there was nothing quite like it in terms of scale and impact on the entire British Empire. The imperialists were well aware of the publicity potential of the Punjab canals.

By then, among the largest river projects undertaken were the Krishna and Godavari delta systems (1868), together serving close to 1 million hectares of farmland; the Western Yamuna canal system (1892, 500,000 hectares); Sirhind canal (1887, 1 million hectares); the Cauvery delta system (1889, 425,000 hectares); Upper and Lower Ganga canals (1854–1878, 1.3 million hectares); and Sarda canal (1926, about 500,000 hectares). Smaller works that had considerable localized impact included the Sone canal (1879), the Nira Valley system (1938), and the Upper Bari Doab canal (1879).

The most dramatic effect of the Punjab canals was the "colonization" of wastes or the conversion of pastures into farms. The total cropped area about doubled, and the area irrigated as a percentage of the cropped area increased from 12 to 22 between 1885 and 1938. The expansion occurred mainly in government canals and in private wells. Canals and rivers together served practically all the major urban centers of Punjab, located in British or princely territories. Once railway communication started, the towns developed thriving businesses with extensive industrial, financial, and commercial dealings. On the other hand, the canals led to waterlogging, salinity, and malaria like in the relatively flat plains of the United Provinces.[15]

---

[15] Indu Agnihotri, "Ecology, Land Use and Colonisation: The Canal Colonies of Punjab," *Indian Economic and Social History Review*, 33(1), 1996, 59–68.

DAMS AND DRILLS 141

Figure 7.2 Richard Baird Smith (1818–1861)
An engineer in the service of the East India Company, Baird Smith's report on the prospects of a network of canals crisscrossing the Punjab rivers fed by Himalayan snowmelt was crucial in the government's decision to build the project. Baird Smith did not live to see any of it, though his last office was the head of the Indian Public Works. He died from a wound sustained in the Siege of Delhi in 1857. The Punjab canals would soon become the best testimony of the British Empire's contributions to Indian development.
Source: Alamy Stock Photos

142   WATER AND DEVELOPMENT

Whether the impressive economic impact on farmers' livelihoods and diversification justified these costs is a matter of opinion. The canals also induced the pastoral groups to cultivate. As a result, the quality of livestock declined.

The key feature of all these projects was their ability to access large waterbodies that withstood seasonal variations. India's monsoon and the Himalayan snow created that possibility only in Punjab, Sind, the United Provinces, and the South Indian deltas. The gravity projects that emerged in this vast region recycled water from a secure source to water-scarce areas using the slope of the land. New ideas, including silt control and basin management, allowed these to serve much more extensive areas than the past Indian regimes could do.[16] This concept was unworkable anywhere else in India, with a few minor exceptions. It was unworkable also in most parts of the tropics. The Nile Basin, like the Punjab, was another exception.

Egypt was under British colonial rule from 1882 until 1922, when it became partly independent. When the rule began, the British did not bring in any new economic ideas but took seriously the legacy of Muhammad Ali and his successors. These regimes had been keen to expand commercial agriculture, especially the growing of cotton and sugar, which would require land extension, and the use of land in seasons outside that (July–November) when the Nile flooding and floodwater recession made cultivation possible. Ali and his successors encouraged using pumps, canals, and barrages to increase water flow to dry fields in summer. Later, some of these systems suffered from poor maintenance. Further, drainage had been overlooked, resulting in some arable land being degraded.

The British approach was to first install a trusted officer at the head of this enterprise. Colin Scott-Moncrieff had earlier worked in the Ganges Canal in India. His appointment as the head of the public works department affirmed that colonial policy, otherwise not very interventionist, would not treat irrigation lightly. In the next few years, more engineers were recruited into senior positions and placed in charge of different areas. In this way, a fundamentally modern engineering package consisting of basin management, flood control, land reclamation, masonry dams, and dredging came to Egypt from India, where it had been active for several decades.

As in India, colonial engineering often started by building on ancient works. The new public works body started with an abandoned barrage near

---

[16] David Gilmartin, "Scientific Empire and Imperial Science: Colonialism and Irrigation Technology in the Indus Basin," *Journal of Asian Studies*, 53(4), 1994, 1127–1149.

DAMS AND DRILLS 143

Cairo. The barrage's foundation was unstable and had almost rotted away from disrepair. A deeper foundation using concrete would be too costly. The solution was to prolong the foundation enough so the barrage would not collapse when water percolated underneath the mud and sand base. This idea had been tested in the South Indian deltas earlier. From the late 1880s, work began on a dam in Aswan to serve Middle and Upper Egypt. The dam's height had to be curtailed to appease Western critics who protested the possible submergence of the Philae Islands. Overall, there was some increase in sown area, though not much gain in land productivity.[17]

These projects became embroiled in a subsidiary debate about how construction labor should be recruited to work. The default system, it was believed, was corvée (see Chapter 5): unpaid labor. An intuitive way to justify unpaid labor was that construction happened when there was seasonal unemployment and that the suppliers of labor services were the future peasants with access to water and more income. In short, corvée was a tax to fund the building. The justification did not have much persuasive power. It resembled slavery, and yet forced labor might indeed have been a part of the older way of constructing public works. The colonialists did not know how to get rid of it, nor could they happily accept it. Similar dilemmas appeared in British Ceylon, as we have seen (Chapter 5). David Mosse suggests that the early colonial rulers in Tamil Nadu believed that the maintenance of tanks by harnessing forced labor was a part of Indian tradition.[18] No one knew for sure if it was or not.

In Sudan, colonial engineering on the Nile began with an ambitious project (1904–1914). In the first quarter of the twentieth century, a cotton-growing operation emerged in Gezira, the interfluve of the Blue Nile and the White Nile. A public-private partnership expanded the year-round cultivation of grain and cotton. A barrage (Sennar) constructed in 1925 over the Blue Nile made more water available in the region. Using electric pumps to recycle river water and channeling it into canals, the area under intensive cultivation expanded. This was the Gezira Scheme, a showpiece for British colonial rule, much like Punjab had been a generation before (Figure 7.3).

Other tropical African regions were just too dry for colonial engineering to make much impact. Pumps, however, found quite extensive use. One

[17] Robert L. Tignor, "British Agricultural and Hydraulic Policy in Egypt, 1882–1892," *Agricultural History*, 37(2), 1963, 63–74.
[18] David Mosse, "Colonial and Contemporary Ideologies of 'Community Management': The Case of Tank Irrigation Development in South India," *Modern Asian Studies*, 33(2), May 1999, 303–338.

Figure 7.3 The Gezira Cotton Scheme, 1951

Reservoirs and canals served about a million acres (forty thousand hectares) of land and made possible the use of mechanical plows.
Source: Alamy Stock Photos

example was in southern and western Zimbabwe. Here, rainfall was low, evaporation high, and cultivation or stock-rearing depended on groundwater availability in the shape of wells or river water. Although human settlement gravitated toward the rivers, the rivers ran dry in summer. After 1893, Cecil Rhodes's wars with the Matabele kingdom and clearance of parts of Matabeleland for white settlement forced many people to resettle in the sparsely populated Shangani reserves. While rivers sustained the settlers, their increasing numbers created water scarcity. In the 1920s and 1930s, an agricultural policy for the area developed. The administration would raise taxes from newly developed areas to invest in boreholes. These boreholes left a curious legacy. During the civil war in the 1960s and the 1970s, access to borehole pumps and storage were used as a weapon of war.

Shortly after World War I, when colonial economic development emerged as a new priority for the British Empire, the Colonial Office asked a British geologist, Frank Dixey, to design a plan for the development of arid Kenya. Dixey was one of the very few experts on groundwater in Africa. His book, reissued in 1950 with the title *A Practical Handbook of Water Supply*, was the standard text on the subject until modern hydrogeology, hydro-engineering, and better methods of finding underground water advanced in the mid-twentieth century. Under the Dixey Scheme, water reservoirs were to be erected in places within the pastoral orbit, an enormous area, so that grazing could concentrate around these projects. By and large, the scheme failed because the aridity problem was too big to be solved in this way. The creation of new externally funded and supplied assets led to competing claims and counterclaims between clans anxious to secure access to these reservoirs, generating fresh conflicts.

By contrast with the Indus tributaries or the Nile, the Niger Basin carried less water. Still, the seasonality of the flow raised the same hope that more could be done there with canals. The resultant scheme, the Office du Niger, was a mixed success at best, and a struggle from its start.

The Office du Niger

In 1919–1920, French colonial engineer Emile Bélime toured the Niger Basin in south-central Mali and drafted a program of irrigation development over nearly two million hectares of semi-arid and seasonally cultivable land by diverting excess water from the Niger and its tributaries. Bélime was giving shape to an ambition to develop the colonies, integrate the economies of France and its West African territories more closely, integrate industry and raw material supplies, and create a self-reliant entity—a developmental ideology captured in the phrase Colonisation Indigène—of which a prominent advocate was Albert Sarraut, the minister for the colonies. The plan failed to gather financial support from the metropolitan government, but the idea stayed, and with loans raised in the center, a scaled-down version of it became a reality (1927–1931). Bélime and his colleagues were in charge.

The engineers and agronomists who set it up believed that plantations run by Europeans were more efficient than the dryland or flush farming methods used in the basin. The use of a heavy plow and deep plowing were crucial to intensive cultivation and high yields, it was believed. But such farming practices from Europe needed more water and more controlled application of it. Any improvement in farming would have to start with water. When fully developed, the scheme had a dam, Markala, a few miles downstream from the historic Ségou town, from which water from the Niger River was redirected into a network of canals.

146 WATER AND DEVELOPMENT

Historians who have studied the project believe that conditions on the ground constrained the ambition and that Indigenous farmers had a significant agency in shaping how the project would unfold.[19] The plan was scaled down to less than half the original size, and a small proportion of the revised plan (possibly as little as one-tenth) was actively irrigated in the long run. The plan had numerous detractors, critics, and enemies within the French imperial establishment, who made Bélime's work challenging. In effect, the work progressed because the office had concentrated enough power to become a political-administrative entity in its own right. "Bélime was the true king, not to be disturbed in his task of developing a part of the empire for the benefit of the mother country."[20]

Further, the project required the resettlement of farmers. One of the challenges was the area's very low population density. The original plan envisioned a kind of grand plantation where resettled or immigrant African farmers would supply labor, working under the direction of French technical experts. The resettlement did not work according to the plan. Office agents went to designated villages to recruit newcomers and offered land, tools, and tax remission. They depended on the local chiefs to supply immigrants. The chiefs would try to eliminate people who were unsuitable in their view, such as rivals or poorer villagers. Some people escaped the draft by bribing officers. Once drafted, the selected individuals were forced to join the project, a controversial element of the scheme that lasted until World War II.[21]

The interests of the settlers and managers diverged. Whereas the primary aim of the Colonisation Indigène was the production of long-staple cotton for the French textile industry, the crop that succeeded more was rice for mainly local consumption. Long-staple cotton proved generally unsuitable in the soil. The interest of the colonial officers was specialization in crops to suit the French economy, and that of the settlers was to grow a wide variety to reduce risk and sell in the local markets. The farmers cultivated land outside the scheme, using inherited methods, and changed the crop mix depending on relative prices. The officers worried that the farmers would be harder to

---

[19] Monica M. van Beusekom, "Colonisation Indigène: French Rural Development Ideology at the Office du Niger, 1920–1940," *International Journal of African Historical Studies*, 30(2), 1997, 299–323.

[20] Mamadou Diawara, "Development and Administrative Norms: The Office du Niger and Decentralization in French Sudan and Mali," *Africa: Journal of the International African Institute*, 81(3), 2011, 434–454, cited text on p. 441.

[21] Jean Filipovich, "Destined to Fail: Forced Settlement at the Office du Niger, 1926–45," *Journal of African History*, 42(2), 2001, 239–260.

negotiate with once armed with legal private titles. Negotiations were needed to settle the fees for using the system and to agree on crops and methods.

To remain operational, the project needed to spend significant money on small-scale irrigation infrastructure, extension services, and tools. Fees paid to use water did not cover the cost. It was subsidized throughout its career. Between World War II and 1959, the Office du Niger received 30 percent of all French spending in the region, maintaining its position as the hub of colonial agriculture. At the same time, as a colonial enterprise or showpiece, it was facing serious problems. The rise in population density in the scheme area and intensive cultivation had led to environmental degradation and reduced soil fertility. A part of the scheme area received floodwaters and had groundwater close to the surface. As a result, excess water drainage was always challenging, and poor drainage led to alkalization and salinization.[22] The office had lost control of its labor policy a long time ago. French technical expertise, too, was abandoning the project. The modernization ideology, as much as the idea of a self-reliant empire, was long dead.

Nevertheless, the office remained a critical economic base after independence. Irrespective of the regime ruling the country, the head of the project (in Mali) was a politically significant figure whom the regime trusted. Furthermore, the Office du Niger gained in importance substantially after the 1970s–1980s Sahelian famines, mainly because the region received migration from the heavily stressed areas on an extensive scale. Most immigrants did not return to the lands they came from. During the 1970s famine, the office was the only major agricultural tract to increase its production.

The Office du Niger is a well-researched subject. However, the accent in the historiography falls upon the development paradigm, conflicts of interest between those who designed it (who were initially affiliated with the imperial policymaking setup) and those who implemented it, and in relation to all this, the politics of the project.[23] Its significance for the book is elsewhere, in the conception of Bélime that monsoon tropical rivers must be used in a certain way for development. The challenge was not the diversion of water where little was available but trapping water when the seasonal flow exceeded local needs. That distinct technical paradigm—for

---

[22] J. Tricart and J.-P. Blanck, "L'Office du Niger, mirage du développement au Mali?" *Annales de Géographie*, 98(549), 1989, 567–587.

[23] Monica M. van Beusekom, "Disjunctures in Theory and Practice: Making Sense of Change in Agricultural Development at the Office du Niger, 1920–60," *Journal of African History*, 41(1), 2000, 79–99.

148 WATER AND DEVELOPMENT

which the immediate context was tropical seasonality, not imperialism or developmentalism—needs stressing.

That geographical dimension helps to understand the enduring appeal of an "unremunerative irrigation scheme that, forty years later, still requires regular injections of foreign aid simply to remain operational."[24] The appeal stems from the commonsense knowledge that there is no better way to provide water in a monsoon tropic than to trap seasonal excess, yet there is no easy way to make that project pay its economic cost. Besides that obvious point so often overlooked, self-reliance in foodgrains has an appeal in drought-prone tropics that cannot be debated. The office area accounts for nearly all of Mali's rice supply and a substantial part of sugarcane supplies.

The notion that river water was an ingredient in development became accepted in Africa mainly through the Nile and Niger and associated treaties.[25] In the interwar period, those who believed in this idea joined hands with the engineers to deliver a design to trap runoff. The inspiration was the United States.

The Conquest of Arid America

Irrigation development in the arid West of the United States is a well-known case of state intervention. After a battle between politicians from dry areas and water-rich ones, the Reclamation Act of 1902 sanctioned the use of public money for water projects, subject to user fees. The typical project tried to do what people in tropical regions have been trying to do for millennia: trap rainwater and recycle water between seasons. The money came from selling federal land in states with large tracts under public ownership.

Not until the Great Depression years was reclamation a success story. Financial costs, unfriendly terrain, and bad engineering hampered progress. The breakthrough came in the 1930s, creating a network of large canals. In the long run, the constructions "welded the West together; . . . made homes, towns, and cities; [and] made the Western states significant members of the family of states," a 1952 assessment concluded.[26] This revolution in

---

[24] Filipovich, "Destined to Fail," 260.

[25] For examples from Africa, the Nile Waters Agreement (1929) and the Century Storage Scheme (after 1952), suggesting an "unmistakable shift" in the assessment of rivers, see Tiyanjana Maluwa, "Legal Aspects of the Niger River under the Niamey Treaties," *Natural Resources Journal*, 28(4), 1988, 671–697.

[26] J. Karl Lee, "Irrigation Policy for Arid Lands," *Journal of Farm Economics*, 34(5), 1952, 751–755.

landscape transformation owed to two types of water projects, groundwater extraction and multipurpose dams, in that chronological order. Both classes required institutional intervention and compromised with private property rights in land and water.

Vast artesian basins existed in southern California, New Mexico, and the Mexican Northwest. The use of artesian wells in the United States began in the last quarter of the nineteenth century. Throughout the tropical Americas, where artesian basins were exploited, intensive cultivation and orchards grew so fast, aided by private capital, that it would diminish water flows within a few years. At different times in the early twentieth century, the issue of discord between private property rights and the sustainability of groundwater basins came to the US courts. Geography challenged and destabilized the idea of absolute private ownership rights that came from a "humid country [English] heritage" and "individualism" and was protected by law, politics, and constitutions.[27] Through droughts and disputes, the notion of reasonable use, correlative rights, or fair share of all users emerged as groundwater use principles.

These grounds were impossible to apply in practice without another radical step, the state claiming rights of appropriation over all water resources, which required knowing over what resources the state was exercising that right. Much energy was used to map groundwater and the features of the artesian basins in the United States. Although, in effect, some version of the appropriation doctrine became universal, the principle formally contradicted private property protected by the constitution of some arid states. However, most of the groundwater rights negotiations and settlements were delivered to the US courts, making this legal and not administrative shaping of rights a distinctive case in the modern history of groundwater use.

The intuition is an old one: that expanding arid area livelihood requires laws to balance water use and recharge. In an 1878 book, John Wesley Powell, an American geologist, called for linking land distribution policy to water availability in arid western states of the United States.[28] That idea was before its time. As groundwater pumping spread from the 1920s, the prospect of an imbalance initially receded. Yet by the early 1950s in California, data on electricity consumption would show a level of draft upon groundwater that was several times higher than the capacity of these resources to replenish

---

[27] Robert G. Dunbar, "The Adaptation of Groundwater-Control Institutions to the Arid West," *Agricultural History*, 51(4), 1977, 662–680, cited text on p. 675.

[28] John Wesley Powell, *The Arid Lands*, Lincoln: University of Nebraska Press, 2004.

150   WATER AND DEVELOPMENT

themselves. Degenerating aquifers raised the cost of extraction via energy charges or the need to install bigger machines capable of pumping water from greater depths. However, private profits did not yet face significant pressure with energy charges falling because of larger energy supplies.

Conservation efforts in groundwater-dependent areas of the Americas started relatively late, in the 1970s. Water rights had been based on historic practices and administrative rules. Therefore, when use exceeded recharge potentials, and the existing institutional means failed to provide solutions, significant changes occurred in the institutional setup. There was no one blueprint for these moves. For one example of reform, in the Colorado River Basin states, legislation on new users, "safe use" rules, and storage (water bank) significantly reduced the cities' dependence on groundwater.[29]

A part of northern Mexico is arid but groundwater-rich. In Mexico City and its suburbs, until the mid-nineteenth century, the wealthy residents and the government relied on water that came to the city via aqueducts from distant natural springs and shallow wells that tapped underground water. The poorer residents used the water from common sources, such as streams, pools, and wells, which were both scarce and of dubious quality. Through these uses, the knowledge about underground resources had become entrenched. As the city grew, large-scale groundwater exploitation in and near Mexico City from the late nineteenth century brought about the "beginning of an age of hydraulic opulence."[30]

During agricultural expansion in the hyper-arid Mexican Northwest in the early twentieth century, private investment in deeper wells using new technology for drilling opened hundreds of artesian wells. Indigenous forms of irrigated farming existed in some of these areas. These systems used seasonal river water, drawing it via channels. In the 1930s and 1940s, the federal government built a cluster of dams in central Mexico, utilizing rivers flowing eastward from the Sierra Madre to generate water for irrigation and power to light up commercial towns. Canal irrigation developed further in the early twentieth century in the Mexican Colorado Delta with investments by American companies that had acquired rights over a large tract

---

[29] Sharon Megdal, "Arizona Groundwater Management," The Water Report, October 15, 2012, https://wrrc.cals.arizona.edu/sites/wrrc.arizona.edu/files/azgroundwater-management.pdf. See also Maurice M. Kelso, William E. Martin, and Lawrence E. Mack, *Water Supplies and Economic Growth in an Arid Environment*, Tucson: University of Arizona Press, 1973.

[30] Casey Walsh, *Virtuous Waters: Mineral Springs, Bathing, and Infrastructure in Mexico*, Berkeley, University of California Press, 2018, title of Chapter 5.

DAMS AND DRILLS   151

of land for development into commercial plantations. In 1937, these lands were sequestered, and serious colonization started in the Northwest.

In most areas, canals and reservoirs created by the river valley works continued to supply irrigation water. However, on the Hermosillo coast, groundwater extraction was the dominant irrigation type. An arid area with little rainfall, the geology of Hermosillo allows rich aquifers to exist, fed by intense, if short-lived, summer rains. Heat dries up nearly all surface water, leaving only dry habitat plants or cacti able to survive. A region that sustained nomadic life and some river-water-dependent agriculture before 1800 started to extend cultivation as European settlers dug shallow wells to access the water underground. With steam engines from the late nineteenth century, water was extracted at bigger volumes from greater depths than before. With the help of canals, it was spread farther afield.

Groundwater extraction began in estates that were bigger on average than the canal-fed ones, giving rise to a newly rich farming class. Within decades, water extraction had far exceeded recharge rates in the area, whereas in the canal areas, salinization threatened soil fertility, especially among the older settlements. Between 1946 and 1963, land distribution laws permitted the formation of cooperative and private estates, especially in areas with no recent history of intensive cultivation. After 1963, land distribution under the public domain was legally restricted to communal property, though extralegal holdings continued.[31]

Dams, reservoirs, aqueducts, and canals appeared in several places in the arid regions of the southwestern US from the turn of the twentieth century. In terrain that did not have enough locally sourced fuel to make cement or good transport access, construction of systems that would withstand floods and could divert water on a scale that the growing population and farming demanded was not easy. Still, engineers, entrepreneurs, and city administrations persisted. The Depression years saw a significant breakthrough. As water from local resources ran out for Los Angeles in the 1920s, the Colorado River Aqueduct, built over eight years in the 1930s, recycled water from the Colorado River to the city and farmlands in southern California while drawing water away from the Mexican Northwest. In the 1930s, the Tennessee Valley projects and the Hoover Dam encouraged engineers to be even more ambitious.

---

[31] David A. Henderson, "Arid Lands under Agrarian Reform in Northwest Mexico," *Economic Geography*, 41(4), 1965, 300–312.

152 WATER AND DEVELOPMENT

Thus, engineering knowledge prevailed over nature for the time being. Knowledge was only one impetus. The other was private investment, supported by prior appropriation rules or common law principles favoring early users. Land reclamation here, like elsewhere, significantly relied on community effort. These were not egalitarian communities. Ownership was unequally distributed. The indigenous peoples and their rights were usually overridden. And inequalities emerged between early and later settlers. The regional states still backed up the legal process tied to reclamation.

Dam construction, however, was beyond communities to fund and needed significant use of taxpayers' money. Dam-building continued in earnest for at least three decades after the end of World War II. From the 1980s, environmentalists pushed against dams. The collapse of a large dam in Idaho in 1976 revealed the significant risks to lives and landscapes that unknown geographical parameters could cause. When the reclamation drive slowed, projects under the Reclamation Bureau supplied water to about one-fifth of the irrigated acreage in the western states. The projects were more successful in producing hydroelectricity.[32] The prospect of solving two problems at once, water and power, made the multipurpose dams an attractive idea.

Dams Become Global

The knowledge that dams enabled moisture control on a large scale reached tropical Asia, Africa, and Latin America in the interwar period. The colonial states knew about this potential in the 1930s. They were too poor to fund large projects, but they did construct a few.

The Mettur dam on the Kaveri was possibly the largest in the world when finished around 1935. The dam involved "mobilization of engineering expertise from across the world . . . the changing political scenario in British India and . . . local water politics."[33] The dam sustained intensive cultivation in one of the drier regions of South India. The electric power generated in the dam and the thermal plant near it supplied energy to a cluster of engineering and textile towns in northern Tamil Nadu. As

[32] The US Bureau of Reclamation website has a nice bite-size history: https://www.usbr.gov/history/index.html.
[33] Aditya Ramesh, "Water Technocracy: Dams, Experts and Development in South India," PhD thesis, SOAS University of London, 2019, cited text on p. 2.

mentioned before, the most important large water project in Mali, the Markala dam, was built in the 1930s and early 1940s to encourage cotton cultivation in the northeastern part of the inland Niger Delta. Although the cotton scheme did not materialize, canals taken from the dam helped rice cultivation.

Small dam construction began in the drylands of Brazil in the nineteenth century. Coffee and rubber cultivation zones and mining areas absorbed migrants from the drought-hit northeast. The great El Niño drought of 1876–1877 that caused famines and devastation throughout the tropics killed large numbers in northeastern Brazil and pushed the imperial state to act. The action plan consisted of building reservoirs to trap rainwater and to transfer water from the Sao Francisco River via a canal. The imperial government also constructed several dams and reservoirs. "Primitive earthworks paved with stone," most were washed away within a few decades.[34] A second wave of dam construction started after extensive geological and climatological surveys of the region around 1910. Thus, the construction of large hydro projects began early, but the drive took off later when electricity for industrialization became an additional necessity.

The Middle East and North Africa offered little scope for dam building. The rivers did not receive enough moisture flow, the topography did not permit storage construction, the rivers were too seasonal, the headwaters did not carry enough, and the evaporation losses were too large.[35] Where Europeans ruled, settlers tried to trap and use more water than before. These projects were local and limited to narrow strips of land near the seaboard and the deltas. A case in point is Somalia. Lack of surface water was acute in the Horn of Africa, one region where there was little scope to create dams, canals, reservoirs, and deep wells. Geography—the lack of perennial rivers and easily accessible groundwater—limited the prospects of projects that might work. Except Somalia, to a limited extent, the countries in the Horn did not have significant transboundary water to share either. These conditions persisted into the late twentieth century because the states in the region earned too little money and were too exposed to the risk of contestations to consider large public projects. Instead of water harvesting, the economies adapted via the composition of trade, relying on the import of "water-rich"

[34] Freidrich W. Freise, "The Drought Region of Northeastern Brazil," *Geographical Review*, 28(3), 1938, 363–378, cited text on p. 374.
[35] Gabi El-Khoury, "Water Resources in Arab Countries," *Contemporary Arab Affairs*, 7(2), 2014, 339–349.

154   WATER AND DEVELOPMENT

goods like rice and exporting water-conserving goods like arid-area animals. Puntland is a prime example of adaptation to aridity through trade.[36]

In North Africa, the most promising region for big schemes was Morocco. Although it was known that Morocco had the greatest water resources of all the colonized lands in North Africa, harnessing this resource was not a simple matter. It was unevenly distributed, much of the rainfall and snowmelt water was trapped in a mountainous area where extensive cultivable plains did not exist, the rivers were short, and their flow seasonal. The Atlas Mountains, however, created a unique scope for harvesting water downstream. Using that opportunity, eleven dams were planned and constructed in Algeria around 1920. Their combined capacity when fully functional was estimated at a little over 6 percent of cultivable land. Still, these were significant projects because they did not rely on reviving ancient waterworks or even follow the same principle. Using this resource by erecting dams would first require serious mapping. This effort began in the 1920s, yielding precipitations and surface flow data. In 1941, the Centre des études hydrologiques was established in Rabat, which made a census of wells and bores.

In the 1920s, Théodore Steeg became the governor of Morocco and Algeria. His time in office earned him the nickname "the water governor." A string of dams was planned to supply irrigation and drinking water for cities and to produce hydropower. The oldest was El Kansera on the River Beht, designed in the late 1920s and constructed over the next ten years. A French engineer built a barrage on the Nfiss River south of Marrakesh in the 1930s, which generated a conflict with indigenous users of the seasonal water flow. The Mellah Dam was a small storage dam to supply drinking water to Casablanca, again a 1930s project. The Bin al-Widan, the last colonial-era project, came up in the Atlas in the late 1940s, mainly to generate power.

What did the colonial projects add up to? The colonial-era dams were small by international standards. The El Kansera could irrigate twenty-four to twenty-eight thousand hectares but irrigated a fraction of that capacity. In contrast, the contemporary Mettur Dam in South India could irrigate two hundred thousand hectares. However, projects designed soon after Moroccan independence were more extensive in scale. The scale of extension of intensive or commercial cultivation was small. But these did give rise to a "developed area" growing export crops like olives, fruit trees, and cereals

---

[36] Melvin Woodhouse and Abdi Hassan Muse, "Water Policy in Puntland State, Somalia," *Waterlines*, 28(1), 2009, 79–88.

in the relatively green Tadla Plains in the country's center. The big hope, wheat, was a successful export only because of a favorable tariff regime in France.

Extracting water from hundreds of feet below ground was expensive in the nineteenth century. But the cost came down substantially in the mid-twentieth century with growing knowledge of hydrogeology.

Groundwater in Australia

Like Brazil, Australia was a mixture of arid and wet land zones. The first settlers arriving at the turn of the nineteenth century found cultivable lands in well-watered valleys, river basins, and cleared forests. The move by graziers toward the arid interior occurred decades later, and as riparian pastures were in limited supply, they depended on exploiting artesian well water.[37] Eighty percent of Australia is forbiddingly arid. Where seasonal rains occurred at all, herding was possible. The aboriginal population of the continent, who lived in the interior or were pushed back there by the European settlers, had been nomadic. One of their key assets was knowledge of where the waterholes were. From observing these groups, the Europeans could see that herding was possible on the fringes of arid tracts. Between 1850 and 1880, the government gave grazing leases to many settlers willing to go to the arid fringe. For decades, settler pastoralism sought seasonal surface water and river basins, much like the indigenous inhabitants had done. Flock sizes increased but were also vulnerable to droughts. Some ranchers created large storage tanks for sheep grazing over a wide area. No human action, however, was enough to evade droughts.

The conditions changed dramatically with the discovery of groundwater and the construction of large waterworks. In 1879, the Great Artesian Basin, a large (over 656,000-square-mile) waterbody spread over central and northern Australia, was discovered.[38] Borewells rapidly increased in number after that. Between 1880 and 1913, Queensland sheep stock about tripled "due largely to the greatly improved water supply derived from the artesian

---

[37] R.L. Heathcote, *Back of Bourke: A Study of Land Appraisal and Settlement in Semi-arid Australia*, Melbourne: Melbourne University Press, 1965.

[38] Craig D. James, Jill Landsberg, and Stephen R. Morton, "Provision of Watering Points in the Australian Arid Zone: A Review of Effects on Biota," *Journal of Arid Environments*, 41(1), 1999, 87–121.

156 WATER AND DEVELOPMENT

sources."[39] Around 1914, there were over two thousand of these, and the combined water extraction was estimated at 700 million gallons daily.[40] With a total population of 2.2 million people in 1881, that level of extraction translates into a per capita daily entitlement (350 gallons) that must have been among the world's highest ever (an average person is believed to need a minimum of 20 gallons per day). A severe drought could still affect this resource; a shallow well might turn brackish. However, the basin provided a level of water security unparalleled in any other dry region except northern Mexico.

A completely different kind of water regime took shape in the southeast, near the mountains that gave rise to almost all of Australia's major rivers and lakes. In this landscape, the settlers built a network of "dams, pipes, channels and drains." They "chose an economic path of exporting a select set of water-intensive products using increasingly water-intensive infrastructure."[41]

Among tropical countries, Australia was extraordinarily lucky with water. But this was not an advantage in isolation from others. Being a settler colony, it was a major destination for British capital export. Also, as a settler colony, pastoralism and farming could develop side by side from scratch. There were no ancient privileges that farmers would take away from herders. The aboriginal population had declined and did not operate on the scale the settlers did. Most pastures were private, ranch-style assets rather than open-access property.

Groundwater in the Middle East

In the Arabian Peninsula, during the twenty-odd years between establishing Saudi dominion after World War I and the discovery and development of oil in the 1940s, the king actively explored technological options to harvest and store water. No part of the peninsula received more than about a foot of rain annually, and all of it was hyper-arid. However, in the southwest, in regions bordering the Persian Gulf, there was enough rainfall to sustain seasonal agriculture. The peninsula also had aquifers in the center (Najd), east (Al-Hasa), and northwest (Hijaz, areas bordering Jordan), and almost none

[39] Griffith Taylor, "Agricultural Regions of Australia. Instalment I," *Economic Geography*, 6(2), 1930, 109–134, cited text on p. 132.

[40] Anon., "The Great Artesian Basin of Australia," *Journal of the Royal Society of Arts*, 62(3202), 1914, 438–440.

[41] Kylie Carman-Brown, *Following the Water: Environmental History and the Hydrological Cycle in Colonial Gippsland, Australia, 1838–1900*, Canberra: ANU Press, 2019, 16.

in the south and southeast (Rub al-Khali). Some of that water occurred in sedimentary rock layers, making it expensive and potentially nonrenewable to extract.

In the 1930s, these aquifers' capacity was unknown, nor had they been accurately mapped. The kingdom had emerged from Najd, which had artesian wells, and as it expanded control in the interwar period, the king began to believe that "water was the key to political power."[42] Acting on that belief, he invited American engineers to survey water resources and suggest ways to expand irrigated agriculture. The water mapping project did not deliver dramatic results. But a closer look below ground led to the world-changing discovery of oil deposits (in Al-Hasa). The kingdom continued the water exploration project, but water was no longer a "key" to its power.

As the introduction to this chapter mentioned, not all solutions to seasonality relied on big engineering. Dry farming, disease prevention and control, and urban water systems were less capital intensive, but challenging in other ways.

Dry Farming

In the 1890s, US agronomists and farmers experimented with dry farming or farming with little or no irrigation. The most famous idea was "packing," or firming the subsoil and retaining a thin surface soil cover so that moisture naturally occurring in the subsoil withstood evaporation. As it became known, the Campbell system was designed in the US Great Plains. Hardy Campbell was a farmer with unusually keen observation power who discovered specific soil properties that dry farming utilized. However, his system was never universally accepted in the United States. There were many skeptics. Of the different soil types in the Great Plains, only one suited dry farming. The idea initially enthused "settlers" struggling with aridity in South Africa and Palestine around the turn of the twentieth century.[43] In South Africa, opinion later became divided, and some observers thought that expanding agriculture in marginal lands at the expense of grazing land on the promise of the Campbell method would be a risk.

---

[42] Toby C. Jones, "State of Nature: The Politics of Water in the Making of Saudi Arabia," in Alan Mikhail, ed., *Water on Sand: Environmental Histories of the Middle East and North Africa*, Oxford: Oxford University Press, 2012, 231–250, cited text on p. 239.

[43] Sarah T. Phillips, "Lessons from the Dust Bowl: Dryland Agriculture and Soil Erosion in the United States and South Africa, 1900–1950," *Environmental History*, 4(2), 1999, 245–266.

158   WATER AND DEVELOPMENT

Dry farming contained a whole package of measures besides packing—adaptation of plants from Central Asia, for example. Packing, which came with the dramatic claim that it made agriculture possible without any artificial irrigation, was the most famous element in the package. But another aspect, the practice of long fallow, became more popular. Farmers noticed that even if the physics behind it was disputed, long fallow enabled land to regain subsoil moisture better than continuous cultivation. The large farms in the plains of the southwestern United States made the practice feasible.[44] Moving southward, as average summer temperatures rose nearer the border with Mexico and the Tropic of Cancer, the concept of agriculture without irrigation became unpromising because of the extreme dryness of the soil. The dry farming dream never caught on, and the Dust Bowl's prolonged drought and wind erosion showed how great a struggle (and disaster risk) agricultural expansion in these vulnerable climates could be. In the second half of the twentieth century, mechanization, groundwater extraction, and irrigation development reduced these conservation experiments to a memory.

Croplands were not the only places the modern states wanted to reshape. Cities were another.

Water to the Cities

Except for canal projects in India and Egypt, the city was the main site of the application of large-scale hydraulics in the nineteenth-century colonies. Where the European colonialists took over an indigenous town, as the French did in Algiers, the settlers appropriated and sometimes inadvertently destroyed part of a preexisting water infrastructure.[45] Eventually, the appropriation meant that the wealthy had greater water access than the urban poor, though all consumed significantly less water per head than city-dwellers in Europe in the late nineteenth century. The former also had access to more secure water sources than the latter. That is, the rich were less susceptible to seasonal fluctuations. Where the colonial city emerged from Indo-European trade, as in Bombay, Madras, and Calcutta,

[44] Mary W.M. Hargreaves, "The Dry-Farming Movement in Retrospect," *Agricultural History*, 51(1), 1977, 149–165.
[45] Brock Cutler, "Imperial Thirst: Water and Colonial Administration in Algeria, 1840–1880," *Review of Middle East Studies*, 44(2), 2010, 167–175.

the infrastructure was rudimentary for all, but there was still an inequality: the rich had homestead wells, and the poor relied on surface water or common wells.

From this foundation, the city authorities tried to centralize the water supply to treat water better and distribute it more widely. The urban bias stemmed from growing anxiety over cholera and enteric diseases as migration increased without either more drinking water or adequate sewage. Migrants had to accept a life that provided little clean water. The administrators thought the Indian cultural sensibility was an obstacle to improvements in hygiene. "At home and abroad," writes the author of a study of urban water supply in colonial India, "rulers and reformers identified the same practical problems, the unhygienic habits of the working class or native city dweller, and the same abstract predicament, the moral degeneration of townspeople living among 'filth,' and applied the same environmental solutions."[46] It was plain enough that no one was immune to an epidemic that spread quickly in an urban setting. The rich came around to funding piped supplies, or a central storage containing treated water. In cities administered by the colonial authorities, like Delhi, the discussions on piped water supply reflected anxieties about Indian cultural practices more directly, leading to a similar outcome.[47]

Despite inequality, the city became more water-secure than the countryside and drew in migrants. As the settlers managed to lay claims on the water-secure croplands in French Algeria, more farmers migrated to the city. In Libya, the same thing happened.[48] In India, famines in the dry Deccan Plateau in 1896 drove many people into Bombay at the end of the nineteenth century. The overcrowded slums were the site of a plague epidemic that killed thousands the next year.

In part, the urban bias came from an institutional difference between the rural and the urban. Colonial states, such as British India, did not see most infrastructure as a pure public good and were keen to have all projects self-funded. Collecting a water tax from canal water was much more complicated and expensive because of high monitoring costs than collecting a water tax from city residents. In the cities, private parties were willing to spend money

---

[46] John Broich, "Engineering the Empire: British Water Supply Systems and Colonial Societies, 1850–1900," *Journal of British Studies*, 46(2), 2007, 346–365.

[47] Awadhendra Saran, *In the City, Out of Place: Nuisance, Pollution, and Dwelling in Delhi, c. 1850–2000*, Delhi: Oxford University Press, 2014.

[48] Mattia Bertazzini, "The Effect of Settler Farming on Indigenous Agriculture: Evidence from Italian Libya," *Economic History Review*, 76(1), 2023, 33–59.

160   WATER AND DEVELOPMENT

on water or partner with the state in the projects. The fact that wealthy residents often self-governed the cities made this partnership easier. No one paid taxes happily for projects that would help the nontaxpayers, too. Still, the anxiety that the rich merchants and industrialists felt about cholera and plague translated into action plans.

Disease was a vital target of these plans.

Disease Control

The intuition that tropical development required water intervention was reinforced by the experience of dealing with animal and human epidemics that came and went with droughts. Water quality varied by season. Diseases like cholera and schistosomiasis were directly associated with the quality of water, which was ordinarily poor in arid lands and worsened during droughts. Sanitation engineers, therefore, were inducted into the geoengineering enterprise. The water treatment and supply interventions eventually contributed to what Abdel Omran called the "receding pandemics" phase of an epidemiologic transition.[49] Public health and medicine to tackle just a few waterborne diseases could substantially bring down deaths from droughts.

This was not a linear movement from bad to better. It appears that in both South Asia and Africa, the initial effect of colonialism—focused on market integration and commercialization—was a rise in epidemic incidence, especially cholera, malaria, trypanosomiasis, and rinderpest. Around 1900, cholera, smallpox, plague, and malaria accounted for twenty-four out of a total forty deaths per one thousand people in South Asia, possibly a higher ratio than in the 1880s. By 1940, however, deaths from the four diseases fell below fourteen per thousand. The turning point came in 1920, after which the Indian population started to grow much faster. "Populations [in Africa]," writes Patrick Manning, "rose at a very modest rate from 1890, then accelerated from 1920 to 1950."[50] Manning's figures stand revised, but the revision does not change the inflection point.[51] In both regions, a part of

[49] A.R. Omran, "The Epidemiologic Transition: A Theory of the Epidemiology of Population Change," *Milbank Memorial Fund Quarterly*, 49(4), 1971, 509–538.

[50] Patrick Manning, "African Population, 1650–2000: Comparisons and Implications of New Estimates," in Emmanuel Akyeampong, Robert H. Bates, Nathan Nunn, and James Robinson, eds., *Africa's Development in Historical Perspective*, Cambridge: Cambridge University Press, 2014, 131–150.

[51] Ewout Frankema and Morten Jerven, "Writing History Backwards or Sideways: Towards a Consensus on African Population, 1850–2010," *Economic History Review*, 67(4), 2014, 907–931.

the actions that led to the epidemiologic transition involved water purification and a centralized supply of filtered water, significantly reducing cholera deaths and deaths during droughts. In India, the cities saw the first systematic attempts to filter water. African demographic history confirms the role of intervention in urban water supply. Life expectancy increased significantly (with inequalities persisting) in Cape Colony between 1900 and 1950, partly owing to smallpox control and water control.[52]

That is not all. The recent history of water in India suggests that a change in access and quality owed less to a top-down statist desire to improve welfare and more to many local and initially disjointed efforts: the municipal water supply schemes funded by merchants, easement law, movements for equality, press campaigns, and legislative autonomy.[53]

Equality movements played a powerful role in western India. Caste rules forbade the use by a lower-caste person of wells and tanks that the upper-caste people used. During the Deccan famines, these rules came under strain, and administrative officers sometimes overrode them. In the interwar period, an organized movement emerged to challenge these rules. The movement campaigned in the newly elected legislature, the courtroom, and the press. One of the pivotal moments in modern Indian history was the Mahad Satyagraha of 1926 when a spontaneous movement emerged from the people forbidden from using a town's public tank to assert their right to its water. Surely, such protests had happened before, and around this time, such protests were not confined to western India. But this event stands out for three reasons. First, it highlighted how universal the exclusion had been in a region where famines had hit hard only a generation ago. Second, it helped B.R. Ambedkar emerge in national politics, later becoming the most influential campaigner for caste equality. Third, the movement failed on the field but succeeded in the court. Water discrimination persisted into the late twentieth century with tenacity, but the caste rules sanctioning discrimination became legally and morally unstable.

Regional estimates confirm. For example, in the Senegal Basin, the population growth rate rose from well below 1 percent per year in the 1896–1920 period, to 1.4 percent in 1920–1954, accelerating further. "This period is characterized by the disappearance of famines followed by high mortality rates from the 1930s." Monique Chastanet, "Survival Strategies of a Sahelian Society: The Case of the Soninke in Senegal from the Middle of the Nineteenth Century to the Present," *Food and Foodways*, 5(2), 1992, 127–149, cited text on pp. 144–145.

[52] Charles Simkins and Elizabeth van Heyningen, "Fertility, Mortality, and Migration in the Cape Colony, 1891–1904." *International Journal of African Historical Studies*, 22(1), 1989, 79–111.

[53] Tirthankar Roy, *Monsoon Economies: India's History in a Changing Climate*, Cambridge, MA: MIT Press, 2022.

162 WATER AND DEVELOPMENT

Like human diseases, cattle diseases in the tropics were partly seasonal and environmental. The efforts to combat these diseases were attempts to overcome the environment. Cattle disease had a devastating impact on the pastoralist economy. How often these events happened, why, and even the exact disease remain obscure in documents from before the great rinderpest outbreak in the 1890s. But the causal link with droughts was obvious enough. "In Ethiopia and the Nilotic Sudan, rinderpest coincided with a drought in 1888–89."[54] The connection with droughts was evident not so much in the etiology of the disease but in transmission. During periods of exceptional dryness, cattle crowded into small areas with more water, spreading the disease quickly. Thus, the disease spread more in dry-season grazing lands than in wet-season grazing lands, which were more dispersed.

The impact of the cattle epidemic was not only the loss of assets for the herders. It weakened the clan leaders, whose power stemmed from livestock holdings, and sometimes encouraged them to try out predatory taxation. A precolonial method of restocking after diseases—raids—was no longer available in the late nineteenth century. Replenishing stock by purchasing animals was unsafe due to the risk of reigniting the epidemic. More international trade in livestock in the late nineteenth century provided a way to restock quickly. At the same time, it exposed the indigenous stock to the transmission of new diseases. There is a theory that the rinderpest came from Indian cattle imported into east-central Africa. Eventually, disease control contributed to a sharp rise in livestock (in East Africa) and, in turn, to overgrazing and declining quality of pastures.[55]

Conclusion

The colonial states' modest financial capability limited the impact of geo-engineering in Asia and Africa. The one exception to this statement was water treatment for disease control, which initiated a fall in death rates and a demographic transition, apparently throughout the arid tropics. Water engineering also created fresh patterns of inequality. Still, these moves defined the role of the state in water. Dams needed states even more because they

---

[54] Holger Weiss, "'Dying Cattle': Some Remarks on the Impact of Cattle Epizootics in the Central Sudan during the Nineteenth Century," *African Economic History*, 26, 1998, 173–199.

[55] Harold F. Heady, 'Rangeland Development in East Africa,' in David Brokensha, ed., Ecology and Economic Development in Tropical Africa, Berkeley: University of California Press, 1965, 73–82.

were costly projects. If some colonial states could at least consider borrowing abroad, few independent states could do that. Some princely states in India wanted to build dams, but British India refused to guarantee their borrowings. Sharing power with feudal chiefs, these rulers could not risk radical tax reform.

Globally, in the interwar years, dams were changing the idea of economic development of the arid tropics. A dam constructed near the headwaters of a river could store enough water to last the dry season. It could generate electricity. Thus, a dam would serve the needs of wet and dry areas, the countryside and the cities, commercial agriculture, and industrialization. The enthusiasm for the multipurpose river valley projects, therefore, signified the arrival of a new model of world development. The model implied that if greening the arid tracts proved costly, industrialize them. From a theory that said "the problem was a lack of water, so the solution was to accumulate water," the thinking said that the region needed to industrialize to reduce its dependence on rainfed, low-yield season-bound agriculture.[56] One stone would kill two birds—poverty and overdependence on agriculture—and this was the multipurpose river valley project centered on a large dam. Aided by funding arrangements, the newly independent nation-states profoundly impacted advancing that agenda.

---

[56] A quote by an academic, cited in Ariaster B. Chimeli, Carolyn Z. Mutter, and Chet Ropelewski, "Climate Fluctuations, Demography and Development: Insights and Opportunities for Northeast Brazil," *Journal of International* Affairs, 56(1), 2002, 213–234.

Chapter Eight
The Big Push

Geoengineering—deep drilling, dams, reservoirs, interbasin transfers, basin management, and hydroelectric power for cities and industries—so inspired economists and politicians in the newly independent states of the mid-twentieth century that development became by default a state responsibility. In the 1980s, the sociologist Peter Evans coined the phrase *developmental state* to define a type of state that existed to make development. Such a state stood apart from lobbies and interest groups, sometimes holding dictatorial power.[1] The concept is useful, but misleading. Most users use the term to mean that developmentalism was a tool for industrialization and a new idea that was adopted because it sounded good. Not so. Developmentalism was necessary to address an ancient idea, indeed an ancient state matter—water control—only with more money and better science than in ancient times. States in tropical societies might want to become developmental in water matters, but they could not access the financial and knowledge resources to meet that aim. Late-twentieth-century states could do that because they commanded more credit internationally, thanks to their image of serving development, foreign aid, and mobile capital.

Investing in water was a life-and-death matter for new states. Traditional livelihoods in the countryside depended on rains and floods. Colonial development policy concentrated on trade and the cities even if the countryside delivered the export articles. The land yield was low, and the farmers were poor. Agriculture and pastoralism were environmentally sustainable because they adapted to natural moisture influx. However, they were not economically sustainable from the 1920s on as population growth rates rose. The new states needed to control rather than merely adapt to natural moisture influx.

On that ambition, there was a deep connection between colonial and postcolonial developmentalism. It was more of an ideological bridge.

---

[1] For a restatement, see Peter B. Evans, "Predatory, Developmental, and Other Apparatuses: A Comparative Political Economy Perspective on the Third World State," *Sociological Forum*, 4(4), 1989, 561–587.

Water and Development. Tirthankar Roy, Oxford University Press. © Oxford University Press (2025). DOI: 10.1093/oso/9780197802397.003.0008

THE BIG PUSH   165

A Continuity

Water was always present in the conception of development and state leadership. The colonial scientists and bureaucrats had placed it there. Historians sometimes imply that the colonial development policy was a matter of consolidating and justifying foreign rule. Colonial agricultural plans came from a misreading of nature, reflecting a representation of nature—possibly false, certainly ill-informed, and one that entailed beliefs in the superiority of European science and a disdain for indigenous science.[2] The scientists and officers blamed indigenous land management techniques for the degradation of land and indirectly justified foreign rule for its access to superior science, settler agriculture, and laws of access. The hangover of that discourse, historians claim further, persists into the present day, and has even been reinforced under the specter of climate change and resource scarcity.[3]

The thesis that colonial knowledge was a bundle of politically charged rhetoric has left a legacy. The postcolonial development plans, according to many anti-dam activists and scholars, imbibed the colonial sentiment, as much driven by representations, beliefs, rhetoric, and "globally dominant governmentalities," and with as little regard for local knowledge and the welfare of real people, as the colonial thinking had displayed.[4] "Technical knowledge," according to one study of North Africa, "is more appreciated than traditional knowledge, considered as obsolete."[5] A big part of the anti-dam campaign in the developing world in the late twentieth century takes that position.

This position recycles a legend that is not completely consistent with the facts. Indigenous knowledge was not demonstrably capable of dealing with poverty and population growth. Colonial knowledge was not a static thing. It needed to adapt and learn, precisely because it failed to deliver significant results. Over time, there was a serious engagement with climate, drought risk, monsoons, and seasonality. Postcolonial states inherited that new learning and built on it. "Flood and famine," said the National Planning

---

[2] See several essays in Diana K. Davis and Edmund Burke III, eds., *Environmental Imaginaries of the Middle East and North Africa*, Athens: Ohio University Press, 2011.

[3] Tor A. Benjaminsen and Pierre Hiernaux, "From Desiccation to Global Climate Change," *Global Environment*, 12(1), 2019, 206–236.

[4] Paola Minoia, "Mega-irrigation and Neoliberalism in Postcolonial States: Evolution and Crisis in the Gharb Plain, Morocco," *Geografiska Annaler*, Series B, 94(3), 2012, 269–286, cited text on p. 269.

[5] Ibid, 1.

166 WATER AND DEVELOPMENT

Committee (India) in 1947, "are two aspects of one problem, development of the water resources of the country."[6] The committee repeated an idea that had long been familiar in the tropics. As we saw in Chapter 4, ancient canals were often created for flood control or spreading water across space, while reservoirs and cisterns for storage and recycling water between seasons were famine-prevention tools. Both types of work would exist side by side.

Another colonial-era discourse, mistakenly attributed to crude Malthusianism, was that resources were threatened by population growth. On the contrary, it reflected not so much anxiety about overpopulation but anxiety about the vulnerability of the resources in question. In drier regions than India, livestock and the human population started rising sharply from the second quarter of the twentieth century, making food production a life-and-death matter and raising the pressure on pastoral orbits. These trends began in the colonial era but intensified in the postcolonial years, so older discussions on desiccation or land degradation returned. There was a parallel discussion about demography. In analyses of the 1970s Sahelian famines, when large numbers of herders moved from the desert fringes toward relatively well-watered agricultural areas, some authors reflected on a process of overexpansion and stressed pastures that had preceded this crisis and led to it in a sense.

In West and East Africa, around World War II, the colonial authorities had invested in boreholes and wells, which continued after independence with international funding. These water sources and immunization programs increased the number and quality of cattle. Some of the experts involved in this development had warned West African governments that range management was compromised with herds' growth among pastoralist and farming populations.[7] The great droughts exposed the imbalance starkly.

And Two Forms of Discontinuity

On the other hand, in two ways, the nation-states changed the colonial inheritance. One way was the reallocation of property rights (Chapter 4). Settler and corporate landholdings went to indigenous owners, though the process happened at variable speeds between regions and between types of landholdings (a slower process in plantations than farmlands). In some

---

[6] Cited in Tirthankar Roy, *Monsoon Economies: India's History in a Changing Climate*, Cambridge, MA: MIT Press, 2022.

[7] Nicole Ball, "Drought and Dependence in the Sahel," *International Journal of Health Services*, 8(2), 1978, 271–298.

THE BIG PUSH   167

cases, as with the Sri Lankan or Indian tea industry, where ownerships changed or foreign owners were forced out, a whole business was threatened. Little research is available on the business collapse following decolonization and the capital flight.

Whether the settlers had grabbed the best land, depriving indigenous farmers, or not, the reverse grabbing and exodus that happened after independence was almost uniformly damaging as it disrupted the flow of capital, managerial capability, and market access. In North Africa (and elsewhere), large estates became the fields of collectivization experiments with often disastrous results. In Algeria, the hurried exit of settler farmers caused a retreat of capital and business assets. "The financially sound, modest European farms that dominated the region have been replaced with a sequence of cooperative settlement types that were economically and technologically unsuccessful."[8] Algeria lost a lucrative market for wine in France, which the settler farmers had served before. In parallel with a deindustrialization following the retreat of expatriate business in India and Indonesia, "with rare exception, farming regression has followed all Third World colonial departures."[9] This was true of Morocco as well, where large capital-intensive French farming estates were either nationalized or occupied by the indigenous elite, reducing the flow of investment and managerial capability into these businesses.

The second and more positive way national governments departed from colonial history was in the scale of infrastructure investment. They did in the 1970s and the 1980s precisely the things the colonial governments had done in the 1930s—build dams and dig deep underground. The difference was not in ideology or commitment. The difference was in financial capacity. The nation-states built thousands of dams, whereas their predecessors had built a few.

In the World's Arid Areas, a Revolution Had Begun

The history of damming rivers in poorer countries forms a vast literature. Scholars contributing to it often write as if dams were an expression of a political project: the display of imperial power or nationalism. The historian Daniel Klingensmith calls India's dam-building drive in the 1950s

---

[8] Edward Karabenick, "A Postcolonial Rural Landscape: The Algiers Sahel," *Yearbook of the Association of Pacific Coast Geographers*, 53, 1991, 87–108, cited text on pp. 106–107.
[9] Ibid., 107.

168 WATER AND DEVELOPMENT

and the 1960s "nationalist engineering" (Figure 8.1).[10] Others attribute the dam drive to a late-twentieth-century "blind belief" that these expensive projects "can be uncritically accepted as panaceas for the problems of underdevelopment."[11]

Individual politicians may have pushed projects to satisfy their ego or ideological beliefs, but there were powerful grounds to justify dams—so much so that the idea was rooted in the culture of the places that suffered extreme seasonal variations in temperature and rainfall. That damming a stream when it was in full flow was the best way to deal with water shortages in the dry seasons, just as creating a canal to divert excess rainwater was necessary in the wet season, was common sense. It did not need the support of science or imperialism to be persuasive. Its appeal was intuitive, universal, and ancient. Advances in hydroengineering, however, added a lot more data on the degree of seasonality in water flows.

The extent of seasonality the data revealed was staggering. Around 1900, the mighty Godavari would have a million cubic feet of water flow per second on an exceptionally wet October day near its confluence. In contrast, the river's upper reaches were reduced to "a series of shallow pools" in April or May.[12] The variation in seasonal moisture influx between the dry and the wet seasons in Niger and Logon Basins was of a similar order.[13] Before a string of dams (1965–1985) came up, the Niger in northwestern Nigeria had a ratio of summer to spring flow of seven to one. Its tributary Benue in east-central Nigeria had a September-March ratio of fifty to one.[14] In 1965, over 60 percent of the annual flow in the Sokoto River, a significant source of surface water in northwestern Nigeria, occurred in three months of the year.[15] Around 2000, "the Indus River measured at Kalabagh can change from 70 km^3 during the summer to 12 km^3 during the winter."[16] In the 1920s, Melvin Knight reported results of measurements in major artesian systems in North

[10] Daniel Klingensmith, *One Valley and a Thousand: Dams, Nationalism, and Development*, Oxford: Oxford University Press, 2007.

[11] Rohan D'Souza, Pranab Mukhopadhyay, and Ashish Kothari, "Re-evaluating Multi-purpose River Valley Projects: A Case Study of Hirakud, Ukai and IGNP," *Economic and Political Weekly*, 33(6), 1998, 297–302, cited text on p. 297.

[12] Bombay, *Report on the Famine of the Bombay Presidency*, Bombay: Government Press, 1903, 8.

[13] See, for example, Jean Cabot, *Le Bassin du Moyen Logone*, Paris: ORSTOM, 1965.

[14] P.J. Wagland, "Kainji and the Niger Dams Project," *Geography*, 54(4), 1969, 459–463.

[15] W.M. Adams, "Traditional Agriculture and Water Use in the Sokoto Valley, Nigeria," *Geographical Journal*, 152(1), 1986, 30–43.

[16] Undala Z. Alam, "Questioning the Water Wars Rationale: A Case Study of the Indus Waters Treaty," *Geographical Journal*, 168(4), 2002, 341–353.

Figure 8.1 Jawaharlal Nehru and M. Visvesvaraya, c. 1947
Two individuals, a politician and an engineer, greatly influenced India's water policy because both believed that river valley projects would serve India best. Visvesvaraya (1861–1962) was a civil engineer with worldwide experience in constructing dams to regulate water velocity. As a senior officer of Mysore state, serving in several capacities, he supervised the construction of a major multipurpose dam in the southern Deccan, the Krishna Raja Sagar, which started in 1911.
Source: Alamy Stock Photos

Africa; the flow of one of these systems (the Chelif) varied in the ratio of one to three hundred, and a second (the Macta) one to four hundred, between seasons in the same year.[17]

[17] Melvin M. Knight, "Water and the Course of Empire in North Africa," *Quarterly Journal of Economics*, 43(1), 1928, 44–93.

170   WATER AND DEVELOPMENT

It did not require complex thinking to imagine what could be done if the extra water could be tamed, stored, and made usable in the dry seasons. What these ideas did need, and received in the twentieth century from the US West, was the knowledge of how to do this on a scale big enough to create whole new cities or thousands of square miles of farmlands and orchards from barren fields. Governments everywhere embarked on "expansive development projects" to grow the scale and change the hardware in water sector development.[18]

The golden age of dam building began when Western European governments and the World Bank offered cheap loans to finance the projects. After the postwar reconstruction boom ended, the Western governments wanted to generate business for factories and engineering firms. Dams were enormously expensive to build. Their high capital cost tended to rise during construction, which never ran according to plan. Besides a significant draft on taxpayers' money, dam projects needed foreign aid or the commitment to sell cheap power or mineral contracts.

Beginning in the 1940s with the Bhakra Dam in Punjab and the Hirakud in Orissa, the Indian government grew ambitious. In the next decade, it designed major projects on the Rihand and Chambal in central India, Koyna in the west, and Krishna and Tungabhadra in the southern Deccan Plateau. Between the 1950s and the 1970s, more than a thousand small and large constructions appeared in India, mainly in the Deccan Plateau.

Dam projects began in Africa in the 1950s, first in perennial river systems: the Nile (the Aswan High), Zambezi, and Volta. The Volta River project in Ghana was started to supply power to an aluminum smelting company, which was a partner in the endeavor. The Sahelian drought of the 1970s strengthened the impulse to build more dams. The 1950s and 1960s saw rapid population growth in Sahel-Sudan, accompanied by a rise in livestock numbers, destruction of woodlands for fuel, and expansion of farmland. Human intervention led to a decline in pasture vegetation, grass species, and soil erosion. The droughts generated a discussion on the spread of the Sahara southward. No matter the cause, building more dams and extending farmlands seemed to be the only effective response to climate change. The Manantali dam in the Senegal River Basin (1976–1992) was West Africa's

---

[18] Anna Bohman and Kaisa Raitio, "How Frames Matter—Common Sense and Institutional Choice in Ghana's Urban Water Sector," *Journal of Environment and Development*, 23(2), 2014, 247–270.

"version of the High Aswan to master the river and to remake the valley" and a legacy of the 1970s drought.[19]

The Sahelian droughts also focused attention on Lake Chad. In the past, the sustainability of the lake had been much discussed (Figure 8.2). Although its water level was not directly influenced by local rainfall variations, the lake did shrink considerably after the prolonged droughts of the 1970s and 1980s. Usually a shallow lake, its extent proved particularly vulnerable to climate effects. As population and livestock numbers grew in the area around the lake (which now has one of the world's highest population growth rates), pressure on resources became intense, often breaking out into conflicts over land and water. The extreme variability of water in Lake Chad and of rainfall in the areas where the water came from forced the locals to combine various livelihood options, from farming to fishing, trading, and circular and seasonal migrations. Most development projects tend to be rooted in an area—in this case, projects needed to work on source regions much farther away.[20]

In Nigeria, two large projects were implemented in the 1970s: the South Chad Irrigation Project and the Baga Polder. The former involved channeling excess water into fields to grow better varieties of millets. The infrastructure appeared, but in a year when the lake had receded. Thereafter, it never delivered the promised expansion of cultivation and was practically abandoned. Baga Polder was a similar land reclamation scheme using water drawn from the lake, producing mixed results. The problem in all cases was that when the lake receded, the infrastructure consisting of pumps, dams, and channels lay idle, and some could not be used anymore. In addition, Nigeria constructed twenty-seven dams on the rivers feeding water into Lake Chad in the 1970s. Subsequently, siltation, water diversion, and groundwater mining in these basins reduced water flow into the lake.

The Moroccan state started large-scale hydraulic planning in the 1970s. The most important project to follow was the Projet Sebou. Sebou is the most important river in North Africa, and its origin is in the Middle Atlas. The project began in 1970 with public investment and foreign funding, including from the World Bank. The plan included ten large dams, forty-four

---

[19] President Diouf, cited in Frans J.G. Padt and Juan Carlos Sanchez, "Creating New Spaces for Sustainable Water Management in the Senegal River Basin," *Natural Resources Journal*, 53(2), 2013, 265–284, cited text on p. 273.

[20] Martin Evans and Yasir Mohieldeen, "Environmental Change and Livelihood Strategies: The Case of Lake Chad," *Geography*, 87(1), 2002, 3–13.

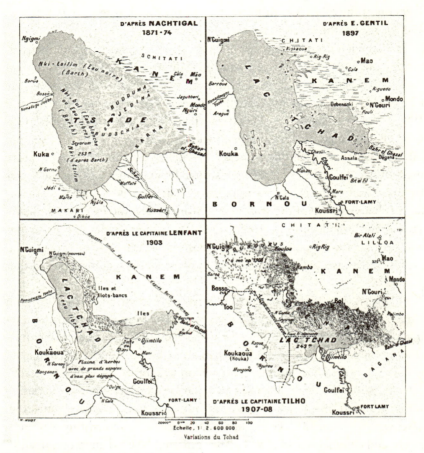

Figure 8.2 Variations in Lake Chad
A 1914 map from Grande Geographie Bong Illustree shows the lake's extent over a thirty-five-year period. Three years shown were years of severe droughts in the northern hemisphere tropics. However, the lake water was not too sensitive to rainfall in the region and did not shrink for that reason. As a result, the lake could provide insurance during drought years.
Source: Alamy Stock Photos

small dams, and thousands of pumping stations, wells, and canals. As with dams elsewhere, bureaucratic, financial, logistical, and political challenges delayed implementation. Forty years later, the project was still growing.[21] In the end, what took pressure off the Moroccan Atlas was not success with water schemes but outmigration, first toward the cities in Morocco and later

---

[21] Minoia, "Mega-irrigation and Neoliberalism."

toward France. The struggle to work harder on poor land with uncertain rainfall was unwinnable without this escape route. The same thing happened in the Senegal Basin, as described later.

After independence from colonial rule, the Tunisian state invested heavily in water. Dams were erected in the semi-arid zone, where river water was available. In the Kairouan alluvial plain of Central Tunisia, following floods that badly affected the Kairouan town, a dam was constructed in the Zeroud River Basin (Sidi Saad, 1982) for flood control and irrigation. The most dramatically ambitious scheme in North Africa was the Great Man Made River Project in Libya, which involved extracting underground water in the Sahara (also called fossil water because of its ancient geological age) and transporting it to the cities in the north. Explorations for oil created the first maps of underground water. The project took decades to mature and started delivering water to Tripoli and other coastal cities in the 1990s.

From the 1930s, the Mexican government pumped in big money for the construction of dams in the Sonora Basin. Between 1950 and 1970, irrigated agricultural land in the province doubled. The dam construction was not entirely a statist intervention. Private landholders and foreign investors played a supportive role in the policy. As the green revolution picked up, land degradation inevitably followed. To compensate for this, more chemical fertilizers were used, causing further stress.[22] See Chapter 5 on the definition of the green revolution as a water-fertilizer-seeds induced rise in land yield. As more water was made available, private "water grab, which occurred in diverse local contexts across Mexico, set the conditions for the burst of economic growth during the postwar years (1940–1970) known as the 'Mexican miracle.'"[23] A burst of private investment in deep wells in Mexico supported "the golden age of agriculture" (the 1940s).[24] Like water diversion in Soviet Central Asia to grow cotton, dams would "industrialize nature" and "rebuild nature."[25] "The triumph of the bull-dozer and the mechanical excavator," wrote a 1956 study, made "an agrarian revolution" imminent in central Sudan.[26] In the late twentieth century, privately funded

---

[22] Sterling Evans, "Dams in the Desert," *Global Environment*, 12(1), 2019, 182–205.

[23] Casey Walsh, "Mineral Springs, Primitive Accumulation, and the 'New Water' in Mexico," *Regions and Cohesion*, 5(1), 2015, 1–25, cited text on p. 22.

[24] José Luis Moreno, "'A Never-Ending Source of Water': Agriculture, Society, and Aquifer Depletion on the Coast of Hermosillo, Sonora," *Journal of the Southwest*, 54(4), 2012, 545–568.

[25] Paul Josephson, "Stalin's Water Workers and Their Heritage: Industrialising Nature in Russia, 1950–Present," *Global Environment*, 10(1), 2017, 168–201.

[26] J.H.G. Lebon, "Rural Water Supplies and the Development of Economy in the Central Sudan," *Geografiska Annaler*, 38(1), 1956, 78–101, cited text on p. 100.

deep drilling from groundwater-rich America or Australia became global, spreading rapidly as economic growth and liberalization advanced capital accumulation in emerging economies. The state, by then, had retreated somewhat from waterworks. But the "global groundwater revolution" had taken hold.[27]

What did these efforts amount to? The world's water dataset is patchy and often difficult to read. Still, what there is would suggest that, in the late twentieth century, even the driest countries, like those in the Sahel, increased their annual freshwater withdrawal levels, total and per head. The India data are richer, suggesting that the trajectory had begun around 1880 and accelerated in the twentieth century (see also Figure 1.2).[28] A recent reconstruction of water use data for country groups answers the question. Figure 8.3 shows that there was a worldwide acceleration in the scale of water harvest from the 1950s, though the rising trend began in all regions of the world from the early twentieth century. This may seem like an attempt to catch up with population growth, which it was—to some extent. But there are two crucial differences between regions.

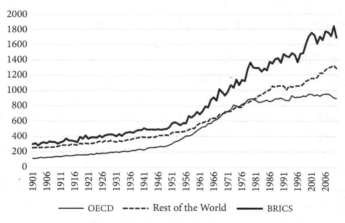

Figure 8.3 Annual Freshwater Withdrawal, 1901–2000 (billion cubic meters)

Source: Hannah Ritchie and Max Roser, "Water Use and Stress," https://ourworldindata.org/water-use-stress. BRICS stands for Brazil, Russia, India, China, and South Africa.

---

[27] Jac van der Gun, "The Global Groundwater Revolution," Oxford Research Encyclopedia, Environmental Science, https://doi.org/10.1093/acrefore/9780199389414.013.632.
[28] Roy, *Monsoon Economies*.

First, domestic and industrial use of freshwater dominated the richer countries' total, whereas agriculture did in poorer countries. World Bank data show that more than 90 percent of freshwater withdrawal in South Asia in 2017 was used in agriculture. In sub-Saharan Africa, nearly 80 percent is used in agriculture. In other words, relatively more water in these regions is allocated to food production. This is so because of the much higher risk of drought and famine in some of these areas and because intensive agriculture is naturally more water-intensive in many of them.

The second difference, vast water access inequality, stems from geography. Members of the Organisation for Economic Co-operation and Development (OECD) have 28 percent of the world's renewable freshwater, South Asia 4 percent, and sub-Saharan Africa 10 percent. The combined population of South Asia and sub-Saharan Africa is well over double that of the OECD members. This imbalance is not a result of economic growth. The availability of freshwater is a geographical parameter and external to the economy. The cost of extracting water is also primarily geographical and is substantially higher in the tropics.

Therefore, whereas the desire to catch up with the West was a powerful sentiment in the 1950s, the actions that followed had a hydraulic dimension. That dynamism varied a lot between regions.

Regions

India and Pakistan

The immediate impetus to expand the Indus Basin canal system came from the Partition of Punjab into two parts: one in Pakistan and the other in India. Punjab canals were an impressive system, but by 1940 they did not meet the demands of the four million hectares of irrigated land that had come into existence. The Himalayan rivers did carry water throughout the year. However, in winter, the level dropped enough to starve the canal system. "Vast quantities of water go to waste in the summer, but there is not enough to go round in the winter."[29] Canals were beginning to be run only in winter, with limited effect. Where they could, Punjab farmers borrowed money to

---

[29] R. MacLagan Gorrie, "Soil and Water Conservation in the Punjab," *Geographical Review*, 28(1), 1938, 20–31.

176 WATER AND DEVELOPMENT

dig wells. After all that, the demand for water in the canal colonies in 1947 exceeded the system's capacity.

The Partition of India created a further complication. The sources for all five Punjab rivers were in India, whereas four basins occurred mainly in Pakistan territory. Both countries were committed to expanding the system's capacity because resettling peasant migrants was an urgent need. Both countries had limited options to plan such expansion. India acted on the Bhakhra Dam Project, first proposed in 1919, to impound the Sutlej and extend the Sirhind Canal to a larger area. Pakistan was keen to build reservoirs in the upper valleys, including Kashmir. The Indus Treaty (see Chapter 10) created a framework for regulated water use, though the treaty came under strain occasionally.

A few years before Indian independence, a modern flood control embankment on an Eastern Indian river, the Damodar, broke. The 1943 breach was not unusual as a breach. In this monsoon-fed river and its tributaries, the water level fluctuated a lot every season, and breaches happened occasionally. Flood control embankments were present in the region for centuries, perhaps millennia. No one knows how effective these were in preventing ancient floods. Indian scientists and engineers imbued with a nationalistic spirit argued, in the 1940s, that the ancient system had been neglected or built over by poorly planned flood control and railway construction works since the nineteenth century. This was true to some extent.

No matter the causes, the 1943 breach generated much heat and alarm because it stopped food transport when a war famine raged in Bengal. India was under a dual government at the time—not the best setup to design ambitious plans. Though state finances were in dire straits, a plan to build a series of dams to regulate the seasonality of the Damodar and its tributaries did take shape.[30] In 1944, the government of Bengal invited a senior designer of the Tennessee Valley project to plan flood control systems for Damodar and its tributaries, mainly Barakar. Four relatively low-capacity dams were planned, which came up in different years soon after India's independence in 1947. Although seen as projects with the combined aim of flood control and irrigation, the former objective was more important because much of the basin was not exactly arid. Subsequent assessments

---

[30] Sayantoni Datta, "Remembering the DVC Dream: Of Nationhood and Development Visions," Indian Institute of Advanced Studies, Shimla, 2013.

of its successes and failures—some by the early campaigners themselves—considered this one aim above others. By that aim, the Damodar project in its first three decades was a mixed blessing, for the dams and reservoirs were not large enough to hold excess water in exceptionally wet seasons. During heavy monsoons, the dams had to release water at the worst possible time only to save themselves, causing worse floods than before. This problem has not entirely disappeared even now. A massive investment then followed this initial boost in the upland rivers in southern and eastern India. The 1970s green revolution further endorsed the investment in canals.

The Nile Basin

In the 1950s, Egypt's second president, Gamal Abdel Nasser, took decisive steps to generate economic development. The drive was new, but the instrument was old: a big dam. The Aswan High Dam was conceived. The Aswan High Dam plan included an enormous reservoir spread about four hundred miles north and south. The southern tip of the lake would be inside Sudan. Sudan opposed the project, and in retaliation, Egypt withdrew its help from constructing a reservoir at Roseires in Sudan. Following military rule in Sudan, negotiations began again, ending in a water-sharing treaty in 1959. The structure of the 1959 agreement was like that of 1929, except that Egypt declared a slightly larger entitlement for itself—and for Sudan an even larger entitlement of the annual flow—leaving significantly less than before "unallocated" or usable by other countries. The dam came up with Soviet help in the 1960s. It made a significant impact on irrigation.

As Ahmad Shokr has shown in a study of the origin of the Aswan High Dam and the reservoir that formed in its wake, the concept of the dam and the idea of state involvement in water projects were not new to the Nile Basin.[31] A nationalist sentiment or a display of power might have reinforced the drive to build but did not lead to it. In the early twentieth century, colonial administrators discussed how interventions could be scaled up to meet the needs of a growing population and export commodities. An older commercialization experience based on cotton and canals, the availability

---

[31] Ahmad Shokr, "Hydropolitics, Economy, and the Aswan High Dam in Mid-century Egypt," *Arab Studies Journal*, 17(1), 2009, 9–31.

178   WATER AND DEVELOPMENT

of engineering expertise, and economic and geological data to forecast the future maintained continuity in policy. Already in that time, attention was starting to shift from canals to reservoirs.

Sustaining the capacity of the Aswan dam was always a problem, partly because of its enormous scale. The White Nile was more promising because it flowed through water-rich countries. Since the 1960s, an information network called Hydromet has been working to collect data on the equatorial lakes. An ambitious plan to drain the vast Sudd swamps in South Sudan to feed the White Nile was defeated by South Sudanese defense forces, then a liberation army fighting for independence.

After the revised Nile Waters Agreement gave more water to Sudan, the Sudanese government set up more "pump schemes," extracting and selling water to lands accessible from these pumps. The original Gezira Scheme was located close to the Blue Nile on its west bank. After independence, pumping extended westward to the east bank of the White Nile. Dykes protected the water channels and the lands they served from Nile floods. The farmers fortunate enough to have land near these "permanent water-regulating" systems were "well-to-do, and enjoy the security of not having their livelihood subject to the vagaries of the Nile flood."[32] Some of the more substantial farmers obtained bank loans to install diesel pumps. Most farmers in the scheme and its offshoots were "tenants" after full nationalization of the scheme in 1957. Their tenancy was secure. The state agencies that invested in the scheme did not make profits; the farmers did. Taxpayers' money was transferred to the emerging farm lobby, an almost universal way farming bias worked in late-twentieth-century green revolution areas.

The area of intensive cash-crop cultivation based on these pump schemes was not small but by no means representative of agricultural conditions in Sudan. In 1980, a historian reflected, "Life away from the rivers is a harsh and constant struggle."[33] Not much changed. Most lands with any influx of river water depended on the "flush"—the annual flooding—or rainfall. In both cases, the land would remain idle for an extended period of the year. Relatively low-valued sorghum (dura, millet) was the main crop grown this way. Outside the riparian floodplains, agriculture was a part of an agropastoralist lifestyle. Groundwater played little or no role in plans to expand commercial agriculture because of northern Sudan's pre-Cambrian rocks.

[32] Ibid., 56.
[33] K.M. Barbour, "The Sudan since Independence," *Journal of Modern African Studies*, 18(1), 1980, 73–97, cited text on p. 80.

However, the development project had not been confined to the riparian area. Shortly before independence, an agricultural plan took shape in Kassala and Gedaref in eastern Sudan and east of the Blue Nile. This region had comparatively good seasonal rainfall and some forest cover. Until the 1950s, herders and millet-growing smallholders lived in this area. There are rivers in the region, but with little water in them in the dry seasons. The government scheme, partly funded by merchants, took some of the grazing lands and forest patches—eventually turning the smallholders into wage workers for the scheme—and introduced mechanization and commercial crops (chiefly sesame). The eastern Sudan projects quickly became a showpiece of environmental degradation. Until these schemes appeared, the area was thinly populated. As the population grew and urbanization proceeded, drinking water shortages became acute. Deforestation and the forced confinement of herders in limited grazing lands degraded these lands. The land yield fell.[34]

The Volta Basin

The Volta River dam plan was one of the earliest projects to start after colonialism ended in West Africa. The government of Ghana revived a British plan of 1914 to build a dam on the Akosombo Gorge to generate electricity and supply power to an aluminum smelting plant. Ghana's president Kwame Nkrumah gave that plan a lofty justification. "Newer nations, . . . which are determined by every possible means to catch up in industrial strength," he said in 1961, "must have electricity in abundance before they can expect any large-scale industrial advance."[35] Industrialization, more than irrigated farming, was the priority.[36] However, the formation of a reservoir was a potential asset for farmlands, especially to resettle displaced people, and that aspect became more prominent as the dam began to be used. In the long run, the river projects delivered power and irrigation water, yet they also showed the vulnerability of multipurpose projects in the face of extreme seasonality.

[34] Galal El-Din El-Tayeb and Anne Lendowski, "Environmental Degradation in Gedaref District," *Sudan Notes and Records*, 1, 1997, 135–157.

[35] Cited in D. Paul Lumsden, "The Volta River Project: Village Resettlement and Attempted Rural Animation," *Canadian Journal of African Studies*, 7(1), 1973, 115–132, cited text on p. 117.

[36] David Hart, *The Volta River Project: A Case Study in Politics and Technology*, Edinburgh: University of Edinburgh Press, 1980.

180 WATER AND DEVELOPMENT

Droughts could still reduce the water flow to such low levels as to cause power outages.

Volta was an example of how the Cold War intruded in African development. US president John F. Kennedy decided to help that aspiration and promised funding, which would be the first serious expression of his commitment to Africa's development and political neutrality. Nkrumah needed and welcomed the decision, for US participation would enable matching finances from other parties, including an American company that would set up the smelting firm. But, the loud anti-US and pro-communism political rhetoric that was part of Nkrumah's international image alarmed the foreign partners. Should the United States offer money and wean him away from full-blown communism or punish him by denying finance?[37] In the end, the former stance won, and the project happened.

The Zambezi Basin

In the second half of the 1950s, colonial authorities designed and built the Kariba Dam on the Zambezi mainly to generate electricity for the industrial and copper mining towns. Constructed with European engineers and World Bank money, the dam became a symbol simultaneously of development and displacement.[38] Since its commissioning, the reservoir has been among the largest in the world, and the dam itself has delivered water for agriculture and power for the major cities in Zambia and Zimbabwe.

The Cahora Bassa dam on the Zambezi was planned and implemented by the colonial ruler of Mozambique and opened days before the regime ended. When designed in the 1960s, the plan offered the same promises as multipurpose river valley projects elsewhere in the world: expansion of intensive agriculture, flood control downstream, power generation, and modern enterprises, especially in mining. One dam would have the capacity to transform lives in the Zambezi Valley. The ecology of the region around the dam site and the delta region were different. Both were exposed to the violence of tropical seasonality but in different ways. Some of the downstream region

[37] Thomas J. Noer, "The New Frontier and African Neutralism: Kennedy, Nkrumah, and the Volta River Project," *Diplomatic History*, 8(1), 1984, 61–79.
[38] Julia Tischler, *Light and Power for a Multiracial Nation: The Kariba Dam Scheme in the Central African Federation*, London: Palgrave, 2013.

was exposed to sudden devastating floods. Farther inland, the lower Zambezi valley was semi-arid, with agriculture dependent on the soils formed by the river, areas farther away being grasslands.

Constructed in a region racked by anticolonial guerilla war, the aim had to be reduced to electricity generation, mainly for export to South Africa. Political realities forced the regime to ally with the apartheid regime in South Africa and enter a deal. Because of the agreement, power lines symbolized the axis between the racist regime and the colonialists and came under attack.

Compared with other projects of similar scale, the dam had a limited impact on agriculture. Like dams elsewhere, this one submerged prime lands earlier enriched by the river's sediments and deprived the lands that escaped submergence of nutrients. New lands available for resettlement, therefore, were of poor quality. The obstructed sedimentation process affected the delta, and obstructed flows affected fishing, a significant business there.

That legacy persisted long after Mozambique's independence in 1975. For the socialist government that took over state power, industrialization and energy were priorities, and the shortage of foreign exchange was dire. The dam delivered energy to the cities and for export, but relatively little irrigation water or electricity to the villages. "The cash-starved nation," writes Allen Isaacman, "lacked the capital to develop the agricultural and industrial sectors that could utilize the cheap energy."[39] Socialist collectivization of agriculture reduced incentives for private investment.

Curiously, whereas for the expert who came from another world, Cahora Bassa was a symbol of failure and past exploitation, for insiders, it symbolized hope and showed the way for the future. Led by that sentiment, the socialist regime planned a second large dam on the Zambezi, the Mphanda Nkuwa. The project hoped to gather capital from nonlocal sources. A deal was signed with the Export-Import Bank of China in 2006 to finance the dam. This time around, nongovernmental organizations took an active interest in any dam project. International Rivers, an organization that works to protect and research river valleys and takes a generally anti-dam stance, criticized the second project, drawing a sharp reaction from the Mozambican government.

---

[39] Allen Isaacman, "Cahora Bassa Dam and the Delusion of Development," *Daedalus*, 150(4), 2021, 103–123, cited text on p. 111.

182 WATER AND DEVELOPMENT

The Senegal and Niger Basins

The colonial strategy that prioritized freedom of navigation on their rivers was abandoned by the newly formed republics of Africa, particularly those situated in the basins of Niger and Senegal. These states instead explicitly changed the legal regimes for water use as input in comprehensive development programs, including irrigation, power generation, and fishing.[40] The accent on trade and cargo movements went down.

Immediately after the 1970s droughts, an organization of the countries sharing the Senegal river basin decided to create a dam upstream in Manantali in Mali. A second dam, Diama, was planned closer to the delta to stop saltwater inflow upstream. The Diama dam, however, also encouraged rice cultivation. The Manantali dam was expected to supply water for power generation and agriculture. Not a large dam by world standards, the project was still far too expensive for local resources to fund. Potential foreign donors and funders did come forward, but the project also generated significant skepticism from the World Bank. It took decades for power generation to be functional. Irrigation potentials remained considerably below the level expected.

The dam gave the population living in the basin more water security and helped convert grazing lands into farmlands. But it was no answer to the desiccation of the western Sahel. Even as the water projects were getting ready, emigration to France speeded up. In the eyes of the locals, this was the most secure way to stabilize livelihoods. Emigration continued throughout the 1960s and the 1970s, and the economy grew dependent on remittances. That dependence persisted into the post-dam years.

After colonialism ended around 1960, the rulers of the newly independent countries sharing the Niger Delta made commitments to industrialization and intensive cultivation as their preferred development models, which further eroded herder power and brought in groups of peasants into the wetland zones. Dam-building projects added to the tendency, to which there were reverses and reactions, for the ruling elite did not have complete control over the territory, but law, development, and water projects combined to push in the same direction.[41] The integrated water-cum-power

---

[40] B.A. Godana, *Africa's Shared Water Resources: Legal and Institutional Aspects of the Nile, Niger and Senegal River Systems*, London: Frances Pinter, 1985.

[41] A. Benjaminsen and Boubacar Ba, "Farmer-Herder Conflicts, Pastoral Marginalisation and Corruption: A Case Study from the Inland Niger Delta of Mali," *Geographical Journal*, 175(1), 2009, 71–81.

development model upset the seasonal cycle in pastoralism by reducing access to dry-season pastures, which turned into irrigated farmland.

The Awash Basin

Awash is the only large river that originates and ends within Ethiopia. Its source is the highlands near Addis Ababa, and it ends after a roughly northeastern journey at Lake Abbe on the Ethiopia-Djibouti border. The river is rainfed, reducing its flow in the dry months (September to June). Some of the minor tributaries of the river dried up entirely in the dry season. But during the rains, the river overtopped and spread nutrient-rich silt over a wide area that sustained large herds of cattle.

The Awash Valley refers explicitly to the Afar region in northeastern Ethiopia. The Afar was the largest among several ethnic groups that peopled the valley, forming a small proportion of the country's population. Still, they commanded political significance because that number was spread over Djibouti, Eritrea, and Ethiopia. The region contained the territory of the Afar Imamate of Aussa (Awsa), the most significant controller of land in the area until the revolution in 1974, and the controller of farmland near the riverbanks. Because the sultanate could collect rent from tenant farmers, it could also spend more on protecting trade routes.

In the 1950s, the imperial state had grown interested in river valley projects in the Awash Basin. A hydroelectric project appeared in 1960 south of the Afar area (Koka dam). The dam proved helpful in controlling the seasonal water flow that would cause flash floods in the north earlier. This was not an unmixed benefit, however. The reduction in the floods also reduced the extent of dry season pastures. Therefore, the dam caused displacement of pastoralist groups.

In the next few years, the United Nations Development Programme and the Ethiopian government conducted surveys to develop a plan to control the flow of the Awash River. Now the aim was irrigation and power. The surveys claimed that the area under irrigation could rise a little over fourfold from 40,000 to 170,000 hectares if a few more dams were built at the right places. Early studies concluded that if this potential materialized, "more opportunities would be opened for the establishment of processing industries." Sulfur and potash were believed to exist in the valley. With the expansion of intensive agriculture, factories would process these materials

184   WATER AND DEVELOPMENT

and produce fertilizers.[42] The planned dams would produce power for these industries and supply water to their customers so that they demanded more of their goods. The dream of self-reinforcing economic growth needed just one step.

From the early 1970s, the Awash Valley projects "to administer" the river's waters had begun to encourage commercial cultivation in the basin.[43] Intensive agriculture spread after the dams. Sugar and cotton were the priorities ahead of the needs of the herders. Large firms with capital contributions from the state produced cotton at a much higher productivity than in rain-fed cultivation and produced sugar where no industry existed before. For the sultanate, the decision to encourage commercial cultivation was a matter of survival. The state could, in principle, nationalize any land, having proceeded to do that with some pastures.

The growth of agriculture and industry in the valley created some jobs for migrant workers, mainly from the highlands, but exposed the pastoralists to starvation. The basin lands formerly used for pastures were earmarked for commercial cultivation. Many Afar who never held legal titles migrated to marginal lands, where the quality of the pasture was poor, and consequently malnutrition among the herds spread. These projects also dried up the river and Lake Abbe. In the valley's lower reaches, the "process of underdevelopment" was stark. "[The] sedentary farming population had sharply increased after control of malaria."[44] Consequently, overstocking and competition over dwindling grazing lands increased too. The Awash Valley Authority's command over water and Afar claims to dry-season pastures clashed repeatedly. Conflicts also broke out regarding the rival claims over the project's water.

Against this backdrop of turbulence, the 1972–1974 famine began. By one popular account, the Ethiopian famine, intense among Afar pastoralists dependent on the Awash River plains, had owed partly to the government's move to develop hydroelectric plants and corporate plantations in the same area and using the same waters. There were other factors. Drought conditions prevailed from the end of the 1960s. As water quality deteriorated, a cholera epidemic killed large numbers. The 1972–1973 drought in the wake of these tragedies caused a "total loss of animals."[45] After the famine, some

---

[42] Addis Anteneh and Hailu Yemanu, "Development of the Awash Valley," c. 1970, available at https://www.ajol.info/index.php/ajol.

[43] Lars Bondestam, "People and Capitalism in the Northeastern Lowlands of Ethiopia," *Journal of Modern African Studies*, 12(3), 1974, 423–439.

[44] Helmut Kloos, "Development, Drought, and Famine in the Awash Valley of Ethiopia," *African Studies Review*, 25(4), 1982, 21–48, cited text on p. 33.

[45] Ibid., 35.

THE BIG PUSH   185

herders tried to rebuild their herds, but others became dependent on irrigated agriculture as wage laborers to obtain water and access famine relief. Farther south, near Koka, dam-induced displacement pushed some herders to take up fishing.

Famine returned in 1984–1987 and wrecked the Marxist regime, as a famine had wrecked imperial rule ten years earlier (Figure 8.4). With that knowledge, the coalition that ruled Ethiopia from 1988 needed no push to turn developmental. "Economic growth" became "a crucial component of the EPRDF's claim for legitimacy," and poverty was seen as "an existential threat" to the state.[46] The obstacle remained the same. Herders and smallholders lived on a resource that yielded little. Seasonality of rainfall made farmlands produce little. Herders were under pressure to turn into farmers. The solution was also old, inviting concessionary companies to develop farming and encourage the sedentarization of herders. From the late twentieth century, Ethiopia emerged as the leading land-lease country in Africa. On this occasion, the policy to promote intensive agriculture succeeded in the highlands.

So far, all the examples have been of multipurpose dams. In several other regions of the world, governments have built dams mainly for electricity generation, concentrated on canals, or failed to act because the environment did not permit many options.

Northeast Brazil

The northeastern region of Brazil, Sertão, is semi-arid. Investments in water to deal with droughts began in the nineteenth century. The first large-scale construction, Usina, was done in 1883. Several smaller dam projects followed with private investment. The import-substituting industrialization strategy that unfolded in the middle decades of the twentieth century did not bypass the arid northeast but failed to reduce the vulnerability of the people to droughts. In the end, industrialization encouraged a great flight of capital and labor from the northeast.[47] A part of this flow followed an older pattern of migration to get closer to the fringes of the Amazon rainforest.

---

[46] Fana Gebresenbet, "Land Acquisitions, the Politics of Dispossession, and State-Remaking in Gambella, Western Ethiopia," *Africa Spectrum*, 51(1), 2016, 5–28, cited text on p. 6.

[47] Douglas H. Graham, "Divergent and Convergent Regional Economic Growth and Internal Migration in Brazil: 1940–1960," *Economic Development and Cultural Change*, 18(3), 1970, 362–382.

Figure 8.4 Monument to Honor the Derg Army in Ethiopia

In the 1970s, Marxist regimes in the poorer tropics pursued a welfare policy, the cornerstone of which was land reform. Redistributing poor-quality and underwatered land made the policy either meaningless or a disaster. Another aspect of the socialist approach was public investment in water infrastructure, which delivered more benefit. Neither served the Derg (council) regime in Ethiopia (1974–1987) well, which gave up power after a famine. The monument honors Cuban and Ethiopian soldiers and was partly sponsored by North Korea. A panel shows distressed, possibly famine-hit, people being rescued by soldiers.
Source: Alamy Stock Photos

THE BIG PUSH   187

In the 1980s, two northeastern states contributed to more than two-thirds of the migrants into this area. At the same time, there was a move to shift more public resources to the northeast in response to criticisms that regional inequality had reached unsustainable levels.

Large-scale intervention in water started a few years after military rule began in 1964. Military rule was established as the industrialization drive had started to flag. The regime needed to invest in infrastructure, attract private investment, and redress regional inequality. One of the areas it focused on was large-scale water projects for drought prevention and hydropower generation. The projects would serve both energy and irrigation. A substantial literature suggests that big projects created for drought control had limited impact on living standards because inequality was already quite deep. While new projects generated employment, they also displaced people.[48] The environment was another casualty. Unprecedented hydropower expansion took place in the 1960s and the 1970s during a burst of authoritarian developmentalism. The projects forged ahead with little regard for the environment. Environmental impact assessments were done after and not before construction had begun, and the concerned ministry had little financial or regulatory capacity to change anything. The public investment did encourage fast economic growth, but the dynamism was mainly confined to the coastal area, where most people lived. "Poverty is highest among rural workers and immigrants" living in the suburbs of the coastal cities. A drought in 1987 revealed another syndrome. A great deal of the governmental relief supplies to restore agricultural production went to the larger farmers, encouraging "paternalism" between the rich and the poor but with little impact on the vulnerability of the poor to such shocks.[49]

An economic crisis slowed the process in the 1980s. When "developmentalism" returned under left-wing governments after 2003, an environmental movement was present, and it had become international. The constitution included a provision to protect indigenous people and their habitats. In their second coming, the scale and design of dams tried to adapt to these demands, becoming smaller, "run-of-the-river" types with significantly reduced displacement and deforestation effects. But environmental regulation continued to suffer from low bureaucratic capacity compared to ministries dealing with energy or industry that wanted the dams.[50]

---

[48] Eve E. Buckley, *Technocrats and the Politics of Drought and Development in Twentieth-Century Brazil*, Chapel Hill: University of North Carolina Press, 2017.

[49] Grant Burrier, "The Developmental State, Civil Society, and Hydroelectric Politics in Brazil," *Journal of Environment and Development*, 25(3), 2016, 332–358.

[50] Ibid.

Sri Lanka

Sri Lanka contains a north-south aligned arid zone, which originates in the geology and the monsoon wind pattern of tropical South Asia. The limited extent of land suitable for rice cultivation has always been a challenge for the state and led, in the 1920s, to the establishment of a research station that collected information on the dry zone. After independence in 1948, the drive to expand rice cultivation in the dry zone became necessary. A nationalist sentiment that the dry area was the home of classical Sri Lanka reinforced the movement. The research station in Kandy (later known as the Field Crops Research and Development Institute) had done significant work in the 1950s. The results became useful when a major initiative was undertaken to push dryland cultivation in the 1960s and 1970s. The Mahaweli scheme, a cluster of dam-canal-power-reservoir projects, would be the state's input into the plan.

The scheme enabled an expansion of cultivation at the cost of rising inequality.[51] In part, the inequality stemmed from the logic of gravity-flow projects, that someone gets less for everyone who gets more. On top of that, this period of Sri Lankan history saw increasing disaffection among a part of the Tamil population. The main working force in the plantation industry, many lost jobs as a leftist state imposed excessive regulation on the foreign-owned firms that dominated the tea plantations. The colonization scheme was exclusionary by pandering to the ethnic Sinhala sentiment. From two ends—a decline of tea where many Tamil workers were employed and the exclusion from the agrarian plans—state policy encouraged ethnic strife.

The Horn of Africa

The Horn of Africa is one large region of arid Africa where river morphology does not permit the construction of big dams and canals. Here, institutional measures, for what they were worth, were often the only ones available. These made no difference in combating seasonality. With states lacking money power to impose their will, the enforcement of policies was weak.

---

[51] Bryan Pfaffenberger, "The Harsh Facts of Hydraulics: Technology and Society in Sri Lanka's Colonization Schemes," *Technology and Culture*, 31(3), 1990, 361–397.

In 1963, the government of independent Somalia announced its first seven-year plan. The plan wanted to solve two problems with one strategy. The three significant challenges were the pastoralists' poverty, the prospect of overgrazing as animal health improved, and the heavy dependence of a famine-prone region on food import. The strategy was to turn as many pastoralists as possible away from herding and draw them into farming. That would develop agriculture while reducing the pressure upon available pastures. That expectation was based on a trend that had begun from the interwar period. The proportion of the population dependent on cultivation had risen significantly between 1931 and 1953 but in the agriculturally more promising South.[52] Sedentarization of the nomads had begun too, but it was still a region-bound process, and there was little chance of creating the conditions of large-scale infrastructural investment to speed up the process. With the collapse of the state from the end of the twentieth century, the top-down drive to effect such changes dissipated.

The Groundwater Revolution

Among tropical drylands, Australia, the Dust Bowl states, southern California, and north-western Mexico have accessible aquifers. The history of exploiting this resource on a large scale starts at different times in different regions. The 1970s were a watershed decade in the global history of the tube well for two reasons: the green revolution offered an opportunity to those farmers with secure access to well water to make money, and deep drilling started to become cheaper. In northwest Mexico, the combined pathway had been taking shape since the 1940s. Deep pumping took off, gradually turning a desert landscape green. Wheat and cotton cultivation expanded, and cities grew, reflecting the projects' success. The boom led to "the concentration of land and water in the hands of a relatively small number of local elites."[53]

It was believed water was "limitless," but its extraction from one hundred meters underground was expensive. In the 1960s, when the green revolution package of high-yielding seeds arrived, water extraction had already exceeded recharge rates, resulting in saltwater intruding into the aquifer. From that time onward, restrictions were imposed on the extraction of groundwater. Still, the steady growth in demand and the fact that "water . . .

---

[52] Ibid.
[53] Moreno, "A Never-Ending Source of Water," cited text on p. 551.

190   WATER AND DEVELOPMENT

fell under the control of a few powerful families" defeated regulations.[54] In the long run, the enforcement of rules did not keep pace with legislation. Capitalism and inequality alone do not explain this syndrome, however. Throughout, disputations persisted over data on the capacity of the aquifers and the extraction rate. All over the world, the capacity of underground aquifers tends to be less well served with technical data compared with surface water resources, which uncertainty plagues regulation and encourage free riding.

In South Asia for centuries, private wells tapped groundwater. Most such wells came up in the alluvial soils of the Indo-Gangetic Basin, where water was nearer the surface and the soil was easy to bore through. The hard rocks of most of South India did not offer either condition. Water did exist, between hard rock layers. Only the wealthiest in the countryside could afford to dig a well, and often the effort to dig one ended in failure to get enough. The introduction of more powerful boring devices and mechanisms to pump water from great distances raised the prospect that a borewell revolution was possible in one of the driest areas of India.

One officer more than the others realized this potential: Alfred Chatterton (1866–1958), an engineer, teacher, administrator, and corporate consultant. Chatterton worked in India roughly between 1888 and 1930. The most important post he held was Industries Director Madras, an office that came with little money or power. Chatterton made a difference by using his position to do experimental research and publicize his findings. He believed that farmers and artisans held the key to Indian development and that they needed useful knowledge about affordable tools. He talked to farmers and artisans to find out what these innovations might be and zeroed in on four ideas. One of these was the borewell, the other three being chrome tanning, improved handloom, and wind power. For an effective policy of famine prevention and rural development, he wrote in 1912, "the Government and the educated classes in this country [must have] an accurate conception of the real value of water."[55] Among his many proposals for lift irrigation and the use of underground water, one was the construction of wells in arid areas run with power-driven pumps.

Chatterton's prediction came true. A century later, India has one of the highest densities of wells in the world. The dam-building drive declined

---

[54] Ibid., 559.
[55] A.C. Chatterton, *Industrial Evolution in India*, Madras: Hindu Office, 1912, 90.

THE BIG PUSH 191

in the late twentieth century because of these projects' environmental and human costs (see Chapter 9). The strategy shifted. Incentives and cheap loans were offered to private investors in tube wells. Many were small farmers. In India, Pakistan, and Bangladesh, tube well construction surged. The area irrigated by tube wells rose from less than 1 percent in India in 1960 to 25 percent in 1980. Some tube wells replaced the old dug wells operated with Persian wheels. In another thirty years, tube wells would emerge as the most important form of irrigation, supplying water to about 45 percent of the arable land. A similar trend was present in Pakistan and Bangladesh.

The whole agricultural strategy was, in some sense, a response to the stalling industrialization drive under state leadership. For forty years after independence in 1947, the Indian state used taxpayer money, control over banks, and high tariffs to generate industrialization based on chemicals, metals, and machinery production. When that drive lost steam in the 1980s, having created a string of mostly useless factories, the state started to retreat from industry. Soon after, it would retreat from big dams too, which had been connected to the industrialization policy via electric power. Ironically, tube wells encouraged industrialization of another kind as the demand for pipes and motors exploded. Small-town industrial clusters developed to produce these goods, and these clusters could supply small machines for various purposes, including engines and pumps to lift, transfer, and sell water from surface sources.[56]

As of today, India, China, and the United States are the largest groundwater-based irrigation users—but groundwater occurs in many regions at varying levels of depth and with varying extraction costs depending on rock types. Most aquifers extend beyond national boundaries; their scale is an advantage, but cross-national appearance an obstacle to conservation. The trend toward deep drilling was universal, however. In Africa, groundwater withdrawal took off from the 1980s, mainly to supply water in city homes. One exception was South Africa, where farmlands had private wells built earlier. By and large, in South Africa, the water infrastructure relied on riparian projects. Then there were regions—like North Africa, Yemen, and Baluchistan—where there was little scope for riparian projects

---

[56] Stephen Briggs and Scott Justice, *Rural and Agricultural Mechanization A History of the Spread of Small Engines in Selected Asian Countries*, Washington, DC: IFPRI, 2015. See also Khalid Aftab and Eric Rahim, "The Emergence of a Small-Scale Engineering Sector: The Case of Tubewell Production in the Pakistan Punjab," *Journal of Development Studies*, 23(1), 1986, 60–76.

192 WATER AND DEVELOPMENT

and a significant rise in average water use in the late twentieth century resulting from deep drilling.

Conclusion

Tropical regions were not the only ones experimenting with big dams in the 1960s and the 1970s. It was the cornerstone of development policy in arid Soviet Central Asia, where, Paul Josephson says, the bioengineering project to retrieve the "white gold for Russia . . . ran amok."[57] It was present in the Mekong Valley in Southeast Asia, where "development has been predicated on the exploitation of . . . natural resources" and "lax social and environmental governance."[58]

The drive for big dams slowed down everywhere at the end of the century. The real check came not from good judgment but from these projects' environmental and political costs, which became too great and obvious to ignore. Frequently, arguments broke out between the possessors of superior and inferior water rights. "Contrary to the depictions of dams as symbols of modernity . . . in the 1960s and 1970s . . . dams . . . today have often become sites of heated, if not violent, confrontation."[59] Until that point, engineers fed the politicians' dream with the conceit that tropical seasonality was a problem that science was waiting to solve given a chance and enough funding.

---

[57] Josephson, "Stalin's Water Workers and Their Heritage," cited text on pp. 182, 193.
[58] Pichamon Yeophantong, "China and the Accountability Politics of Hydropower Development," *Contemporary Southeast Asia*, 42(1), 2020, 85–117. Cited text on p. 86.
[59] Ibid., 90.

Chapter Nine
Paying For Green Revolutions

Dams and drills had universal appeal because they served agricultural growth, as well as industrialization, via the promise of cheap energy and water for cities. Rain-dependent agriculture and pastoralism formed a sustainable model of exploitation of nature, while the population growth rate was near zero. The scale and modern forms of water control placed sustainability under strain. A resolve to end poverty made the developmental agenda overlook the potential costs of irrigation projects, as "overriding priority was mostly placed on the first-order effects of technology and economic growth."[1]

The withdrawal of freshwater as a percentage of renewable sources touched unsustainably high levels in the semi-arid tropics. A primary measure of water stress is the risk of running out of freshwater. Around 2016, water stress levels and freshwater withdrawal as a percentage of renewable sources ranged from 42 percent in India to 105 percent in Pakistan and similarly high levels in parts of sub-Saharan Africa. The levels were considerably lower in the temperate countries in Western Europe, North America, Japan, and China.[2] Water stress did not just mean water running out. Modern forms of water control led to a fall in water and soil quality, new inequality in access, and deforestation and desertification. This chapter describes some of the more well-known examples.

The paradoxical history of big dams is a good place to begin.

The Paradox of Dams

Initially, the enthusiasm for large-scale water projects stemmed from a colonial-era faith that the biological knowledge that had made Western

---

[1] Margaret R. Biswas and Asit K. Biswas, "Complementarity between Environment and Development Processes," *Environmental Conservation*, 11(1), 1984, 35–44.

[2] World Resources Institute, "Water Stress by Country," 2024 (accessed on December 5, 2024), https://www.wri.org/data/water-stress-country.

Water and Development. Tirthankar Roy, Oxford University Press. © Oxford University Press (2025).
DOI: 10.1093/oso/9780197802397.003.0009

194   WATER AND DEVELOPMENT

European agriculture yield much more output per hectare was trans-
plantable if only the seasonal water problem was handled somehow. However, biological knowledge often failed to deliver dramatic results or proved
impossible to transplant. Extracting and storing water entailed such enormous costs that water productivity (flow per unit cost) fell to low levels.
Such projects were rarely economical for private entrepreneurs and needed
a heavy dose of taxpayers' money. When environmental costs are added,
the state takes on the dual role of investor and regulator. In this way, dams
entailed an enlargement of the states.

The expansion of the state for this purpose was potentially disputatious.
The environment was the root of the disputes. The global environmental
movement consolidated through anti-dam protests. With almost thirty years
gone after anti-dam sentiment and activism peaked in Latin America and
India, the costs of tropical dams are no longer matters of debate. Dams solved
one problem, water, by creating another: reduced soil fertility because silts
accumulated behind the dams rather than scattering on the cultivable surface. All dams, tropical or not, trap rich silts, thus depriving the downstream
of nutrients while encouraging algae and vegetation growth in the reservoir,
potentially silting it. In India, big dams damaged forests; caused waterlogging, salination, and diseases; displaced people; and possibly increased
earthquake risk.[3] Tropical dams universally evened out the seasonal flow in
rivers, thus affecting and sometimes decimating anadromous fish species.
These species migrate from the sea inland and back again as water temperature and volume vary between seasons. In the West African basins, the dams
of the 1980s reduced the river floods, with an unanticipated fall in groundwater recharge at the same time. Where dams urged people to move from
one agricultural tract to another, inevitably younger men could make the
move more easily than women and older people.

In rain-fed rivers throughout India, enormous reservoirs were built after
1947. Several reservoirs attached to the dams silted fast; the silting happened on too large a scale to make dredging possible. The Hirakud Dam,
built on the Mahanadi in eastern India, was one of these projects. The reservoir emerged from submerged farmlands and about a hundred square miles
of forest. The dam generated electricity, which encouraged industrial and
mining enterprises around it. However, effluents from these sites polluted

---

[3] Satyajit K. Singh, "Evaluating Large Dams in India," *Economic and Political Weekly*, 25(11),
1990, 561–574. For a short historical account of the river projects and the controversies around them,
see Michael H. Fisher, *An Environmental History of India: From Earliest Times to the Twenty-First
Century*, Cambridge: Cambridge University Press, 2018.

the river, affecting irrigated agriculture yield. Since the 1980s, industrialization, mining, effluent release, and paddy cultivation have taken a heavy toll on the reservoir and water quality. The Manantali dam in West Africa changed the basin's ecology from brackish aquatic to freshwater space. Waterborne disease incidence rose. Farmers with more resources and credit access migrated to the irrigated tracts, which the poorer local farmers resented. The Senegal River projects affected recession agriculture by reducing floods without compensating those affected.[4]

Canals redistributing reservoir waters encouraged wastage at the head-reach and caused a shortage at the tail end.[5] Farmers adapted cropping patterns to seasonal scarcity and devised rules to contain discords.[6] However, informal cooperation usually worked only on a small scale. Losses in the conveyance of water from the source to points of use were high, partly because of evaporation but also sometimes because of poor management and engineering.[7] Weakly lined canals caused a lot of water to percolate underground.[8] In a water-scarce economy, cheap or free water leads to a level of use that can create scarcity for others. Reservoirs and canals often generated more inequality than growth.[9]

In the 1990s, the campaign against dams crystallized around a big target, the Indian Narmada Valley project (Figure 9.1). International NGOs rallied to the campaign against its construction, pointing at the displacement of people mainly, and forced the World Bank to reassess its funding commitment to the project.[10] After the World Bank withdrew in 1993 from funding the Narmada Valley dam project—in a widely publicized move many anti-dam activists saw as a victory—the enthusiasm for dams receded

---

[4] Frans J.G. Padt and Juan Carlos Sanchez, "Creating New Spaces for Sustainable Water Management in the Senegal River Basin," *Natural Resources Journal*, 53(2), 2013, 265–284.

[5] Ashok K. Mitra, "Underutilisation Revisited: Surface Irrigation in Drought Prone Areas of Western Maharashtra," *Economic and Political Weekly*, 21(17), 1986, 752–756; on the problem in the Krishna Basin, the largest field of irrigation development in the Deccan Plateau, see Bret Wallach, "Irrigation Developments in the Krishna Basin since 1947," *Geographical Review*, 74(2), 1984, 127–144.

[6] "The rules are resources that are called upon when needed." Peter Mollinga, *On the Waterfront: Water Distribution, Technology and Agrarian Change in a South Indian Canal Irrigation System*, Hyderabad: Orient Longman, 2003, 181.

[7] Ashok K. Mitra, "Joint Management of Irrigation Systems in India: Relevance of Japanese Experience," *Economic and Political Weekly*, 27(26), 1992, A75–A82.

[8] Several examples of disputes over river water and attempts at resolving these are discussed in Madhav Gadgil and Ramachandra Guha, *Ecology and Equity: The Use and Abuse of Nature in Contemporary India*, London: Routledge, 1995, 76–81; and V. Saravanan, *Water and the Environmental History of Modern India*, London: Bloomsbury, 2021. The second book discusses disputes resulting from the clash between agricultural and urban demand for water in a South Indian basin.

[9] Esther Duflo and Rohini Pande, "Dams," *Quarterly Journal of Economics*, 122(2), 2007, 601–646.

[10] Robert H. Wade, "Muddy Waters: Inside the World Bank as It Struggled with the Narmada Projects," *Economic and Political Weekly*, 46(40), 2011, 44–65.

Figure 9.1 The Old Shoolpaneshwar Temple

A popular religious site was submerged during the construction of the Narmada Valley projects around 1990 and later rebuilt on a new site. Determined resistance by the Narmada Bachao Andolan (save Narmada movement), whose flag is showing, led to foreigners withdrawing financial assistance. The movement was almost certainly the highest-profile anti-dam protest in the world.
Source: Alamy Stock Photos

a little. The Narmada project came up but marked a slowdown in the drive to build multipurpose river valley projects. Funding these hugely capital-intensive projects with taxpayers' money alone and without foreign help was, and remains, beyond the reach of most countries in tropical Asia and Africa. Multilateral foreign donors hesitated to work against the sentiment built up during the movement.

The pro-dam sentiment did not die, however. The anti-dam activists tried to hijack the discourse by projecting it as a conflict between environmentalism and capitalism, implying that the pro-dam interests represented private economic interests. Where foreign money or foreign aid was involved, the pro-dam politics was called imperialist or neocolonial. The root of the political framing went back to the 1970s when radical leftist movements emerged in the developing world. Experts on development and its discontents did not always accept this framework. The tropical regions did not know ways to mitigate seasonality other than trapping water. Even if trapping water caused damage, the instinct of many experts was to manage the crisis and not give up on dams. David Hart, the author of a study of the Volta River project in Ghana in the 1970s, saw how unhelpful politics was in understanding water projects; "it may be best to leave aside the accusatory polemic of most theories of imperialism neo-colonialism and dependency economies."[11]

Eventually, the reality hit. There were no known alternative means to supply the growing population, cities, and businesses with water and power except by building more dams and impounding more rainwater. Groundwater was not available everywhere. Even where there was groundwater, its extent was unknown, and extraction was often done by private parties that excluded others. And wells, however deep, did not generate electric power. At the end of the twentieth century, regional political lobbies working to create jobs and water for cities and environmental activists increasingly came at loggerheads. Not surprisingly, the largest dam projects ever undertaken came up in China, where the balance of politics was heavily tilted on the developmental side. China entered a series of partnerships in Africa to build projects, at least one of which—the Ethiopian Grand Renaissance—was much larger than previous projects in Africa.

"The international debate around dam construction in Africa appear[ed] to be changing" from around 2010.[12] Old plans were revived and new partners were sought. China came forward with funding plans. In Sudan, Saudi Arabia promised money to build three large river valley projects. Outside the arid tropics, plans larger in scale than anything done before were designed (China, Congo). Analysts of the turnaround saw this return of the dams as a geopolitical tendency, reflecting new alliances forming. It was more than that. The resurgence of dams came from the impossibility of the anti-dam stance in a geography where no Plan B existed to solve problems of seasonality and drought. Plus, worries over climate change and clean energy revived interest in hydroelectricity.

Even where water was resourced in other ways, intensive cultivation imposed costs. Agricultural expansion in an arid tropical setting can give rise to a hazardous chain: agrarian change depletes the very resources— water, loamy soil, retention of moisture in soil—that are in short supply to begin with, encouraging farmers to apply more intensive methods, further causing environmental stress.[13] The Indo-Gangetic Basin, an agricultural

---

[11] David Hart, *The Volta River Project. A Case Study in Politics and Technology*, Edinburgh: University of Edinburgh Press, 1980.

[12] Harry Verhoeven, "Briefing African Dam Building as Extraversion: The Case of Sudan's Dam Programme, Nubian Resistance, and the Saudi-Iranian Proxy War in Yemen," *African Affairs*, 115(460), 2016, 562–573, cited text on p. 572.

[13] Tirthankar Roy, "Land Quality, Carrying Capacity, and Sustainable Agricultural Change in Twentieth-Century India," in Gareth Austin, ed., *Economic Development and Environmental History in the Anthropocene: Perspectives on Asia and Africa*, London: Bloomsbury, 2017, 159–178.

198 WATER AND DEVELOPMENT

tract in continuous cultivation for millennia, has witnessed the struggle to maintain land yield for a long time. The British Indian canals sometimes degraded or created environmental hazards.[14] In the western part of the basin, where subsoil water was used for cultivation, groundwater reservoirs were already being depleted in the early twentieth century. "With the continuous multiplication of population not upon the rivers but upon the subsoil reservoirs ... south of the Jumna, the ground water supply is becoming more and more precarious, leading to an agricultural crisis," said a witness appearing in the Royal Commission on Agriculture in 1927. In some tracts in the Indo-Gangetic Basin, the uncertainty raised the cost of constructing a well and the cost of water extraction.[15] In deltaic Bengal, agricultural expansion and dense settlements changed the natural flooding pattern of the rivers and, in turn, reduced soil fertility.

After independence in 1947, the construction of dams in the Himalayan rivers somewhat stemmed the crisis. However, after the 1970s green revolution, water use rose so much in these breadbaskets that the supply ran short. New dams were becoming harder to build because the rivers were shared between India and Pakistan and because of anti-dam activism. States responded to the farmers' needs by subsidizing water and electricity used to run pumps, which led to the overuse of water. The shift to paddy in the arid areas is a good example of the syndrome. Arid-land crops require moist soil when the plants are young but can withstand dryness. Therefore, they are better suited to arid monsoon conditions than rice varieties that require moisture throughout their life cycle. But rice is traded over wider areas and promises more profits, and if the costs are reduced, it marches on.

Groundwater

Wells offered an alternative source of water where groundwater was available. However, extracting water was costly, especially when water occurred in fissures between hard rock layers. Wells, therefore, remained confined to the alluvial river valleys.

---

[14] Elizabeth Whitcombe, *Agrarian Conditions in Northern India*, vol. 1, Berkeley: University of California Press, 1972; Indu Agnihotri, "Ecology, Land Use and Colonisation: The Canal Colonies of Punjab," *Indian Economic and Social History Review*, 33(1), 1996, 59–68.
[15] India, *Royal Commission on Agriculture*, vol. 7, Delhi: Government Press, 1927, evidence taken in the United Provinces, 377–279.

PAYING FOR GREEN REVOLUTIONS 199

There was extensive well irrigation in colonial India. Wells were relatively affordable in the alluvial lands and more expensive to construct, as well as of uncertain value in the drier Deccan Plateau (see Chapter 7). In 1920, for example, the percentage of area irrigated by wells was the highest in the alluvial tracts (7.3 percent) and smallest in the Deccan Traps (2.4 percent). The former received more rainfall and the latter little rainfall. Since deep drilling was still not technologically feasible, well construction was easier and the returns from wells were most secure where subsoil water was plentiful and seasonal variation in the water level was moderate. In the riparian Gangetic plains, this condition was fulfilled. The water table varied between ten and thirty feet. It was easy to construct a temporary well in a year of shortage and give it up when the water supply became normal. In the Deccan Traps, on the other hand, the water table was forty to fifty feet even in the monsoon months, and locating a well site here was not easy. The winter was drier and hotter. Nearly all wells in dry South India were permanent constructions, very wide (twenty to one hundred feet), and, on average, irrigated a smaller quantity of land.

Some arid regions have little choice in the matter. After Baluchistan was incorporated into the state of Pakistan (1955–1970), its most arid areas' economy still relied upon traditional modes of irrigation. Small dams and reservoirs were built, but in the highlands. In the drier regions, the karez and rainwater harvesting continued. A change, however, had set in. With government encouragement, considerable private investment went into the construction of tube wells, with a positive but small impact on land yield.[16] The karez was a communal property, but the tube well was a private property often controlled by the substantial shareholders in the karez system. Groundwater being limited, tube wells placed great pressure on the sustainability of the traditional systems and increased the burden upon small farmers to maintain wells. In many cases, the karez was abandoned or had collapsed. "In these circumstances, conflicts were inevitable," a 1995 study stated. "Neither under customary law nor under government jurisdiction did rules exist to resolve these dilemmas."[17]

---

[16] Akhtar Husain Siddiqi, "Baluchistan (Pakistan): Its Development and Planning Policy," *Geo-Journal*, 22(1), 1990, 5–19.

[17] Frank van Steenbergen, "The Frontier Problem in Incipient Groundwater Management Regimes in Balochistan," *Human Ecology*, 23(1) 1995, 53–74, cited text on p. 58. See also Daanish Mustafa and Usman Qazi, "Karez versus Tubewell Irrigation: Comparative Social Acceptability and Practicality of Sustainable Groundwater Development in Balochistan, Pakistan," in Lisa Mol

On the Indian side, in Punjab, Haryana, or the South Indian deltas, canals and wells were both critical. In Pakistan, canals were essential assets of the green revolution of the 1970s. Almost 80 percent of the Punjabi canal zone had become a part of Pakistan in 1947. But from the 1980s, as drilling became more economical, the green revolution spread to areas where groundwater could be accessed mechanically. By then, canals and dams were insufficient to keep pace with the rising urban and agricultural demand for water, and groundwater exploitation was allowed to speed up.

When India's economic miracle began thirty years ago, borewells and urbanization became interdependent. From 18 percent in 1951, the urban population rose to 30 percent in the 2000s. The environmental sustainability scholarship acknowledges a link between rapid urbanization and modern models of water access.[18] Attempts in the mid-twentieth century to treat city water projects as a public good ran into problems of undersupply, poor maintenance, and corruption. From the late twentieth century, that model yielded to private supply in country after country.[19] Eighty percent of urban and industrial water in India now comes from wells.

The pressure on underground water was reaching a breaking point. Between 1995 and 2004, the proportion of the Indian population living in "unsafe" districts—unsafe being defined as the aquifers' declining capacity to recharge and sustain current levels of water extraction—increased from 7 to 35 percent.[20] In northern districts that once led the green revolution and yet received low rainfall, groundwater exploitation in the 1990s reached levels that far exceeded the capacity of the aquifers to sustain. The main issue was not supply, but that groundwater appeared as a private good to the users, whereas it came from a common pool. The crisis was more dire in Pakistan. By 2010, many aquifers in desperately water-scarce Pakistan were saline (Sindh) or overused (Baluchistan).

The potential for groundwater running out was almost universal in the 2000s, but the threat materialized faster in two types of areas. One type

---

and Troy Sternberg, eds., *Changing Deserts: Integrating People and Their Environment*, Cambridge, UK: White Horse Press, 2012, 129–153.

[18] "As India urbanises, the growing proportions of its population would come into contact with formal water service providers," which implies reduces barriers to access. Tushaar Shah and Barbara van Koppen, "Is India Ripe for Integrated Water Resources Management? Fitting Water Policy to National Development Context," *Economic and Political Weekly*, 41(31), 2006, 3413–3421.

[19] Akin Mabogunje, "Water Resources and Economic Development in Nigeria," in David Brokensha, ed., *Ecology and Economic Development in Tropical Africa*, Berkeley: University of California Press, 1965, 147–159, and other chapters in this book.

[20] P.S. Vijay Shankar, Himanshu Kulkarni, and Sunderrajan Krishnan, "India's Groundwater Challenge and the Way Forward," *Economic and Political Weekly*, 46(2), 2011, 37–45.

occurs in Gujarat and Rajasthan in India, where the monsoon is relatively weaker and surface water scarcer. The second type appears in the Indo-Gangetic Basin, from Punjab to Bengal, where successive green revolutions placed a heavy draft on underground water. These two areas have seen the sharpest fall in aquifer levels, a simple measure of which is the average depth of the wells.

One example of the arid land type is Kachchh, the western Indian region where groundwater extraction in the 1980s caused salination and a fall in the groundwater capacity. Historically, most of Kachchh was more suitable for pastoralism than agriculture. The region being partly deltaic, water was often available in riverbeds and borewells; the pastoralists relied on the knowledge of where it was available and controlled some of these resources. Large population concentrations were few. Bhuj, the principal town, was served by one of the largest humanmade lakes in the region, constructed in the sixteenth century and rebuilt and repaired many times since then. In the late twentieth century, the tube-well wave took over, replacing some of the traditional water extraction systems. Agriculture and urban water supply began to depend on groundwater. By 2000, the infrastructure was under strain due to overextraction.[21]

At about the same time, and for the same reasons, the water table fell in other parts of Gujarat, which were already more agricultural than Kachchh. Water and climate scholar Navroz Dubash's 2002 study of two villages in Mehsana district to the east of Kachchh showed how the crisis developed.[22] Well construction became more expensive, making well owners more powerful. Well power reinforced caste power and social inequality. Gujarat is often cited as an example of an active water market in operation, again a market that tube wells made possible. However, caste cartels sometimes influence the working of these markets.

Semi-arid and hyper-arid Rajasthan represented another way the syndrome developed. A mountain range spread in a northeast-southwest direction in the middle of this large state divides it into broadly two ecological zones: arid or extremely arid lands to the west of the range and lands to the east, again short in rainfall but rich in groundwater. One relatively small area in the north receives canal water from the Indus complex. If that area is excluded, then pastoralism and rainfed agriculture dominated the land

[21] Charul Bharwada and Vinay Mahajan, "Drinking Water Crisis in Kutch: A Natural Phenomenon?" *Economic and Political Weekly*, 37(48), 2002, 4859–4866.

[22] Navroz K. Dubash, *Tubewell Capitalism: Groundwater Development and Agrarian Change in Gujarat*, Delhi: Oxford University Press, 2002.

202 WATER AND DEVELOPMENT

use pattern on the western side, except in small enclaves where water was found nearer the ground. In the east, well-irrigated agriculture was long established. As in Gujarat, the tube-well revolution in Rajasthan led to an expansion of intensive agriculture, water markets, consolidation of caste power, and an inevitable fall in the water table and deterioration of water quality. Occurrence of fluoride and nitrate is a problem in most of Rajasthan.

In Punjab, the problem appeared differently. In climatic terms, Punjab is as dry as Kachchh or arid Rajasthan. The Indus Basin waters made canal irrigation possible. Until the 1970s, canals sustained wheat cultivation. However, canal water dropped during the dry seasons, and canals could flood lands, thus causing waterlogging and salinity in some places. The tube well reduced the dependence on this hazardous asset. More than that, it enabled the cultivation of profitable rice. A new crop rotation pattern became possible. Rice is water-intensive, and the high-yield summer rice variety grows in the dry season when the water table drops. As private investment moved into well building and the water table fell, less was available to farmers with smaller landholdings. Wells, again, caused inequality and drove some farmers out of business.[23] They also encouraged water trading.

The accent on deep wells in Punjab started in the 1960s as a response to the salinity problem. The policy achieved some effect at a high cost. When private investment in tube wells took off, the state agency withdrew from groundwater management. The subsequent story has similarities with Indian Punjab. Wealthy landholders invested in wells, with the help of easier trade rules for importing cheap diesel engines. Inequality increased. But land yield in tube-well-served holdings rose too. The official mood was upbeat and discounted any prospect of an environmental crisis.[24] By 2000, the fall in the water table was common knowledge. In addition to the environmental stress, there was a regulatory crisis. The government had withdrawn from managing this resource, making it difficult for it to return to the task. Despite many plans, committees, seminars, and announcements, there was "less respect for the law, unavailability of needed data and information, lack of political will and institutional arrangements."[25]

[23] Daizo Sugimoto, "Groundwater Depletion Effects on Punjab Agriculture," *Senri Ethnological Studies*, 96, 2017, 35–46.
[24] Robert Johnson, *Private Tube Well Development in Pakistan's Punjab: Review of Past Public Programs / Policies and Relevant Research*, Colombo: International Irrigation Management Institute, 1989.
[25] Asad Sarwar Qureshi, "Groundwater Governance in Pakistan: From Colossal Development to Neglected Management," *Water*, 12, 2020, 1–19, cited text on p. 1.

PAYING FOR GREEN REVOLUTIONS   203

South Asia has an unparalleled concentration of wells among the world's tropical countries. It is also an overresearched field. From hundreds of articles and books on the subject, one would hear the same story: how tube wells and private investment raised farm output and reduced the water table. However, South Asia is luckier than most regions because of the heavy monsoons, which make managing artificial recharge more promising. Where this prospect does not exist, well irrigation is a potential disaster. At another end of the spectrum from India stands Yemen. One of the world's driest countries and completely dependent on stored water, Yemen's agricultural development scheme discovered the tube well in the early 1970s. In the next thirty years, arable land increased tenfold, a big part of the rise supported by tube wells.[26] Expatriate Yemenis invested their remittance into tube wells or in the water trade. By 2000, the water table had dropped so low that new wells had to dig nearly three thousand feet underground to access aquifers. In Gujarat, a well three hundred feet deep would cause concern. Yemen was at another level.

This was not all. As water became scarcer, private well-owners had more power. Some of that power also came from the commercial success of qat or khat, a cathinone-containing green leaf used as a stimulant and medicine. Profits from qat trade made the heavy investments worthwhile. But the economics opened a front of dispute between farmers and qat grower firms that often came from the outside and started their operations by drilling an unlicensed tube well. The government had by 2005 set up a series of water initiatives that lacked enough power to enforce licensing on private investors but did create local user committees. Organized protests against commercial wells continued to grow.

If in Yemen, deep wells were the asset for the wealthy, in Baluchistan, "it was often the 'have-nots,' the farmers that did not have a share in the kareze [communally managed underground channels], that were the first to use the opportunities offered by the new technology."[27] Because wells thus appeared as the more democratic technology, digging wells did not stop, and the groundwater levels fell in the 1990s and the 2000s, despite laws that insisted on licensing of wells. The tendency was slowed, if not reversed, in a few areas where the kareze-owner bodies formed strong collectives and

---

[26] Gerhard Lichtenthaeler, "Water Conflict and Cooperation in Yemen," *Middle East Report*, 254, 2010, 30–35.

[27] Frank van Steenbergen, "Promoting Local Management in Groundwater," *Hydrogeology Journal*, 14, 2006, 380–391, cited text on p. 382.

204 WATER AND DEVELOPMENT

outnumbered the well diggers. These and a few other examples from South Asia showed that group management of common property was nowhere a democratic institution. Effective groups would consolidate traditional forms of power, and work to prohibit outsiders from investing money in these ventures.

Conclusion

Since the dam drive started to wane in the 1990s, numerous initiatives emerged in India to build smaller projects and regulate access to the water that these yielded. The central government's employment programs enabled the construction of watershed projects. Common property management principles emerged, which caste associations modified. At the same time, these projects never became a genuine alternative to dams and drills. Even in hyper-arid western Rajasthan, where watershed projects and small dams appeared, poorer villagers pooled money and labor to install shallow tube wells, and wealthier villagers drilled deeper underground.[28] Rallying many people behind small and sustainable projects is hard because the trade-off between water security and the environment is rooted in seasonality. The solutions to heat and seasonality may damage the landscape, yet no one is ready to compromise on water security.

Besides changing the landscape in adverse ways, water interventions also created inequality and disputes because securing water for one group led to potential insecurity for the others. Chapter 10 is about these discords.

---

[28] N.C. Narayanan and Lalitha Kamath, "Rural Water Access: Governance and Contestation in a Semi-arid Watershed in Udaipur, Rajasthan," *Economic and Political Weekly*, 47(4), 2012, 65–72.

Chapter Ten
Inequality And Discord

"The utilization of water, more than any other resource has experienced tremendous conflicts," writes the geographer Josephine Msangi.[1] Controlled water harvesting on a large scale unleashed three types of conflict. First, there was a potential variance between two principles in transboundary river sharing. One of these asserted sovereign territorial rights over resources, and the other wanted to maintain the unity of the source. Countries in different places in a river basin chose the principle that best suited their interests.

Second, the accent on intensive agriculture made the coexistence of farmers and herders as two specialist livelihood groups unworkable, especially on lands that could be used for farming and herding in different seasons. Third, water security and insecurity led to not just interpersonal differences but also interregional and interethnic inequality. Where regions had different cultures, water quarrels merged into and fed ethnic wars. "Coping with drought [and] shift between agricultural and pastoralism" writes an analyst of the Darfur conflict, "have been not only adaptive processes, but have also been characterized by shifts in identities."[2]

The awkward history of basin sharing is a good place to start.

The Nile Basin

From the start, Ethiopia was left out of the Nile Basin treaties for no other reason than no one had colonized Ethiopia (Italian occupation lasted for too short a time to count), and the origin of these treaties was owed to Anglo-French dialogues. Ethiopian rulers may have felt left out by these negotiations, but water was of less concern to them. The rulers lived in the highlands and had little financial capacity to build large water projects. Their

---

[1] J.P. Msangi, "Water Resources Conservation in the Semi-arid Parts of Tanzania," *Journal of Eastern African Research and Development*, 17, 1987, 63–73, cited text on p. 63.

[2] Leif Manger, "Resource Conflict as a Factor in the Darfur Crisis in Sudan," Chr. Michelsen Institute, accessed November 23, 2024, https://www.cmi.no/file/1816-Manger---Resource-Conflict-as-a-Factor.pdf.

Water and Development. Tirthankar Roy, Oxford University Press. © Oxford University Press (2025). DOI: 10.1093/oso/9780197802397.003.0010

206   WATER AND DEVELOPMENT

main instrument of developing the semi-arid areas was to offer concessions to plantation companies willing to invest locally in water supply and use the water to grow cotton and sugar. All that changed with the Welo famine of 1972–1974, followed by the empire's fall.

The regime publicly asserted that the Ethiopian state had full rights over any water in its territory. It protested an Egyptian plan to divert Nile water to Sinai. However, it could not afford to build its own water storage. An upstream country, Ethiopia resented the skewed distribution of Nile water between Egypt and the others. Scholars based in Ethiopia blamed British colonialism. "A grossly inequitable *status quo*," one of them called the legacy.[3] Colonialism was not the real problem; Egypt's aridity was. With a history of disputes and negotiations over the Nile behind it, any single country trying to change the flow of the Nile risked a war with Egypt and possibly Sudan. A militarily and economically stronger Ethiopia took a risk to build the Grand Ethiopian Renaissance Dam in the 2010s. Some see the dam as an inevitable response to the growing threat of droughts and power shortages. Others see it as a sign that Nile treaties are failing.

Nile treaties were mainly a bilateral exercise between Sudan and Egypt. Disputes did break out between them, but Sudan was not powerful enough to threaten the treaty—so Egypt's interest was protected. Oil exports from Sudan after 2000, however, changed the balance. A number of large hydraulic and infrastructure projects were conceived since then. Of these, the most significant was the Merowe dam. The idea first took shape during colonial rule and seemed too expensive to become a reality until oil exports made it affordable. Since 1999, the Nile Basin Initiative managed to bring eleven countries to the negotiating table. Although it can intervene locally and on a small scale and organize information exchange, the initiative cannot devise a fresh sharing rule.

Southern Asia

The most famous and complex international agreement in South Asia is the Indus Waters Treaty between India and Pakistan.[4] Both countries rely heavily on the major rivers of the Indus Basin for irrigation and power.

---

[3] Dereje Zeleke Mekonnen, "The Quest for Equitable Resolution of the Nile Waters Dispute," *International Journal of Ethiopian Studies*, 7(1–2), 2013, 77–100, cited text on p. 78.

[4] The section draws on my *Monsoon Economies: India's History in a Changing Climate*, Cambridge, MA: MIT Press, 2022.

All these rivers originate inside India, four of which flow inside Pakistan. The Indus Waters Treaty in 1960 allowed Pakistan to exploit the Western rivers more intensively while allowing India rights to the Eastern rivers. Although the two countries often fought wars, the treaty survived. Between 2002 and 2012, threatening words were exchanged over the Treaty, and in the 2020s, tensions rose again.[5] On the Eastern borders, India's decision to build a barrage on the Ganges on the Bangladesh border (1973–1974) caused much uneasiness between the two countries. Comparatively speaking, river-sharing arrangements between India and Nepal and India and Bhutan were more peaceful.

Within South Asia, which contains over a fifth of the world's population and 8 percent of global freshwater and which relies critically on freshwater harvested from shared rivers, the prospect of going to war over water is not beyond imagination.[6] As of now, the nations of South Asia cooperate more than disputing their rights to riparian resources. Critics believe that the terms of negotiation reflect the economic weight of the countries more than ecological considerations.[7] In addition, the prospect of climate change shifts the geographical knowledge base on which some of the treaties were drawn.

Countries as critically dependent on a river basin as Pakistan and India are on the Indus and its tributaries chose to cooperate rather than fight over water because it was rational to cooperate, despite many other differences.[8] But when perceptions of water deprivation exist, friction over other issues can be harder to resolve. The Arab League's plans to divert the headwaters of the Jordan River were one of the sources of the divergence that led up to the 1967 war.[9] Water security was behind South Africa's 1998 decision to send its army to Lesotho, the source of the Orange River. The operation officially served as a "restoration of democracy" after a flawed election.

The history of agreements to share the Kaveri waters in South India goes back to the early-twentieth-century treaties between the princely state of

[5] On the treaty and disputes in the early-2000s, see Ramaswamy R. Iyer, "Indus Waters Treaty 1960: An Indian Perspective," March 16, 2014, https://www.boell.de/en/2014/03/16/indus-waters-treaty-1960-indian-perspective.

[6] Brahma Chellaney, *Water: Asia's New Battleground*, Washington, DC: Georgetown University Press, 2011.

[7] Paula Hanasz, "Power Flows: Hydro-Hegemony and Water Conflicts in South Asia," *Security Challenges*, 10(3), 2014, 95–112.

[8] Undala Z. Alam, "Questioning the Water Wars Rationale: A Case Study of the Indus Waters Treaty," *Geographical Journal*, 168(4), 2002, 341–353.

[9] Meredith Giordano, Mark Giordano, and Aaron Wolf, "The Geography of Water Conflict and Cooperation: Internal Pressures and International Manifestations," *Geographical Journal*, 168(4), 2002, 293–312.

208 WATER AND DEVELOPMENT

Mysore and the British-ruled Madras presidency. A larger share of the waters went to the agriculturally developed deltaic Tamil Nadu region, whereas a larger share of the basin fell in the Karnataka region. The waters sustained intensive cultivation in the Thanjavur rice belt. The agreements limited intraterritory usage, dam building, and reservoir capacity in the river's upper reaches. From the 1970s, the green revolution, industrialization, and urban demand increased water usage throughout the basin. After 1990, the negotiations gave way more often to disputation. On two occasions, in 1995 and 2002, failure of the seasonal rains reduced peak water flow in the river and the reservoirs, compelling Karnataka to capture a larger share of water than before and causing a mass protest in Tamil Nadu. Although an independent regulatory body, a river authority, now oversaw the sharing arrangements, the disputants were not happy with its ruling, and an appeal against the orders was filed in the supreme court.

The principle on which river sharing is based is now known as *integrated water resource management* (IWRM). It builds on the intuition that the sustainability of surface water resources depends on sustaining a river basin, irrespective of political boundaries. This idea influenced governance and legislation from soon after independence in India. For example, the Rivers Board Act in India (1956) permitted the federal government to set up a board to investigate and advise disputing states (provinces) over a basin's water. The Constitution of India (1950) placed water on the list of subjects over which the states had exclusive authority—but this move had exposed river basins to interstate disputes, hence the Interstate River Water Disputes Act of 1956, which set out the grounds and process for setting up a tribunal to settle disputes.

Experience shows that few interstate disputes were solved despite this infrastructure. "While appealing in principle, practical implementation [of IWRM] has often been problematical," asserts an article on the Krishna River Basin dispute.[10] The process of adjudication took time: tribunal awards stayed in place for decades while population, use patterns, and even the geography changed; every drought generated a fresh dispute; and oversight of groundwater and potential links between extraction of groundwater and flow levels in the river defeated the purpose of the award.

---

[10] Jean-Philippe Venot, Luna Bharati, Mark Giordano, and François Molle, "Beyond Water, beyond Boundaries: Spaces of Water Management in the Krishna River Basin, South India," *Geographical Journal*, 177(2), 2011, 160–170, cited text on p. 168.

Disputes over river water, therefore, tested the structure of Indian federalism as no other issue did. Interstate disputes go back to the busiest dam construction period, in the 1960s and 1970s. The power of the Congress Party, which ruled New Delhi and most riparian states, contained the force of these disputes. The dispute reemerged as Congress disintegrated in the 1990s and regional parties gained popularity. Courtroom battles over the Kaveri River water partly resulted from the breakdown of political decision-making.

A recent case is the argument between Chhattisgarh and Odisha (Orissa) states over the Mahanadi waters. The river originates in Chhattisgarh, a part of the Madhya Pradesh state when the Hirakud dam in Odisha was erected in the early 1950s.[11] The upstream state was not happy about the dam and the displacement of people in its territory. Fifty years later, the upstream state, Chhattisgarh since 2000, started building dams in their territory, allegedly empowered by the tacit support of the central government (the same political party ruled Chhattisgarh and the center) and ignoring the objections of the downstream state. The counterargument was that the Mahanadi Delta was water-surplus, and the diversion upstream would have little impact on the dam's contribution to agriculture and industry. Nevertheless, media reports on the dispute fed the narrative that political arm-twisting was the answer to interstate river-sharing disagreements. That Hirakud faces deteriorating potentials due to silting added fuel to these contestations.

River Sharing Elsewhere

In the tropical Americas, transboundary collaboration mainly took the form of knowledge exchange on aquifers rather than sharing physical water volumes as in the Asian and African rivers. Seasonal floods were also a field of collaboration on the US-Mexico border and the Argentina-Chile border close to the Atacama Desert. These temperate but "transitional" landscapes are seen as areas "subject to threshold shifts from Mediterranean to semi-arid" climate types with global warming.[12]

---

[11] Sailen Routray, Patrik Oskarsson, and Puspanjali Satpathy, "A Hydrologically Fractured State? Nation-Building, the Hirakud Dam and Societal Divisions in Eastern India," *South Asia: Journal of South Asian Studies*, 43(3), 2020, 429–445.

[12] Christopher A. Scott, Francisco J. Meza, Robert G. Varady, Holm Tiessen, Jamie McEvoy, Gregg M. Garfin, Margaret Wilder, Luis M. Farfán, Nicolás Pineda Pablos, and Elma Montaña, "Water

210 WATER AND DEVELOPMENT

Within borders, it is often harder to create dispute settlement systems, in the absence of which "the potential for political instability over domestic water distribution and development" becomes real every day. A study of the Indus Basin shows that these differences do not directly stem from absolute scarcity. Rather, they are entangled in the discourses on entitlement to water and relate to broader political processes such as "democratization, . . . social justice, [articulation of] ethnic, religious, and linguistic identity," and perceptions of groups of claimants about justice and economic security.[13]

Recent interstate disputes on rivers are also about the adverse effects of dams, which are disproportionately distributed between the upstream and the downstream. Fierce disputes broke out in 2018 between Turkey and Iraq over Turkey's decision to build the Ilisu dam and reservoir on the Tigris River. The region is already severely water-scarce and facing a rise in aridity. The dam promises development upstream and deprivation downstream. That cities in the downstream were since the 2010s caught up in war practically broke down negotiations for several years. The Grand Ethiopian Renaissance Dam on the Blue Nile is primarily power-generating in a relatively wet part of East Africa but has potentially adverse implications for Sudan's water supply. In the Indian section of the River Jhelum, construction of another hydropower project, Kishanganga (2007–2018), generated a dispute with Pakistan, which feared reduced water flows into the country. In the Mekong Basin, China's construction of a series of dams raises the fear of reduced supply and poorer-quality water for the downstream countries.

Basin Sharing with China

Most of China is not tropical, but because it is an upstream state, it holds vital importance for the tropics. Overall, China is more water-secure than most intertropical countries. It has considerably greater renewable water resources per head, and its dependence on inflow from sources external to its borders is less than 1 percent; for contrast, the dependency numbers are 30 percent for India, 90 percent for Bangladesh, and 40 to 74 percent

Security and Adaptive Management in the Arid Americas," *Annals of the Association of American Geographers*, 103(2), 2013, 280–289.
[13] Daanish Mustafa, "Social Construction of Hydropolitics: The Geographical Scales of Water and Security in the Indus Basin," *Geographical Review*, 97(4), 2007, 484–501.

INEQUALITY AND DISCORD   211

in mainland Southeast Asia. Most of the sources feeding these countries or regions originate in China. If water-secure on average, China requires hydropower and considerable drinking water for the arid western region. Since 1990, a series of substantial projects have come up, and more are under construction to regulate, use, and divert the waters of the major rivers, including the Brahmaputra and the Mekong.

How was the river-sharing arrangement with neighbors managed? Being the source of most rivers in Asia, China does conduct negotiations with the stakeholders, but on a bilateral level. Where cross-border trade relied on navigation, river sharing and conservation treaties worked better. Treaties were relatively conflict-free, where the partners were politically and militarily less relevant. Thus, a peaceful arrangement under China's "impossibly large presence" has been in place in the Mekong Basin for some decades.[14] The arrangements were more opaque and tense with the Brahmaputra. India and Bangladesh, the downstream countries, have no effective treaty with China, and both stand to lose if there is a significant impact on the source of the rivers on which they depend. The asymmetry between the Mekong and Brahmaputra stems from China's sharing of rivers with a bigger military rival, India, in the west.[15] On the Mekong, substantial literature suggests that dam-building in Yunnan has started altering the basin's hydrology, including the direction of water flow into Tonle-Sap Lake, which sustains the agricultural economy of Cambodia.[16]

If these tense negotiations involved states and were around public investment, raw scarcity generated intergroup clashes.

West Africa after Droughts

Land and water are in shortage in sub-Saharan Africa. In the backdrop of a pervasive shortage, when the state intervened to distribute land or water or redraw administrative boundaries—which often ended up with one political unit being populated by mainly one ethnic group—the moves could

---

[14] Milton Osborne, cited in Thanakvaro Thyl De Lopez, "Natural Resource Exploitation in Cambodia: An Examination of Use, Appropriation, and Exclusion," *Journal of Environment and Development*, 11(4), 2002, 355–379, cited text on p. 360.
[15] Lobsang Yangtso, "China's River Politics on the Tibetan Plateau: Comparative Study of Brahmaputra and Mekong," *The Tibet Journal*, 42(2), 2017, 49–58.
[16] Yos Santasombat, *The River of Life: Changing Ecosystems of the Mekong Region*, Chiang Mai: Mekong Press, 2011.

212   WATER AND DEVELOPMENT

trigger anxieties about losing access, attempts to grab resources, and violent conflict.[17] Periods of extreme and long-lasting dryness intensified the process.

From a climatic point of view, the nineteenth century was relatively benign in northern and western Africa. Droughts returned in the twentieth century. The drought of 1911–1914 was a great shock in northern Nigeria. A railway link between the coast and Kano had possibly reduced the scale of trans-Saharan trade in central Sahel-Sudan. The colonial governments already interfered in tribute and tax payments. Military operations in the region involved the requisition of animals and disruption to trade. World War I brought further stress, a Tuareg revolt, and brutal repression. The desert economy saw an exodus of nomads and marginal farmers toward the south and sedentary occupations. Although overland trade did not disappear, and transhumance and interdependence continued, the gradual decline of the Tuareg economy persisted throughout the twentieth century.

The next fifty years were relatively drought-free. Droughts returned in the 1970s, in some cases starting in 1968 and ending six years later. The nature of the effect varied. South of the Sahara, it devastated the economy of the nomadic groups, who earlier dealt with droughts by relying on their trading partners and dependents in the savanna but on this occasion could not do that anymore. "The decline of the desert-edge sector," wrote two historians just as the shadow of the great drought was beginning to recede, "was one of the most underestimated impacts of colonialism."[18]

The two successive waves of drought in Mali, 1968–1974 and 1984–1985, had a lasting impact on traditional livelihoods. The still mainly nomadic Tuareg of the north lost some of their livelihood and became dependent on relief.[19] Younger Tuareg migrated. "Traditionalists sought explanations for the fact that their revered way of life was unravelling, and their communities were dying. The government served as a convenient culprit."[20] The feeling was strong that the government, like its colonial predecessor, did more for the farmers than the herders. "Whether or not relief was deliberately withheld, Mali's resources were limited, and the options of the national

---

[17] Hanne Seter, Ole Magnus Theisen, and Janpeter Schilling, "All about Water and Land? Resource-Related Conflicts in East and West Africa Revisited," *GeoJournal*, 83(1), 2018, 169–187.

[18] Paul E. Lovejoy and Stephen Baier, "The Desert-Side Economy of the Central Sudan," *International Journal of African Historical Studies*, 8(4), 1975, 551–581.

[19] Thurston Clarke, *The Last Caravan*, New York: G.P. Putnam's Sons, 1978. For a more detailed treatment, see Edmond Bernus, *Dates, Dromedaries and Drought: Diversification in Tuareg Pastoral Systems*, New York: Guilford Press, 1990.

[20] Kalifa Keita and Dan Henk, "Conflict and Conflict Resolution in the Sahel: The Tuareg Insurgency in Mali," Strategic Studies Institute, US Army War College, 1998, 27.

government were severely constrained."[21] In this way, drought made a weak state weaker. The Saharan states had negotiated settlements with the Tuareg on several occasions in the past (1962–1963, 1990–1996, and 2006–2009), which often collapsed. The droughts changed the pattern fundamentally by pushing many younger people into insurgency. While a connection between insurgency and pastoralism is obvious, it is unclear which way the causality runs. A crisis in pastoralism, it is said, fuels militancy in the Sahel.[22] But militancy fuels a crisis in pastoralism via the collapse of land governance and of land and water access, and causing frequent dislocation of herds. The circular chain was deadly for a vast area in the Sahel.

Large water projects made things worse. Analysis of the Senegal-Mauritania dispute in the 1980s attributed a significant role to the river valley projects. In the Senegal River Basin, the dam projects envisaged the expansion of farmlands, which reduced the land marked as pasture. The Mauritanian economy was substantially dependent on livestock, and the basin provided extensive dry-season pasture for groups sharing the land on the banks of the river. Much of this was effectively lost or under threat of conversion when the Diama dam came up.

The 1989 conflict that broke out into a riot had roots in French colonial rule, when the regime pushed for settled agriculture, effectively discriminating against the pastoralists. Different ethnic groups dominated these livelihoods. On the Mauritanian side, "Black African" peasants and "white African" pastoralists of Berber-Arab descent shared the rights to the basin lands. Ethnic rivalry and strife had grown since Mauritanian independence in 1960. The 1989 outbreak was the most severe episode and was induced by two immediate factors. First was the 1980s droughts that reduced pastures available for the dry season and pushed many nomadic herders to become farmers. The second factor was the two dams that started in 1988. The dam projects weakened the basis for cooperation between herders and farmers. Lands that could now be used throughout the year were up for grabs. On the Mauritanian side, speculators captured land where irrigated agriculture could develop. The land rights allocation system had already changed in Mauritania in anticipation of the dams, enabling the authorities to disregard the customary uses of local peasants. The conflict quickly spread to the towns. The role of the competition over farmland was not so proximate or

---

[21] Ibid., 12.

[22] Anouar Boukhars and Carl Pilgram, "Crisis of Pastoralism Coming Due," in *In Disorder, They Thrive: How Rural Distress Fuels Militancy and Banditry in the Central Sahel*, Washington, DC: Middle East Institute, 2023.

214 WATER AND DEVELOPMENT

large behind the violence. But it explained the riots' timing and the persistent and fierce competition for basin land within Mauritania.[23]

Sudan

Sudan is another example of how politics combined with vulnerable geography to fuel ethnic wars. The concentration of business and intensive agriculture in the riverine areas and the main urban-industrial center of Khartoum was aided, if not created, by the colonial accent on commercialization. The "alliance of riverine, northern Arab elites" sustained ethnoreligious nationalism, which had formed in reaction to British rule. This northern nationalism, drawing on reinvented precolonial tradition, alienated groups in the south. Outside the Nile Corridor, there was little scope for urbanization or intensive agriculture because water was scarce and seasonal.

The paradox of Sudan—whether colonial or postcolonial—was that it was also too weak and impoverished a state to impose a strong form of federalism, notwithstanding its militaristic orientation and development of the Nile Basin economy. In Darfur, the elites could provide only logistical and moral support in a battle about land and water. That battle turned fierce in the wake of the droughts in the 1970s. As pastures reduced, herders threatened to encroach on farmers' lands. Ethnicity made the dispute brutal for the noncombatants, as the farmer-herder conflict took on shades of ethnic conflict. Droughts of the 1980s pushed migrants into the cultivation zones. Incomplete land titling initiatives had left landed property vulnerable to capture. "Environmental stress on a vulnerable landscape ... forced some to defend their land and others to migrate or find new land."[24]

East Africa

In the 1970s, the cliché that Ethiopia was Africa's breadbasket and granary collapsed. The absence of irrigation, high seasonality, the unreliability of fluctuating rainfall, low land yield, and regional inequality in water access and water security were recognized as problems to which no easy and inexpensive solution existed. The so-called Wollo famine was the third

---

[23] Andrea Nicolaj, "The Senegal Mauritanian Conflict," *Africa: Rivista trimestrale di studi e documentazione dell'Istituto italiano per l'Africa e l'Oriente*, 45(3), 1990, 464–480.
[24] Scott Straus, *Making and Unmaking Nations: War, Leadership, and Genocide in Modern Africa*, Ithaca, NY: Cornell University Press, 2015, cited text on p. 250.

and the most severe to occur in the north of the country within fifteen years. Few lessons had been learned from the previous episodes. Eventually, military officers and students brought down the imperial regime, but some of the affected people continued to resist the new government. The famine in 1972–75 showed how precarious the economic conditions were. Relief operations took off, in the country and internationally, but the effort was insufficient and allegedly misdirected (Figure 10.1). In 1985, famine returned to the country.

For decades before the famines (1974, 1985), population pressure in the northern regions caused widespread deforestation and loss of pasture. The process led to soil erosion in the drier climates of the north. Lowland cultivation zones that received migrants became more dependent on rainfed agriculture and the erratic spring rains. Before the famine, development policy involved giving away pastures and suitable land to commercial farming companies, some foreign-owned.[25] This long-term pattern of livelihood

Figure 10.1 An Arax Airlines cargo plane bringing relief supplies during the Sahel famine, 1972

Arax Airlines was a Lagos-based company formed in the early 1970s with foreign aid. It closed operations in 1989.
Source: Alamy Stock Photos

[25] Abdul Mejid Ahssein, ed., *Rehab: Drought and Famine in Ethiopia*, London: International African Institute, 1976.

216 WATER AND DEVELOPMENT

change "substantially increased the proportion of the population susceptible to climatic variations."[26] Cultivation extended into wet pastures used for herding in the wet seasons, reducing the capacity of the agricultural system to sustain livestock for cultivation. Droughts thus created shortages of oxen and made the return to normal agriculture more difficult. The average land yield stayed low.[27]

In 1975, a military coup led to establishing a Marxist dictatorship in Ethiopia. Regions to the south and west of the capital, Addis Ababa, had developed commercial agriculture more successfully than the semi-arid areas in the north and were less affected by the 1974 famine. Still, the regime was held responsible. "The 1974 revolution [in Ethiopia] was in many ways a response to the state's long-term failure to transform agrarian production in the 1960s and early 1970s."[28] The Marxist regime, acting on the belief that unequal property rights in natural resources predisposed the society to famines, initiated land reforms. It began a large-scale project of collectivization and resettlement of drought-affected populations in the country.[29] Land reforms generated more problems than they solved. Nationalization of land and abolition of landlord property in the 1970s reduced investment in land. The state was too weak to make large-scale public investments, relying on migration instead. The resettlement program encouraged Eritrean and Tigrayan secessionist movements by generating the fear that the resettlement aimed to depopulate their support bases. The program also failed because it did not supply enough infrastructure, including water, in the settlements. "Peasant entitlements to the benefits of economic growth . . . in the cities and in the south and west . . . failed to materialize for small farms in the northern and central parts of the country where famine is endemic."[30]

What factors caused the Ethiopian famines? Three theories exist. One blamed crises on capitalism: "the profit incentive . . . is the underlying cause of the present process of underdevelopment in the northeastern lowlands."[31]

---

[26] James C. McCann, "A Great Agrarian Cycle? Productivity in Highland Ethiopia, 1900 to 1987," *Journal of Interdisciplinary History*, 20(3), 1990, 389–416, cited text on p. 394.

[27] In one surveyed region about 500 kilograms of grain per acre, and with a 1.2-acre-per-household landholding on average, that meant less than a year's supply of subsistence in a year.

[28] McCann, "A Great Agrarian Cycle?," cited text on p. 416.

[29] Marina Ottaway, "Drought and Development in Ethiopia," *Current History*, 85(511), 1986, 217–220, 234.

[30] McCann, "A Great Agrarian Cycle?," cited text on p. 390.

[31] Lars Bondestam, "People and Capitalism in the Northeastern Lowlands of Ethiopia," *Journal of Modern African Studies*, 12(3), 1974, 423–430.

A second blamed property rights: "the state's failure to develop traditions and institutions for the secure ownership and transmission of property." Specifically, land tenure and property were not secure enough to incentivize peasants to invest in and improve the land.[32] A third interpretation emphasized resources, suggesting that the demographic transition in an already vulnerable resource environment increased vulnerability and made it more likely that a drought would cause a famine in the agriculturally marginal northeast.[33]

These explanations are not mutually exclusive. The common factor is the seasonality of semi-arid tropics. Population growth made food production—or the state's ability to import food—critical. Commercial farming was potentially a solution to low land yield and low tax taken from herders. The legally weak property rights of the pastoral groups over lands that could be used for the purpose no doubt aided the transfer of assets. Against this backdrop, the Marxist regime's attempts to control land and its produce caused agricultural growth to fall to near-zero, making a recovery from 1974 elusive and a second famine likely. Famine broke out in 1985.

Since the 1990s, farmer-herder conflicts emerged in the west, bordering South Sudan. The migration of seminomadic Nuer into Ethiopia made interethnic clashes more likely. A study of this discord cautions against attributing it too readily to resource crises, among other reasons, because pastoralism and agriculture were often combined, contestations occurred within groups, and external politics impinged on these contests. The study does, however, suggest a reason why resource competition had the potential to turn into a clash between identities.[34] Farming populations carry an identity defined by attachment to a territory, sometimes backed up by legally protected territorial claims, but not always. "The nomadic Nuer are perceived as new to the area, having come there to use the vast scrublands for pasture."[35] The distinction between the long-settled and strangers is deep-rooted in farmers' sense of themselves and easily transmitted into political discourses. For the migrants, on the other hand, land entitlement

---

[32] Merid W. Aregay, "Society and Technology in Ethiopia: 1500–1800," *Journal of Ethiopian Studies*, 17, 1984, 127–147; and discussion of Aregay's work more generally in Donald Crummey, "Society, State, and Nationality in the Recent Historiography of Ethiopia," *Journal of African History*, 31(1), 1990, 103–119.

[33] McCann, "A Great Agrarian Cycle?"

[34] Jon Harald Sande Lie and Axel Borchgrevink, "Layer upon Layer: Understanding the Gambella Conflict Formation," *International Journal of Ethiopian Studies*, 6(1/2), 2012, 135–159.

[35] Ibid.

218   WATER AND DEVELOPMENT

was tied to the *use* of land rather than territorial heritage. An unused land did not belong to anyone.

Politics added fuel to these contests. The Sudanese civil war, as well as droughts, drove more people into Ethiopia. Depending on the state's sympathies for the mainly Christian South Sudan movement and which ethnic groups allied with the cause, federalism entailed distributing favors and public goods unequally between regions and ethnic groups. A study of farmer-herder dispute in Mieso—in eastern-central Ethiopia, on the border of the Oromia and Somali regional states—illustrates how ethnic conflicts were rooted in changing land use. The region is not particularly arid, but the seasonality of its rainfall sustained both farming and herding. However, with the expansion of farming and the conversion of many herders into agro-pastoralists, the competition over the remaining pastures became intense. Disputes had occurred here since the 1930s when the imperial government allocated farmland to companies. When that happened, farmers and herders jointly resisted and defeated the move.[36] That collaboration ended with population growth, especially after the land reform of the 1970s.

The government allocated nationalized land to users, turning some herders to till these lands and others to resist that move by claiming the land was common property. Governments had few, if any, choices about containing these clashes. Indeed, federal politics often worsened them, usually by creating loyal groups, complicating and changing interclan relationships. These alliances made negotiated and legal solutions to these disagreements elusive. Ideas about history, inheritance, and ancient entitlements also intruded.

A 1996 book on the civil war in Somalia described the war as a "struggle for resources."[37] Before the civil war of the 1990s, smallholders and pastoralists shared common water resources. Disputes had happened, but these were between clans and internalized within them. They spilled over and turned pan-regional because of population growth and the state's developmental activities. Development entailed the expropriation of pastoralists from pastures that could sustain irrigated agriculture. Somalia again

[36] Fekadu Beyene, "Property Rights Conflict, Customary Institutions and the State: The Case of Agro-Pastoralists in Mieso District, Eastern Ethiopia," *Journal of Modern African Studies*, 47(2), 2009, 213–239.
[37] Catherine Besteman and Lee V. Cassanelli, eds., *The Struggle for Land in Southern Somalia: The War behind the War*, Boulder, CO: Westview, 1996.

illustrated how everything that development meant in postwar Africa—explosive urban growth, foreign aid, agricultural intensification, emigration, and remittances—induced the shift of resources from traditional livelihoods toward meeting the consumption needs of a limited set of people. This inequality was "a central theme in modern Africa's rural history."[38]

In Somalia, since the 1990s, struggles for control over fertile land, pasture, and water have caused violent clashes between clans. "The lack of any recognized authority to address these conflicts increases their significance." The construction of Ethiopian dams complicated the situation because of the prospects of redistributing water and the absence of a framework for negotiating interregional water-sharing.[39] Disputes over pastures among pastoralist clans have always been common. The growth of human and animal populations and possibly drying of the climate worsened these, and the influx of cheap light weapons made clashes increasingly and brutally violent. Mogadishu was often called the arms hub of Africa.

Throughout the 1990s, as clan conflicts intensified, those who could repeatedly targeted food and water sources to weaken their opponents. Conflicts did not even mean bloodshed but simply starving the opponent, which was a relatively easy thing to do in interior Somalia and an effective weapon of war. Baidoa, a major city bordering an agricultural tract, saw a famine in 1992 from such circumstances and earned the epithet "the city of death," due to its situation at the intersection of conflicts.

Most recent studies of failed states like Somalia—with high levels of violence, competing authorities and jurisdictions, absence of viable negotiating platforms, and other ills—offer as a solution the creation of institutions, provision of public goods like education, and the rule of law, and essentially to bring development back on the government's agenda.[40] The prescription sounds hollow. Development costs money. The problem is that the domestic resource base—given the unrelentingly arid climate—does not supply enough resources to the central state to do any of this, or indeed, even to maintain an army that can prevail over the factions. Similarly, in diagnosing the state's failure in Somalia, many studies harp on the toxic inheritance of clan-based politics—a perennial contest without a referee, without sufficient

---

[38] Jon Unruh, "Resource Sharing—Smallholders and Pastoralists in the Lower Shabeelle Valley," in Besteman and Cassanelli, eds., *The Struggle for Land in Southern Somalia*, 115–130.

[39] World Bank, *Conflict in Somalia: Drivers and Dynamics*, Washington, DC: World Bank, 2005, cited text on p. 30.

[40] For example, Mwangi S. Kimenyi, John Mukum Mbaku, and Nelipher Moyo, "Reconstituting Africa's Failed States: The Case of Somalia," *Social Research*, 77(4), 2010, 1339–1366.

220 WATER AND DEVELOPMENT

recognition of what the contest has been over, which is decreasing per-capita access to land, grazing, and water.

Cities

As economies grew and diversified, cities and the countryside increasingly competed for river water. India's generally rapid economic growth since the 1990s added to the fear that nonagricultural demand for water was growing too fast. The worry came from near-reckless private groundwater exploitation by farmers or city-dwellers. Water clashes have grown in India's mega-cities, where "a combination of institutional path dependence and a neoliberal restructuring" has "extended the ability of [the cities] to establish new forms of water entitlement in rural and peri-urban areas."[41] India's federalism and the lobbying power of farmers and urban elites have kept the contestation under check, for now at least.

Political ecology scholarship shows how drinking water shortages have intensified and sometimes caused conflicts in the cities. During several episodes in North Africa, large-scale political shifts followed. The Arab Spring in 2011 in Tunisia led to an increase in informal connections to drinking water networks. Uncontrolled building activities increased, and the price of water fell because of unregulated access. At the same time, seasonal shortages and breakdown of the network became more common.[42] In the backdrop of extreme aridity, the diversion of water from sources used by rural communities to serve urban needs has been a potent root of low-key conflicts and legal disputations. Sonora in Mexico is another example.[43]

Conclusion

Not all conflicts in the tropics are about resources. However, some of the most lasting ones suggest that the inequality of water access and poor productivity of land and pasture have contributed to these. International

[41] Bharat Punjabi and Craig A. Johnson, "The Politics of Rural-Urban Water Conflict in India: Untapping the Power of Institutional Reform," *World Development*, 120, 2019, 182–192.

[42] M. Hassen Baouab and Semia Cherif, "Revolution Impact on Drinking Water Consumption," *Social Indicators Research*, 132(2), 2017, 841–859. See also M.L. Bouguerra, *Les batailles de l'eau: pour un bien commun de l'humanité*, Paris: Enjeux Planète, 2003.

[43] Lucero Radonic, "Environmental Violence, Water Rights, and (Un) Due Process in Northwestern Mexico," *Latin American Perspectives*, 42(5), 2015, 27–47.

hydropolitics warms up and wanes, depending on the effectiveness of the negotiating platforms. The occasional threat of war notwithstanding, the negotiated model has become more acceptable and deep-rooted in some places more than others. We do not know yet why the trade-off between development and water stress broke out in civil war in one place and was negotiated in another.

Will climate change make it worse? Chapter 12 returns to this question. Before that, we need to gather some thoughts on pastoralism, the natural livelihood of the semi-arid.

Chapter Eleven
Tropical Pastoralism

Savannas or grasslands cover about 20 percent of the earth's land area, often merging into the desert edge in the world's tropics. Animal herding is usually the only livelihood possible in these lands. Herders appear in the previous chapters many times. What is their story? The legend everyone seems to believe is that pastoralism has declined—in some cases, from the colonial era in the nineteenth century. "Today," the World Bank wrote in 2008, "mobility of pastoralists is increasingly being constrained, which is causing the effectiveness of the pastoral system to deteriorate fast."[1] Regional historiographies confirm the diminishing capacity of pastoralists to cope with droughts and famines. In the late 1960s, a study of Somalia observed "a strong and persistent tendency for the proportion of the nomads to shrink." "In the latter half of the twentieth century," writes a study on Western Sahara, "traditional nomadic societies have come under increasing pressure to change or adapt their precarious way of life."

In India, the decline began in the late nineteenth century, when the vast grasslands of Punjab, the bār, were converted into "canal colonies" by engineers working for the British colonial state. Historians of North India think that the British Indian state did not like nomadic peoples for many reasons and wanted to suppress them when they had a chance. Elsewhere, prolonged droughts delivered the final blow. In the late twentieth century, "there [was] more than 50 percent decline in the area of commons and grazing pasture lands in the country."[2] "Pastoralism in Ethiopia is under increasing pressure, caught in a downward spiral of resource depletion and diminishing resilience against shocks and stresses."[3] A study of Fulani herders in Nigeria

---

[1] World Bank, *Sustainable Land Management Sourcebook*, Washington, DC: World Bank Publications, 2008, 209.

[2] Kanna K. Siripurapu, Sushma Iyengar, Vasant Saberwal, and Sabyasachi Das, *An Overview of Mobile Pastoralism in Andhra Pradesh and Telangana States of the Deccan Plateau Region of India*, New Delhi: Centre for Pastoralism, 2018, 52.

[3] Tagesse Melketo, Martin Schmidt, Michelle Bonatti, Stefan Sieber, Klaus Müller, and Marcos Lana, "Determinants of Pastoral Household Resilience to Food Insecurity in Afar Region, Northeast Ethiopia," *Journal of Arid Environments*, 188, 2021, 1–11, cited text on p. 1.

Water and Development. Tirthankar Roy, Oxford University Press. © Oxford University Press (2025).
DOI: 10.1093/oso/9780197802397.003.0011

observed in 1995 that "only about a third of the Fulbe live a nomadic to semi-nomadic lifestyle at this time."[4] Similar stories are told about Sudan, Kenya, and the Fulani of Mali.[5] The decline story implies a competition over land that farmers and herders fought over, and the farmers won.

But not all the decline was unhappy or forced. Mineral discovery led to more benign forms of decline. Diamonds in Botswana, oil drilling in the Arab Peninsula, and phosphate mining in Mauritania and the Western Sahara led to either sedentarization of the nomads in the cities or where herding survived, to heavy subsidization of the herding activity. Some former pastures were converted into wildlife reserves, and the pastoralists were reemployed as reserve workers. These are exceptions.

The generally accepted story is one of decline and retreat, initiated by European colonialists and sustained by nation-states. But this is a legend and it is not true. It is based on myths, not facts. Global land use data do not show that pastures are in absolute decline. Pastures had been growing as a proportion of land surface for centuries before the present. The growth accelerated after 1800 and was rapid between 1850 and 1970 (5 to 22 percent).[6] These numbers contradict the fact that European colonialists disliked nomads and nomadism. Colonialism aided pastoralists by fixing property rights on land, in effect demarcating those lands where the pastoralists could move around undisturbed. The global meat market exploded, encouraging pastoralists to expand stocks. Stocks grew in the interwar period because droughts and epidemic diseases were managed better. Some of the most significant pastoralist peoples, like the Tuareg, Fulani, or Maasai, were studied, and their histories were documented in these times. All of that happened during a golden age for pastoralists in tropical Africa.

Pasture growth stopped around 1970, at about 22 to 24 percent of the global land surface. The golden age ended in the 1970s because the Sahelian climate was becoming drier. The midcentury droughts in Asia and Africa also reinforced the states' resolve to build more dams, subsidize the green

---

[4] Wendy Wilson, "The Fulani Model of Sustainable Agriculture: Situating Fulbe Nomadism in a Systemic View of Pastoralism and Farming," *Nomadic Peoples*, 1995 (36/37), 35–51, cited text on p. 37.

[5] Essays in J. Markakis, ed., *Conflict and the Decline of Pastoralism in the Horn of Africa*, Basingstoke: Palgrave Macmillan, 1993. Also Sara Pantuliano, "Oil, Land and Conflict: The Decline of Misseriyya Pastoralism in Sudan," *Review of African Political Economy*, 37(123), 2010, 7–23; Suzette Heald, "Agricultural Intensification and the Decline of Pastoralism: A Case Study from Kenya," *Africa: Journal of the International African Institute*, 69(2), 1999, 213–237.

[6] Kees Klein Goldewijk, Arthur Beusen, Gerard van Drecht, and Martine de Vos, "The HYDE 3.1 Spatially Explicit Database of Human-Induced Global Land-Use Change over the Past 12,000 Years," *Global Ecology and Biogeography*, 20, 2011, 73–86.

224   WATER AND DEVELOPMENT

revolution, and convert semi-arid lands into agricultural land. When many governments embarked on development in the late twentieth century, the specialist herders' position became unstable because rural development usually concentrated on converting pasture into farmland.[7] People who had been exclusively dependent on livestock shed that dependence and tried to acquire farmlands. On the other side, population growth and growth of meat consumption encouraged pastoralism to expand. Under these contradictory forces, the net gain of pastoral land hit zero. The crucial agent in this alternative story is water, not land. Water projects promised conversion. Land conversion did not end herding but adversely affected transhumant herding, favoring ranch-style herding in combination with farms where that option was feasible. I develop this story in the present chapter.

Two qualifications are necessary at the outset. First, the chapter is not about pastoralism nor all arid areas where herding exists. It is about pastoralism *in semi-arid tropical regions*. The key feature of that environment is seasonality. The foraging grounds are seasonal, and since the strength and pathway of the monsoon rains are variable, the grounds shift from one year to another. That condition contrasts with Central Asian steppes, where seasonality has a different meaning. Map 11.1 makes the distinction more explicit.

A second qualification is necessary to explain why even if there was no overall and absolute decline, nor a retreat of herding, pastoralists could still get caught up in disputatious claims over resources. If not a retreat, there was still a transformation: the progressive integration of herding with farming. I suggest that the integration was a specific feature of semi-arid tropical pastoralism. It stemmed from the fact that some pastures had potential uses as farmlands if water projects could mitigate seasonality. That integration, I also suggest, was disturbed and generated discords because pastures were historically underlegislated. The right to a converted land was open to interpretation because it did not previously exist. The crucial agent in this narrative is water, not land. Water projects promised converting land from one use to another, from pasture to farm. The prospect of converting seasonal fields to perennial grazing-cum-farmland rests at the heart of the modern pastoralist transition.

The rest of the chapter consists of three themes: the default analytical narratives, the long-range history of tropical pastoralism inferred from the

---

[7] A series of studies compiled in a collaborated work published in 1990 revisit these themes for the Sahelian and East African agropastoral groups. Mette Bovin and Leif Manger, eds., *Adaptive Strategies in African Arid Lands*, Uppsala: Scandinavian Institute of African Studies, 1990.

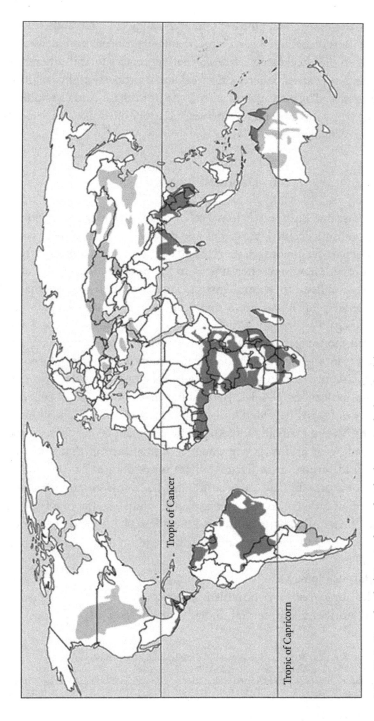

Map 11.1 Grasslands (Tropical grasslands shown in darker shade).
Source: Data in public domain.

226 WATER AND DEVELOPMENT

evolution of the monsoonal climatic and archaeological data, and regions and cases of transformation. By and large, the desert fringe is excluded from the regional studies because the transformation came late and differently from the semi-arid areas, where waterworks and property rights reforms had more agency. The narrative that emerges from these studies is different from the tragic folklores that historians and economists like to tell about pastoralism. What are these folklores?

Two Declinist Legends

One legend says that European colonial rule in Asia and Africa was responsible for pastoralism's decline. Europeans assumed governance of these lands without a deep understanding of the dryland environment so different from Western Europe. They were often hostile to the nomadic herders because the latter were difficult to tax and govern. The states tried to collect taxes from the herders, but it was not a significant source of state income nor a secure one against the risk of cattle disease and droughts. Farmers and planters paid more taxes than herders.[8] Because tropical pastoralism was an adaptation to a geographical condition, it embodied distinct forms of knowledge. Colonial administrators thought they knew how to farm better than the Indigenous peoples. By pushing that knowledge as superior science, they indirectly devalued Indigenous practices and understandings, some of which were gradually forgotten. The colonial bias for farms stood on a misreading of aridity as a product of human action that scientific practices could reverse or mitigate.[9] Where they could build large water projects to transform the landscape, pastoralists became irrelevant. "Pastoral nomads were of little consequence in a plan as unique as the one laid out for Punjab."[10] An unfamiliarity with what the nomadic life meant hardened the distance. The colonizers were instead "brought up in an old foodgrain civilization."[11]

Social purpose joined the scientific ambition. A pattern of "privileging settled cultivating areas over unsettled pastoral areas repeatedly appeared throughout northern and central India." The division between peasant

---

[8] For Ethiopia in the 1970s, tax made a powerful justification for land conversion.

[9] Diana Davis, *The Arid Lands*, Cambridge, MA: MIT Press, 2018.

[10] Indu Agnihotri, "Ecology, Land Use and Colonisation: The Canal Colonies of Punjab," *Indian Economic and Social History Review*, 33(1), 1996, 37–58, cited text on p. 43. See also Behnke and Kerven, "Replacing Pastoralism."

[11] Jacques Pouchepadass, "Colonialism and Environment in India: Comparative Perspective," *Economic and Political Weekly*, 30(33), 1995, 2059–2067, cited text on p. 2065.

castes and pastoralist and mobile tribes hardened in the colonial mind.[12] Distrust of the transhumant pastoralists as an ungovernable entity reinforced the bias. "To the British," a study of Punjab says, "seemingly fluid landscapes and shifting habitations connoted anarchy. . . . Keen to incorporate pastoral spaces within the settled agrarian order, the British officials moved vigorously to map them as village spaces."[13] A consensus among environmental historians is that the colonial authorities were keen on sedentarizing the nomads from an impulse that was more political than economic.[14]

The political drivers were part fiscal and part military. Most historians of early British rule in India agree about "the [East India] Company's repugnance for mobile social groups."[15] The eighteenth-century political turmoil drew the Indian pastoralist groups into a new set of political relationships and pushed them more than before to take up arms.[16] A fear of rootless mercenaries may have hardened the sentiment. This account of a fall of pastoralism as a by-product of a European military enterprise finds support among Africanists. "The colonial period was, for nomads, one of diminished opportunities. Even when they did settle permanently, they did it as a response to restricted freedom of movement and an inability to maintain their traditional livelihood."[17] In northern-eastern Kenya, "a broader purpose of disciplining and controlling what local officials believed to be unruly Somali pastoralists" lay behind British development plans for the region.[18]

The facts do not support the environmental historian that there was a state-engineered decline in pastoralism. There was no decline. Instead, a rise in pastoralism took place during colonialism. The colonial era in Africa and Asia saw a significant rise in herd animal population, a

[12] Brian Caton, "Social Categories and Colonisation in Panjab, 1849–1920," *Indian Economic and Social History Review*, 41(1), 2004, 33–50, cited text on p. 50.

[13] Neeladri Bhattacharya, *The Great Agrarian Conquest: The Colonial Reshaping of a Rural World*, Ranikhet, India: Permanent Black, 2019, 87.

[14] Diana K. Davis, *Resurrecting the Granary of Rome: Environmental History and French Colonial Expansion in North Africa*, Athens: Ohio University Press, 2007.

[15] Seema Alavi, "The Makings of Company Power: James Skinner in the Ceded and Conquered Provinces, 1802–1840," *Indian Economic and Social History Review*, 30(4), 1993, 437–466, cited text on p. 454.

[16] Around 1800, Begum Samru's army of several thousand soldiers "became the vehicle for the upward social mobility of the semi-pastoral and herdsmen communities ... who had so far remained on the fringe of the Mughal political tradition." Alavi, "The Makings of Company Power."

[17] Victor Azarya, "Pastoralism and the State in Africa: Marginality or Incorporation?" *Nomadic Peoples*, 38, 1996, 11–36, cited text on p. 23.

[18] Hannah Whittaker, "Frontier Security in North East Africa," *Journal of African History*, 58(3), 2017, 381–402, cited text on p. 391.

228 WATER AND DEVELOPMENT

booming trade in animals—export and interregional—and even grassland expansion. The growing livestock trade as transportation costs fell and consumption levels increased encouraged herd sizes beyond the carrying capacity of the pastures. The control of cattle disease led to expansion in herds even as pastures shrank in quantity and quality. This was the case in East Africa and Sudan.[19] Weak states with an overdependence on pastures had an incentive to permit herds to grow. Most colonial regimes tolerated migration. In British Baluchistan in the interwar years, the government allowed migratory herds from Afghanistan to graze pastures and raise finances. "The vegetation of the pastures has everywhere received a setback owing to the increased numbers of animals," a 1945 account reported.[20] Herd sizes rose so much that colonial authorities often campaigned that overgrazing had reached levels high enough to cause desertification.[21]

The bad-colonialism narrative also simplifies how the European mind worked, overstates European agency in the economic history of land use, wrongly suggests that a bias toward sedentary lives was a colonial value, and implies that herders were a distinct set of people from farmers. In Africa, many colonial experts did see transhumant pastoralism as an adaptation to the tropical environment, especially where farmlands and grazing lands were unavailable year-round, savanna abounded, and droughts kept checks on herd size (containing the prospect of overgrazing).[22] A "rangeland paradigm" took shape in the twentieth century that saw pastoral mobility "as ecologically rational in an environment characterized by high variability of natural resources."[23] Herding was an adaptation to the variability of moisture and the scarcity of wet farmlands and a sensible choice on the desert edge, where the tsetse fly was inactive. The roots of that paradigm were colonial expertise.

---

[19] Harold F. Heady, "Rangeland Development in East Africa," in David Brokensha, ed., *Ecology and Economic Development in Tropical Africa*, Berkeley: University of California Press, 1965, 73–82; J.H.G. Lebon, "Rural Water Supplies and the Development of Economy in the Central Sudan," *Geografiska Annaler*, 38(1), 1956, 78–101, cited text on p. 101.

[20] Harold Glover, "Soil Erosion In Baluchistan," *Empire Forestry Journal*, 24(1), 1945, 21–32, cited text on p. 23.

[21] The Otterman cycle: Overgrazing leads to a rise in surface albedo (a measure of diffuse reflection in total solar radiation) and reduced convection.

[22] Andrew Warren, "Changing Understandings of African Pastoralism and the Nature of Environmental Paradigms," *Transactions of the Institute of British Geographers*, 20(2), 1995, 193–203.

[23] See discussion in Hanne Kirstine Adriansen, "Understanding Pastoral Mobility: The Case of Senegalese Fulani," *Geographical Journal*, 174(3), 2008, 207–222, cited text on p. 207.

Recent economic history scholarship suggests that the tropical colonial states did not have the fiscal capacity to act on the impulse to change resource use radically. And they did not discover nor create a drive toward sedentarization. The nomadic and the sedentary were never separated. "A process of continuous sedentarization," writes a history of nomadism, in the long run "has to be recognized as a normal aspect of nomadism." In pre-colonial West Africa and West Asia, nomads lived in the cities, specialized as bankers and merchants, and settled down on land when that option seemed sensible (during a famine) or feasible (when open access land was available for farming). "The richest and the poorest among the nomads tend to sedentarize: the richest, when the size of their flocks exceeds the capacity of the grazing land available to the tribe; the poorest, when loss of livestock reduces their flock below the minimum need."[24]

Sedentarization as a permanent move toward plow agriculture was also an older thing. D.D. Kosambi, a historian of India, believed that pastoralism and slash-and-burn agriculture represented a primitive production system compared with settled agriculture and that "[t]heir decay followed the spread of a superior production complex (or mode of production), based on plough agriculture."[25] Kosambi's timespan was much longer than the nineteenth century.

Neither were farmers and herders distinct, nor were they rivals. Transhumance was a strategy for maintaining cattle stock that suited the seasonality of the tropical climate; farmers and herders both knew the value of doing this. In the twentieth century, as transhumant groups cultivated on the side, sedentary farming communities raised cattle if possible. In the western Sahel, the farmers kept cattle for meat and milk. Deep plowing with bullock power was rare because the soil was not suitable for deep plowing. Pastoralists had access to rock salt layers that met the sedentary peoples' demand for salt. The presence of sedentary people within the same communities gave the purely transhumant people better access to pastures than when the farmers

---

[24] M.B. Rowton, "Autonomy and Nomadism in Western Asia," *Orientalia*, 42, 1973, 247–258, cited text on p. 254.

[25] Sumit Guha, "States, Tribes, Castes: A Historical Re-exploration in Comparative Perspective," *Economic and Political Weekly*, 50(46–47), 2015, 50–57, cited text on p. 52. Kosambi was voicing an Indianist impulse to explain how castes became distinct from tribes. Plow agriculture was associated with castes, and pastoralism with tribes. The impulse to divide ancient societies into two types— one built around lineages like family and clan and another with a weak sense of lineage, commonly called tribal—reappears in other places, the tribal being identified with nomadic herding. See Daniel T. Potts, *Nomadism in Iran: From Antiquity to the Modern Era*, Oxford: Oxford University Press, 2014.

230 WATER AND DEVELOPMENT

represented other ethnic groups.[26] The distinction disappears again when we consider lands suitable for different uses in different seasons.

What was unique about colonialism was not a biased attitude but faith in coding private property rights. The legal definition of private property was a work in progress, but pastoralist rights were almost everywhere outside the law. Therefore, allocating private rights sometimes took away land used by the herders, as in Punjab. More universally, the move defined farmlands and, by default, grazing lands. Paradoxically, that made it easier for pastoralist peoples to grow their herds, and when the herds grew too large, to degrade the pasture.

A second story builds on economists' distinction between "open access" and "common pool" and the claim that a legally secure right ensures efficient use of assets. No recognized or enforceable property rights protect open-access natural resources.[27] Since no user can legally exclude competing users of the same asset, they fight it out or overuse and degrade the property. In short, open access entails the risk of conflict, capture, and decline.[28] A stylized history follows: In the beginning, most pastoral property was open access. Open access is also exposed to capture by politically backed private entrepreneurs, like European settlers in a colonial regime. Hence the crisis of pastoralism. Garrett Hardin's "tragedy of the commons" paper was the first concise statement of the possibility.[29]

Once again, this model is unhelpful as a theory of the history of pastoralism. It presumes a decline and then explains it with a political logic. But there was no decline. In a 2003 review of the field, Arun Agarwal criticized the property rights paradigm for its inattention to external forces like "demographic change, market penetration, and state policies."[30] One can add to this list dams and drills to convert pastures into farmlands.

If tropical pastoralism is an outcome of the climatic condition, it should be easy to re-create the baseline from long-range climate and land-use data.

---

[26] Wilson, "The Fulani Model of Sustainable Agriculture."

[27] Vincent Ostrom and Elinor Ostrom, "Public Goods and Public Choices," in E.S. Savas, ed., *Alternatives for Delivering Public Services: Toward Improved Performance*, Boulder, CO: Westview Press, 1977.

[28] Dean Lueck and Thomas J. Miceli, "Property Law," in A. Mitchell Polinsky and Steven Shavell, eds., *Handbook of Law and Economics*, Amsterdam: Elsevier, 2007, 186–257.

[29] Garrett Hardin, "The Tragedy of the Commons," Science, n.s., 162, no. 3859, 1968, 1243–48. Commons, a potential response to this problem, are a field where an identified user group or a government working for them has an enforceable legal right. That right mimics private property rights in that it can exclude those outside the designated group.

[30] Arun Agrawal, "Sustainable Governance of Common-Pool Resources: Contexts, Methods, Politics," *Annual Review of Anthropology*, 32, 2003, 243–262, cited text on p. 250.

The Arid Tropics and the Rise of Pastoralism

A rainfall level of 250 mm (about 10 inches) is the minimum necessary for any farming.[31] Most of North Africa, the Middle East, the Horn of Africa, and Namibia have less; other tropical countries have extensive areas with less rainfall. However, even low levels of seasonal moisture influx can create grasslands, making it possible for livestock to survive, provided they move to moist areas in the dry season. For this reason, transhumant pastoralism was extensive and well adapted to the tropical environment for much of the Holocene, when the present-day pattern of monsoons emerged in Asia and Africa.

Climatic conditions during the Holocene were not stable. There were episodes of "savannization." There is debate over whether the process was anthropogenic or climatic. Current research suggests that it was the latter in the Neolithic periods. Warming and cooling of climate happened in the past, though evidence does not show that these occurred synchronously around the globe.[32] Based on lake sediments from Lonar Crater in peninsular India, a study reconstructs climate history in the recent millennia.[33] In South Asia, the Holocene warming and cooling episodes were unique because the impact depended mainly on the effects of snowmelt and the summer monsoon, factors not present (as prominently) elsewhere in the tropical world. However, conditions in South Asia were not similar. The riparian north that received meltwater and the dry rainfed peninsula would differ in human response to climate change.

A warming early- to mid-Holocene (8000–5000 BP, or 8–5 kybp) raised insolation, the summer monsoon strengthened, and meltwater levels rose. The urban-riparian Indus Valley settlements emerged in this phase. The first farming villages in the north appeared at 5–4 kybp, and in the Deccan, after 4 kybp, though these were agropastoral. A subsequent cooling (4–3.3 kybp) reduced monsoon strength and meltwater levels. The Harappan settlements declined. In the riparian Indo-Gangetic Basin, farming continued. In the rain-dependent Deccan Plateau, savannization caused the abandonment of settlements for mobile herding.

---

[31] Thomas Vettera and Anna-Katharina Rieger, "Ancient Water Harvesting in the Old World Dry Belt—Synopsis and Outlook," *Journal of Arid Environments* 169, 2019, 42–53.

[32] Raphael Neukom, Nathan Steiger, Juan José Gómez-Navarro, Jianghao Wang, and Johannes P. Werner, "No Evidence for Globally Coherent Warm and Cold Periods over the Preindustrial Common Era," *Nature*, 571, 2019, 550–554.

[33] Nils Riedel, Dorian Q. Fuller, Norbert Marwan, Constantin Poretschkin, Nathani Basavaiah, Philip Menzel, Jayashree Ratnam, Sushma Prasad, Dirk Sachse, Mahesh Sankaran, Saswati Sarkar, and Martina Stebich, "Monsoon Forced Evolution of Savanna and the Spread of Agro-Pastoralism in Peninsular India," *Scientific Reports*, 11, 2021, 1–13.

232 WATER AND DEVELOPMENT

A puzzle is the Minoan Warming. During the Minoan Warming, the average temperature in peninsular India was 3°C higher than in the late twentieth century and about 2° higher than 4000 BP (4 kybp). The warming peaked at around 3.3–3 kybp. According to previous logic, the summer monsoon was stronger. Archaeological evidence from the Deccan Plateau shows that early farmers abandoned sedentary lives and took to pastoralism in many "southern-neolithic" sites. Archaeologists attributed the shift to pastoralism to increased aridity, pointing at another warming effect: surface water evaporation.[34] I read the evidence to mean that farming was not abandoned, but the population adapted to agropastoralism. In the Indo-Gangetic Basin, the farming and cattle-based settlements spread, turning political (the Mauryan Empire's rise began around this time).[35]

There were subsequent cooling and warming episodes, but the entrenchment of agriculture, which also stabilized the grazing zones and the adoption of dry crops, may have moderated the impact on livelihoods. It is safe to speculate that in the Common Era, climate changes were regional (as discussed), and local anthropogenic forces operated more strongly behind livelihood modulations. Pollen data analysis suggests that agriculture and pastoralism were stable in the Common Era in peninsular India.

These patterns of change cannot be generalized to the tropical world. India and its summer monsoons have been studied more than the climate history of Africa. One thing seems certain. Changes taking place in the twentieth century were an outcome of institutional, technological, and demographic variables that took shape in these times. These agents produced contradictory results, sometimes encouraging herding and sometimes suppressing it. More universally, it brought the two nearer, giving rise to "ranch-style" or sedentary herding rather than transhumant mobile types. A few regional examples of the dual process can be helpful to understand the transformation from nomadic herding to agro-pastoralism. I restate the analytical narrative explaining the story at the end of the chapter.

Why is long-run climate history important for my purpose? Because it explains that the farming-herding combination in the long past fluctuated according to climatic warming phases. We cannot just build legends of decline and fall without checking with climate history data first. What had

---

[34] M.K. Dhavalikar, "Farming to Pastoralism: Effects of Climatic Change in the Deccan," in Juliet Clutton-Brock, ed., *The Walking Larder. Patterns of Domestication, Pastoralism, and Predation*, London: Unwin Hyman, 1989, 156–168.

[35] Gayatri Kathayat, Hai Cheng, Ashish Sinha, Liang Yi, Xianglei Li, Haiwei Zhang, Hangying Li, Youfeng Ning, and R. Lawrence Edwards, "The Indian Monsoon Variability and Civilization Changes in the Indian Subcontinent," *Science Advances*, 3, 2017, 1–8.

happened since the twentieth century was a permanent shift in this modulation. It happened due to human intervention *in water*, a dimension of the Anthropocene not emphasized enough.

With a set of region studies, the rest of the chapter illustrates the point.

West Africa (Senegal and Niger Basins)

In the nineteenth century, nomadism was widespread on the western fringes of the Sahara, from Algeria and Morocco to Mauritania and further south in Senegal and Mali. Few serious studies were conducted on the communities engaged in nomadism and herding in this broad region, with occasional exceptions (Figure 11.1). More substantial material to interest the historian exists for the riparian areas in the south, in Mali and Senegal.

Figure 11.1 *Nomads of Bechar*, by Antonio Beato, 1864

Antonio (Antoine) Beato (1832–1906) was a British-Italian photographer. With his brother Felice Beato, he popularized documentary-style photography. Beato traveled extensively in the Middle East and North Africa. This family of herders was based in Bechar, an area in western Algeria, where grazing was one of the three main occupations, the other two being agriculture in the oases and the trans-Saharan trade. Tourism and transportation access changed the livelihood pattern beginning in the late twentieth century.
Source: Alamy Stock Photos

234   WATER AND DEVELOPMENT

The territory of Mali can be divided into northern nomadic and southern farming regions. The division based on livelihood was reinforced by the governmental institutions of the south penetrating the north. The northern part belonged to the French colonial empire. The colonialists governed at arm's length by promising nomadic groups their independence if they acknowledged formal French authority. That type of peace also meant that the government underinvested in these areas compared to the farmland areas. The arm's-length relationship continued after independence. Government officers were reluctant to go on postings to the north, investment in communication was limited, and attempts to reclaim power provoked rebellion.

The nomadic herders in these desert fringe areas have traditionally been only pastoralists, exchanging goods with farmers and taxing them but rarely engaging in farming. They also had little in common with the agricultural southern half of Mali, which had held political power since independence. Tuareg rebellions of the 1960s were a reaction to this divergence, deepened by socialist economic policies that made little accommodation to pastoralism. The drought of 1968–1974 hit the nomads of Malian Sahel hard. Many left for city jobs, moved into refugee camps, left the country, and took up agriculture. The sense remained that the government did not see the pastoral nomad as a political ally or an economic asset. Tuareg communities became a recruitment ground for various rebel groups in the region.[36] In turn, the communal element made alliances more fractious.

In relatively water-rich Niger, also home to a significant Tuareg population, the government invested money in the 1960s and the 1970s in water schemes for the pastoral nomads, and more Tuareg joined the administration and the army. Still, a sense of "homeland" prevailed, and attempts to retain control over it provoked resistance. From the late twentieth century, uranium mining in this homeland complicated the scenario.

In the inland Niger Delta, the nature of pastoralism and the groups involved are different; with a land almost 3 million hectares in extent, a land use pattern had come into existence centuries ago. The wetlands in the delta enabled rice farming during and after the rains and dry-season

[36] David Michel, "Case Study: Mali," in US Institute of Peace, *Water Conflict Pathways and Peacebuilding Strategies*, Washington, DC: US Institute of Peace, 2020, 14–17, cited text on p. 17.

pasture for the rest of the year. The Fulani herders had considerable political and military power before French colonial rule was established in 1892. Expansion of colonial rule made interregional migration and dispersal of the pastoralists easier.[37] Some of these groups settled elsewhere as farmers. In the early twentieth century, areas bordering the Sahel developed close cooperation between settled groups and migrant herders, secured by their shared interest in animals as a productive resource and an article of growing trade. A cattle tax encouraged the colonial authorities to take an interest.

The 1970s drought and the Niger dam projects permanently shrank this active delta, and the reliance upon artificial irrigation systems increased. In the 1970s, the World Bank funded the reconstruction of dykes used in lowland rice cultivation. Canals and dykes empowered some communities with access to these technologies. Those nearer the hyper-arid areas faced "an inexorable process of erosion and desertification."[38] Thus, in the late twentieth century, in the inland Niger Delta, there was a gradual shift away from pastoralism toward agropastoralism.

Early-twentieth-century accounts of pastoralism in wetter Cameroon and Nigeria again harp on cooperation. German colonial rule had ended in Cameroon in 1916. The successor regime welcomed the cross-border migration of the herders. The farmers in this relatively green plateau benefited from the presence of the herders because much land lay either permanently or seasonally fallow. The herders also paid taxes. In Nigeria, again, the parties depended on each other via "an unspoken contract involving the exchange of dung for [millet] stubble" in the dry season.[39] "The town and cattle Fulani," wrote a 1991 study of the group in Nigeria, "are half brothers."[40]

While not breaking out in wars, the symbiosis became unstable in the late twentieth century. With continued migration, overgrazing and discord emerged as serious issues in Cameroon.[41] In Nigeria, the relentless conversion of grazing lands into lands suitable for year-round farming and changes

---

[37] Adebayo, "Of Man and Cattle."
[38] Derrick J. Thom and John C.C. Wells, "Farming Systems in the Niger Inland Delta, Mali," *Geographical Review*, 77(3), 1987, 328–342.
[39] M.O. Awogbade, "Fulani Pastoralism and the Problems of the Nigerian Veterinary Service," *African Affairs*, 78 (313), 1979, 493–506, cited text on p. 502.
[40] Adebayo, "Of Man and Cattle."
[41] Martin Z. Njeuma and Nicodemus F. Awasom, "The Fulani and the Political Economy of the Bamenda Grasslands, 1940–1960," *Paideuma: Mitteilungen zur Kulturkunde*, 36, 1990, 217–233.

236   WATER AND DEVELOPMENT

in feeds and fertilizers reduced the interdependence in the late twentieth century. Herders would use pastures next to these lands when crops stood on farmlands late in the wet season. This was a perennial source of dispute because animals could also damage crops.

Sudan

Before colonial schemes like Gezira began in Sudan, pastoralism prevailed as one of the main livelihoods away from the Nile and its tributaries. As in French West Africa, the British in Sudan dealt with the pastoralists marginally, not knowing what to do about them. The British, however, believed in property rights and initiated a drive to reform those rights. Practice was another matter. Administrative capacity and information on preexisting rights were limited, and one reformer, Herbert Kitchener, left titling common lands in British Sudan entirely out of the scope of the legislation. His successor, George Wingate, engaged with it, but only when he tried to offer land to an American business to develop cotton plantations and discovered that he lacked the legal means to do so. The officer in charge believed that documentary evidence to support claims of collective use was unreliable, and no other form of evidence was available.[42]

After independence in Sudan in 1956, the national government added another element to the reform program: "The assumption that all nomads have to proceed to higher standards of living through settlement and adoption of agriculture."[43] The instrument was public investment in water. In parallel, a reluctance to intervene in pastoralist lives persisted because the administration had little reliable data on how many nomads there were.[44]

The Gezira Scheme was for farmers who had long settled in the area. But other plans taken up after independence—using the waters of the Atbara in the far east of the country and a small tributary to the Blue Nile, the Rahad—appeared in areas where nomadism had been one of the main livelihoods. Around 1970, "recently sedentarized" nomadic groups near the Nile

---

[42] Steven Serels, "Political Landscaping: Land Registration, the Definition of Ownership and the Evolution of Colonial Objectives in the Anglo-Egyptian Sudan, 1899–1924," *African Economic History*, 35, 2007, 59–75.

[43] Salih A. El-Arifi, "A Regional Approach to Planning and Development of Pastoral Nomads in the Sudan," *Sudan Notes and Records*, 56, 1975, 147–159, cited text on p. 148.

[44] "Basically you were recorded as 'nomadic' only when the enumerator could not put you in another category!" Sameer Alredaisy, Abdel Aziem Tinier, and Jack Davies, "Farming, Herding, Water and Rangeland in the Butana," *Sudan Studies*, 44, 2011, 57–69, cited text on p. 64.

floodplains practiced some flush cultivation.[45] Droughts in the 1970s pushed many of them deeper into agriculture. Decades into their operation, the irrigation projects divided the nomadic herder peoples into several groups. There were still many who developed no ties with farmland. However, a substantial number also held tenancies in the irrigated area. In short, the herders adapted to farmland development in the river valley by diversifying or even becoming farmers, with their herds on the rise.

What about the animal herders farther away? Little was known about them until the Darfur conflict in 2003 revealed the presence of Arabic-speaking herders dispersed over a large region. They came under attention when they were caught up in the contest between the Arab militia and the farmers.

Southern Africa

A large savanna land was located on the borders of Angola and Namibia, where cattle population and cattle export rose sharply beginning in the twentieth century. The local rulers were as keen as the colonial powers controlling the region to develop trade and the "cattle commodification" on which trade was built. With the growth of the livestock trade, and the retreat of rinderpest, animals became so attractive an asset that "formerly agricultural people" of the region "became a pastoral people."[46]

In the highlands, underlegislation of pastoral property was less of a problem than intergroup competition for limited pasture. The formation of the Basotho nation in the 1820s set the stage for a contest over scarce land between the Boer herders and the agropastoral population of the region. The highlands received enough rains to sustain farmlands, good pastures, and a cattle population. Milk and stored grain provided insurance against droughts. The white settler areas were too dry to maintain intensive farming and depended on herding. Cattle did not adapt easily to the pasture available; sheep could. Boers who had migrated from the Cape Colony saw a potential to export wool and specialized in raising wool-bearing sheep. The

[45] David R. Lee, "The Location of Land Use Types: The Nile Valley in Northern Sudan," *Economic Geography*, 46(1), 1970, 53–62, cited text on p. 57.
[46] Emmanuel Kreike, "De-globalisation and Deforestation in Colonial Africa: Closed Markets, the Cattle Complex, and Environmental Change in North-Central Namibia, 1890–1990," *Journal of Southern African Studies*, 35(1), 2009, 81–98.

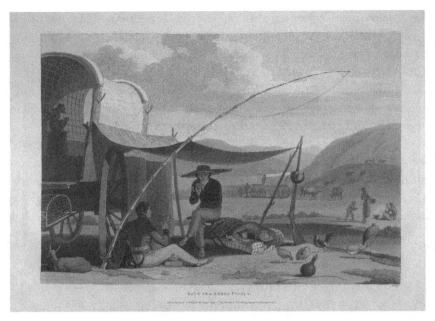

Figure 11.2 "Halt of a Boer's Family," 1804 engraving by Samuel Daniel

Migration from the coast to the interior was a core part of the legend of the Dutch-descendant peoples of southern Africa and inspired many images and photographs. For nomadic Boers, movements were a search for pastures, sometimes leading to contests with other nomadic groups and farmers.
Source: British Library

offer of cheap land grants encouraged land speculation, driving the Boers further into pastoralism (Figure 11.2).

From the 1830s, droughts exposed the settlers to considerable stress. Settlers in the coastal areas were better off accessing the seaborne trade in food grains. Those in the interior lived with a nonexistent trade and transport system and unreliable pastures. The grain trade relied on draft oxen. Droughts made it impossible to feed the animals on the move and stopped the caravan trade.[47] The rivers were not navigable, and the first railways were built in the 1880s. The switch to wool-bearing sheep had reduced the meat supply. "The Boers . . . experienced famine for the first time in 1863."

Raiding the dry-season pasture lands was an inevitable response. Such raids had happened before. In the 1860s, the raids led to the transfer of

---

[47] Elizabeth A. Eldredge, "Drought, Famine and Disease in Nineteenth-Century Lesotho," *African Economic History*, 16, 1987, 61–93.

control over a large part of the king's territory to the settler-pastoralists. At the same time, population growth, immigration of refugees, the disappearance of wildlife, and the loss of cattle exposed the king's territory to famines. Arable land continued to expand at the expense of the pastures as the opportunity to export grain rose. "By the end of the nineteenth century, the Basotho had lost their capacity to withstand periods of food scarcity."[48]

This story is unique in the tropical world because of the high proportion of European farmers and herders in South Africa (more than a third of the population in the early twentieth century). The history was somewhat different in Botswana, where significant changes in the position of the pastoralists followed the discovery of minerals. About 5 percent of the land area in the country is suitable for cultivation. High temperatures and low rainfall make surface water scarce and unstable, even in the floodplains of the two main rivers. Botswana remained free of the kind of contests for land that happened in South Africa.

From the mid-twentieth century, the Botswanan economy became dependent on diamond mining. In the 1970s and 1980s, as famines raged in northern and central Africa, the Botswanan government used its "very favourable foreign exchange position" to build a rural drilling program for small settlements. "Basically all the population, except nomads, has been able to obtain enough water for human consumption on a regular basis."[49] The program could not cover all nomadic herders because some lived in areas where drilling would not succeed. Overall, pastoralism received help and survived, if not profitably. Thanks to diamonds, pastoralism could remain an economic mainstream. Oil and phosphate mining near the Sahara produced a similar pattern, subsidizing nomadism. "A discriminatory [government] expenditure pattern," wrote a study of drought response, "favouring livestock development over arable production . . . serves to facilitate the transition by a traditional dominant group of cattle owners to a contemporary capitalist class of commercial farmers and industrialists."[50]

---

[48] Ibid., 85.

[49] John D. Holm and Richard G. Morgan, "Coping with Drought in Botswana: An African Success," *Journal of Modern African Studies*, 23(3), 1985, 463–482, cited text on p. 468.

[50] Roy Love, "Drought, Dutch Disease and Controlled Transition in Botswana Agriculture," *Journal of Southern African Studies*, 20(1), 1994, 71–83. Also, Kwaku Osei-Hwedie, "Food Policy: Managing Drought and the Environment in Botswana," *Africa Development*, 23(2), 1998, 61–83.

240 WATER AND DEVELOPMENT

East Africa

In the second half of the nineteenth century, the growing meat trade on the Somalian coast induced the Majeerteen clans to expand stocks and use pastures intensively. The gum and livestock trade made merchants who traded in the Arabian Sea grow rich. Ships from Bombay and Aden brought tobacco, rice, textiles, and iron. Their control over the trade cut the herders from the spot markets where they had sold earlier. The trade suffered from frequent drought conditions. Still, in the twentieth century, the meat trade expanded, trade in hides expanded, which made pastoralists money even as premium grazing lands receded.[51]

From the mid-twentieth century and before the great drought of the 1970s, the Somali nomads constructed cemented water reservoirs to trap rainwater. In the wet season, the herds moved over the orbit containing pastures. In the dry season, it would return to these reservoirs. According to a 1968 study, the reservoirs "[revolutionized] the economy of the nomad by almost trebling the numbers of his livestock and are creating permanent settlements which are slowly developing into pastoral/agricultural villages with the resultant need for social services."[52]

Unlike the driest pastures of Somalia or the Sahel desert edge, the Rift Valley grasslands are moist, and the farmland soil is potentially high-yielding. Considerable cultivation existed here in the seventeenth century, when many Maasai households began to give up mixed occupations and specialize as nomadic herders while maintaining close economic ties with cereal farmers.[53] British and German rules created a border between two extensive rangelands in a region that had no clear political boundary before. British rule in Kenya initially led to conflicts between the colonizer and the pastoralists, whom the former saw as an exclusive warlike group fiercely attached to their homeland. At the turn of the twentieth century, the two had found a way to live in peace. In Tanganyika, by contrast, tensions persisted. Partly as a result of continuing hostility and partly the expansion of European settler farming, in the first half of the twentieth century, pastoralists in Kenya,

---

[51] See contributions in Markakis, ed., *Conflict and the Decline of Pastoralism in the Horn of Africa*.

[52] Mohamed Haji Ibrahim Egal, "Somalia: Nomadic Individualism and the Rule of Law," *African Affairs*, 67(268), 1968, 219–226, cited text on p. 220.

[53] Thomas Spear and Richard Waller, eds., *Being Maasai: Ethnicity and Identity in East Africa*, Athens: Ohio University Press, 1993.

Tanganyika, and Uganda were confined to reserves, which restricted their economic opportunities but protected their access to the now more limited land available as pastures.

After independence in 1963, the farming bias became stronger, now reinforced by the fear that the pastoralists might damage good land by overgrazing. At the same time, new ideas on herd and pasture management promoted commercial and sedentary ranches. The pastoralists adapted by taking up farming when possible and joining the livestock trade more readily. In the process, their exclusive territory shrank significantly. Whereas the continuous land loss in evidence elsewhere affected the East African pastoralists, the forces leading to land loss also made the groups more unequal. "Increased commoditization of the livestock economy," for example, "has led to a growing polarization of pastoralists into haves and have-nots, particularly in Maasai areas close to urban markets."[54]

Ethiopia

Land conversion in Ethiopia was linked to the state's encouragement of capitalist farming. In 1895 a British firm, the Tendahao company, diversified from mining and engineering interests in South Africa to cotton in Ethiopia. The imperial state had promised the firm a large chunk of Afar grazing land. The regional ruler, the sultan of Awsa, was a minority shareholder and controller of farmland in the area. The sultan acquired lands bordering the plantation to preempt further such offers.[55]

The pressure to encourage more such farms grew after World War II when the discourse on development picked up in Ethiopia. The consensus was that the resettlement of herders on farmlands held the best prospect for all. Which land? The state stepped in around 1955 with a revised constitution that declared grazing lands to be state property, denying legal status to the user rights on which the Afar had depended. There was no actual dispossession because the state collected a cattle tax and, in return, implicitly recognized Afar rights to use but not own pastures. But the balance of sentiment had turned against the herders, and the state had asserted a

---

[54] Fratkin, "East African Pastoralism in Transition," cited text on p. 9.

[55] John H. Harbeson, "Territorial and Development Policies in the Horn of Africa: The Afar of the Awash Valley," *African Affairs*, 77(309), 1978, 479–498.

242   WATER AND DEVELOPMENT

territorial claim that could now be used to reallocate land for developmental purposes. The Marxist regime went much further along that road, with damaging consequences, as Chapter 10 has shown.

Madagascar

Madagascar illustrates differently the retreat of pastoralism and expansion of commercial cultivation. Ecological regions were sharply divided here during colonial rule. French colonialism led to growth of export crop cultivation: rice and coffee. This expansion happened in the wetter highlands and eastern plains. Hydraulic projects such as marshland conversion and dams and canals—in Lake Alaotra in the northeast—aided intensive cultivation. French settlers cultivated these lands until independence in 1960.

In colonial times, the pastoralist areas were spared because they were too distant from the core farming zones and unsuitable for conversion into arable lands. "The arid south became a labor reserve" instead.[56] In the long run, the development of commercial agriculture did not leave the arid southwest untouched. As a demographic transition began in the early twentieth century, taking off in the 1950s, the shift toward agropastoralism in the available river basins accelerated.[57] The retreat of the spiny thickets, a vegetation pattern in the southwest that sustained herding, placed pastoralist groups under pressure in the late twentieth century.[58]

India

Transhumant pastoralism was once extensive in India. Much of it disappeared in the nineteenth century, well before a similar tendency unfolded in Africa with the expansion of farmlands. The history of its decline in the Indo-Gangetic Basin was linked to population growth and expansion of agriculture and cattle-owning farmers. British colonial reforms pushed that

[56] Lucy Jarosz, "Defining and Explaining Tropical Deforestation: Shifting Cultivation and Population Growth in Colonial Madagascar (1896–1940)," *Economic Geography*, 69(4), 1993, 366–379, cited text on p. 370.

[57] The Linta basin in the southwest is an example, studied in Jeffrey C. Kaufmann and Sylvestre Tsirahamba, "Forests and Thorns: Conditions of Change Affecting Mahafale Pastoralists in Southwestern Madagascar," *Conservation and Society*, 4(2), 2006, 231–261.

[58] Karen Middleton, "Who killed 'Malagasy Cactus'? Science, environment and colonialism in southern Malagasar (1924-1930)," *Journal of Southern African Studies*, 25(2), 1999, 215-248.

TROPICAL PASTORALISM   243

tendency. The case of Punjab was mentioned earlier. Canals also came up in the western Gangetic Basin. Conditions resembling precolonial Punjab persisted in western Rajasthan (formerly Rajputana), where nomadic groups reared sheep and camels. The material to write a continuous history of these regions and these groups is hard to find.[59]

In the Deccan, two areas had extensive areas of pastoralism. One of these falls in a BSh zone bordering the present Andhra Pradesh and Karnataka states. In this very dry area, where, in 1876, a massive famine broke out, sheep herding by groups known as Kuruba or Kurumba was the main livelihood in the nineteenth century. The sheep breeds indigenous to the area did not produce a lot of wool or very fine wool, but they did yield quite sturdy wool, which was cheap. The herders also wove this into blankets and sold some of the wool to carpet and blanket makers in small towns in the area. This industry in the twentieth century did not exactly collapse but became slowly obsolete as forest reservations deprived some Kurubas of pasture, and others lost their market to imported wool.[60]

The second smaller region was located further south. The Kangayam grasslands in South India stretch over 1500 square miles in the north-central part of the Tamil Nadu state. This area received a lot more rain than the northern arid tracts, but not enough for rainfed paddy growing. Still, the grass here was rich enough to sustain cattle herding. Until the twentieth century, the grasslands were thinly populated, with few towns. The low density resulted in part from repeated famines in the region. Literary sources suggest that the influx of cattle-raising pastoral people from outside the area led to competition for pasture in the first millennium of the Common Era.[61] During the second millennium, there was a slow expansion of cultivation in the river valleys, even as pastoralism remained significant.

In the late eighteenth century, when the East India Company took over the administration of this region, records still described it as a land of shrubs and bushes. But the river valleys had received migrants for a long time. In the nineteenth century, there was a significant expansion of cultivation

---

[59] Among exceptions to that statement, studies on the Rabari must be mentioned. See Sigrid Westphal-Hellbusch, "Hinduistische Viehzüchter Nordwest-Indiens und Probleme ihrer gegenwärtigen Umstellung, an den Rabari exemplifiziert," *Sociologus*, 22(1/2), 1972, 49–75. More recently, Rabari textile heritage drew attention. Photographer Steve McCurry helped make the Rabari famous.

[60] Tirthankar Roy, "Changes in Wool Production and Usage in Colonial India," *Modern Asian Studies*, 37(2), 2003, 257–286.

[61] Anil Kumar, S. Natarajan, Nagaratna B. Biradar, and Brij K. Trivedi, "Evolution of Sedentary Pastoralism in South India: Case Study of the Kangayam Grassland," *Pastoralism*, 1(7), 2011, 1–18.

244 WATER AND DEVELOPMENT

and population. The growth did not happen at the pastoralists' expense; it was achieved by allocating grazing lands to the farmers, many of whom had received canal water from the Kaveri River. In this way, agropastoralism expanded. The government first took over pastures and then privatized them, and the nomadic herders were pushed to marginal lands, becoming increasingly obscure in the records.

I have called the two declinist interpretations of the history of tropical pastoralism legends. What is my story?

To End with a Reinterpretation

In recent decades, there was not a decline of pastoralism but a combination of contradictory forces. These forces were not, as we may think, capitalism, colonialism, and population growth. These variables did not have one-directional impacts. The meat trade encouraged the pastoralists, and the grain trade worked against them. The growth of herds due to better epidemic control was good news when there was the growing demand for meat, but bad news because the growth of humans and farmlands restricted the pastoralists' access to good grazing lands.

What happened since the 1970s was the accent on farming backed up by irrigation, in addition to public appropriation of pastures or eminent domain encouraging pastoralists to take up farmlands and farmers to keep herds. Droughts reinforced the trajectory. Transhumance declined, but there was no overall fall in pastoralism. In places. this process was disputatious because grazing lands had not entailed individual rights. There was no guidance from historical records about who had owned land that converted from one use to another. In colonial Punjab, the British Indian state solved this in one way. In many cases, the state might step in to allocate rights, but lobbying and force would derail the process.

Why was the right to pasture underlegislated? For two reasons: intrayear variation in moisture and interyear variation in moisture. Within-year seasonality made herders and farmers use the same plot. Farmers and herders had nonrival rights on the same plot, their lands being usable as farms or pastures in different seasons. From this baseline, any external push to change the land use from seasonal to year-round would threaten these arrangements. The external push came primarily from water projects, especially in areas served by a big dam.

The second reason that pastures are hard to regulate is that pastures are not one plot of land used yearly but a shifting domain, an orbit. In drier savannas, "grazing resources . . . are highly variable in space and time."[62] The transhumant pastoralists do not know where the best land is available in a specific season. Therefore, the potential grazing lands in a region formed the "macro pastoral orbit."[63] In drought years, the orbit would expand, and in rainy years, it would contract. "Arid lands are typically unstable," and pastoralist practices are a response to that geographical instability.[64] Another way to understand the orbit concept is via "key resources."[65] The pastoral orbit includes some areas that may not be used in average years but provide insurance, sometimes a tiny patch of land that survives droughts and provides dry-season pasture.

Tropical pastoral lands did not develop a clear notion of property because the orbit was not demarcated or, being variable, was impossible to demarcate. And because property rights were not needed, the state was not required either—making, in extreme cases, "econom[ies] without states."[66] Even as the colonial states emerged in such lands, "the notion of pastoral land rights was considered an oxymoron."[67] "Administrative organization, or the State, in the European sense of the term, cannot exist among peoples always on the move."[68] Occasional attempts notwithstanding, colonial authorities did not legislate for pastures. In modern parlance, these landscapes would be called "ungoverned" spaces. Pastoral areas were essentially ungoverned spaces, because geography made them so.

---

[62] M. Moritz, "Open Property Regimes," *International Journal of the Commons*, 10(2), 2016, 688–708, cited text on p. 689.

[63] Stephen Pastner, "Ideological Aspects of Nomad-Sedentary Contact: A Case from Southern Baluchistan," *Anthropological Quarterly*, 44(3), 1971, 173–184. This 1960s study of Baluchistan found that access to the orbit was not a legal right but a social-cultural one, strengthened by rituals and symbols. Most marriages were contracted between groups within the orbit.

[64] Elliot Fratkin, "East African Pastoralism in Transition: Maasai, Boran, and Rendille Cases," *African Studies Review*, 44(3), 2001, 1–25, cited text on p. 7.

[65] Roy Behnke and Carol Kerven, "Replacing Pastoralism with Irrigated Agriculture in the Awash Valley, Northeastern Ethiopia: Counting the Costs," paper presented at the International Conference on Future of Pastoralism (Institute of Development Studies, University of Sussex and the Feinstein International Center of Tufts University), 2011, cited text on p. 1.

[66] William Reno, review of Peter D. Little, *Somalia: Economy without State*, Bloomington: Indiana University Press, 2003, in *Journal of Modern African Studies*, 42(3), 2004, 474–475.

[67] John G. Galaty, "Land Grabbing in the Eastern African Rangelands," in Andy Catley, Jeremy Lind, Ian Scoones, and Jeremy Lindeck, eds., *Pastoralism and Development in Africa: Dynamic Change at the Margins*, Abingdon: Routledge, 2012, 143–153, cited text on p. 144.

[68] Melvin M. Knight, "Water and the Course of Empire in North Africa," *Quarterly Journal of Economics*, 43(1), 1928, 44–93, cited text on p. 48.

246 WATER AND DEVELOPMENT

From the late 1960s, a prolonged drought permanently reduced pastures in the Sahel, opening many fronts in a similar dispute. Reserving forests and forest fringe areas for tourism or protecting biodiversity curtailed the herders' capacity to survive droughts.[69] In an earlier era, these episodes drove them to the areas where moist pastures were available within their known orbit. As the orbit shrank or fractured in the late twentieth century, more pastoralists took up farming while not giving up herding, a move that can be understood also as insurance against climate shocks. Population growth created a "competition between the demand for land for the production of foodgrains to feed the human population, and for the natural production of grass to feed animals."[70] Agropastoralism grew by absorbing grazing lands into farmlands when political conditions encouraged the move.

There was, however, the legacy of an institutional vacuum, making this process deeply fraught. Farmers and herders moved into lands that were enclosed by extra-legal means.[71] Rivalry emerged, and the missing property right kicked in. "In all cases," says a study of the Fulani in northern Nigeria, "the question of land ownership looms on the horizon, but in all places, people are afraid to discuss it. The result has been clashes between pastoralists and their hosts."[72]

[69] Bilal Butt, Ashton Shortridge, and Antoinette M.G.A. WinklerPrins, "Pastoral Herd Management, Drought Coping Strategies, and Cattle Mobility in Southern Kenya," *Annals of the Association of American Geographers*, 99(2), 2009, 309–334.

[70] Sunil Ray, "Declining Production Conditions of Raw Wool: Analysis of Emerging Conflicts in Sheep Husbandry in Rajasthan," *Economic and Political Weekly*, 34(2), 1999, 1209–1214, cited text on 1212.

[71] For an analytical model of "incomplete" (not geographically bounded and defined) and "contingent" (unaffected by nature) grazing rights where weather shocks and uneven occurrence of foraging grounds between seasons make complete and noncontingent rights over a definite parcel of land impractical, see Rachael E. Goodhue and Nancy McCarthy, "Traditional Property Rights, Common Property, and Mobility in Semi-arid African Pastoralist Systems," *Environment and Development Economics*, 14(1), 2009, 29–50.

[72] A.G. Adebayo, "Of Man and Cattle: A Reconsideration of the Traditions of Origin of Pastoral Fulani of Nigeria," *History in Africa*, 18, 1991, 1–21, cited text on p. 16.

Chapter Twelve
The Future of the Trade-Off

The book discusses a trade-off between economic development and water stress. Mitigating stress depends on the promise of success from institutional steps taken by states and societies. A new variable in this mix is global climate change, which can potentially change not only temperatures but, with it, aridity, climate variability, and moisture inflow patterns and volumes. What are the tools available to deal with the trade-off? Will markets, laws, regulations, or new technologies work to mitigate the crisis? Will the crisis get worse with global warming? This chapter attempts to answer these two questions.

Predicting what might happen with global warming must begin by distinguishing between the average and dispersion. The norm is a combination of monthly distributions of moisture flow and temperatures or seasonality of an order that can be predicted easily. Deviations imply extreme events like floods and famines. These are low-probability events, but form two ends of the same probability distribution. Most popular or media discourses about the effects of warming on the tropics concentrate on extreme events and their becoming more severe than in the past (more accurately, the probability of such events rising overall). I show later in the chapter that the evidence to believe that extreme events will be more severe is patchy at worst, and stronger for some regions than others at best. And the evidence that the average will change does not (yet) exist. The book conducts a historical study on the assumption that societies and states primarily adapt to the norm, because it is a known form of uncertainty. Whether societies and states also adapt to extreme events—and how they do, and how these change—is a much harder question to answer. There is no evidence that warming will affect the norm.

But that topic comes later in the chapter. First, let us consider another question. If the solutions to seasonality produce adverse side effects, what are the chances of managing these effects better?

Water and Development. Tirthankar Roy, Oxford University Press. © Oxford University Press (2025).
DOI: 10.1093/oso/9780197802397.003.0012

Will Markets, Laws, and Regulations Work?

Economists, activists, and scientists offer a variety of solutions to water stress. Water markets are one potential solution, but pricing water from the commons is complicated and does not necessarily help conservation. Conservation technologies like drips and sprinklers, diguettes (mounds built to reduce runoff), and watershed management do work. Some work on a small scale, and others, like overground drips, work better for a few commercial plants and rarely for the main food grains. Cooperation to control the use and contain conflict sometimes worked locally, but the principle rarely succeeded or was even tried regionally or nationally. This was so because in a diverse group, caste and other forms of deep-rooted inequality undermined cooperation. Outsiders cannot often see how hierarchies entrench within cooperative bodies.

The European legal doctrines governing water use—riparian and prior appropriation rights—presume surface water sources. Both can be extended to groundwater. More recently, water quality has been addressed via legislation or case laws, again usually in the context of surface water bodies. All these rules are about establishing property rights on resources, in disregard of the sustainability of the resource. The common law principle that a well belongs to the owner of the land where it is situated is a good example of this oversight. In South Asia, which is among the world's largest groundwater users, sustainability issues properly emerged as challenges for policymaking and topics for public discourse after the peak of the green revolution was over and the depletion of underground water became more apparent.

Ideally, property rights on the commons should recognize that one person's use affects the others' entitlements (correlative rights). This is good ground for asserting public trust—the idea that the state should manage a waterbody, which needs correlative rights to be better protected.[1] In practice, in many societies, another rule can exist: users who accessed the resource in the past would have a superior right to access it (prior appropriation). The public trust then contradicts historical entitlements. When these rules are simultaneously asserted, there is a field of dispute, and the law offers no easy way out.

Public trust is a new type of legislation in many tropical countries, though the principle was well known in the past. The Ottoman Civil Code in the

---

[1] Erin Ryan, "A Short History of the Public Trust Doctrine and Its Intersection with Private Water Law," *Virginia Environmental Law Journal*, 38(2), 2020, 135–206.

THE FUTURE OF THE TRADE-OFF   249

late nineteenth and early twentieth centuries incorporated it. In the late nineteenth century, officers of the state in charge of famine relief in western India sometimes requisitioned wells from their private owners without any legal sanction. They did this to clean the water of bacteria and to open access to these to famine-hit peoples, some of whom were barred by their caste status from accessing ponds and wells. However, asserting and enforcing public trust can be tortuous, especially when prior appropriation is a long-established convention. Think again of the private well, whose owner may lose the right to draw water if public trust in the aquifer is established. As far as one can see, law has nowhere gone to the extreme of derecognizing prior appropriation rights to the well. In the famine-hit Deccan Plateau, requisitioning a private well that belonged to an upper-caste person for the use of others would be seen as an insult to religion.

Furthermore, in parts of the world where colonialism gave shape to neo-customary land rights, like sub-Saharan Africa, prior appropriation took precedence over state rights. As the population rose, the competition for water and limited land resources intensified. Since the customary land rights system defined rights by ethnicity, the competition for resources became an interethnic competition.

One potential model of legally regulating groundwater use is the tradeable permit. The user has a fixed entitlement, and any excess use requires the purchase of a license from another user who does not use the entitlement to the full. This system was introduced in Mexico, which nationalized groundwater and then regulated it via user concessions.[2,3] In Chennai (Madras) city, a 1987 law to regulate wells had the same purpose. The method worked better when the users were large municipalities. The monitoring and information cost with agricultural well-owners was just too large. With South Asian well-ownership at two thousand times that of Mexico, the potential costs of a permit system would be too high.

The scholarship on the regulation of water use makes an interesting point. The groundwater revolution, which the state let happen but did not invest in, created local alliances between farmers and drilling firms. The consolidation of regional power in this way made any top-down intervention harder.[4] The same story occurred in the cities, where the beneficiaries of groundwater

[2] M.W. Rosegrant and R.G. Schleyer, "Establishing Tradable Water Rights: Implementation of the Mexican Water Law," *Irrigation and Drainage Systems*, 10, 1996, 263–279.

[3] Tushaar Shah, Aditi Deb Roy, Asad S. Qureshi, and Jinxia Wang, "Sustaining Asia's Groundwater Boom: An Overview of Issues and Evidence," *Natural Resources Forum*, 27, 2003, 130–141.

[4] Trevor Birkenholtz, "Contesting Expertise: The Politics of Environmental Knowledge in Northern Indian Groundwater Practices," *Geoforum*, 39, 2008, 466–482.

250   WATER AND DEVELOPMENT

were the most affluent apartment-owning elites. In contrast, later migrants and poorer residents continued relying on a limited municipal water supply.

The 1990s scholarship on the tragedy of the commons often claimed that participatory management, where the potential gainers and losers came together to manage a resource, would lead to sustainable use. However, local cooperation can also perpetuate and strengthen local inequalities without a third party to redress the power imbalance. "Though participation can work in small operations," concludes a study of South Africa, "to make the assumption that magic can be worked at scale and that heterogeneity of stakeholders does not have an impact on participatory processes is deeply flawed."[5]

Most governments do not seem to believe that the ancient systems of using the commons and participatory management are the answer to the needs of large populations. Public policy relies heavily on entrepreneurial agriculture and large infrastructure projects. There is little ground to believe that the conditions for the success of small-scale waterworks—conditions that Elinor Ostrom called design principles—are robust, especially in the face of commercial agriculture accessing the same resources with more intrusive technology (foggara versus drilling) or environmental change. Cooperation was neither widespread nor even tried in waterworks serving large groups of people.

From the early 2000s, water experts in South Asia began to discuss the prospects of groundwater recharge and rainwater harvesting. Both systems follow the same principle: trap and recycle rainwater when it is in excess. Trapping rainwater on a small scale and at the household or community level is a low-technology system. Artificial recharge of underground aquifers under threat is not. Success requires geological data and significant investment. Success is not guaranteed. Since 2008 in India, the government took over the initiative to plan, research, and sponsor projects. Most projects were local and under construction, so it is not yet possible to know how much of a difference the plan will make.

Some development experts advocate reduced water intensity in development rather than giving up on development to protect the environment. Ecological modernization theorists suggest that not all trade-offs can be solved by choice. They suggest that whereas industrialization and consumption caused environmental degradation, the solution is not

---

[5] Julia Brown, "Assuming Too Much? Participatory Water Resource Governance in South Africa," *Geographical Journal*, 117(2), 2011, 171–185, cited text on p. 183.

THE FUTURE OF THE TRADE-OFF   251

reducing industrialization, or reducing consumption, or adding to regulation. These drives tend to fail. Industrialization and consumption have radically molded lives, made people live longer, and made them acquire more skills and interests, so it is futile to campaign for a return to a more elemental way of life. What's more, regulation of the commons entails significant enforcement problems. Instead, the emphasis falls upon "reduced use of resources" while sustaining industrialization and consumption at roughly the present levels.[6]

Trading in water is a well-used concept within countries and over smaller areas. All irrigation societies have been familiar with it. But can water be traded internationally, virtually like carbon permits, between surplus and shortage areas? International trade in water-intensive products (say, the product of a water-intensive crop like sugarcane) follows an environmental logic. What about water itself? There is no working model to show the commercial and infrastructural logistics needed to make this prospect a reality. A 2020 paper concludes, using a model that predicts surplus and excess countries, that trading in water permits would be common within the twenty-first century.[7]

Will Science Deliver Solutions?

Some examples to help answer that question come from advances in emissions and pollution control in industries that once produced a lot of air and water pollution. However, the practical steps are not exclusively technological. In practical terms, the perspective of urban consumption rather than farmland irrigation seems more promising. For example, water-conserving washing machines and toilets have reduced household use of water considerably. Irrigation of farmlands, which uses the most water, is much harder to control.

No single tool or idea promises to solve the water problem on a world scale, but some hold more promise than others. Seeking radical solutions to seasonality has been going on for decades. Cloud seeding and snowpack enhancements have been used since the 1940s. Large-scale use is probably

---

[6] Frederick H. Buttel, "Environmental Sociology and the Explanation of Environmental Reform," *Organization and Environment*, 16(3), 2003, 306–344, cited text on p. 323.

[7] Neal T. Graham, Mohamad I. Hejazi, Son H. Kim, Evan G. R. Davies, James A. Edmonds, and Fernando Miralles-Wilhelm, "Future Changes in the Trading of Virtual Water," *Nature Communications*, 11(3632), 2020, 1–7.

252 WATER AND DEVELOPMENT

still confined to their original home, the western United States. Dry ice or silver iodide are released in the atmosphere to induce ice crystal formations. Where this is done in snow-packed mountains, the technology could potentially increase streamflow in the plains. It is expensive, and despite a few attempts in Morocco, Mali, and Burkina Faso, it has rarely been used in tropical regions. In the majority of cases, the results were uncertain at best.

Perhaps the leading candidate is the desalination of seawater, which is already in extensive use in Australia and on a small scale in many countries. Desalination produces about one hundred million cubic meters per day worldwide, less than 1 percent of the daily water requirement (roughly 26 gallons per person per day) of the 1.5 billion people living in arid or semi-arid areas. The fact that the technology can work on a large scale is evident. In the 2010s, desalination plants developed fast around the world. The largest plants came up in West Asia and Australia. There is a reason the oil-producing Middle East has more of them than any other world region. Seawater desalination generally requires about ten times more energy than pumping water from wells, though the costs are decreasing. The energy comes from oil. Wider use of the technology depends on fossil fuel and extensive subsidization of the final price of water.[8]

Will Climate Change Make It Worse?

Emissions from fossil fuels are changing the world's climate. The tropical and the extratropical are coming nearer, a process often described as tropical widening. We know the story. We may still make the mistake that it is all happening due to fossil fuel emissions in the last few decades. Other human-centric processes of climatic change worked over centuries. Cultivated land and pastures increased from almost three million square miles in 1750 to nineteen million square miles in 2000, or from 5.4 to 34.7 percent of the global land surface.[9] These numbers suggest the staggering extent of deforestation that happened. Deforestation contributes to carbon emissions, and by changing surface albedo it can affect the pathway of the

[8] Farida Helmy, "Can Desalination Help Keep Peace in the Middle East?," *Corporate Knights*, 12(3), 2013, 34–36.

[9] Kees Klein Goldewijk, Arthur Beusen, Gerard van Drecht, and Martine de Vos, "The HYDE 3.1 Spatially Explicit Database of Human-Induced Global Land-Use Change over the Past 12,000 Years," *Global Ecology and Biogeography*, 20, 2011, 73–86.

intertropical convergence zone.[10] A significant proportion of the global land surface outside these areas is affected by human action in other ways.

Awareness about climate change and its roots in human action has been growing since the end of the last millennium, if not before. The scholarship on prediction of what will happen and predictions about water took off in the 2010s. A large number of new journals appeared. Climate change debates and discourses changed the prediction methodology from local to large-scale modeling. The currently used models are large-scale in three senses: basin-wide predictions, which are crucial for transboundary river water sharing negotiations; the use of more statistical data than before; and the use of hydrological models (like MIKE-SHE), which integrate all sources of flow in the predictive scenarios. However, this scholarship has serious limitations. Almost without exception, geographers predict the impact of climate change without factoring in politics and policies to worsen, control, regulate, or reverse the effect.

Where does that scholarship take us? Contrary to the dire predictions in the popular press, the scientific-statistical forecasts do not yield a unanimous or clear verdict on the question, would climate change make the choices even harder? Climate change and global warming are expected to affect agriculture by reducing the recharge level in the rainfed river basins. The nonagricultural and urban demand for water should increase its share in total water use from 15 to 20 percent in 2020 to over 30 percent in 2050. Even without the effects of global warming, nearly a fifth of the population of India and a much larger proportion of India's urban population will live under extreme water scarcity conditions by 2050.[11] But this is too broad a statement.

The Intergovernmental Panel on Climate Change (IPCC) was established in 1988 by the United Nations Environment Programme and the World Meteorological Organization. Since then, the IPCC has periodically gathered scientific data to suggest scenarios for the future that could in theory inform policymakers. On water, the IPCC is consistently more negative than hydrological research suggests. The 2008 assessment report unambiguously predicted that climate change will make water scarcer and insecurity (risks)

---

[10] N. Devaraju, G. Bala, and A. Modak, "Effects of Large-scale Deforestation on Precipitation in the Monsoon Regions: Remote versus Local Effects," *Proceedings of the National Academy of Sciences of the United States of America*, 112(11), 2015, 3257–3262.

[11] B. Venkateswarlu and J.V.S.N. Prasad, "Carrying Capacity of Indian Agriculture: Issues Related to Rainfed Agriculture," *Current Science*, 102(6), 2012, 882–888.

254 WATER AND DEVELOPMENT

more significant in the arid areas. The claim was strange for the time it was made because forecasting precipitation levels was still at an early stage. The 2021 assessment report marginally revised the claim by adding "potentially": "The main climate change contribution to water insecurity is the potential for reduced water availability."[12]

There are five ways hydrological research is not consistent with this strong form of prediction. First, the extent of temperature change cannot be accurately measured until at least 2035. Second, the impact of aridity on human life depends not just on the average rise but also on the amplitude of month-by-month fluctuations. We do not know enough about how warming or an increase in the average surface temperature affects the amplitude. Third, the consequences of an average temperature increase for individual regions are difficult to predict. Fourth, while climate change will increase aridity or evapotranspiration, the total effect depends on another variable to which a lot of uncertainty attaches: rains, floods, and streamflow (surface water flow fed by all sources). It is impossible to know how streamflow changes in different parts of the world because the hydrological models rely on past data, whereas the causal model may change.

Fifth, there is no agreement on the methodology used to predict the impact of climate change. Using historical data to predict the future is sustained by the assumption of stationarity, meaning the assumption that the variability in streamflow stays within observed historical variability. A study to test the robustness of the assumption found (with catchments data from around the world but relatively few from the tropics) that the variability of extreme values associated with floods and droughts did indeed stay largely stationary in catchments exclusively affected by climate change, but not in those where human interventions were extensive.[13]

A similar openness exists in the prediction of drought occurrence and intensity. Three variables interact to cause a drought: moisture deficit, unusual warming, and low initial streamflow, or the volume of water in surface waterbodies before the occurrence of a monsoon failure. The first two factors dry up the soil and the plants directly and by reducing streamflow—the combined prospect is called a meteorological drought. The

---

[12] M.A. Caretta et al., "Water," in H.-O. Pörtner et al., eds., *Climate Change 2022: Impacts, Adaptation and Vulnerability. Contribution of Working Group II to the Sixth Assessment Report of the Intergovernmental Panel on Climate Change*, Cambridge: Cambridge University Press, 551–712, cited text on p. 563.

[13] Zhengrong Wang and Yuting Yang, "Stationarity of High and Low Flows under Climate Change and Human Interventions across Global Catchments," *Earth and Space Science*, 11, 2024. https://doi.org/10.1029/2023EA003456.

third factor, baseflow, can counteract the effect to some extent.[14] Consider an environment where warming causes more meteorological droughts but raises baseflow via snowmelt. It becomes difficult to say that more warming will cause more drought.

Despite the disagreements and openness about the link between warming and water stress worldwide, local data suggest stronger forms of prediction. There appears to be enough consensus that arid areas of California and Mexico will see drier conditions by the middle decades of the twenty-first century.[15] Both regions may have some unused underground water. In the arid areas served by a perennial river but with little precipitation, the impact of a rise in aridity or evapotranspiration can be one-directional and less uncertain. Egypt is a significant case. Here, an increase of aridity will likely cause a fall in groundwater levels around mid-century.[16] But even in Egypt, which has few rainy days in a year, the future depends on how the two sources of the Nile that do get a lot of rain and are both far away from Egypt change.

The health of Lake Chad, a shallow waterbody that changes in size every year and one that sustains the lives of millions of people, is vital for the economic and political well-being of the Sahel. Since the 1970s famine, many experts predicted the progressive shrinking of the lake. However, the source of most of its water was not local; it was located several hundred miles to the southeast in the Logon Basin, a semiequatorial area. According to most estimates, this area should see greater variability and intensity of rainfall due to climate change, raising the risk of floods and droughts. While the lake may not recover to the size it had in the early 1960s, its catchment area can receive occasional heavy rains.[17]

Forecasting streamflow takes place all over the semi-arid tropics. The exercise did not begin recently in response to the prospect of climate change. It started about a hundred years ago when states stepped in to solve seasonality. Forecasts are done by feeding past data into a statistical model, in which some of the main causal variables are precipitation, snow water,

---

[14] Rajesh Singh and Vimal Mishra, "Atmospheric and Land Drivers of Streamflow Flash Droughts in India," *Journal of Geophysical Research: Atmospheres*, 129, 2024, https://doi.org/10.1029/2023JD040257.

[15] Alejandro Yáñez-Arancibia and John W. Day, "Water Scarcity and Sustainability in the Arid Area of North America," *Regions and Cohesion*, 7(1), 2017, 6–18.

[16] M.G. Eltarabily, I. Abd-Elaty, A. Elbeltagi, M. Zelenáková, and I. Fathy, "Investigating Climate Change Effects on Evapotranspiration and Groundwater Recharge of the Nile Delta Aquifer, Egypt," *Water*, 15(572), 2023, 1–16.

[17] Peter Schmidt and Robert Muggah, "Impacts of Water Fluctuation in the Lake Chad Basin," in *Climate Change and Security in West Africa*, Rio de Janeiro: Igarape Institute, 2021.

256 WATER AND DEVELOPMENT

and soil moisture. Using such a model, the US Department of Agriculture provides seasonal streamflow forecasts for watersheds across the arid western states. In Africa, the quality of data and modeling vary from country to country. Overall, the density of stations collecting streamflow and weather data is thin compared with the United States, Australia, or India.

One significant by-product of the forecasting exercise is the hydrological drought index, which measures the shortfall in streamflow from the long-term average. The measures for Africa show that the 1980s saw an almost unbroken episode of hydrological drought like no other registered since the data began to be recorded nearly a century earlier. In west-central Africa, baseflow (precipitation-led addition to streamflow) decreased from 1950 to 1980, and an increasing trend appeared from 1981 to 2018. In North Africa, the decrease continued.[18] Some studies contend that a declining trend in moisture inflow began decades, even centuries, before anthropogenic climate change became a prospect.[19]

The periodic assessment reports of the IPCC permit the broad generalization that the monsoons will be stronger and droughts more intense in the near future. However, whether some semi-arid regions will turn into arid ones or stay semi-arid remains hard to predict because the impact on evapotranspiration and precipitation is not synchronous. It is helpful to delve into more details of the measurement to see why.

Assessing the impact of climate change begins with two measures: potential evapotranspiration, which reflects the effect of a global temperature increase modified by local factors like types of vegetation, solar radiation, relative humidity, and wind speed; and climate aridity index, the ratio of potential evapotranspiration to actual precipitation. The computation of potential evapotranspiration follows methods developed in the 1940s. The high-resolution global database is a recent addition. The first set of aridity index data appeared in 2009; since then, the data have been revised several times. Available from WorldClim, the dataset is a standard basis for building predictions about sustainability, agriculture, pastoralism, and drought risk.[20]

---

[18] Jessica R. Ayers, Gabriele Villarini, Yves Tramblay, and Hanbeen Kim, "Observed Changes in Monthly Baseflow across Africa," *Hydrological Sciences Journal*, 68(1), 2023, 108–118.

[19] Sharon E. Nicholson, "Climatic and Environmental Change in Africa during the Last Two Centuries," *Climate Research*, 17(2), 2001, 123–144.

[20] Robert J. Zomer, Jianchu Xu, and Antonio Trabuco, "Version 3 of the Global Aridity Index and Potential Evapotranspiration Database," *Scientific Data*, 9, 2022.

One set of standard measures widely used to predict droughts considers precipitation, leading to at least three criteria: standardized precipitation; standardized precipitation evaporation index (SPEI), calculated as the difference between precipitation and evapotranspiration (which captures temperature or aridity effect); and a refinement of the latter that factors in net evapotranspiration. The aridity index is a variation of SPEI.

The aridity index is an essential tool in human geography; it is widely used to measure the risk of meteorological drought. The greater the index, the greater the risk. There is some openness on where the semi-arid is located between the maximum values of 0 and 1. An index value of around 0.5 indicates a semi-arid state, and an index of 0.8 or above a hyper-arid state. A surface temperature increase can potentially increase precipitation. The monsoon rains happen because the amplitude of surface temperature is greater on land than on the sea. An average rise in temperature does not alter that process. In short, a change in potential evapotranspiration may not imply a similar change in the aridity index.

Drought risk depends on short-term changes in precipitation; predictions about such changes carry large margins of error. This is so because, in the northern semi-arid tropics, precipitation is influenced by several climatic systems (Arctic Oscillation, Siberian High, and El-Nino Southern Oscillation). Moreover, the historical correlation between these factors and monsoon strength appears to be changing, making it more difficult to predict short-term changes in monsoon strength even with more data.[21] Existing models predict mean annual rainfall, the spatial spread, and variation in rainfall within a season. The year 1997–1998 saw one of the most significant departures in sea surface temperatures in recorded history, but the summer monsoon was near-normal in India. Not surprisingly, drought prediction indices offer divergent predictions, and more than one study finds that the aridity index is not a good predictor of drought intensity.[22]

What about long-term changes in monsoon strength? Considerable research now exists on the future of the South Asian monsoon, and these predictions are reported in IPCC assessments. Comparatively less research

---

[21] Chenxi Xu, Y. Simon Wang, Krishna Borhara, Brendan Buckley, Ning Tan, Yaru Zhao, Wenling An, Masaki Sano, Takeshi Nakatsuka, and Zhengtang Guo, "Asian-Australian Summer Monsoons Linkage to ENSO Strengthened by Global Warming," *Climate and Atmospheric Science*, 6(8), 2023, 1–10.

[22] Hongli Zhang, Liang Zhang, Qiang Zhang Qian Liu, Xiaoni You, and Lixia Wang, "Analysis of the Difference between Climate Aridity Index and Meteorological Drought Index in the Summer Monsoon Transition Zone," *Remote Sensing*, 15, 2023, 1–17.

258 WATER AND DEVELOPMENT

exists for the other semi-arid tropical zones. It is impossible to generalize for specific regions based on South Asia, but South Asia indicates broad tendencies. The South Asian historical data show a marginal decline in precipitation volume between 1950 and 2000 and a marginal rise after that.[23] The IPCC and some scholars attribute this shift to global warming and predict that the northern hemisphere's southwest or summer monsoon is strengthening. That prediction is repeated in blogs, press, and social media writings with added color: "Climate change is making the South Asian monsoon increasingly violent and erratic," said the *New York Times* in 2022. In the short run, more intense monsoons cause floods and landslides. There is some evidence that these problems associated with intensity have aggravated in South and Southeast Asia in the last decade or so.

This book is about the long term. In the semi-arid tropics, the long-term impact of changes in precipitation would depend less on "violence" as journalists call it and more on precipitation seasonality. A change in seasonality would mean the pattern of crop choices will need to change, and ways to store monsoon runoff will need a rethinking. The climate seasonality index is a measure that combines mean annual rainfall with monthly rainfall. The index moves in a range of 0 to 1.83. If rainfall is evenly distributed throughout the year, the index becomes zero, and if rainfall is concentrated in one month, the index takes a value of 1.83. A semi-arid seasonality index is typically around 1.2 to 1.3, suggesting that most rains occur in a two-month window. In the semi-arid monsoon, a rising seasonality combined with increasing aridity might suggest a more pressing need and a more complex challenge to store monsoon runoff. There is a shortage of studies on seasonality. The studies that do exist do not lead to a singular prediction. For example, based on historical data, a study on Western India shows that the seasonality and aridity indexes have risen in recent decades, but the trends are not statistically significant.[24]

As mentioned earlier, the link between warming and water stress depends crucially on the impact of snowmelt on streamflow. The impact of temperature changes is difficult to reconstruct for riparian regions because changing monsoon patterns and the El Niño–Southern Oscillation both

---

[23] A. Katzenberger, A. Levermann, J. Schewe, and J. Pongratz, "Intensification of Very Wet Monsoon Seasons in India under Global Warming," *Geophysical Research Letters*, 49, 2022, 1–10.

[24] Akanksha Rani, Devesh Sharma, Mukand S. Babel, and Aditya Sharma, "Spatio-Temporal Assessment of Agro-Climatic Indices and the Monsoon Pattern in the Banas River Basin, India," *Environmental Challenges*, 7, 2022, 1–10.

THE FUTURE OF THE TRADE-OFF   259

contribute to river flows directly or indirectly through snowmelt. Warming could cause faster snowmelt and more streamflow, but warming could also lead to smaller snow accumulation and a long-term decline in streamflow. Using different assumptions about snowmelt can lead to the prediction of a basin getting wetter or drier.[25] Most trends in streamflow are not statistically significant. Paleotemperatures are often not a reliable guide to prediction. Research on this topic seems to be in the preliminary stages, with considerable uncertainty attached to forecasts. The uncertainty stems from, as a study of semi-arid Andean headwaters suggests, insufficient knowledge of snow depth and density over seasons and across space.[26]

A final piece in the puzzle is the relationship between groundwater recharge and increasing climatic aridity. This relationship is nonlinear. Recharge rates are disproportionately slower in more arid areas, and recharge is likely to be affected more in arid areas (potential evapotranspiration exceeding precipitation) than in temperate ones. This finding suggests an emerging water inequality between the temperate and heavy-monsoon areas (like Southeast Asia, part of India) on the one hand, where predicted rise in precipitation due to stronger monsoons can lead to proportionately greater recharge potential, and the arid and hyper-arid areas in Africa, India, Australia, and the southwestern United States on the other, where predicted decrease in precipitation combines with low recharge sensitivity to cause a fall in supply.[27]

Conclusion

So, will climate change make the trade-off harder to manage? There is no clear answer available to this question from current research. What we do

[25] For two studies on the Brahmaputra Basin offering contradictory results, see Sarfaraz Alam, Mostafa Ali, Ahmmed Zulfiqar Rahaman, and Zahidul Islam, "Multi-model Ensemble Projection of Mean and Extreme Streamflow of Brahmaputra River Basin under the Impact of Climate Change," *Journal of Water and Climate Change*, 12(11), 2021, 2026–2044; Fadji Z. Maina, Augusto Getirana, Sujay V. Kumar, Manabendra Saharia, Nishan Kumar Biswas, Sasha McLarty, and Ravi Appana, "Irrigation-Driven Groundwater Depletion in the Ganges-Brahmaputra Basin Decreases the Streamflow in the Bay of Bengal," *Communications Earth and Environment*, 5 (169), 2024, https://doi.org/10.1038/s43247-024-01348-0.

[26] Gonzalo Navarro, Shelley MacDonell, and Remi Valois, "A Conceptual Hydrological Model of Semiarid Andean Headwater Systems in Chile," *Progress in Physical Geography*, 2023, 1–19.

[27] Wouter R. Berghuijs, Raoul A. Collenteur, Scott Jasechko, Fernando Jaramillo, Elco Luijendijk, Christian Moeck, Ype van der Velde, and Scott T. Allen, "Groundwater Recharge Is Sensitive to Changing Long-Term Aridity," *Nature Climate Change*, 2024, https://www.nature.com/articles/s41558-024-01953-z.

260 WATER AND DEVELOPMENT

know is that even within the arid and semi-arid tropics, the impact will differ. A new pattern of inequality awaits the generation who will live through the middle decades of the twentieth century. There is not enough data yet to reduce that pattern to slogans about tropical suffering due to climate change.

Does that matter? Not really. No matter whether heat or seasonality levels rise, or where they do, the available solutions remain the same—source more water, recycle more between seasons, and deal with the side effects of these actions. I end the book with that message.

Chapter Thirteen
Conclusion

I do not want to subject the reader to a lengthy restatement of the book's argument. It has been repeated enough times already. But some of my claims need stressing one more time. Aridity afflicts a large part of the world. That world does not interest me. The book is not about a problem or an obstacle to population growth and income growth that has no practical solution. It is about a *solution* to the aridity problem. The solution is potentially available in *those arid areas that receive a seasonal influx of moisture.* Most of these areas appear on or near the two tropics. The solution involves extracting, storing, and recycling excess water, for use when the rains fail, or during dry seasons, or in cities. In the semi-arid tropics, that enterprise picked up since the nineteenth century and occurred on a scale the people living there could only dream of even a hundred years earlier. With the wider use of that solution, the poorer countries in the semi-arid areas experienced relatively rapid economic and demographic change in the late twentieth century.

With that initial claim, I make several other claims about the process that the book has called "emergence." First, the solution did not stem from a big political shift or a particular "ism"—whether nationalism, developmentalism, or any other. As archaeological evidence shows, the solution was well known in semi-arid tropical societies for millennia. European colonialism in Asia and Africa brought in new expertise and ambitions. These experts found the tropical geography baffling at many levels and made mistakes when reading it. But they also gathered useful data and captured its fundamental character—seasonality. Several institutional interventions were designed to mitigate seasonality, with limited success. Canals did better under strict conditions. Dams and wells came late. Sanitation and water treatment did very well.

Thanks to these interventions, roughly between the 1920s and the 1960s, the tropical societies did better at reducing mortality than raising productivity. The outcome was a sharp rise in population growth but a low income growth rate. We see these societies as failures if we assess performance by per capita income trends. Instead, they successfully solved one

Water and Development. Tirthankar Roy, Oxford University Press. © Oxford University Press (2025).
DOI: 10.1093/oso/9780197802397.003.0013

262 WATER AND DEVELOPMENT

problem—shorter lives—with tools that did not solve the other problem: low incomes.

Late-twentieth-century states used the same instruments to support industrialization, urbanization, and cash crop production. Aided by taxpayers' money, international aid, and loans, they could build many more dams and reservoirs than the colonial states could do. These states followed and did not reverse the colonial pattern of intervention. There was substantial continuity between these eras. The difference was a much higher technical and fiscal capacity to perform large-scale geoengineering.

Second, the solution had limits and side effects. They were confined to areas served by heavy seasonal rains and floods; otherwise, there was no water to trap. Drier areas that fell behind did not see how development benefited them. These projects created cultivable lands out of pastures, but no one knew who owned them. Fierce battles and lobbying broke out. Dams caused controversies. Where available, groundwater was exploited more heavily in response to the flagging dam drive. In some areas, these resources were technically plentiful, but groundwater mining was expensive. Groundwater extraction triggered a legal problem the colonial regimes avoided. The tap or well above ground is legally protected private property. The water below the ground is an open-access resource. Creating a law about the shared water resources underground would not always solve this issue if not enough is known about the water below. Entire nations and large regions have little underground water anyway. Above all, extracting water in any form for mass consumption and production is expensive and seldom pays for itself without taxpayers' money.

Why does government after government persist with an uneconomical model with adverse side effects? Political ecologists would point to vested interests. I disagree. Climate scientists, climate historians, and archaeologists tell us that persistence is nothing new in the tropical world. A single idea has been pursued through various regimes in the tropical world for hundreds of years: recycle water, and when that fails, take up herding. Despite the costs of water recycling with modern means, the idea is still popular and will remain so. This has nothing to do with power, lobbying, or state-building. It has everything to do with common sense.

Persistence stems from three instincts: one old and two new. The old one is that the solution to seasonal aridity is so obvious—trap excess inflow for use later—that it is crazy not to use it. A new one is that dams and drills create gainers, sustain cities, and generate green revolutions. The costs are high;

the gains are, too. A second new instinct is this: in regions that have seen frequent droughts and famines in recent decades, self-sufficiency in foodgrain production is a goal to achieve no matter the cost. Water projects are not just instruments to push GDP growth; they serve security broadly and are worth paying for, no matter the monetary return. Asking the water-stressed people in the tropics to consume less is useless because these instincts are powerful and cannot be argued against. Other solutions need to be found.

My third claim concerns the future, specifically climate change effects. The media hype about the dire future awaiting the tropical world may not be all wrong but is based on an incomplete and unfinished research project and a patchwork of data and results that do not converge into definite predictions. But that is not the point. The important thing is that whether climate effects get better or worse, *the solution does not change*. It cannot change. In the foreseeable future, the semi-arid tropics will continue using the limited set of instruments, dams, or drills that the people here have used forever. The best that these societies can do is mitigate the side effects as much as possible. It is not an easy road by far, but history shows it is the only way forward.

References

Aaronsohn, Ran (1995), "The Beginnings of Modern Jewish Agriculture in Palestine: 'Indigenous' versus 'Imported,'" *Agricultural History*, 69(3), 438–453.

Adams, Adrian (1977), "The Senegal River Valley: What Kind of Change?," *Review of African Political Economy*, 10, 33–59.

Adams, W.M. (1986), "Traditional Agriculture and Water Use in the Sokoto Valley, Nigeria," *Geographical Journal*, 152(1), 30–43.

Adebayo, A.G. (1991), "Of Man and Cattle: A Reconsideration of the Traditions of Origin of Pastoral Fulani of Nigeria," *History in Africa*, 18, 1–21.

Adriansen, Hanne Kirstine (2008), "Understanding Pastoral Mobility: The Case of Senegalese Fulani," *Geographical Journal*, 174(3), 207–222.

Agarwal, Arun (2003), "Sustainable Governance of Common-Pool Resources: Contexts, Methods, Politics," *Annual Review of Anthropology*, 32, 243–262.

Agnew, C.T. (1982), "Water Availability and the Development of Rainfed Agriculture in South-West Niger, West Africa," *Transactions of the Institute of British Geographers*, 7(4), 419–457.

Agnew, Clive T., Ewan Anderson, W. Lancaster, and F. Lancaster (1995), "Mahafir: A Water Harvesting System in the Eastern Jordan (Badia) Desert," *GeoJournal*, 37(1), 69–80.

Agnihotri, Indu (1996), "Ecology, Land Use and Colonisation: The Canal Colonies of Punjab," *Indian Economic and Social History Review*, 33(1), 37–58.

Ahssein, Abdul Mejid, ed. (1976), *Rehab: Drought and Famine in Ethiopia*, London: International African Institute.

Alam, Sarfaraz, Mostafa Ali, Ahmmed Zulfiqar Rahaman, and Zahidul Islam (2021), "Multi-model Ensemble Projection of Mean and Extreme Streamflow of Brahmaputra River Basin under the Impact of Climate Change," *Journal of Water and Climate Change*, 12(11), 2026–2044.

Alam, Undala Z. (2002), "Questioning the Water Wars Rationale: A Case Study of the Indus Waters Treaty," *Geographical Journal*, 168(4), 341–353.

Alavi, Seema (1993), "The Makings of Company Power: James Skinner in the Ceded and Conquered Provinces, 1802–1840," *Indian Economic and Social History Review*, 30(4), 437–466.

Alredaisy, Sameer, Abdel Aziem Tinier, and Jack Davies (2011), "Farming, Herding, Water and Rangeland in the Butana," *Sudan Studies*, 44, 57–69.

Amrith, Sunil (2018), *Unruly Waters: How Rains, Rivers, Coasts, and Seas Have Shaped Asia's History*, New York: Basic Books, 2018.

Anon (1914), "The Great Artesian Basin of Australia," *Journal of the Royal Society of Arts*, 62(3202), 438–440.

REFERENCES 265

Anon (1976), "Report of the Symposium on Arid Zone Development," *Bulletin of the American Academy of Arts and Sciences*, 29(7), 12–17.

Anon (2017), "India's Water," *The Economic Times*, https://economictimes.indiatimes.com/news/politics-and-nation/the-precarious-situation-of-indias-water-problem/articleshow/57965416.cms?from=mdrInland.

Anteneh, Addis, and Hailu Yemanu (1974), "Development of the Awash Valley," c. 1970. Available at https://www.ajol.info/index.php/ajol.

Aragey, Merid W. (1984), "Society and Technology in Ethiopia: 1500–1800," *Journal of Ethiopian Studies*, 17, 127–147.

Arkell, Thomas (1991), "The Decline of Pastoral Nomadism in the Western Sahara," *Geography*, 76(2), 162–166.

Arnold, David (2000), "'Illusory Riches': Representations of the Tropical World, 1840–1950," *Singapore Journal of Tropical Geography*, 21(1), 6–18.

Atchi Reddy, M. (1990), "Travails of an Irrigation Canal Company in South India, 1857–1882," *Economic and Political Weekly*, 25(12), 619–628.

Austin, Gareth (2009), "Cash Crops and Freedom: Export Agriculture and the Decline of Slavery in Colonial West Africa," *International Review of Social History*, 54(1), 1–37.

Awogbade, M.O. (1979), "Fulani Pastoralism and the Problems of the Nigerian Veterinary Service," *African Affairs*, 78 (313), 493–506.

Ayers, Jessica R., Gabriele Villarini, Yves Tramblay, and Hanbeen Kim (2023), "Observed Changes in Monthly Baseflow across Africa," *Hydrological Sciences Journal*, 68(1), 108–118.

Azarya, Victor (1996), "Pastoralism and the State in Africa: Marginality or Incorporation?," *Nomadic Peoples*, 38, 11–36.

Baier, Stephen (1976), "Economic History and Development: Drought and the Sahelian Economies of Niger," *African Economic History*, 1, 1–16.

Baier, Stephen (1980), *An Economic History of Central Niger*, Oxford: Clarendon Press.

Balbo, Andrea L., Erik Gómez-Baggethun, Matthieu Salpeteur, Arnald Puy, Stefano Biagetti, and Jürgen Scheffran (2016), "Resilience of Small-Scale Societies: A View from Drylands," *Ecology and Society*, 21(2), https://www.ecologyandsociety.org/vol21/iss2/art53/.

Ball, Nicole (1978), "Drought and Dependence in the Sahel," *International Journal of Health Services*, 8(2), 271–298.

Ballard, Charles (1986), "Drought and Economic Distress: South Africa in the 1800s," *Journal of Interdisciplinary History*, 17(2), 359–378.

Baouab, M. Hassen, and Semia Cherif (2017), "Revolution Impact on Drinking Water Consumption," *Social Indicators Research*, 132(2), 841–859.

Barbour, K.M. (1980), "The Sudan since Independence," *Journal of Modern African Studies*, 18(1), 73–97.

Beaumont, Peter (1974), "Water Resource Development in Iran," *Geographical Journal*, 140(3), 418–431.

Behnke, Roy, and Carol Kerven (2011), "Replacing Pastoralism with Irrigated Agriculture in the Awash Valley, Northeastern Ethiopia: Counting the Costs," Paper presented at the International Conference on Future of Pastoralism (Institute of Development Studies, University of Sussex and the Feinstein International Center of Tufts University) Addis Ababa, March 21-23, 2011.

Bellucci, Stefano, and Massimo Zacearia (2014), "Wage Labor and Mobility in Colonial Eritrea, 1880s to 1920s," *International Labor and Working-Class History*, 86, 89–106.

Below, Regina, Emily Grover-Kopec, and Maxx Dilley (2007), "Documenting Drought-Related Disasters: A Global Reassessment," *Journal of Environment and Development*, 16(3), 328–344.

Benjaminsen, A., and Boubacar Ba (2009), "Farmer-Herder Conflicts, Pastoral Marginalisation and Corruption: A Case Study from the Inland Niger Delta of Mali," *Geographical Journal*, 175(1), 71–81.

Benjaminsen, Tor A., and Pierre Hiernaux (2019), "From Desiccation to Global Climate Change," *Global Environment*, 12(1), 206–236.

Berghuijs, Wouter R., Raoul A. Collenteur, Scott Jasechko, Fernando Jaramillo, Elco Luijendijk, Christian Moeck, Ype van der Velde, and Scott T. Allen (2024), "Groundwater Recharge Is Sensitive to Changing Long-Term Aridity," *Nature Climate Change*, https://www.nature.com/articles/s41558-024-01953-z.

Bernus, Edmond (1990), *Dates, Dromedaries and Drought: Diversification in Tuareg Pastoral Systems*, New York: Guilford Press.

Bertazzini, Mattia (2023), "The Effect of Settler Farming on Indigenous Agriculture: Evidence from Italian Libya," *Economic History Review*, 76(1), 33–59.

Besteman, Catherine, and Lee V. Cassanelli, eds. (1996), *The Struggle for Land in Southern Somalia: The War behind the War*, Boulder, CO: Westview.

Beyene, Fekadu (2009), "Property Rights Conflict, Customary Institutions and the State: The Case of Agro-Pastoralists in Mieso District, Eastern Ethiopia," *Journal of Modern African Studies*, 47(2), 213–239.

Bhattacharya, Neeladri (2019), *The Great Agrarian Conquest: The Colonial Reshaping of a Rural World*, Ranikhet, India: Permanent Black.

Biasillo, Roberta, and Claiton Marcio da Silva (2019), "Cultivating Arid Soils in Libya and Brazil during World War Two," *Global Environment*, 12(1), 154–181.

Butt, Bilal, Ashton Shortridge, and Antoinette M.G.A. WinklerPrins (2009), "Pastoral Herd Management, Drought Coping Strategies, and Cattle Mobility in Southern Kenya," *Annals of the Association of American Geographers*, 99(2), 309–334.

Binswanger, Hans P. (1978), "Risk Attitudes of Rural Households in Semi-arid Tropical India," *Economic and Political Weekly*, 13(25), A49–A62.

Biswas, Asit K. (1985), "Ancient Urban Water Supply Systems," *GeoJournal*, 11(3), 207–213.

Biswas, Margaret R., and Asit K. Biswas (1984), "Complementarity between Environment and Development Processes," *Environmental Conservation*, 11(1), 35–44.

Black, Richard, and Mohamed F. Sessay (1997), "Refugees, Land Cover, and Environmental Change in the Senegal River Valley," *GeoJournal*, 41(1), 55–67.

Blainey, Geoffrey (1985), "Australia: A Bird's-Eye View," *Daedalus*, 114, 1–27.

Bloom, David E., and Jeffrey D. Sachs (1998), "Geography, Demography, and Economic Growth in Africa," *Brookings Papers on Economic Activity*, 2, 207–295.

Bohman, Anna, and Kaisa Raitio (2014), "How Frames Matter—Common Sense and Institutional Choice in Ghana's Urban Water Sector," *Journal of Environment and Development*, 23(2), 247–270.

Bombay (1903), *Report on the Famine of the Bombay Presidency*, Bombay: Government Press.

Bondestam, Lars (1974), "People and Capitalism in the Northeastern Lowlands of Ethiopia," *Journal of Modern African Studies*, 12(3), 423–439.

Boserup, Ester (1983), "The Impact of Scarcity and Plenty on Development," *Journal of Interdisciplinary History*, 14(2), 383–407.

Bouguerra, M.L. (2003), *Les batailles de l'eau: pour un bien commun de l'humanité*, Paris: Enjeux Planète.

Boukhars, Anouar, and Carl Pilgram (2023), "Crisis of Pastoralism Coming Due," in *In Disorder, They Thrive: How Rural Distress Fuels Militancy and Banditry in the Central Sahel*, 4-6, Washington, DC: Middle East Institute.

Bourguignon, François, and Christian Morrisson (2002), "Inequality among World Citizens: 1820–1992," *American Economic Review*, 92(4), 727–744.

Bovin, Mette, and Leif Manger, eds. (1990), *Adaptive Strategies in African Arid Lands*, Uppsala: Scandinavian Institute of African Studies.

Broich, John (2007), "Engineering the Empire: British Water Supply Systems and Colonial Societies, 1850–1900," *Journal of British Studies*, 46(2), 346–365.

Brown, Julia (2011), "Assuming Too Much? Participatory Water Resource Governance in South Africa," *Geographical Journal*, 117(2), 2011, 171–185.

Buckley, Eve E. (2017), *Technocrats and the Politics of Drought and Development in Twentieth-Century Brazil*, Chapel Hill: University of North Carolina Press.

Burke, Edmund, III (2009), "The Transformation of the Middle Eastern Environment, 1500 B.C.E.–2000 C.E.," in Edmund Burke III and Kenneth Pomeranz, eds., *The Environment and World History*, 81–117, Berkeley: University of California Press.

Burke, Edmund, III, and Kenneth Pomeranz, eds. (2013), *The Environment and World History*, Berkeley: University of California Press, 2009.

Burrier, Grant (2016), "The Developmental State, Civil Society, and Hydroelectric Politics in Brazil," *Journal of Environment and Development*, 25(3), 332–358.

Buttel, Frederick H. (2003), "Environmental Sociology and the Explanation of Environmental Reform," *Organization and Environment*, 16(3), 306–344.

Cabot, Jean (1965), *Le Bassin du Moyen Logone*, Paris: ORSTOM (office de la recherche scientifique et technique outre-mer).

Caretta, M.A., et al., "Water," in H.-O. Pörtner et al., eds. (2022), *Climate Change 2022: Impacts, Adaptation and Vulnerability. Contribution of Working Group II to the Sixth Assessment Report of the Intergovernmental Panel on Climate Change*, Cambridge: Cambridge University Press, 551–712.

Carman-Brown, Kylie (2019), *Following the Water: Environmental History and the Hydrological Cycle in Colonial Gippsland, Australia, 1838–1900*, Canberra: ANU Press.

Caton, Brian (2004), "Social Categories and Colonisation in Panjab, 1849–1920," *Indian Economic and Social History Review*, 41(1), 33–50.

Chappell, John E., Jr. (1970), "Climatic Change Reconsidered: Another Look at 'The Pulse of Asia,'" *Geographical Review*, 60(3), 347–373.

Chastanet, Monique (1992), "Survival Strategies of a Sahelian Society: The Case of the Soninke in Senegal from the Middle of the Nineteenth Century to the Present," *Food and Foodways*, 5(2), 127–149.

Chatterton, A.C. (1912), *Industrial Evolution in India*, Madras: Hindu Office.

Chellaney, Brahma (2011), *Water: Asia's New Battleground*, Washington, DC: Georgetown University Press.

Chen, Martha Alter (1991), *Coping with Seasonality and Drought*, New Delhi: Sage.

Chimeli, Ariaster B., Carolyn Z. Mutter, and Chet Ropelewski (2002), "Climate Fluctuations, Demography and Development: Insights and Opportunities for Northeast Brazil," *Journal of International Affairs*, 56(1), 213–234.

Clarke, John I. (1959), "Studies of Semi-nomadism in North Africa," *Economic Geography*, 35(2), 95–108.

Clarke, Thurston (1978), *The Last Caravan*, New York: G.P. Putnam's Sons.

Clayton, Daniel (2012), "Militant Tropicality: War, Revolution and the Reconfiguration of 'The Tropics' c.1940–c.1975," *Transactions of the Institute of British Geographers*, 38(1), 2012, 180–192.

Cleaver, Frances (1995), "Water as a Weapon: The History of Water Supply Development in Nkayi District, Zimbabwe," *Environment and History*, 1(3), 313–333.

Collins, Robert O. (2002), *The Nile*, New Haven, CT: Yale University Press.

Comstock, Charles (1934), "The Mir Alum Dam," *Military Engineer*, 26(148), 254–257.

Crummey, Donald (1990), "Society, State, and Nationality in the Recent Historiography of Ethiopia," *Journal of African History*, 31(1), 103–119.

Curtin, Philip D. (1974), "The Black Experience of Colonialism and Imperialism," *Daedalus*, 103(2), 17–29.

Cutler, Brock (2010), "Imperial Thirst: Water and Colonial Administration in Algeria, 1840–1880," *Review of Middle East Studies*, 44(2), 167–175.

Dainelli, Giotto (1931), "The Agricultural Possibilities of Italian Somalia," *Geographical Review*, 21(1), 56–69.

Datta, Sayantoni (2013), "Remembering the DVC Dream: Of Nationhood and Development Visions," Indian Institute of Advanced Studies, Shimla.

Davis, Diana K. (2007), *Resurrecting the Granary of Rome: Environmental History and French Colonial Expansion in North Africa*, Athens: Ohio University Press.

Davis, Diana K. (2016), *The Arid Lands: History, Power, Knowledge*, Cambridge, MA: MIT Press.

Davis, Diana K., and Edmund Burke III, eds. (2011), *Environmental Imaginaries of the Middle East and North Africa*, Athens: Ohio University Press.

De Lopez, Thanakvaro Thyl (2002), "Natural Resource Exploitation in Cambodia: An Examination of Use, Appropriation, and Exclusion," *Journal of Environment and Development*, 11(4), 355–379.

Demangeot, Jean (1978), *Les espaces naturels tropicaux: Essai de geographie physique*, Paris: Masson.

REFERENCES 269

Derr, Jennifer L. (2019), *The Lived Nile: Environment, Disease, and Material Colonial Economy in Egypt*, Stanford, CA: Stanford University Press.

Devaraju, N., G. Bala, and A. Modak (2015), "Effects of Large-Scale Deforestation on Precipitation in the Monsoon Regions: Remote versus Local Effects," *Proceedings of the National Academy of Sciences of the United States of America*, 112(11), 3257–3262.

Dhavalikar, M.K. (1989), "Farming to Pastoralism: Effects of Climatic Change in the Deccan," in Juliet Clutton-Brock, ed., *The Walking Larder: Patterns of Domestication, Pastoralism, and Predation*, 156–168, London: Unwin Hyman.

Diamond, Jared M. (2017), *Guns, Germs, and Steel: The Fates of Human Societies*, New York: W.W. Norton & Company.

Diawara, Mamadou (2011), "Development and Administrative Norms: The Office du Niger and Decentralization in French Sudan and Mali," *Africa: Journal of the International African Institute*, 81(3), 434–454.

Dixon, Charles George (1850), *Sketch of Mairwara*, London: Smith, Elder.

Djurfeldt, Agnes Andersson (2012), "Seasonality and Farm/Non-Farm interactions in Western Kenya," *Journal of Modern African Studies*, 50(1), 1–23.

Dobby, E.H.G. (1961), *Monsoon Asia*, Chicago: Quadrangle Books.

Doolittle, William E. (1995), "Indigenous Development of Mesoamerican Irrigation," *Geographical Review*, 85(3), 301–323.

D'Souza, Rohan (2003), "Canal Irrigation and the Conundrum of Flood Protection: The Failure of the Orissa Scheme of 1863 in Eastern India," *Studies in History*, 19(1), 41–68.

D'Souza, Rohan, Pranab Mukhopadhyay, and Ashish Kothari (1998), "Re-evaluating Multi-purpose River Valley Projects: A Case Study of Hirakud, Ukai and IGNP," *Economic and Political Weekly*, 33(6), 297–302.

Duflo, Esther, and Rohini Pande (2007), "Dams," *Quarterly Journal of Economics*, 122(2), 601–646.

Dumont, René (1964), "Le développement agricole spécialement tropical exige un enseignement totalement repensé," *Revue Tiers Monde*, 5(1), 13–38.

Dunbar, Robert G. (1977), "The Adaptation of Groundwater-Control Institutions to the Arid West," *Agricultural History*, 51(4), 662–680.

Durrill, Wayne K. (1986), "Atrocious Misery: The African Origins of Famine in Northern Somalia, 1839–1884," *American Historical Review*, 91(2), 287–306.

Edgerton-Tarpley, Kathryn (2013), "Tough Choices: Grappling with Famine in Qing China, the British Empire, and Beyond," *Journal of World History*, 24(2), 135–176.

Edgerton-Tarpley, Kathryn (2016), "Between War and Water: Farmer, City, and State in China's Yellow River Flood of 1938–1947," *Agricultural History*, 90(1), 94–116.

Egal, Mohamed Haji Ibrahim (1968), "Somalia: Nomadic Individualism and the Rule of Law," *African Affairs*, 67(268), 219–226.

El-Arifi, Salih A. (1975), "A Regional Approach to Planning and Development of Pastoral Nomads in the Sudan," *Sudan Notes and Records*, 56, 147–159.

El-Bushra, El-Sayed, and Mohammed Osman El Sammani (1977), "Urban and Rural Water Supplies in the Sudan," *Ekistics*, 43, 36–42.

REFERENCES

El-Din El-Tayeb, Galal, and Anne Lendowski (1997), "Environmental Degradation in Gedaref District," *Sudan Notes and Records*, 1, 135–157.

Eldredge, Elizabeth A. (1987), "Drought, Famine and Disease in Nineteenth-Century Lesotho," *African Economic History*, 16, 61–93.

El Jihad, Moulay Driss (2001), "L'eau de la montagne et le pouvoir étatique au Maroc: entre le passé et le present," *Annales de Géographie*, 110(622), 665–672.

El-Khoury, Gabi (2014), "Water Resources in Arab Countries," *Contemporary Arab Affairs*, 7(2), 339–349.

Eltarabily, M.G., I. Abd-Elaty, A. Elbeltagi, M. Zelenáková, and I. Fathy (2023), "Investigating Climate Change Effects on Evapotranspiration and Groundwater Recharge of the Nile Delta Aquifer, Egypt," *Water*, 15(572), 1–16.

Endfield, Georgina H., and Sarah L. O'Hara (1997), "Conflicts over Water in 'The Little Drought Age' in Central México," *Environment and History*, 3(3), 255–272.

Evans, Martin, and Yasir Mohieldeen (2002), "Environmental Change and Livelihood Strategies: The Case of Lake Chad," *Geography*, 87(1), 3–13.

Evans, Peter B. (1989), "Predatory, Developmental, and Other Apparatuses: A Comparative Political Economy Perspective on the Third World State," *Sociological Forum*, 4(4), 561–587.

Evans, Sterling (2019), "Dams in the Desert," *Global Environment*, 12(1), 182–205.

Fazle Karim Khan, Muhammad, and Muhammad Nawaz (1995), "Karez Irrigation in Pakistan," *GeoJournal*, 37(1), 1995, 91–100.

Federico, Giovanni, and Antonio Tena-Junguito (2017), "Lewis Revisited: Tropical Polities Competing on the World Market, 1830–1938," *Economic History Review*, 70(4), 1244–1267.

Fei, J.C.H., and A.C. Chiang (1968), in W.W. McPherson, ed., *Economic Development of Tropical Agriculture: Theory, Policy, Strategy, and Organization*, Gainesville: University of Florida Press.

Fenske, James (2013), "Does Land Abundance Explain African Institutions?," *Economic Journal*, 123(4), 1363–1390.

Fenske, James, and Namrata Kala (2015), "Climate and the Slave Trade," *Journal of Development Economics*, 112, 19–32.

Filipovich, Jean (2001), "Destined to Fail: Forced Settlement at the Office du Niger, 1926–45," *Journal of African History*, 42(2), 239–260.

Fisher, Michael H. (2018), *An Environmental History of India: From Earliest Times to the Twenty-First Century*, Cambridge: Cambridge University Press.

Frank, Charles R., Jr. (1969), Review of John de Wilde, ed, Agricultural Development in Tropical Africa, Baltimore, Johns Hopkins University Press, 1967, *Economic Development and Cultural Change*, 17(3), 1969, 438–441.

Frankema, Ewout, Erik Green, and Ellen Hillbom (2016), "Endogenous Processes of Colonial Settlement. The Success and Failure of European Settler Farming in Sub-Saharan Africa," *Revista de Historia Economica—Journal of Iberian and Latin American Economic History*, 34(2), 237–265.

REFERENCES 271

Frankema, Ewout, and Morten Jerven (2014), "Writing History Backwards or Sideways: Towards a Consensus on African Population, 1850–2010," *Economic History Review*, 67(4), 907–931.

Fratkin, Elliot (2001), "East African Pastoralism in Transition: Maasai, Boran, and Rendille Cases," *African Studies Review*, 44(3), 1–25.

Freise, Freidrich W. (1938), "The Drought Region of Northeastern Brazil," *Geographical Review*, 28(3), 363–378.

Gadgil, Madhav, and Ramachandra Guha (1995), *Ecology and Equity: The Use and Abuse of Nature in Contemporary India*, London: Routledge.

Galaty, John G. (2012), "Land Grabbing in the Eastern African Rangelands," in Andy Catley, Jeremy Lind, Ian Scoones, and Jeremy Lindeck, eds., *Pastoralism and Development in Africa: Dynamic Change at the Margins*, Abingdon: Routledge, 143–153.

Gallup, John Luke, Jeffrey D. Sachs, and Andrew D. Mellinger (1999), "Geography and Economic Development," *International Regional Science Review*, 22(2), 179–232.

Garchitorena, A., S.H. Sokolow, B. Roche, C.N. Ngonghala, M. Jocque, A. Lund, M. Barry, E.A. Mordecai, G.C. Daily, J.H. Jones, J.R. Andrews, E. Bendavid, S.P. Luby, A.D. LaBeaud, K. Seetah, J.F. Guégan, M.H. Bonds, and G.A. De Leo (2017), "Disease Ecology, Health and the Environment: A Framework to Account for Ecological and Socio-Economic Drivers in the Control of Neglected Tropical Diseases," *Philosophical Transactions: Biological Sciences*, 372(1722), 1–12.

Gebresenbet, Fana (2016), "Land Acquisitions, the Politics of Dispossession, and State-Remaking in Gambella, Western Ethiopia," *Africa Spectrum*, 51(1), 5–28.

Geertz, Clifford (1972), "The Wet and the Dry: Traditional Irrigation in Bali and Morocco," *Human Ecology*, 1(1), 23–39.

Gilmartin, David (1994), "Scientific Empire and Imperial Science: Colonialism and Irrigation Technology in the Indus Basin," *Journal of Asian Studies*, 53(4), 1127–1149.

Giordano, Meredith, Mark Giordano, and Aaron Wolf (2002), "The Geography of Water Conflict and Cooperation: Internal Pressures and International Manifestations," *Geographical Journal*, 168(4), 2293–2312.

Gjersø, Jonas Fossli (2015), "The Scramble for East Africa: British Motives Reconsidered, 1884–95," *Journal of Imperial and Commonwealth History*, 43(5), 831–860.

Glover, Harold (1945), "Soil Erosion in Baluchistan," *Empire Forestry Journal*, 24(1), 21–32.

Godana, B.A. (1985), *Africa's Shared Water Resources: Legal and Institutional Aspects of the Nile, Niger and Senegal River Systems*, London: Frances Pinter.

Goldewijk, Kees Klein, Arthur Beusen, Gerard van Drecht, and Martine de Vos (2011), "The HYDE 3.1 Spatially Explicit Database of Human-Induced Global Land-Use Change over the Past 12,000 Years," *Global Ecology and Biogeography*, 20, 73–86.

Goldsmith, Raymond W. (1983), *The Financial Development of India, Japan and the United States*, New Haven, CT: Yale University Press.

Goodhue, Rachael E., and Nancy McCarthy (2009), "Traditional Property Rights, Common Property, and Mobility in Semi-arid African Pastoralist Systems," *Environment and Development Economics*, 14(1), 29–50.

272 REFERENCES

Goodman, R. David (2012), "Demystifying 'Islamic Slavery': Using Legal Practices to Reconstruct the End of Slavery in Fes, Morocco," *History in Africa*, 39, 143–174.

Gorrie, R. MacLagan (1938), "Soil and Water Conservation in the Punjab," *Geographical Review*, 28(1), 20–31.

Gourou, Pierre (1949), "Qu'est-ce que: Le monde tropical?," *Annales. Histoire, Sciences Sociales*, 4(2), 140-148.

Graham, Douglas H. (1970), "Divergent and Convergent Regional Economic Growth and Internal Migration in Brazil: 1940–1960," *Economic Development and Cultural Change*, 18(3), 362–382.

Graham, Neal T., Mohamad I. Hejazi, Son H. Kim, Evan G. R. Davies, James A. Edmonds, and Fernando Miralles-Wilhelm (2020), "Future Changes in the Trading of Virtual Water," *Nature Communications*, 11, 3632, 1–7.

Grolle, John (2015), "Historical Case Studies of Famines and Migrations in the West African Sahel and Their Possible Relevance Now and in the Future," *Population and Environment*, 37(2), 181–206.

Groningen Growth and Development Centre, http://www.ggdc.net › horizontal-file_02-2010.

Guadagni, Marco M.G. (1978), "Colonial Origins of the Public Domain in Southern Somalia (1892–1912)," *Journal of African Law*, 22(1), 1–29.

Guha, Sumit (2015), "States, Tribes, Castes: A Historical Re-exploration in Comparative Perspective," *Economic and Political Weekly*, 50(46–47), 50–57.

Gunawardene, R.A.L.H. (1971), "Irrigation and Hydraulic Society in Early Medieval Ceylon," *Past and Present*, 53, 3–27.

Habib, Irfan (1969), "An Examination of Wittfogel's Theory of 'Oriental Despotism,'" in K.S. Lal, ed., *Studies in Asian History, Proceedings of the Asian History Congress, New Delhi*, London: Asia Publishing, 378–392.

Hall, Bruce S. (2005), "The Question of 'Race' in the Pre-colonial Southern Sahara," *Journal of North African Studies*, 10(3–4), 339–367.

Halvorsen, Kjell H. (1978), "Colonial Transformation of Agrarian Society in Algeria," *Journal of Peace Research*, 15(4), 323–343.

Hanasz, Paula (2014), "Power Flows: Hydro-Hegemony and Water Conflicts in South Asia," *Security Challenges*, 10, 95–112.

Harbeson, John H. (1978), "Territorial and Development Policies in the Horn of Africa: The Afar of the Awash Valley," *African Affairs*, 77(309), 479–498.

Hardin, Garrett (1968), "The Tragedy of the Commons," *Science*, 162(3859), 1243–1248.

Hargreaves, Mary W.M. (1977), "The Dry-Farming Movement in Retrospect," *Agricultural History*, 51(1), 149–165.

Hart, David (1980), *The Volta River Project: A Case Study in Politics and Technology*, Edinburgh: University of Edinburgh Press.

Havinden, Michael, and David Meredith (1996), *Colonialism and Development: Britain and Its Tropical Colonies, 1850–1960*, London: Routledge.

He, Wenkai (2015), "Public Interest and the Financing of Local Water Control in Qing, China, 1750–1850," *Social Science History*, 39(3), 409–430.

REFERENCES 273

Heady, Harold F. (1965), "Rangeland Development in East Africa," in David Brokensha, ed., *Ecology and Economic Development in Tropical Africa*, 73–82, Berkeley: University of California Press.

Heald, Suzette (1999), "Agricultural Intensification and the Decline of Pastoralism: A Case Study from Kenya," *Africa: Journal of the International African Institute*, 69(2), 213–237.

Heathcote, R.L. (1965), *Back of Bourke: A Study of Land Appraisal and Settlement in Semi-arid Australia*, Melbourne: Melbourne University Press.

Helmy, Farida (2013), "Can Desalination Help Keep Peace in the Middle East?," *Corporate Knights*, 12(3), 34–36.

Henderson, David A. (1965), "Arid Lands under Agrarian Reform in Northwest Mexico," *Economic Geography*, 41(4), 300–312.

Hicks, John (1987), "The Production Function," in Hicks, *Capital and Time: A Neo-Austrian Theory*, 177–184, Oxford: Oxford University Press.

Hill, Polly (1982), *Dry Grain Farming Families: Hausaland (Nigeria) and Karnataka (India) Compared*, New York: Cambridge University Press.

Hirsch, Abraham M. (1961), "Some Aspects of River Utilization in Arid Areas: The Hydro-Economics of Inadequate Supply," *American Journal of Economics and Sociology*, 20(3), 271–286.

Hoag, Heather J. (2013), *Developing the Rivers of East and West Africa: An Environmental History*, New York: Bloomsbury Academic.

Hoffmann, Clemens, Gabrielle Daoust, and Jan Selby (2022), *Divided Environments: An International Political Ecology of Climate Change, Water and Security*, Cambridge: Cambridge University Press.

Holm, John D., and Richard G. Morgan (1985), "Coping with Drought in Botswana: An African Success," *Journal of Modern African Studies*, 23(3), 463–482.

Ibrahim, Moussa, Dominik Wisser, Abdou Ali, Bernd Diekkrüger, Ousmane Seidou, Adama Mariko, and Abel Afouda (2017), "Water Balance Analysis over the Niger Inland Delta—Mali: Spatio-Temporal Dynamics of the Flooded Area and Water Losses," *Hydrology*, 4(1), 1–23.

Idda, Salem, Bruno Bonté, Marcel Kuper, and Hamidi Mansour (2021), "Revealing the Foggara as a Living Irrigation System through an Institutional Analysis: Evidence from Oases in the Algerian Sahara," *International Journal of the Commons*, 15(1), 431–448.

Iliffe, John (2007), *Africans: The History of a Continent*, Cambridge: Cambridge University Press.

India (1880), *Report of the Indian Famine Commission. Part I: Famine Relief*, London: HMSO.

India (1927), *Royal Commission on Agriculture*, Vol. VII, Delhi: Government Press.

Isaacman, Allen (2021), "Cahora Bassa Dam and the Delusion of Development," *Daedalus*, 150(4), 103–123.

Iyer, Ramaswamy R. (2014), "Indus Waters Treaty 1960: An Indian Perspective," March 16, 2014, https://www.boell.de/en/2014/03/16/indus-waters-treaty-1960-indian-perspective.

274 REFERENCES

James, Craig D., Jill Landsberg, and Stephen R. Morton (1999), "Provision of Watering Points in the Australian Arid Zone: A Review of Effects on Biota," *Journal of Arid Environments*, 41(1), 87–121.

Jansen, M. (1989), "Water Supply and Sewage Disposal at Mohenjo-Daro," *World Archaeology*, 21(2), 177–192.

Jarosz, Lucy (1993), "Defining and Explaining Tropical Deforestation: Shifting Cultivation and Population Growth in Colonial Madagascar (1896–1940)," *Economic Geography*, 69(4), 366–379.

Jeevananda Reddy, S. (1983), "Climatic Classification: The Semi-arid Tropics and Its Environment—A Review," *Pesquisa Agropecuária Brasileira*, 18(8), 823–847.

Jodha, N.S., and V.S. Vyas (1969), *Conditions of Stability and Growth in Arid Agriculture*, Vallabh Vidyanagar, India: Agroeconomic Research Centre.

Johnson, Harry G. (1971), "Review of W.A. Lewis, *Aspects of Tropical Trade, 1883–1965*," *Journal of International Economics*, 1, 131–136.

Johnson, Martha C., and Meg Smaker (2014), "State Building in De Facto States: Somaliland and Puntland Compared," *Africa Today*, 60(4), 3–23.

Jones, Toby C. (2012), "State of Nature: The Politics of Water in the Making of Saudi Arabia," in Alan Mikhail, ed., *Water on Sand: Environmental Histories of the Middle East and North Africa*, Oxford: Oxford University Press, 231–250.

Josephson, Paul (2017), "Stalin's Water Workers and Their Heritage: Industrialising Nature in Russia, 1950–Present," *Global Environment*, 10(1), 168–201.

Kalb, Martin (2022), *Environing Empire: Nature, Infrastructure and the Making of German Southwest Africa*, New York: Berghahn Books, 2022.

Kaneda, Hiromitsu (1969), Review of W.W. McPherson, ed., *Economic Development of Tropical Agriculture: Theory, Policy, Strategy, and Organization, Pakistan Development Review*, 9(3), 346–349.

Kapteijns, Lidwien (1989), "The Historiography of the Northern Sudan from 1500 to the Establishment of British Colonial Rule: A Critical Overview," *International Journal of African Historical Studies*, 22(2), 251–266.

Karabenick, Edward (1991), "A Postcolonial Rural Landscape: The Algiers Sahel," *Yearbook of the Association of Pacific Coast Geographers*, 53, 87–108.

Karaman, K.K., and Sevket Pamuk (2010), "Ottoman State Finances in European Perspective, 1500–1914," *Journal of Economic History*, 70, 593–629 (with http://www.ata.boun.edu.tr/sevketpamuk/JEH2010articledatabase).

Kassambara, Abdoulaye Abakar (2010), "La Situation Économique et Sociale du Tchad de 1900 à 1960," PhD dissertation, Université de Strasbourg.

Kathayat, Gayatri, Hai Cheng, Ashish Sinha, Liang Yi, Xianglei Li, Haiwei Zhang, Hangying Li, Youfeng Ning, and R. Lawrence Edwards (2017), "The Indian Monsoon Variability and Civilization Changes in the Indian Subcontinent," *Science Advances*, 3, 1–8.

Katzenberger, A., A. Levermann, J. Schewe, and J. Pongratz (2022), "Intensification of Very Wet Monsoon Seasons in India under Global Warming," *Geophysical Research Letters*, 49, 1–10.

Kaufmann, Jeffrey C., and Sylvestre Tsirahamba (2006), "Forests and Thorns: Conditions of Change Affecting Mahafale Pastoralists in Southwestern Madagascar," *Conservation and Society*, 4(2), 231–261.

Kebbede, Girma (1988), "Cycles of Famine in a Country of Plenty: The Case of Ethiopia," *GeoJournal*, 17(1), 125–132.

Keita, Kalifa, and Dan Henk (1998), "Conflict and Conflict Resolution in the Sahel: The Tuareg Insurgency in Mali," Strategic Studies Institute, US Army War College.

Kelso, Maurice M., William E. Martin, and Lawrence E. Mack (1973), *Water Supplies and Economic Growth in an Arid Environment*, Tucson: University of Arizona Press.

Kerr, Ian J. (2006), "On the Move: Circulating Labor in Pre-colonial, Colonial, and Postcolonial India," *International Review of Social History*, 51(1), 85–109.

Kibreab, Gaim (2001), "Property Rights, Development Policy and Depletion of Resources: The Case of the Central Rainlands of Sudan, 1940s–1980s," *Environment and History*, 7(1), 2001, 57–108.

Kimenyi, Mwangi S., John Mukum Mbaku, and Nelipher Moyo (2010), "Reconstituting Africa's Failed States: The Case of Somalia," *Social Research*, 77(4), 1339–1366.

Klingensmith, Daniel (2007), *One Valley and a Thousand: Dams, Nationalism, and Development*, Oxford: Oxford University Press.

Kloos, Helmut (1982), "Development, Drought, and Famine in the Awash Valley of Ethiopia," *African Studies Review*, 25(4), 21–48.

Klute, Georg (1996), "The Coming State. Reactions of Nomadic Groups in the Western Sudan to the Expansion of the Colonial Powers," *Nomadic Peoples*, 38, 49–71.

Knight, Melvin M. (1928), "Water and the Course of Empire in North Africa," *Quarterly Journal of Economics*, 43(1), 44–93.

Konczacki, Z. A. (1967), "Nomadism and Economic Development of Somalia: The Position of the Nomads in the Economy of Somalia," *Canadian Journal of African Studies*, 1(2), 163–175. Cited text on p. 173.

Kosambi, Damodar (1965), *The Culture and Civilisation of Ancient India in Historical Outline*, London: Routledge and Kegan Paul.

Kreike, Emmanuel (2009), "De-globalisation and Deforestation in Colonial Africa: Closed Markets, the Cattle Complex, and Environmental Change in North-Central Namibia, 1890–1990," *Journal of Southern African Studies*, 35(1), 81–98.

Krishnan, Chitra, and Srinivas V. Veeravalli (2006), "Tanks and Anicuts of South India: Examples of an Alternative Science of Engineering," in A.V. Balasubramanian and T.D. Nirmala Devi, eds., *Traditional Knowledge Systems of India and Sri Lanka*, 220-227, Chennai: Centre for Indian Knowledge Systems.

Kumar, Anil, S. Natarajan, Nagaratna B. Biradar, and Brij K Trivedi (2011), "Evolution of Sedentary Pastoralism in South India: Case Study of the Kangayam Grassland," *Pastoralism*, 1(7), 1–18.

Kumar, Mayank (2013), "Peasants, Pastoralists and Rulers: Aspects of Ecology and Polity in Seventeenth- and Eighteenth-Century Rajasthan," Occasional paper, New Delhi: Nehru Memorial Museum and Library.

276 REFERENCES

Kummu, Matti, and Olli Varis (2011), "The World by Latitudes: A Global Analysis of Human Population, Development Level and Environment across the North-South Axis over the Past Half Century," *Applied Geography*, 31(2), 495–507.

Kuznets, Simon (1933), "Seasonal Variations in Industry and Trade: Appendices," NBER Working Paper No. 2204, www.nber.org/chapters/c2204.pdf.

Laitin, David D., and Said S. Samatar (1987), *Somalia: Nation in Search of a State*, Boulder, CO: Westview Press.

Landes, David (1998), *Wealth and Poverty of Nations*, Cambridge, MA: Belknap Press of Harvard University Press.

Lautze, Jonathan, and Mark Giordano (2005), "Transboundary Water Law in Africa: Development, Nature, and Geography," *Natural Resources Journal*, 45(4), 1053–1087.

Leach, E.R. (1959), "Hydraulic Society in Ceylon," *Past and Present*, 15, 2–26.

Lebon, J.H.G. (1956), "Rural Water Supplies and the Development of Economy in the Central Sudan," *Geografiska Annaler*, 38(1), 78–101.

Lecocq, Baz (2015), "Distant Shores: A Historiographic View on Trans-Saharan Space," *Journal of African History*, 56(1), 23–36.

Lee, David R. (1970), "The Location of Land Use Types: The Nile Valley in Northern Sudan," *Economic Geography*, 46(1), 53–62.

Lee, J. Karl (1952), "Irrigation Policy for Arid Lands," *Journal of Farm Economics*, 34(5), 751–755.

Lewis, W. Arthur, ed. (1970) *Tropical Development 1880–1913: Studies in Economic Progress*, London: George Allen and Unwin.

Lie, Jon Harald Sande, and Axel Borchgrevink (2012), "Layer upon Layer: Understanding the Gambella Conflict Formation," *International Journal of Ethiopian Studies*, 6(1/2), 135–159.

Lightfoot, Dale R. (1997), "Qanats in the Levant: Hydraulic Technology at the Periphery of Early Empires," *Technology and Culture*, 38(2), 432–451.

Lisovski, Simeon, Marilyn Ramenofsky, and John C. Wingfield (2017), "Defining the Degree of Seasonality and its Significance for Future Research," *Integrative and Comparative Biology*, 57(5), 934–942.

Loftus, Alex (2009), "Rethinking Political Ecologies of Water," *Third World Quarterly*, 30(5), 953–968.

Love, Roy (1994), "Drought, Dutch Disease and Controlled Transition in Botswana Agriculture," *Journal of Southern African Studies*, 20(1), 71–83.

Lovejoy, Paul E., and Stephen Baier (1975), "The Desert-Side Economy of the Central Sudan," *International Journal of African Historical Studies*, 8(4), 551–581.

Lueck, Dean, and Thomas J. Miceli (2007), "Property Law," in A. Mitchell Polinsky and Steven Shavell, eds., *Handbook of Law and Economics*, 183-257, Amsterdam: Elsevier.

Lumsden, D. Paul (1973), "The Volta River Project: Village Resettlement and Attempted Rural Animation," *Canadian Journal of African Studies*, 7(1), 115–132.

Lydon, Ghislaine (2009), *On Trans-Saharan Trails: Islamic Law, Trade Networks, and Cross-Cultural Exchange in Nineteenth-Century Western Africa*, Cambridge: Cambridge University Press.

Mabogunje, Akin (1965), "Water Resources and Economic Development in Nigeria," in David Brokensha, ed., *Ecology and Economic Development in Tropical Africa*, Berkeley: University of California Press, 147–159.

Mackenzie, Fiona (1996), "Conflicting Claims to Custom: Land and Law in Central Province, Kenya, 1912–52," *Journal of African Law*, 40(1), 62–77.

Maddison Project Database (2020), University of Groningen, https://www.rug.nl/ggdc/historicaldevelopment/maddison/releases/maddison-project-database-2020?lang=en.

"Maddison Database 2010" https://www.rug.nl/ggdc/historicaldevelopment/maddison/releases/maddison-database-2010 (accessed on December 5, 2024).

Maddox, Gregory H. (1998), "Networks and Frontiers in Colonial Tanzania," *Environmental History*, 3(4), 436–459.

Mahony, Martin, and Georgina Endfield (2018), "Climate and Colonialism," *Climate Change*, 9, 1–16.

Maina, Fadji Z., Augusto Getirana, Sujay V. Kumar, Manabendra Saharia, Nishan Kumar Biswas, Sasha McLarty, and Ravi Appana (2024), "Irrigation-Driven Groundwater Depletion in the Ganges-Brahmaputra Basin Decreases the Streamflow in the Bay of Bengal," *Communications Earth and Environment*, 5 (169), https://doi.org/10.1038/s43247-024-01348-0.

Manger, Leif (n.d.), "Resource Conflict as a Factor in the Darfur Crisis in Sudan," Chr. Michelsen Institute, accessed November 24, 2024, https://www.cmi.no/file/1816-Manger—Resource-Conflict-as-a-Factor.pdf.

Manning, Patrick (2014), "African Population, 1650–2000: Comparisons and Implications of New Estimates," in Emmanuel Akyeampong, Robert H. Bates, Nathan Nunn, and James Robinson, eds., *Africa's Development in Historical Perspective*, 131–150, Cambridge: Cambridge University Press.

Markakis, John (1988), "The Nationalist Revolution in Eritrea," *Journal of Modern African Studies*, 26(1), 51–70.

Markakis, John, ed. (1993), *Conflict and the Decline of Pastoralism in the Horn of Africa*, London: Macmillan and Institute of Social Studies.

McCann, James C. (1990), "A Great Agrarian Cycle? Productivity in Highland Ethiopia, 1900 to 1987," *Journal of Interdisciplinary History*, 20(3), 389–416.

McCann, James C. (1999), "Climate and Causation in African History," *International Journal of African Historical Studies*, 32(2/3), 261–279.

McNeill, John (2000), *Something New under the Sun: An Environmental History of the Twentieth-Century World*, New York: W.W. Norton.

McNeill, J.R. (2013), "The Eccentricity of the Middle East and North Africa's Environmental History," in Alan Mikhail, ed., *Water on Sand: Environmental Histories of the Middle East and North Africa*, 27–50, Oxford: Oxford University Press.

Megdal, Sharon (2012), "Arizona Groundwater Management," The Water Report, https://wrrc.cals.arizona.edu/sites/wrrc.arizona.edu/files/azgroundwater-management.pdf.

Mekonnen, Dereje Zeleke (2013), "The Quest for Equitable Resolution of the Nile Waters Dispute," *International Journal of Ethiopian Studies*, 7(1–2), 77–100.

Melketo, Tagesse, Martin Schmidt, Michelle Bonatti, Stefan Sieber, Klaus Müller, and Marcos Lana (2021), "Determinants of Pastoral Household Resilience to Food Insecurity in Afar Region, Northeast Ethiopia," *Journal of Arid Environments*, 188, 1–11.

Michel, David (2020), "Case Study: Mali," in US Institute of Peace, *Water Conflict Pathways and Peacebuilding Strategies*, 14–17, Washington, DC: US Institute of Peace.

278 REFERENCES

Mikhail, Alan (2011), *Nature and Empire in Ottoman Egypt: Studies in Environment and History*, New York: Cambridge University Press.

Mikhail, Alan, ed. (2013), *Water on Sand: Environmental Histories of the Middle East and North Africa*, New York: Oxford University Press.

Miller, Joseph C. (1982), "The Significance of Drought, Disease and Famine in the Agriculturally Marginal Zones of West-Central Africa," *Journal of African History*, 23(1), 1982, 17–61.

Minoia, Paola (2012), "Mega-irrigation and Neoliberalism in Postcolonial States: Evolution and Crisis in the Gharb Plain, Morocco," *Geografiska Annaler*, Series B, 94(3), 269–286.

Mishra, Ashok K., and Vijay P. Singh (2010), "A Review of Drought Concepts," *Journal of Hydrology*, 391, 202–216.

Mithen, Steven (2010), "The Domestication of Water: Water Management in the Ancient World and Its Prehistoric Origins in the Jordan Valley," *Philosophical Transactions: Mathematical, Physical and Engineering Sciences*, 368(1931), 5249–5274.

Mitra, Ashok K. (1986), "Underutilisation Revisited: Surface Irrigation in Drought-Prone Areas of Western Maharashtra," *Economic and Political Weekly*, 21(17), 752–756.

Mitra, Ashok K. (1992), "Joint Management of Irrigation Systems in India: Relevance of Japanese Experience," *Economic and Political Weekly*, 27(26), A75–A82.

Mollinga, Peter (2003), *On the Waterfront: Water Distribution, Technology and Agrarian Change in a South Indian Canal Irrigation System*, Hyderabad: Orient Longman.

Moreno, José Luis (2012), "'A Never-Ending Source of Water': Agriculture, Society, and Aquifer Depletion on the Coast of Hermosillo, Sonora," *Journal of the Southwest*, 54(4), 545–568.

Moritz, M. (2016), "Open Property Regimes," *International Journal of the Commons*, 10(2), 688–708.

Morrissey, Katherine G., and Marcus A. Burtner (2019), "Global Imaginary of Arid Lands," *Global Environment*, 12(1), 102–133.

Mosse, David (1999), "Colonial and Contemporary Ideologies of 'Community Management': The Case of Tank Irrigation Development in South India," *Modern Asian Studies*, 33(2), 303–338.

Msangi, J.P. (1987), "Water Resources Conservation in the Semi-arid Parts of Tanzania," *Journal of East African Research and Development*, 17, 63–73.

Mustafa, Daanish (2007), "Social Construction of Hydropolitics: The Geographical Scales of Water and Security in the Indus Basin," *Geographical Review*, 97(4), 484–501.

Mustafa, Daanish, and Usman Qazi (2012), "Karez versus Tubewell Irrigation: Comparative Social Acceptability and Practicality of Sustainable Groundwater Development in Balochistan, Pakistan," in Lisa Mol and Troy Sternberg, eds., *Changing Deserts: Integrating People and their Environment*, 129–153, Cambridge, UK: White Horse Press.

Mutibwa, Phares M. (1972), "Trade and Economic Development in Nineteenth-Century Madagascar," *Transafrican Journal of History*, 2(1), 32–63.

Myint, Hla (1965), *The Economics of the Developing Countries*, New York: Praeger.

Myrdal, Gunnar (1968), *Asian Drama*, London: Allen Lane.

Narayanan, N.C., and Lalitha Kamath (2012), "Rural Water Access: Governance and Contestation in a Semi-arid Watershed in Udaipur, Rajasthan," *Economic and Political Weekly*, 47(4), 65–72.

Navarro, Gonzalo, Shelley MacDonell, and Remi Valois (2023), "A Conceptual Hydrological Model of Semiarid Andean Headwater Systems in Chile," *Progress in Physical Geography*, 1–19.

Neukom, Raphael, Nathan Steiger, Juan José Gómez-Navarro, Jianghao Wang, and Johannes P. Werner (2019), "No Evidence for Globally Coherent Warm and Cold Periods over the Preindustrial Common Era," *Nature*, 571, 550–554.

Nicholson, Sharon E. (2001), "Climatic and Environmental Change in Africa during the Last Two Centuries," *Climate Research*, 17(2), 123–144.

Nicolaj, Andrea (1990), "The Senegal Mauritanian Conflict," *Africa: Rivista trimestrale di studi e documentazione dell'Istituto italiano per l'Africa e l'Oriente*, 45(3), 464–480.

Njeuma, Martin Z., and Nicodemus F. Awasom (1990), "The Fulani and the Political Economy of the Bamenda Grasslands, 1940–1960," *Paideuma: Mitteilungen zur Kulturkunde*, 36, 217–233.

Noer, Thomas J. (1984), "The New Frontier and African Neutralism: Kennedy, Nkrumah, and the Volta River Project," *Diplomatic History*, 8(1), 61–79.

Oloo, Adams (2007), "The Quest for Cooperation in the Nile Water Conflicts: The Case of Eritrea," *African Sociological Review*, 11(1), 95–105.

Omran, A.R. (1971), "The Epidemiologic Transition: A Theory of the Epidemiology of Population Change," *Milbank Memorial Fund Quarterly*, 49(4), 509–538.

Osei-Hwedie, Kwaku (1998), "Food Policy: Managing Drought and the Environment in Botswana," *Africa Development*, 23(2), 61–83.

Oshima, Harry T. (1986), "The Transition from an Agricultural to an Industrial Economy in East Asia," *Economic Development and Cultural Change*, 34(4), 783–809.

Oshima, Harry T. (1987), *Economic Growth in Monsoon Asia: A Comparative Study*, Tokyo: University of Tokyo Press.

Ostrom, Vincent, and Elinor Ostrom (1977), "Public Goods and Public Choices," in E.S. Savas, ed., *Alternatives for Delivering Public Services: Toward Improved Performance*, 7-49, Boulder, CO: Westview Press.

Ottaway, Marina (1986), "Drought and Development in Ethiopia," *Current History*, 85(511), 217–220.

Padt, Frans J., and Juan Carlos Sanchez (2013), "Creating New Spaces for Sustainable Water Management in the Senegal River Basin," *Natural Resources Journal*, 53, 265–284.

Pantuliano, Sara (2010), "Oil, Land and Conflict: The Decline of Misseriyya Pastoralism in Sudan," *Review of African Political Economy*, 37(123), 7–23.

Park, Mungo (1858), *Travels in the Interior of Africa*, Edinburgh: Adam and Charles Black.

Park, Mungo (1909), *The Travels of Mungo Park*, London: H. Milford.

Parthasarathi, Prasannan (2011), *Why Europe Grew Rich and Asia Did Not: Global Economic Divergence, 1600–1850*. Cambridge: Cambridge University Press.

Pastner, Stephen (1971), "Ideological Aspects of Nomad-Sedentary Contact: A Case from Southern Baluchistan," *Anthropological Quarterly*, 44(3), 173–184.

Pastner, Stephen, and Carroll McC. Pastner (1972), "Agriculture, Kinship and Politics in Southern Baluchistan," *Man*, 7(1), 128–136.

Pearson, Mike Parker (1997), "Close Encounters of the Worst Kind: Malagasy Resistance and Colonial Disasters in Southern Madagascar," *World Archaeology*, 28(3), 393–417.

Peel, M.C., B.L. Finlayson, and T.A. McMahon (2007), "Updated World Map of the Köppen-Geiger Climate Classification," *Hydrology and Earth System Sciences*, 11, 1633–1644.

Pfaffenberger, Bryan (1990), "The Harsh Facts of Hydraulics: Technology and Society in Sri Lanka's Colonization Schemes," *Technology and Culture*, 31(3), 361–397.

Phillips, Sarah T. (1999), "Lessons from the Dust Bowl: Dryland Agriculture and Soil Erosion in the United States and South Africa, 1900–1950," *Environmental History*, 4(2), 245–266.

Potts, Daniel T. (2004), *Nomadism in Iran: From Antiquity to the Modern Era*, Oxford: Oxford University Press.

Pouchepadass, Jacques (1995), "Colonialism and Environment in India: Comparative Perspective," *Economic and Political Weekly*, 30(33), 2059–2067.

Powell, John Wesley (2004), *The Arid Lands*, Lincoln: University of Nebraska Press.

Pritchard, Sara B. (2012), "From Hydroimperialism to Hydrocapitalism: 'French' Hydraulics in France, North Africa, and Beyond," *Social Studies of Science*, 42(4), 591–615.

Punjabi, Bharat, and Craig A. Johnson (2019), "The Politics of Rural-Urban Water Conflict in India: Untapping the Power of Institutional Reform," *World Development*, 120, 182–192.

Radonic, Lucero (2015), "Environmental Violence, Water Rights, and (Un) Due Process in Northwestern Mexico," *Latin American Perspectives*, 42(5), 27–47.

Raj, K.N. (1975), "Agricultural Development and Distribution of Landholdings," *Indian Journal of Agricultural Economics*, 31(1), 1–13.

Ramesh, Aditya (2019), "Water Technocracy: Dams, Experts and Development in South India," PhD thesis, SOAS University of London.

Rani, Akanksha, Devesh Sharma, Mukand S. Babel, and Aditya Sharma (2022), "Spatio-Temporal Assessment of Agro-Climatic Indices and the Monsoon Pattern in the Banas River Basin, India," *Environmental Challenges*, 7, 1–10.

Rao, G.N., and D. Rajasekhar (1994), "Land Use Pattern and Agrarian Expansion in a Semi-arid Region: Case of Rayalaseema in Andhra, 1886–1939," *Economic and Political Weekly*, 29(26), A80–A88.

Ray, Sunil (1999), "Declining Production Conditions of Raw Wool: Analysis of Emerging Conflicts in Sheep Husbandry in Rajasthan," *Economic and Political Weekly*, 34(2), 1209–1214.

Reno, William (2004), Review of Peter D. Little, *Somalia: Economy without State*, *Journal of Modern African Studies*, 42(3), 47–475.

Ricardo, David (1821), *On the Principles of Political Economy and Taxation*, London: J. Murray.

REFERENCES 281

Riedel, Nils, Dorian Q. Fuller, Norbert Marwan, Constantin Poretschkin, Nathani Basavaiah, Philip Menzel, Jayashree Ratnam, Sushma Prasad, Dirk Sachse, Mahesh Sankaran, Saswati Sarkar, and Martina Stebich (2021), "Monsoon Forced Evolution of Savanna and the Spread of Agro-Pastoralism in Peninsular India," *Scientific Reports*, 11, 1–13.

Roberts, Richard (1987), *Warriors, Merchants and Slaves: The State and the Economy in the Middle Niger Valley 1700–1914*, Stanford, CA: Standford University Press.

Roberts, Richard L. (1996), *Two Worlds of Cotton: Colonialism and the Regional Economy in the French Soudan, 1800–1946*, Stanford, CA: Stanford University Press.

Rodríguez-Labajos, Beatriz, and Joan Martínez-Alier (2015), "Political Ecology of Water Conflicts," *WIREs Water*, 2, 2015, 537–558.

Rosegrant, M.W. and R.G. Schleyer (1996), "Establishing Tradable Water Rights: Implementation of the Mexican Water Law," *Irrigation and Drainage Systems*, 10, 263–279.

Ross, Corey (2019), *Ecology and Power in the Age of Empire: Europe and the Transformation of the Tropical World*, Oxford: Oxford University Press.

Routray, Sailen, Patrik Oskarsson, and Puspanjali Satpathy (2020), "A Hydrologically Fractured State? Nation-Building, the Hirakud Dam and Societal Divisions in Eastern India," *South Asia: Journal of South Asian Studies*, 43(3), 429–445.

Rowton, M.B. (1973), "Autonomy and Nomadism in Western Asia," *Orientalia*, 42, 247–258.

Roy, Tirthankar (2003), "Changes in Wool Production and Usage in Colonial India," *Modern Asian Studies*, 37(2), 257–286.

Roy, Tirthankar (2017), "Land Quality, Carrying Capacity, and Sustainable Agricultural Change in Twentieth-Century India," in Gareth Austin, ed., *Economic Development and Environmental History in the Anthropocene: Perspectives on Asia and Africa*, 159–178, London: Bloomsbury.

Roy, Tirthankar (2020), *The Economic History of India 1857–2010*, 4th edition, Delhi: Oxford University Press.

Roy, Tirthankar (2022), *Monsoon Economies: India's History in a Changing Climate*, Cambridge, MA: MIT Press.

Rubenson, Sven (1991), "Conflict and Environmental Stress in Ethiopian History: Looking for Correlations," *Journal of Ethiopian Studies*, 24, 71–96.

Ryan, Erin (2020), "A Short History of the Public Trust Doctrine and Its Intersection with Private Water Law," *Virginia Environmental Law Journal*, 38(2), 135–206.

Sachs, Jeffrey D. (2000), "Tropical Underdevelopment," Center for International Development (Harvard University) Working Paper.

Samatar, A. (1988), "The State, Agrarian Change and Crisis of Hegemony in Somalia," *Review of African Political Economy*, 43, 26–41.

Santasombat, Yos (2011), *The River of Life: Changing Ecosystems of the Mekong Region*, Chiang Mai: Mekong Press.

Saran, Awadhendra (2014), *In the City, Out of Place: Nuisance, Pollution, and Dwelling in Delhi, c. 1850–2000*, Delhi: Oxford University Press.

Saravanan, V. (2021), *Water and the Environmental History of Modern India*, London: Bloomsbury.

282 REFERENCES

Schmidt, Peter, and Robert Muggah (2021), "Impacts of Water Fluctuation in the Lake Chad Basin," in *Climate Change and Security in West Africa*, 15–18, Rio de Janeiro: Igarape Institute.

Schmokel, Wolfe W. (1985), "The Myth of the White Farmer: Commercial Agriculture in Namibia, 1900–1983," *International Journal of African Historical Studies*, 18(1), 93–108.

Scott, Christopher A., Francisco J. Meza, Robert G. Varady, Holm Tiessen, Jamie McEvoy, Gregg M. Garfin, Margaret Wilder, Luis M. Farfán, Nicolás Pineda Pablos, and Elma Montaña (2013), "Water Security and Adaptive Management in the Arid Americas," *Annals of the Association of American Geographers*, 103(2), 280–289.

Sen, Amartya (1981), *Poverty and Famines: An Essay on Entitlement and Deprivation*, Oxford: Clarendon Press.

Sen, Dinesh Chandra (1923), *Purba Banga Geetika*, Calcutta: University of Calcutta Press, vol. 1 of 4.

Sen, Sudipta (2019), *Ganges: The Many Pasts of an Indian River*, New Haven, CT: Yale University Press.

Serels, Steven (2007), "Political Landscaping: Land Registration, the Definition of Ownership and the Evolution of Colonial Objectives in the Anglo-Egyptian Sudan, 1899–1924," *African Economic History*, 35, 59–75.

Serels, Steven (2019), "Small-Scale Farmers, Foreign Experts, and the Dynamics of Agricultural Change in Sudan, Eritrea, and Djibouti before the Second World War," *International Journal of African Historical Studies*, 52(2), 217–230.

Seter, Hanne, Ole Magnus Theisen, and Janpeter Schilling (2018), "All about Water and Land? Resource-Related Conflicts in East and West Africa Revisited," *GeoJournal*, 83(1), 169–187.

Shah, Mihir (2013), "Water: Towards a Paradigm Shift in the Twelfth Plan," *Economic and Political Weekly*, 48, 40–52.

Shah, Tushaar, and Barbara van Köppen (2006), "Is India Ripe for Integrated Water Resources Management? Fitting Water Policy to National Development Context," *Economic and Political Weekly*, 41(31), 3413–3421.

Sheridan, Thomas E. (1988), *Where the Dove Calls: The Political Ecology of a Peasant Corporate Community in Northwestern Mexico*, Tucson: University of Arizona Press.

Shokr, Ahmad (2009), "Hydropolitics, Economy, and the Aswan High Dam in Mid-century Egypt," *Arab Studies Journal*, 17(1), 9–31.

Siddiqi, Akhtar Husain (1990), "Baluchistan (Pakistan): Its Development and Planning Policy," *GeoJournal*, 22(1), 5–19.

Simkins, Charles, and Elizabeth van Heyningen (1989), "Fertility, Mortality, and Migration in the Cape Colony, 1891–1904," *International Journal of African Historical Studies*, 22(1), 79–111.

Singh, Rajesh, and Vimal Mishra (2024), "Atmospheric and Land Drivers of Streamflow Flash Droughts in India," *Journal of Geophysical Research: Atmospheres*, 129, https://doi.org/10.1029/2023JD040257.

Singh, Satyajit K. (1990), "Evaluating Large Dams in India," *Economic and Political Weekly*, 25(11), 561–574.

REFERENCES 283

Siripurapu, Kanna K., Sushma Iyengar, Vasant Saberwal, and Sabyasachi Das (2018), "An Overview of Mobile Pastoralism in Andhra Pradesh and Telangana States of the Deccan Plateau Region of India," New Delhi: Centre for Pastoralism.

Sivasundaram, Sujit (2010), "Ethnicity, Indigeneity, and Migration in the Advent of British Rule to Sri Lanka," *American Historical Review*, 115(2), 428–452.

Smith, Tony (1975), "The French Economic Stake in Colonial Algeria," *French Historical Studies*, 9(1), 184–189.

Spate, O.H.K. (1952), "Toynbee and Huntington: A Study in Determinism," *Geographical Journal*, 118(4), 406–424.

Spear, Thomas, and Richard Waller, eds. (1993), *Being Maasai: Ethnicity and Identity in East Africa*, Athens: Ohio University Press.

Stenning, Derrick J. (1957), "Transhumance, Migratory Drift, Migration; Patterns of Pastoral Fulani Nomadism," *Journal of the Royal Anthropological Institute of Great Britain and Ireland*, 87(1), 57–73.

Straus, Scott (2015), *Making and Unmaking of Nations. War, Leadership, and Genocide in Modern Africa*, Ithaca, NY: Cornell University Press.

Sugihara, Kaoru (2024), "Varieties of Industrialization: An Asian Regional Perspective," in Giorgio Riello and Tirthankar Roy, eds., *Global Economic History*, 2nd edition, 249–269, London: Bloomsbury.

Swain, Ashok (1997), "Ethiopia, the Sudan, and Egypt: The Nile River Dispute," *Journal of Modern African Studies*, 35(4), 675–694.

Tada, Hirokazu (1992), *Indo no daichi to mizu* [Land and water in India], Tokyo: Nihon Keizai Hyouronsha, 1992.

Taddia, Irma (1990), "At the Origin of the State/Nation Dilemma: Ethiopia, Eritrea, Ogaden in 1941," *Northeast African Studies*, 12(2–3), 157–170.

Taylor, Griffith (1930), "Agricultural Regions of Australia. Instalment I," *Economic Geography*, 6(2), 109–134.

Teclaff, Ludwik A. (1996), "Evolution of the River Basin Concept in National and International Water Law," *Natural Resources Journal*, 36(2), 359–391.

Thom, Derrick J., and John C.C. Wells (1987), "Farming Systems in the Niger Inland Delta, Mali," *Geographical Review*, 77(3), 328–342.

Thomas Arkell, "The Decline of Pastoral Nomadism in the Western Sahara," Geography, 76(2), 1991, 162-166. Cited text on p. 162.

Tignor, Robert L. (1963), "British Agricultural and Hydraulic Policy in Egypt, 1882–1892," *Agricultural History*, 37(2), 63–74.

Tilley, Helen (2004), "Ecologies of Complexity: Tropical Environments, African Trypanosomiasis, and the Science of Disease Control in British Colonial Africa, 1900–1940," *Osiris*, 19, 21–38.

Tischler, Julia (2013), *Light and Power for a Multiracial Nation. The Kariba Dam Scheme in the Central African Federation*, London: Palgrave.

Tiyanjana, Maluwa (1988), "Legal Aspects of the Niger River under the Niamey Treaties," *Natural Resources Journal*, 28(4), 671–697.

Tricart, J., and J.-P. Blanck (1989), "L'Office du Niger, mirage du développement au Mali?," *Annales de Géographie*, 98(549), 567–587.

284 REFERENCES

Unruh, John D. (1996), "Resource Sharing: Smallholders and Pastoralists in Shalambood, Lower Shabeelle Valley," in Catherine Besteman and Lee V. Cassanelli, eds., *The Struggle for Land in Southern Somalia: The War behind the War*, 115–130, Boulder, CO: Westview.

Urbano, Annalisa (2017), "A 'Grandiose Future for Italian Somalia': Colonial Developmentalist Discourse, Agricultural Planning, and Forced Labor (1900–1940)," *International Labor and Working-Class History*, 92(1), 69–88.

US Bureau of Reclamation, "Reclamation History" September 11, 2023 (accessed on December 5, 2024) https://www.usbr.gov/history/index.html.

van Beusekom, Monica M. (1997), "Colonisation Indigène: French Rural Development Ideology at the Office du Niger, 1920–1940," *International Journal of African Historical Studies*, 30(2), 299–323.

van Beusekom, Monica M. (2000), "Disjunctures in Theory and Practice: Making Sense of Change in Agricultural Development at the Office du Niger, 1920–60," *Journal of African History*, 41(1), 79–99.

van der Gun, Jac (2019), "The Global Groundwater Revolution," Oxford Research Encyclopedia, Environmental Science, https://doi.org/10.1093/acrefore/9780199389414.013.632.

van Steenbergen, Frank (1995), "The Frontier Problem in Incipient Groundwater Management Regimes in Balochistan," *Human Ecology*, 23(1), 53–74.

Venkateswarlu, B., and J.V.S.N. Prasad (2012), "Carrying Capacity of Indian Agriculture: Issues Related to Rainfed Agriculture," *Current Science*, 102(6), 882–888.

Venot, Jean-Philippe, Luna Bharati, Mark Giordano, and François Molle (2011), "Beyond Water, beyond Boundaries: Spaces of Water Management in the Krishna River Basin, South India," *Geographical Journal*, 177(2), 160–170.

Verhoeven, Harry (2016), "Briefing African Dam Building as Extraversion: The Case of Sudan's Dam Programme, Nubian Resistance, and the Saudi-Iranian Proxy War in Yemen," *African Affairs*, 115(460), 562–573.

Vettera, Thomas, and Anna-Katharina Rieger (2019), "Ancient Water Harvesting in the Old World Dry Belt—Synopsis and Outlook," *Journal of Arid Environments*, 169, 42–53.

Vijay Shankar, P.S., Himanshu Kulkarni, and Sunderrajan Krishnan (2011), "India's Groundwater Challenge and the Way Forward," *Economic and Political Weekly*, 46(2), 37–45.

Wade, Robert H. (2011), "Muddy Waters: Inside the World Bank as It Struggled with the Narmada Projects," *Economic and Political Weekly*, 46(40), 44–65.

Wagland, P.J. (1969), "Kainji and the Niger Dams Project," *Geography*, 54(4), 459–463.

Walker, Thomas S., and James G. Ryan (1990), *Village and Household Economies in India's Semi-arid Tropics*, Baltimore: Johns Hopkins University Press.

Wallach, Bret (1984), "Irrigation Developments in the Krishna Basin since 1947," *Geographical Review*, 74(2), 127–144.

Walsh, Casey (2018), *Virtuous Waters: Mineral Springs, Bathing, and Infrastructure in Mexico*, Berkeley: University of California Press.

REFERENCES   285

Walsh, Casey (2015), "Mineral Springs, Primitive Accumulation, and the 'New Water' in Mexico," *Regions and Cohesion*, 5(1), 1–25.

Wang, Zhengrong, and Yuting Yang (2024), "Stationarity of High and Low Flows under Climate Change and Human Interventions across Global Catchments," *Earth and Space Science*, 11, https://doi.org/10.1029/2023EA003456.

Warren, Andrew (1995), "Changing Understandings of African Pastoralism and the Nature of Environmental Paradigms," *Transactions of the Institute of British Geographers*, 20(2), 193–203.

Webb, James L.A., Jr. (1995), *Desert Frontier: Ecological and Economic Change along the Western Sahel, 1600–1850*, Madison: University of Wisconsin Press.

Webster, J.B. (1980), "Drought, Migration and Chronology in the Lake Malawi Littoral," *Transafrican Journal of History*, 9(1), 70–90.

Weiss, Holger (1998), "'Dying Cattle': Some Remarks on the Impact of Cattle Epizootics in the Central Sudan during the Nineteenth Century," *African Economic History*, 26, 173–199.

Westphal-Hellbusch, Sigrid (1972), "Hinduistische Viehzüchter Nordwest-Indiens und Probleme ihrer gegenwärtigen Umstellung, an den Rabari exemplifiziert," *Sociologus*, 22(1/2), 49–75.

Whitcombe, Elizabeth (1972), *Agrarian Conditions in Northern India*, vol. 1, Berkeley: University of California Press.

Whitcombe, Elizabeth (1983), "Irrigation," in Dharma Kumar, ed., *Cambridge Economic History of India*, vol. 2, 677–736, Cambridge: Cambridge University Press.

Whittaker, Hannah (2017), "Frontier Security in North East Africa," *Journal of African History*, 58(3), 381–402.

Williamson, Jeffrey G. (2013), *Trade and Poverty: When the Third World Fell Behind*, Cambridge, MA: MIT Press.

Wilson, Wendy (1995), "The Fulani Model of Sustainable Agriculture: Situating Fulbe Nomadism in a Systemic View of Pastoralism and Farming," *Nomadic Peoples*, 36/37, 35–51.

Wittfogel, Karl (1957), *Oriental Despotism: A Comparative Study of Total Power*, New Haven, CT: Yale University Press.

Woodhouse, Melvin, and Abdi Hassan Muse (2009), "Water Policy in Puntland State, Somalia," *Waterlines*, 28(1), 79–88.

World Bank (2005), *Conflict in Somalia: Drivers and Dynamics*, Washington, DC: World Bank.

World Bank (2008), *Sustainable Land Management Sourcebook*, Washington, DC: World Bank Publications.

World Bank (2024), "Level of Water Stress," https://databank.worldbank.org/source/world-development-indicators/Series/ER.H2O.FWST.ZS (accessed on December 5, 2024).

Xu, Chenxi, Y. Simon Wang, Krishna Borhara, Brendan Buckley, Ning Tan, Yaru Zhao, Wenling An, Masaki Sano, Takeshi Nakatsuka, and Zhengtang Guo (2023),

"Asian-Australian Summer Monsoons Linkage to ENSO Strengthened by Global Warming," *Climate and Atmospheric Science*, 6(8), 1–10.

Yanagisawa, Haruka (1989), "Mixed Trends in Landholding in Lalgudi Taluk: 1895–1925," *Indian Economic and Social History Review*, 26(4), 405–435.

Yáñez-Arancibia, Alejandro, and John W. Day (2017), "Water Scarcity and Sustainability in the Arid Area of North America," *Regions and Cohesion*, 7(1), 6–18.

Yangtso, Lobsang (2017), "China's River Politics on the Tibetan Plateau: Comparative Study of Brahmaputra and Mekong," *The Tibet Journal*, 42(2), 49–58.

Yeophantong, Pichamon (2020), "China and the Accountability Politics of Hydropower Development," *Contemporary Southeast Asia*, 42(1), 85–117.

Zartman, William (1963), "Farming and Land Ownership in Morocco," *Land Economics*, 39(2), 187–198.

Zhang, Hongli, Liang Zhang, Qiang Zhang, Qian Liu, Xiaoni You, and Lixia Wang (2023), "Analysis of the Difference between Climate Aridity Index and Meteorological Drought Index in the Summer Monsoon Transition Zone," *Remote Sensing*, 15, 1–17.

Zomer, Robert J., Jianchu Xu, Antonio, and Trabuco (2022), "Version 3 of the Global Aridity Index and Potential Evapotranspiration Database," *Scientific Data*, 9.

Index

For the benefit of digital users, indexed terms that span two pages (e.g., 52–53) may, on occasion, appear on only one of those pages.

Abdel Omran, 160
Aden, 66–68, 240
Afar (region, people), 62–63, 183, 184–185, 241–242
Afghanistan, 84, 227–228. *see also* South Asia
Africa. *see* West Africa, Horn of Africa, North Africa, Southern Africa
agricultural productivity, 8–9, 11, 12, 17–18, 21–22, 27, 36–37, 41, 59, 111, 116, 119–121, 124–125, 164, 173–174, 179, 193–194, 197–199, 202, 214–217
agriculture. *see* flush cultivation, rainfed farming, irrigation, dry farming, recessionary agriculture, slash-and-burn
agropastoralism, 91–93, 178, 231–232, 235, 237–238, 242, 243–244, 246
Ahmed Gran, 62
Ajmer-Merwara, 136
Alaotra, Lake, 242
Algeria, 72–74, 108, 113, 119–120, 123, 124–126, 135, 154, 159, 167, 233
Al-Hasa, 156–157
alkalization, 147
Amartya Sen, 38–39
Andean Region, 258–259
Andhra Pradesh, 243
Angola, 51, 96–97, 99–100, 237
Antislavery. *see* slavery
aquifers, 2–3, 12, 21, 23, 44, 59–60, 82, 87, 89, 108, 149–151, 156–157, 189–192, 200–201, 203, 209, 248–250
Arab Peninsula, 223
aridisols, 8–9
Arnold Toynbee, 29–30
artesian wells, 71–72, 84–86, 149, 150–151, 155–157, 168–169
Arthur Cotton, 136–137
Asmara, 66
Aswan High Dam, 170–171, 177–178
Atbara, 59–60, 236–237
Atlas Mountains, 51–52, 71–72, 154, 171–173

Australia, 13–14, 49, 51–52, 89, 155–156, 173–174, 189, 252, 255–256, 259
Awash (river, basin), 61, 63, 183–185

bacterial reservoirs, 19
bacteriology, 19
Baluchistan, 84–86, 107, 191–192, 199, 200, 203–204, 227–228
Bangladesh, 81, 190–191, 206–207, 210–211. *see also* South Asia
baseflow, 254–256
basin management, 20–21, 61, 142, 164
basin-sharing, 115–116, 128, 205, 210–211
Basotho, 237–239
Bay of Bengal, 133
Beht (river), 154
Benadir coast, 52, 64, 66–68, 121
Bengal, 92, 95–96, 111–112, 117, 133, 176–177, 197–198, 200–201
Benue River, 54, 168–169
Bhakra Dam, 170
Bhutan, 206–207. *see also* South Asia
Bihar, 104, 111–112
Bin al-Widan Dam, 154
biodiversity, 8–9, 30, 50, 246
Blue Nile, 52, 58–60, 143, 178–179, 210, 236–237
Boer, 237–238
Bombay, 110, 158–159, 240
Boreholes, 60–61, 91–92, 134–145, 166
Botswana, 51–52, 223, 239
Brahmaputra (river, basin), 210–211
Brazil, 51, 87–88, 134, 153, 155, 174, 185–187
British Empire, 140–141, 144–145. *see also* colonialism
Burkina Faso, 12, 51, 251–252

Cahora Bassa Dam, 180–181
Cairo, 142–143
Calcutta, 158–159
California, 86–87, 89, 149–151, 189, 255

288 INDEX

Cameroon, 51, 235–236
canals, 15, 17–18, 20, 21–23, 31–32, 44, 59, 61, 83–84, 104–111, 115–116, 125–127, 133, 134–145, 148–149, 151, 152–154, 165–166, 171–173, 175–178, 185, 188, 195, 197–198, 200, 202, 235, 242–243, 261
Cape Colony, 160–161, 237–238
carbon emissions, 252–253
Casablanca, 154
Cauvery delta, 140. *see also* Kaveri
Central Asia, 29–30, 158, 173–174, 192, 224
Chad, 12, 22, 51, 54, 58, 99
Chad, Lake, 58, 171, 172, 255
Chambal Dam, 170
Charles George Dixon, 136
Chile, 26, 209
China, 11, 23, 30–32, 112, 174, 181, 191–193, 197, 210–211
cholera, 11, 18, 159–161, 184–185
climate aridity index, 256
climate change, 10, 23, 28, 43, 92–93, 105–106, 165, 170–171, 197, 207, 221, 231–232, 247, 252–260
climatic zones, 2, 30, 49–50, 126–127
cloud seeding, 251–252
coercion, 94–95
colonialism, colonial period, 13–16, 18, 58, 60–61, 67–69, 71, 90–91, 99, 114–132, 160–161, 179–180, 182–183, 196–197, 206, 212, 223, 227–228, 230, 242, 244, 249, 261
Colorado River, 150–151
Colorado River Aqueduct, 151
common pool resources. *see* commons
commons, 113, 129, 130, 148, 200, 222–223, 230, 248, 250–251
Congo, 58–59, 127–128, 197
contracts, 96–97, 117–118, 127, 170
convection, 81
cooperation, 23, 63, 86, 94, 95–96, 98, 126–127, 195, 203–204, 213–214, 234–235, 248, 250
Coromandel coast, 95–96
corvée (unpaid labor), 127, 135, 143
Cuttack, 112

dams, 20–23, 31–32, 34, 44–45, 59, 61, 74, 76, 104, 108–111, 113, 127, 129, 133, 138, 140, 142, 148–156, 162–164, 167–174, 176–177, 181, 183–185, 187, 188, 191, 192–200, 204, 209–210, 213–214, 219, 223–224, 230, 242, 261, 262–263
Darfur, 22, 60, 99, 205, 214, 237

Deccan Plateau, 9, 18, 50, 82, 83, 131, 134, 138, 159, 170, 199, 231, 232, 248–249
Delhi, 99, 101, 140–141, 159, 209
Desalination, 252
Desertification, 193, 227–228, 235
Diama Dam, 182, 213
diseases, 9, 11, 18–19, 61, 99, 110, 159–162, 194, 223. *see also* cholera
Djibouti, 183. *see also* Horn of Africa
Dredging, 142, 194–195
droughts, 9–16, 18–19, 22, 29–30, 35–36, 38–40, 45, 46–47, 51–53, 56–58, 60–62, 64, 68, 79, 82–83, 86, 87–103, 110–112, 115, 124–126, 135, 138, 148, 149, 153, 155–156, 158, 160–162, 165–166, 170–172, 175, 179–180, 182, 184–187, 197, 205–206, 208, 212–218, 222–224, 226, 228, 234, 235–240, 244–246, 254–257, 262–263
dry farming, 41, 67, 71, 73, 75–76, 120, 133–134, 157–158
dykes, 53, 178, 235

East Africa. *see* Horn of Africa, Kenya, Tanzania
East India Company, British, 83, 111–112, 116–117, 127, 136–137, 141, 243–244
ecological modernization (concept), 250–251
ecological specialization (concept), 13–14
economic development, 1, 22, 106–107, 130–131, 133, 144–145, 163, 177, 247
economic history, 1–2, 15, 25–26, 28, 29, 32, 35, 40, 41, 46, 49, 61, 90–91, 96–97, 228–229
economics, 35–36, 40, 41–42, 203
Egypt, 2–3, 17–18, 20, 22–23, 30–32, 45, 49, 58–61, 105, 117–118, 129–130, 133, 142–143, 158–159, 177, 206, 255
El Kansera Dam, 154–155
Elinor Ostrom, 113, 250
Ellsworth Huntington, 29
engineering, 2, 20–21, 28, 32, 44, 78, 104–105, 133, 134, 136, 139, 142–145, 148–149, 152–153, 157, 160, 162–164, 167–168, 170, 177–178, 192, 195, 241, 262
entisols, 8–9
environmental degradation, 34, 147, 179, 250–251
environmental regulation, 187, 248–251. *see also* law
epidemic. *see* diseases
epidemics. *see* diseases, cholera
epidemiologic transition, 160–161
Eritrea, 51–52, 58–59, 64–71, 120, 183, 216
erosion, 5, 77, 158, 170–171, 215–216, 235

INDEX 289

Ester Boserup, 36–37
Ethiopia, 34, 51–52, 58–59, 61–63, 65, 66–69, 116, 129–130, 162, 183–186, 197, 205–206, 210, 214–219, 222–223, 241–242
Euphrates. *see* Fertile Crescent
evapotranspiration, 3–6, 8, 28, 50, 52, 72, 77, 254, 255–257, 259

famine, 10–13, 18–19, 29, 33–34, 38–39, 42, 45–47, 51–52, 62, 69, 82, 83, 90, 92, 94, 95–103, 110, 122, 125–126, 129, 133–136, 138, 140, 147, 153, 159, 161, 165–166, 175, 176–177, 184–186, 189, 190, 205–206, 214–219, 222, 229, 238–239, 243, 247–249, 255, 262–263. *see also* droughts
Fertile Crescent, 52, 75
fishing, 7, 52–53, 58, 77, 171, 181–182, 184–185
flood control, 15, 105, 111–113, 136–139, 142, 165–166, 173, 176–177, 180–181
flush cultivation, 53, 58, 145, 236–237
foggara. *see* qanat
fossil fuel, 27–28, 252–253
France, 56–58, 79, 129, 134–135, 145, 154–155, 167, 171–173, 182
French colonialism, 54–56, 58, 122, 134–135, 145, 213–214, 234–235, 242. *see also* colonialism
French West Africa, 236
freshwater withdrawal, 12, 21–22, 174, 175, 193

Ganges (Ganga), 45, 52, 112, 139, 142, 206–207
Garrett Hardin, 230
Gezira Scheme, 143, 178, 236–237
globalization, 26
Godavari River, 82, 137–138, 140, 168–169
Governance, 42, 68, 86, 102, 192, 208, 212–213, 226
Grand Ethiopian Renaissance Dam, 206, 210
grasslands, 50, 53, 87–88, 126, 180–181, 222–223, 231, 240–241, 243. *see also* savanna, steppe, rangelands, pastoralism
Great Lakes, 78
Great Plains (USA), 157
Great Rift Valley, 92–93
green revolution, 111, 123–125, 173–174, 176–178, 198, 200–201, 207–208, 248, 262–263
Gross Domestic Product (GDP), 3, 12, 26, 262–263

groundwater, 2–3, 5–6, 8–9, 21, 25, 48–49, 51, 52, 59, 75–76, 82, 86–89, 107, 129, 136, 143–145, 147, 148–151, 153–157, 171, 173–174, 178, 189–192, 194, 197–204, 208, 220, 248, 249–250, 255, 259, 262
groundwater recharge, 194, 250, 259
Guinea, 56
Gujarat, 41–42, 100–101, 106, 200–203

hafirs (rock cisterns), 59–60, 106–107
Harry Oshima, 39
Heinrich Barth, 54
Henan, 112–113
Hermosillo, 151
Hijaz, 156–157
Himalayas, 9, 23, 52, 75, 81–82, 86, 104, 133, 135, 140, 141–142, 175–176, 198
Hirakud Dam, 170, 194–195, 209
Holocene, 92, 105–106, 231
Hoover Dam, 21, 151
Horn of Africa, 6–7, 9, 13–14, 48–49, 51, 52, 63, 64–66, 68, 73, 122, 123–124, 153–154, 188–189, 231. *see also* Somalia, Eritrea, Djibouti, Somaliland, Puntland, Ethiopia
hydraulic conductivity, 51
hydraulic societies, 29, 46–47
hydrodynamics, 133
hydroelectric power, 20–21, 152, 164, 183, 184–185, 197
Hydrological Drought Index, 256
hydrological models, 253–254

Idaho, 152
Ilisu Dam, 210
India, 5–10, 14–15, 17–18, 20, 21, 23–26, 30–32, 34, 36, 39, 40–42, 45, 50–51, 63–65, 67–68, 74–75, 78, 79, 81, 82–83, 86, 89–93, 95–100, 102–106, 109–112, 116–118, 125–127, 129, 131–143, 152–155, 158–163, 165–170, 174–177, 190–204, 206–211, 220, 222–223, 226–227, 229, 231–232, 242–244, 248–250, 253, 255–259. *see also* South Asia
Indian Ocean, 45, 52, 65, 78, 79–81, 131
Indo-Gangetic Basin, 22, 31, 45, 49, 52, 81–83, 105–106, 112, 139, 190, 197–198, 231, 232, 242–243
Indus Valley, 31, 105–106, 231
industrialization, 26–27, 38–40, 69, 153, 163, 164, 167, 179–183, 185–187, 191, 193–195, 207–208, 250–251, 262

290   INDEX

inequality, 14–16, 20, 22–23, 25–26, 41–42, 51, 84, 103, 119–120, 123–125, 130–132, 158–159, 162–163, 175, 185–190, 193, 195, 201, 202, 204, 205, 214–215, 218–221, 248, 259–260
insolation, 231
institutions. *see* contract, cooperation, coercion, corvée, slavery, law, property rights
Intertropical Convergence Zone, 5, 58, 87–88, 252–253
Iraq, 74–76, 210
Irrigation, 5–6, 8–9, 14–15, 18, 22, 30–31, 37, 45–46, 62, 66, 71–73, 79, 83–84, 108–109, 119–121, 124–125, 130, 131, 134–140, 142, 145, 147, 148, 150–151, 154, 157–158, 171, 173, 176–177, 179–184, 187, 190–193, 199, 202–203, 206–207, 214–215, 235, 236–237, 251
Israel, 74–76, 104–107

Japan, 12, 39, 193
Jiangsu, 112–113
Johann Heinrich von Thünen, 35–36
Jordan, 21, 74–75, 106–107, 156–157
Jordan River (*also* valley), 15, 31, 32, 75, 76, 207
Jubba River, 64–65

Kaoru Sugihara, 40
karez. *see* qanat
Kariba Dam, 180
Karl Wittfogel, 29–30, 108
Karnataka, 40–41, 82–83, 109, 127, 207–208
Kaveri River, 111–112, 136–137, 152–153, 207–209, 243–244
Kaveri-Coleroon (Kollidam) Basin Dam, 136–137
Kenya, 58–59, 63–64, 144–145, 222–223, 227, 240–241
Khuzestan, 76
Kishanganga Dam, 210
Koka Dam, 183–185
Köppen-Geiger map, 49–50
Kosi River, 111–112
Koyna Dam, 170
Krishna River, 82, 137–138, 140, 170, 208
Kurnool, 138
Kuruba, 243

land conversion, 28, 50–51, 83, 84, 119, 120, 122, 126, 140–142, 182, 213, 222–224, 235–236, 241, 242, 244
land reclamation, 142, 148–149, 152, 171. *see also* land conversion
land yield. *see* agricultural productivity
law, 16, 19, 30–31, 40, 76, 83, 86, 97–98, 109, 116–118, 120, 122, 124–125, 127, 128–129, 132, 134, 149–152, 161, 165, 182–183, 199, 202–204, 207, 219–220, 230, 247–249, 262
legislation. *see* law
leprosy, 9
Lesotho, 207
Libya, 72–73, 119–120, 134, 159, 173
Linta Basin, 242
litigation. *see* law
Logon Basin, 58, 168–169, 255
Lonar Crater, 231
Los Angeles, 151

Madagascar, 51–52, 79, 242
Madras (city), 158–159, 249
Madras (province, Presidency), 23, 190
Madras Irrigation Canal and Navigation Company, 138
Mahad Satyagraha, 161
Mahanadi, 112, 194–195, 209
Malaria, 9, 18, 140–142, 160–161, 184
Malawi, Lake, 92–93
Mali, 58, 145, 227, 233, 234
Manantali Dam, 170–171, 182, 194–195
Markala Dam, 145, 152–153
Marrakesh, 154
Massawa, 62–64
Matabeleland, 143–144
Mauritania, 12, 51, 56, 97–98, 213–214, 223, 233
Mauryan Empire, 232
Mediterranean (region, climate), 72, 74, 84, 209
Mellah Dam, 154
Meltwater. *see* snowmelt
Melvin M. Knight, 71, 168–169
Menelik, 66
Merowe Dam, 206
meteorological drought, 254–255, 257. *see also* drought
Mettur Dam, 152–155
Mexico, 15, 21, 23, 51, 86–87, 89, 109, 149, 150–151, 156, 158, 173–174, 189, 209, 220, 249, 255
Mexico City, 150

INDEX 291

Middle East, 6–7, 10, 26, 45, 51–52, 74–75, 153–154, 156–157, 231, 252
Middle East and North Africa, 52, 74–75, 153–154, 233
migration, 14–16, 27–28, 36–37, 40–42, 53, 56–58, 62, 67, 69–71, 77, 78–79, 88, 90–94, 96, 99–100, 147, 159, 171–173, 182, 185–187, 216, 217–219, 227–228, 235–236, 238–239
Mogadishu, 64, 219
moisture stress, 12–13, 27–28, 38–39, 90
Mombasa, 66
Monsoon Asia (concept), 29, 40
monsoons, 3, 5–10, 12, 14–15, 29, 32, 35–36, 39, 40–42, 44, 45, 48–52, 59, 62, 64, 79–82, 84, 86, 89, 90–91, 105–106, 108, 109, 111, 133, 135, 136–139, 142, 147–148, 165–166, 176–177, 188, 198–201, 203, 224–226, 231–232, 254–259. *see also* seasonality, intertropical convergence zone, tropicality
Morocco, 51–52, 71–74, 97–98, 122, 123–124, 154–155, 167, 171–173, 233, 251–252
Mozambique, 51, 77, 78–79, 97, 180–181
Mungo Park, 54–55, 96

Najd, 156–157
Namibia, 6–7, 51–52, 78, 231, 237
Nepal, 206–207
Net evapotranspiration. *see* evapotranspiration
New Mexico, 87, 149
Nfiss River, 154
Niger (country), 12, 14, 48–49, 51, 58, 234
Niger Basin, 11, 13–14, 52, 96, 145–148, 168–169, 182
Niger Delta, 7, 52–53, 111, 152–153, 182–183, 234–235
Niger River, 7, 21, 49, 52–55, 58, 168–169. *see also* Niger Basin, Niger Delta
Nigeria, 40–41, 51, 54, 111, 168–169, 171, 212, 222–223, 235–236, 246
Nile Basin, *see* Nile River
Nile River, 2–3, 32, 49, 52, 58–61, 92–93, 117–118, 129, 130, 142, 143, 148, 170–171, 177–179, 205–206, 210, 214, 236–237, 255
Nira Valley, 140
nomadism, 50–51, 74–75, 93, 131–132, 189, 212, 222, 223, 226–227, 229, 233–234, 236–237, 239, 240. *see also* pastoralism, transhumance
nomads. *see* nomadism
North Africa, 6–7, 45, 49, 51, 52, 71–75, 107, 108, 118–119, 122, 123, 125–126, 133, 134, 153–154, 165, 167, 171–173, 191–192, 220,

231, 233, 256. *see also* Algeria, Libya, Tunisia, Egypt, Morocco, Middle East and North Africa

Office du Niger, 145–148
open access, 118–120, 229, 230, 248–249
Orissa (Odisha), 112, 138–139, 170, 209

Pakistan, 23, 51, 81, 84–86, 175–176, 190–191, 193, 198–200, 206–207, 210. *see also* South Asia
Paleotemperatures, 258–259
Palestine, 75–76, 157
pastoralism, 6–7, 14, 20–22, 27, 28, 33, 35–36, 51, 53–54, 64, 67–69, 74–75, 77, 78, 81–82, 84, 91–92, 121, 132, 155, 156, 164, 182–183, 193, 201–202, 205, 212–213, 217–218, 222–246, 256. *see also* nomadism, transhumance, agropastoralism
Patna, 112
phosphate mining, 223, 239
Pierre Gourou, 30
political ecology, 42–44, 46–47, 220
pollen data analysis, 232
pollution, 42, 106–107, 251
population growth, 1, 8–9, 11, 15, 18, 20, 23–25, 34, 36–37, 77, 88, 113, 120, 130–131, 164, 165–166, 170–171, 174, 193, 217, 218–219, 223–224, 238–239, 242–244, 246, 261–262
potential evapotranspiration. *see* evapotranspiration
precipitation, 2–5, 29, 49–50, 72, 76, 89, 154, 253–259. *see also* monsoons, rainfall
property rights, 16–20, 22–23, 34, 48, 56, 115–116, 119–120, 125, 126, 134–135, 148–149, 166–167, 216–217, 223, 224–226, 230, 236, 245, 248. *see also* law, riparian rights, water rights
public health, 19, 160
Punjab, 15, 22, 81–83, 134, 140–143, 170, 175–176, 200–202, 222–223, 226–227, 230, 242–244
Puntland, 33, 65, 69–71, 153–154

qanat, 15, 84–86, 106–108
Queensland, 155–156

Rabari, 242–243
Rabat, 154
Rahad, 236–237

292   INDEX

rainfall, 3–8, 10, 12, 29, 39, 48–50, 52–53, 56,
  58, 62, 63, 65, 71, 75–79, 81–89, 108, 135,
  143–144, 151, 154, 156–157, 168, 171–172,
  178–179, 185, 199–202, 214–215, 218, 231,
  239, 255, 257, 258. *see also* precipitation,
  monsoons
rainfed farming, 3, 7–9, 14, 17, 20, 40–42, 53,
  59, 61, 62, 74, 75, 83–84, 95, 118–119,
  123–124, 163, 184, 201–202, 215–216, 243
rainwater harvesting, 199, 250
Rajasthan, 81–82, 104, 109, 200–202, 204,
  242–243
Rajputana, 242–243
rangeland. *see* grasslands
Rangeland paradigm, 228
recessionary agriculture. *see* flush cultivation
Red Sea, 66–71
regulation. *see* environmental regulation, law
renewable water, 12, 210–211
reservoirs, 10, 14–15, 17–23, 31, 32, 59–60, 76,
  104, 108–109, 111, 113, 115–116, 126–127,
  129, 135, 144–145, 151, 153–154, 164,
  165–166, 176–180, 188, 194–195, 197–199,
  207–208, 210, 240, 262. *see also* dams
Richard Baird Smith, 140–141
Rift Valley, 75, 92–93, 240–241
Rihand Dam, 170
Rinderpest, 18, 68, 122–123, 160–162, 237
riparian rights, 128–129
river-sharing. *see* water treaties
Roseires Dam, 177
Rub al-Khali, 156–157
Ruwenzori, 58–59

Sahara Desert, 15–16, 131
Sahel, 6–7, 12, 14, 16–17, 34, 50, 52–54, 58, 91,
  93, 94, 96, 97–98, 115, 147, 166, 170–171,
  174, 182, 212–213, 215, 223–224, 229–230,
  234–235, 240–241, 246, 255
Salinization, 147, 151
Sanitation, 18–19, 116, 125–126, 134, 160, 261
Sao Francisco River, 153
Sarda canal, 140
Saudi Arabia, 197
savanna. *see* grasslands
savannization, 231
schistosomiasis, 9, 160
seasonality, 1–15, 19, 25–29, 33, 35, 39, 41–44,
  46, 49–52, 71–72, 77, 89–92, 95, 103, 113,
  125, 134, 139, 145, 147–148, 157, 165–166,
  168–169, 176–177, 179–181, 185, 188, 192,
  196–197, 204, 214–215, 217, 218, 224,

  229–230, 244, 247, 251–252, 255–256, 258,
  259–261
sedentarization, 185, 189, 223, 229
sedimentary basin, 89
sedimentary rock, 59–60, 156–157
seepage losses, 7
Ségou, 145
semi-arid regions (semi-arid ttropics), 1–3, 18,
  59, 256
Senegal (country), 51, 56, 58, 213, 233
Senegal River, 21, 48–49, 56–58, 88, 98,
  170–173, 182, 194–195
Senegal Valley/Basin. *see* Senegal River
Seraye, 66
Shabelle River, 52, 64
Shangani reserves, 143–144
Sidi Saad Dam, 173
Sind (Sindh), 139, 142, 200
Sirhind Canal, 140, 176
slash-and-burn agriculture, 229
slavery, 63, 94–99, 143. *see also* trading in
  enslaved peoples
snowmelt, 9, 52, 58–59, 71–72, 75, 86, 140,
  141, 154, 231, 254–255, 258–259
snowpack enhancements, 251–252
Sokoto Caliphate, 54
Somalia, 63–71, 120, 121, 153–154, 189,
  218–220, 222, 240–241. *see also* Horn of
  Africa
Somaliland, 52, 64, 65, 67–71, 120. *see also*
  Horn of Africa
Sone canal, 140
South Africa (country), 51, 78–79, 120,
  122–123, 157, 174, 181, 191–192, 207, 239,
  241, 250
South Asia, 6–7, 12, 13–14, 21–22, 26, 39, 45,
  49, 51, 75, 81, 83–84, 91, 95, 105–106, 111,
  112–113, 115, 125–126, 160–161, 175, 188,
  190, 203–204, 206–207, 231, 248–250,
  257–258. *see also* India, Pakistan,
  Afghanistan, Bangladesh, Sri Lanka, Bhutan
South Sudan, 58–59, 178, 217–218
Southeast Asia, 6–7, 37–38, 40, 52, 89, 192,
  210–211, 257–259
Southern Africa. *see also* Namibia, South
  Africa, Botswana, Zimbabwe, Mozambique,
  Angola
Southwest Africa. *see* Namibia
Sri Lanka, 15, 21, 31–32, 81, 83–84, 108–109,
  166–167, 188. *see also* South Asia
Srisailam Dam, 138

INDEX

standardized precipitation evaporation index (SPEI), 257
state capacity, 11
streamflow, 28, 138, 251–252, 254–256, 258–259
Sub-Saharan Africa, 6–7, 21–22, 64–65, 74–75, 175, 193, 211–212, 249
Sudan, 2–3, 6, 10, 12, 17–18, 20, 22–23, 33–34, 49, 58–61, 64, 91, 99, 117–118, 130, 131, 133, 143, 162, 170–171, 173–174, 177, 178–179, 197, 206, 210, 212, 214, 217–218, 222–223, 227–228, 236–237
Suez Canal, 61, 67–68
Sunkesula Dam, 138
surface albedo, 252–253
sustainability, 23–25, 149, 171, 193, 199–200, 208, 248, 256
Sylhet, 111–112
Syria, 74–75

Tamil Nadu, 82–83, 104, 109–111, 127, 143, 152–153, 207–208, 243
Tanganyika, 240–241
tanks, 82–83, 104, 105–107, 109–110, 126–127, 143, 155, 161. *see also* reservoirs
Tanzania, 58–59, 77–78
technology, 1, 16–17, 37, 42–43, 83, 104, 109, 111, 113, 123, 150–151, 193, 203–204, 244, 250–252
Tennessee Valley, 151, 176–177
Tigris. *see* Fertile Crescent
trachoma, 9
trade, trading, 13–14, 16–17, 37–38, 51, 71–72, 81, 115, 123, 130–132, 202, 212–213
trading in enslaved peoples, 15–17, 103
Tragedy of the commons *see* Garrett Hardin
transhumance, 15, 91, 212, 229–230, 244. *see also* nomadism, pastoralism
transmissivity, 51
trans-Saharan caravan trade, 13–14, 16–17, 72, 115, 131, 212, 233
treaties. *see* water treaties
tropicality, 33, 38–39, 41, 45–47, 89
Tungabhadra Dam, 138, 170
Tungabhadra River, 82, 138, 170
Tunisia, 72–74, 123–124, 173, 220

Uganda, 58–59, 63, 240–241
United Provinces, 140–142
Upper and Lower Ganga canals, 140
Upper Bari Doab canal, 140

Urbanization, 75–76, 130–131, 179, 200, 214, 262
USA, 7–8, 12, 21, 30, 51, 87, 109, 133–134, 148–150, 157–158, 180, 191–192, 251–252, 255–256, 259

vapor pressure deficit, 3–5
Victoria, Lake, 77
virtual water trade, 13, 16–17, 90
volcanic eruptions, 82
Volta River, 21, 48–49, 170–171, 179–180, 196–197

W. Arthur Lewis, 37–38, 46–47, 130–131
water access, 23–25, 73–74, 95, 114, 126, 127, 158–159, 175, 200, 212–215, 220–221
water bank, 150
water harvesting, 31, 104–105, 113, 153–154, 199, 205, 250
water management, 61, 202. *see also* governance, institutions, political ecology
water markets, 201–202, 248
water pricing, 248
water quality, 9, 11, 18–19, 99, 115–116, 134, 160, 184–185, 194–195, 201–202, 248
water recycling, 1, 3, 23, 262
water rights, 122, 148–150, 192
water stress, 23, 103, 193, 220–221, 247, 248, 255, 258–259
water trading, 202, 251
water treaties, 19, 23, 115–116, 127–130, 135, 148, 205–208, 211. *see also* basin-sharing
water turbine, 133–134
waterlogging, 139–142, 194, 202
West Africa, 2, 7, 9, 14, 16–17, 21, 23, 45–46, 49, 52–58, 115, 117, 134–135, 145, 166, 170–171, 179–180, 194–195, 211–214, 229, 233–236. *see also* Nigeria, Niger, Burkina Faso, Cameroon, Senegal
West Asia. *see* Middle East
Western Europe, 21, 26, 39–40, 133, 170, 193, 226
Western Sahara, 222–223
White Nile. *see* Nile

Yellow River, 32, 112–113
Yemen, 64, 67, 106, 191–192, 203–204

Zagros Mountains, 75
Zambezi River, 21, 48–49, 170–171, 180–181
Zambia, 180
Zanzibar, 63, 66, 77–78
Zimbabwe, 77, 143–144, 180–181